PHILOSOPHY OF SPORT AND PHYSICAL ACTIVITY

ISSUES AND CONCEPTS

EDITED BY
PASQUALE J. GALASSO

CANADIAN SCHOLARS' PRESS INC.   TORONTO   1988

Philosophy of Sport and Physical Activity: Issues and Concepts

First published in 1988 by
Canadian Scholars' Press Inc.
180 Bloor St. W., Ste. 402
Toronto, Ontario   M5S 2V6

Canadian Cataloguing in Publication Data

Main entry under title:

Philosophy of sport and physical activity

Includes bibliographical references
ISBN 0-921627-42-4

1. Sports – Philosophy. I. Galasso, Pasquale J., 1930–

GV706.P48   1988   796'.01   C89-093028-7

Printed and bound in Canada by Canadian Printco Limited

Publisher's Acknowledgements

Ross, S. (1986). "Cartesian Dualism and Physical Education: Epistemological Incompatibility," in Kleinman, Seymour (Ed). _Mind and Body: East Meets West_ (pp. 15-24). Champaign, IL: Human Kinetics Publishers. Steel, M. (1977). "What We Know When We Know A Game," _Journal of Philosophy of Sport_, IV, 96-103. Thompson, P.B. (1982). "Privacy and the Urinalysis Testing of Athletes," _Journal of the Philosophy of Sport_, IX, 60-65. Ravizza, K. and Daruty, K. (1984). "Paternalism and Sovereignty in Athletics: Limits and Justifications of the Coach's Exercise of Authority Over the Adult Athlete," _Journal of the Philosophy of Sport_, XI, 71-82. Roberts, T.J. (1986). "Sport, Art, and Particularity: The Best Equivocation," _Journal of the Philosophy of Sport_, XIII, 49-63. Kildea, A.E. (1983). "Competition: A Model for Conception," _Quest_, 35, 169-181. Above articles reprinted by permission. _Stress Without Distress_ by Hans Selye, pp. 122-131. Copyright © 1984 Hans Selye. Reprinted by permission of Harper & Row, Publishers, Inc. "Epistemology, Intentional Action, and Physical Education" Nov.-Dec. 1985, pp. 29-33 and "Eating Disorders, Physical Fitness, Persons and Physical Education" by Saul Ross, July-Aug. 1986, pp. 16-20. "The Dimensionality of an Ethical Code" by Earle F. Zeigler, Jan.-Feb. 1988, pp. 15-21. "Rules, Penalties and Officials: Sport and the Legality-Morality Distinction" by D. Shogan, Nov.-Dec. 1988, pp. 1-15. Reprinted by permission from the _Journal_, Canadian Association for Physical Education and Recreation, Ottawa, Ontario, Canada. _Sports and Athletics: Philosophy in Action_ by J. C. Mihalich. Copyright © Rowman & Littlefield Publishers, Inc. Reprinted by permission. "The Philosophy of Excellence: Olympic Performances, Class Power, and the Canadian State" by Bruce Kidd. Paper presented at The First International Conference on the Olympics and East/West and South/North Cultural Exchange in the World System, Aug. 1987. Reprinted by permission. "Competition: Is It What Life's All About" by Bil Gilbert. Previously published in _Sports Illustrated_, May 16, 1988, Vol. 68, No. 20, pp. 88-99. Reprinted by permission. "Sport Organizations and Ethical Concerns" by P.J. Galasso. Presented at the conference of the Canadian Association for Health, Physical Education and Recreation, June 1981. "The Ethics of Eating and Exercising Disorders" by P. J. Galasso. Presented at the CAHPER conference, June 1985. "The Ombudsman for Sport: An Idea Whose Time Has Come" by P. J. Galasso. Presented May 1988. "The Dimensionality of an Ethical Code" by E.F. Zeigler. Previously published in the CAHPER Journal, Jan.-Feb. 1988, pp. 16-21. "Responsibility and Authority in Coaching Philosophy" by Dennis Nighswonger. Paper presented at the CAHPER conference in May, 1988. "Natural Justice in Sport" by P.J. Galasso. Paper presented at The Ontario Sport Centre, Nov. 1987. "Sportsmanship" by Patricia A. Lawson. Paper presented to the CAHPER conference, May 1988.

The publisher would like to thank those contributors who gave their permission to reprint articles.

CONTENTS

i

ACKNOWLEDGEMENTS

This book was made possible by the support of many individuals. I would like to thank my colleagues in the Philosophy of Sport and Physical Activity Committee, Dr. Patricia Lawson, University of Saskatchewan, Dr. Saul Ross, University of Ottawa, Dr. Debra Shogan, University of Alberta and Dr. Earle Zeigler, University of Western Ontario, who have written the majority of the papers. I would also like to thank the other authors who have permitted the reprinting of published work or who have contributed original material.

I am also indebted to the editorial and design staff of Canadian Scholars' Press Inc. for facilitating the publication of this reader.

The co-operation of and assistance from the staff of the Faculty of Human Kinetics, University of Windsor, is gratefully acknowledged.

Kari, Linda and Mike, who decided independently to enter the same field as their parents, offered encouragement throughout the process.

And finally, I cannot say enough to match the contributions of my wife, Jan, through research for my articles, the proofreading of the entire text, and her warmth and strength of presence.

P.J. Galasso, Ph.D.
Editor
Windsor, Ontario
November, 1988

PREFACE

Philosophy of sport and physical activity is a young area of study. It was not until the 1960s, when graduates with advanced degrees in Physical Education and Human Kinetics returned to Canadian universities, that courses were taught in the theory and application of the philosophy of sport. Graduate courses began to emerge in the middle to late 1960s at the master's level. Unfortunately, there is still limited availability within doctoral programs of this area of study in Canada.

In 1971 a conference was held by members of the Ontario Universities Physical Education Association (now defunct), in Toronto, to examine the scope of the development of Physical Education as a subdisciplinary conglomerate, and to identify the composition of these subdisciplines. Philosophy of sport and physical activity was one of the subdisciplines acknowledged as a bona fide area of study.

A major symposium was hosted in 1971 by the Faculty of Physical Education and Health Education at the University of Windsor, with the co-operation of the Philosophy of Sport and Physical Activity Committee (formed in 1969) of the Canadian Association for Health, Physical Education and Recreation (CAHPER). The proceedings were produced and distributed by the Sport Canada Directorate, Department of Health and Welfare, Ottawa, Canada. In 1974, a second major symposium was hosted at the University of Western Ontario as the annual meeting of the Philosophic Society for the Study of Sport. This organization was formed in the early 1970s as an international society. A third major symposium, Persons, Minds and Bodies, was hosted by the University of Ottawa in 1986, and in 1988 the proceedings were published.

In the early 1970s a major grant was acquired by the Canadian Association for Health, Physical Education and Recreation, from Recreation Canada, to enable the subdiscipline committees of CAHPER to function by financing the travel of their executive committees. This subsidy has continued to the present. The Philosophy of Sport and Physical Activity Committee has produced programs at the annual conventions.

The emergence of the study of practical ethics as a major curricular focus can be attributed to the many national and international incidents of moral turpitude which have occurred recently in all phases of society. Many curricular units in universities have initiated courses in practical ethics, thus following the lead of several programs in physical education and human kinetics.

It was gratifying to be part of the Canadian Philosophical Association meeting held at the University of Windsor in 1988, on its twenty-fifth anniversary, as part of the Learned Societies. I attended the first official meeting of the Canadian Society for the Study of Practical Ethics. It is a credit to the discipline of Philosophy for recognizing the legitimacy of practical ethics as an area of study.

This book was initiated because of the need for such a text to provide a basis for class discussion as well as seminars. Most of the papers have been authored by members of the Philosophy of Sport and Physical Activity Special Committee of CAHPER. Additional papers were added in order to round out certain aspects of the field. It should serve as an excellent required text in courses in the Philosophy of Sport and Physical Activity, and Ethics.

SECTION I.

SUPERIORITY AND DOMINANCE

"WE'RE ALL PLAYING GAMES"
THE INCOMPATIBILITY OF ATHLETIC AND ACADEMIC EXCELLENCE

GEORGE HOCHFIELD

Last year, despite a good deal of faculty opposition, the leadership of the State University of New York at Buffalo persuaded the SUNY Board of Trustees to rescind its longstanding rule against the granting of athletic scholarships. This was the first step in carrying out a plan, adopted in the spring of 1987, for the "upgrading" of the athletic program at Buffalo from Division III to Division I. President Steven B. Sample, who was known to think that "you cannot have a first-rate university without Division I," said when the plan was adopted, "We believe the upgrade will be a positive step for students and the university and, indeed, for all of Western New York."

Perhaps the most vocal of the faculty opponents was Professor George Hochfield, who carried his opposition to Division I athletics to the pages of the *New York Times*. Professor Hochfield, who is still nursing his wounds and insisting that the battle is not necessarily over yet, here interviews himself for *Academe*.

Q. Professor Hochfield, why are you so violently opposed to a change that the president sees as beneficial for so many people?
A. I am normally opposed to big-time campus sports, but the violence comes from my bafflement at my university's *choosing*, in this day and age, at a moment when scandal has never been so rife in the world of college sports, to commit itself to a wasteful, corrupt, and degrading system.
Q. Whew! You really don't like it, do you? But after all, in American higher education everybody does it.
A. For repeating that stupid phrase, which I must have heard at least a thousand times during the past year, you deserve strangulation, not a polite response. Was there ever a more idiotic reason for doing anything? Everybody gets drunk; everybody smokes pot and snorts cocaine; and everybody lies, cheats, steals, and commits fornication! No, everybody doesn't. These things are all matters of choice, and so is starting or continuing a big-time sports program. The assurance that everybody is supposed to be doing it only spares people the effort (or embarrassment) of thinking about it.
Q. Well, nevertheless, everybody does do it. They must have good enough reasons.

3

I. Superiority and Dominance

A. I have studied the matter with some attention and I think the reasons are worth very little. There are only two, in point of fact, and the first one is simply publicity. (The second I'll get to in a moment.) That is, when the promoters of the "College Sports Industry" (as the *Times* called it last summer) try to explain the advantages of big-time athletic programs, what they mostly talk about are things like "national attention"; it wasn't sufficiently "visible." Now, by going to Division I, it will demonstrate that it is a "first rate university" and begin to get the "national attention" it craves.

Such attention, of course, is not only a good in itself; it is supposed to bring in money. Presidents and alumni fundraisers characteristically link visions of future wealth with ambitious sports programs. Visitors will flock; alumni pockets will be opened; research grants will be won; not only the university but all of Western New York will flourish. One member of the delegation that went to persuade the SUNY Board of Trustees to change its rule against athletic scholarships was the president of the Buffalo Area Chamber of Commerce.

How much of this is a pipe dream, I don't know. Nor do I know how much money will have to be invested before there are any returns. But, returns or not, I do believe that the whole enterprise is misguided. If one is looking for a way to enhance its reputation, is this the way to do it on the verge of the twenty-first century? Or is it to choose precisely what everybody else has been doing for the past century? I think it is a mindless surrender to conventionality, a mad plunge into the mainstream where all the midwestern whales already occupy the waters. The "visibility" one can hope to achieve there will be minimal, and other, more valuable, possibilities will have to be ignored or sacrificed.

The plain, irreducible truth is that there is no rational connection between higher education and professional sports, and universities ought to do other things than field football and basketball teams as ways of distinguishing themselves. Let them do it by means that *do* have a rational connection with higher education. Institutional public relations, I suppose, is here to stay — the Office of University Relations (as it's called) is the fastest growing administrative component on my campus. But let them make hay out of our scientific research, our music and theater and dance, our splendid libraries. Those are a few of the things that deserve "national attention" at universities. If students are educated well, alumni will know their value and will learn to support them. We degrade our alumni, as well as ourselves, when we sponsor athletic contests as a way of stimulating their generosity.

Q. Are you serious? There isn't a college president in the country who wouldn't tell you that alumni demand sports. The president's job sometimes depends on the success of the athletic program.

A. They deal with the wrong alumni, who have in my terms been badly educated, and they have only themselves to blame if they become the victims of what they themselves have helped to create. If presidents allow sports to become the principal means of "public relations" with alumni, then of course they will have to deal with alumni demands for athletic success. It's hard to feel sympathy for them. Only a few days ago, a friend of mine heard the president of one of the most important public universities in the country call Buffalo's decision to go to Division I "insane." The sports program at his university, he said, was like "a noose around [his] neck." What has he done to loosen its grip? When you get right down to it, he'd rather live with the noose than risk his job by telling people straight out that sports have become insane at his university. But maybe if he did he'd discover a lot of alumni who agree with him and would help him keep his job.

Q. You've referred several times to the corruption associated with sports. Are you thinking of the recent scandals involving drugs, rape, falsification of grades, and so forth?

A. No, something else. Big-time sports infect a campus with hypocrisy and cant. They are an assault on the integrity of the institution — no resistance is possible. I'm not talking now about the inevitable cheating that goes on everywhere: the payoffs, the grade changes, the rule-bending for the sake of admissions and eligibility. Those are the scandals the NCAA is supposed to wring its hands over and punish people for — as they occasionally do with punishments that never deter the crimes.

I'm talking about something more fundamental: the lying that begins with the first and original lie all university presidents have to mouth: "The pursuit of athletic excellence is compatible with the pursuit of academic excellence." Putting aside the probability that most of these gentlemen haven't the foggiest notion of what "academic excellence" is, or would be terrified at the prospect of having to take it seriously, the fact remains that they repeat this untruthful formula ceaselessly, and it's hard to believe they don't know it's untrue, however willing they may be to delude themselves and others.

The pursuit of "athletic excellence," which means winning games and playing in postseason tournaments or bowls and making money at the gate and acquiring a national reputation as a sports power, is simply *not* compatible with "academic excellence." You have first of all to recruit athletes, a highly competitive affair that necessarily leads to the lowering of admission standards (assuming, to be sure, that the "academically excellent" institution actually has admission standards). This happens because the preponderance of athletes worth recruiting are just not likely to be very good students. Why should they be? Their chief interest has been, and will continue to be, elsewhere. They...

Q. But what about...?

5

I. Superiority and Dominance

A. Bill Bradley? You were about to nonplus me with that name, weren't you? Bill Bradley always gets mentioned at this point in the argument. But he's a rare exception, as you know perfectly well. The average college athlete is much more likely not to graduate than to win a Rhodes scholarship and become a United States Senator. And while proceeding to nongraduation, the average college athlete is likely to take a bizarre melange of remedial, trivial, and sport-related courses. How can it be otherwise? If a team is to be "athletically excellent," it must demand a large proportion of the athlete's time. It must take him away periodically from his classes, and confine attention to them within strict limits. The athlete is inculcated with the knowledge that he or she has one serious purpose on campus and that only one kind of performance really counts. The athlete's payment (i.e., scholarship) depends on it as well as any hope for a professional career, and everything else is a farce. The athlete knows what really matters, however often the president (and even his coaches) intone their pious fraud of "academic excellence." Thus the athlete is steeped in hypocrisy from the moment he or she becomes an object of desire to institutions of higher learning.

I sometimes imagine a scene in which the star of the basketball team tells his coach that he's unable to make a road trip because he must catch up on his reading of *The Commedia* or perhaps *Swann's Way.* Our spontaneous response to such a fantasy tells us just how much "academic excellence" means on most American campuses.

Q. Still, isn't it true that many worthy young men and women have been helped to a college education by means of athletic scholarships?

A. Do you really think so? Your question, pardon me for saying it, is only another expression of the hypocrisy I've been talking about: pretended benevolence disguising exploitation. If universities were truly concerned about the education of a few thousand worthy young men and women, they could surely find other means of doing it, and without degrading the quality of the education bestowed.

Q. But surely you do not mean to suggest that all athletes are mercenary?

But not to pull any punches, a lot of these young men don't strike me as very worthy to begin with. They put themselves up for sale. They entertain bids, and they make calculations about their prospects for going on to the pros. They are eager to embrace their corrupters; it's perfect symbiosis. I remember seeing a documentary film a few years ago about a very talented high school basketball player who was being courted by dozens of universities. Which would he choose? It was a question presumed to have serious import. Everyone was spouting their concern for his educational future, but all that he was thinking about — if the barely intelligible words he uttered could truly be regarded as expressions of thought — was how he could best ensure himself a professional career. He was probably ineducable, but he was quite willing (or more likely resigned) to use some university as his stepping stone, and it was willing to use him.

Q. Surely that was an exceptional case. Not all high school athletes are so, well, mercenary.

A. No, I suppose not. But even if the athletes are not all mercenary, the universities are. Division I sports programs are expensive and they must be made to pay for themselves. I understand relatively few of them do, but they all must try. It is another factor intensifying competition for athletes and heightening the pressure on them for success. Of course, all this hustling is cloaked in the same old verbiage of "excellence." The plain realities are that the athletes must pretend to be students, and the universities must pretend to be interested in their education. It says something about the moral character of the acacemic profession that its members accommodate themselves so comfortably to these obvious dishonesties practiced upon and by the students whom it is their life work to educate.

Q. Well, even granting that a certain amount of dishonesty is inevitable in major sports programs, don't you think they add something important to the college experience? Don't they create school spirit and loyalty? Don't they give many people a chance for involvement in an exciting, harmless activity? Don't they "enhance student life"?

A. I won't dwell on your interesting thought that one might overlook a certain amount of dishonesty for the sake of enhancing student life. But you have indeed opened up an important subject. Here is the second reason given in justification of expensive, attention-getting sports on campus: school spirit, loyalty, the good, clean fun of Saturday afternoons at the football game. All of them seen as "enhancing student life" and no doubt linked with the so-called "pursuit of academic excellence."

I have to say that I regard this justification as empty-headed and mischievous. Consider seriously now, what question is really at stake when those phrases about "school spirit," etc., are used in connection with university athletics? It is the central question, to which we always get back one way or another, of the effect that universities ought to have on students, and through them, on the society to which they belong. Or, put in another way, it is the question of the university's relation to popular culture, the culture by which our students are formed, and in which their minds and lives are saturated.

What do you suppose people actually have in mind when they talk about "school spirit," etc.? Not gratification over a biology class or freshman English. Or appreciation for the attentions of the dean of student affairs, or for the quality of the library. So far as I can make it out, "school spirit" is a feeling specifically associated with participation in the ritual of athletic contests: something concocted out of pre-game

I. Superiority and Dominance

rallies, rehearsed cheers, and the joy of being on the winning side (losing is never thought of as conducive to "school spirit"). All of this is supposed to lead to a sort of "patriotism": What a wonderful place is Monumental U where all together we cheer on our teams and feel uplifted by their victories! Thus is student life enhanced.

It hardly needs saying that this "school spirit" tells us nothing about how well students are educated. It's a response to a particular stimulus, essentially the same feeling experienced by New York Yankees or Buffalo Bills fans, with the difference that no one pretends there's a peculiar virtue associated with fandom (as there's supposed to be with "school spirit").

Now we all recognize that there's something childish in the feelings usually aroused by athletic contests. A person for whom the victory or defeat of an athletic team of which he or she is not a member is an important event, who really *cares* about such things, has something undeveloped about him. "School spirit," in my opinion, is precisely the expression of such a lack of development. When a university cultivates it and takes pride in the degree of "school spirit" it has elicited in its predominantly adolescent student body, it is not enhancing student life but debasing it. "School spirit" is a sign of the infantile character of an institution.

Q. Oh, professor, surely this is going too far! An innocent matter like...

A. I've only begun. And you've provided me with just the word I need. What underlies the satisfaction people take in "school spirit"? Why do administrators rub their hands contentedly in its presence, and parents and editorialists smile benignly? Big-time sports on campus are a way of extending the childhood of students, that is to say, their innocence. You should understand that the world outside the university, for all of its credulous faith in the social and economic advantages of higher education, is deeply distrustful of what may happen there. The university is a place of unpredictable intellectual possibilities. Most students, it's true, manage to resist them, or never even encounter them, but many do, and lives can sometimes be changed that way. A new idea, if it takes root in a person, has the power to awaken the critical spirit, possession of which is the only true adulthood.

The world outside — and I include most university administrators in this category — is not especially comfortable with that sort of thing. It wants the university to perform its training function, and for the rest to preserve as much as possible the innocence of the children it sends there. And innocence is made visible in images of the football stadium and basketball court: thousands of excited faces in passionate enthusiasm over a childish contest; cheerleaders in short skirts leaping to the shoulders of their fiercely smiling male counterparts; multitudes of index fingers waving at the television camera as they are identically waved on every

8

campus in the country. These images all confirm the fantasy of college innocence, a world of games.

To provide students with more and more games, therefore, is to pander to their immature selves; it is a betrayal. (You understand, of course, that I'm not talking about the games people actually play but the mass games, the ones performed by a few dozen professional athletes before huge crowds of spectators.) You may take it as a simple rule of thumb: the more "school spirit" whipped up on a campus, the more infantile the student body.

Q. I refuse to believe...

A. This theme of childishness, its preservation and encouragement, is a very important one. It is one of the fundamental attributes of popular culture in America. Ask yourself, please, what cultural experiences a person growing up in America is likely to have had by the time he or she arrives at the university. Perhaps only someone who has tried to raise a child during the past twenty-five years can grasp the full horror of it. Apart from the normal mental vacuity and sports obsession of the American high school, the world of the young consists of the omnipresent commercial media where everything is designed to preserve adolescence as a permanent state of being: the ceaseless music with its baby-talk poetry, the disk-jockey chatter, the talk shows and game shows, the sitcoms, the beer and automobile ads, the movies, the *Playboys* and *People* magazines, Ann Landers and Brenda Starr, football games, basketball games, hockey games, baseball games, bowling, boxing, golf, automobile racing, wrestling! To be sure, no one experiences *only* these things, and some people do outgrow them, more or less, but more and more people know life primarily through them. They are more intimate than one's neighbors; they are the subjects of opinion and conversation; they are the form and substance of consciousness itself! The citizens of Cleveland rejoiced recently at the establishment in their city of the Rock and Roll Hall of Fame.

In such a culture the prospects for the critical spirit are dim. Where is it to find encouragement? Obviously, the university is one possible answer. And so we come back to the question of how universities ought to influence their students. The mass-sports programs sponsored by American universities, programs controlled as much by the demands of television as by the needs of ordinary "live" (as they say) spectators, are simply ways of embracing popular culture. They obliterate the distinction, so fearful and threatening, between the university as a home of ideas and the world outside where a mindless popular culture reigns unchallenged.

Q. I fear you are not only a Utopian. You sound to me suspiciously like — I must say it — an elitist!

9

I. Superiority and Dominance

A. And you sound suspiciously like one of my students. Or perhaps the associate provost for undergraduate education. Of course I am an elitist. What else is higher education for but to convey the best, most truthful, most interesting and important culture that mankind possesses from one generation to the next? The university is by its nature an elitist institution; not all the efforts of presidents and provosts, of alumni associations and chambers of commerce, can quite extinguish that fact. Sport is one of the instruments most favored to hide and smother it: look there's nothing dangerous going on here! We're all playing games!

Q. The critical spirit! Do the honest, hard-working people of this country need that?

A. Don't they?

THE PHILOSOPHY OF EXCELLENCE: OLYMPIC PERFORMANCES, CLASS POWER, AND THE CANADIAN STATE

BRUCE KIDD

On the final day of the the 1983 Olympic Academy of Canada, a residential workshop on the problems and prospects of the Olympic Movement, a group of Olympic athletes attempted an audacious protest. Staging a mock trial, they placed the President of the Canadian Olympic Association, Roger Jackson, in the docket. The indictment:

> the COA, by establishing team selection standards significantly higher than those of the international federations and the International Olympic Committee, thereby denying many deserving athletes the opportunity of participating in the Games, had violated the Olympic Charter.

The prosecution, led by wrestler Howard Stupp, built its case carefully. The COA criteria — requiring a world ranking in the top 16 for Olympic selection, and a "reasonable probability of finishing in one of the top three placings" for the Pan-American Games[1] — were introduced without objection. They had been in effect since 1978 and had been widely circulated. Witnesses were then summoned to confirm that these standards would exclude a number of gifted and popular national champions and that in some sports of rapidly rising participation, such as nordic skiing, Canadians would not be represented at all. British scholar Peter McIntosh, a guest speaker at the Academy, then testified that the pursuit of victory was not the sole purpose of the Games. "Pierre de Coubertin is frequently misquoted as saying that 'the most important thing is not the winning, but the taking part!'" McIntosh argued. "In fact, what he said was 'the most important thing is less to win than to take part.' He made it a matter of priority. In 1980, there were 5472 Olympic competitors. Most were not within striking distance of a medal, but perhaps they got more out of the Games than the people who were."

Stupp then appealed to the jury, his audience of athletes, teachers, coaches, sports administrators, journalists and COA executive members. Surely a Canadian champion, after years of dedicated effort, deserved an opportunity of competing in sport's finest event, he said. How could the Olympics inspire others if no Canadians were involved? This argument evoked little applause, but Stupp pressed on. According to the Olympic

11

I. Superiority and Dominance

Charter, he said, the Olympic Movement sought "to encourage and strengthen friendship between sportspersons from every country," not to restrict the opportunities for such friendships. Slightly more applause. If all NOCs followed the Canadian example, he argued, many of the "cinderella" champions of Olympic legend, including Jackson, would never have been entered — nervous hooting — and there would be only about 2,000 athletes in the Games. That wouldn't be the Olympics, he shouted in conclusion, and sat down to a grudging hand.

Three COA leaders — Jackson, and IOC Members James Worrall and Richard Pound — were then called to defend the criteria. They were each greeted by enthusiastic applause. If the Games were to motivate Canadians to pursue "excellence," the *altius, citius, fortius* of another Olympic motto, tougher standards than the achievement of a Canadian championship were necessary, Pound said. The major Games were not the place for "learners" or "tourists," he explained to rows of nodding heads. No matter how personally worthy, the Canadian champion who finished up the track or was eliminated in the heats inspired no one. "We want Canadians to compete — not just participate — in international competition," Jackson said. Under cross-examination, he explained it was not a question of funds, but of creating the conditions under which Canadians would train harder to move up the ladder. That's the only way Canada had improved its overall Olympic placing from 23rd in 1972, to 10th in 1976, and perhaps 7th or 8th in 1984. This statement touched off prolonged cheering. In his testimony, Worrall responded to the argument about the IOC. Nothing in the Charter required an NOC to send an athlete in every event, he said. If it did, entries would be so great the Games would be unmanageable. By the time the defence summed up — lowering the standards would retard Canada's climb to the top — the outcome was in little doubt. The COA was acquitted by a wide margin.

Not all the major players had taken part — the federal and provincial governments which play an integral role in shaping the Olympic project in Canada were notably absent — but the testimony and argument in the Academy mock trial encapsulated the discourse within the Canadian Olympic community as it prepared for the 1984 Games. The debate over selection would intensify — several athletes even took the COA to a real court[2] — but the COA leadership held firm, knowing it could count on the full support of the membership and ultimately, of the governments.[3] The basis of this consensus was widespread agreement with the COA's "philosophy of excellence" — the view that top athletic performance, as measured by medals, rankings, and records set in international competition, should be the overriding goal for the Olympic Movement, and that all athletes, coaches and administrators should devote themselves to this goal. Some might dispute what ranking constituted the threshold for "excellence" and how particular rankings

12

were to be calculated. Some admitted to other, less urgent, goals such as ensuring the fairness of competition and publicizing the international aspects of the Olympic Movement among school children and the general public. There was some debate about the extent to which sports bodies should support equality for women. The emphasis on high performance was often intertwined with a stern nationalism. In these respects, the values of Canadian Olympic leaders differed from the dominant ideology in North American sport — the "win-at-all-cost" hucksterism of the continentalist and male-exclusive commercial sport cartels, such as the National Hockey League and Major League Baseball. But the vocabulary of "excellence" pervaded all discussion. Even the protesting athletes shared it. Now that the COA has slightly relaxed selection standards for the 1987 Pan-American and 1988 Winter Olympic and Olympic Games, not a protest is to be heard.

The purpose of this paper is to examine the hegemony of "excellence" within the Olympic sports in Canada. I will argue that the promotion of the Canadian variant of "excellence" has been a recent project of a fraction of the male upper middle class, enabled by the absence of any effective challenge to that class and gender's leadership within the Olympic sports, the federal state's response to a deep crisis of legitimacy, and the simultaneous development of neo-conservative ideas. I will also point out that while the programs created to conduct the "pursuit of excellence" have a statist form, they have had the support of and clearly benefit indigenous and multi-national capital. Finally, I will suggest that the "philosophy of excellence" is highly ideological, that through its distillation into everyday commonsense it not only reinforces the domination of partriarchal state capitalism, but blocks the development of more democratic opportunities. Such an argument is hardly new, but it reminds us of the necessity of examining the institutions, practices and beliefs associated with Olympic sport in their historical contingency, and helps advance the process of generating, considering and implementing more beneficial alternatives. That, too, should be a task of sport scholarship.

"The GDR of the Commonwealth"

Canadians in the Olympic sports have not always been preoccupied with the medal hunt. An earlier generation was known as much for its *joie de vivre*, its desire to participate whatever the result, and its eagerness to travel to explore other cultures, as for its prowess on the field. The ideology of "excellence" has only been fashioned and spread during the last 25 years, in the course of the construction of a state-directed system for high performance sport. During that time, federal and provincial

13

I. Superiority and Dominance

governments, often at the instigation of Olympic leaders, have created elaborate mechanisms for the training and support of what are often referred to as "elite" athletes. To achieve the most effective program management, they have transformed the once autonomous, voluntary and largely regulatory sports governing bodies into professionally administered corporations and moved them into centrally located administrative centres. To improve the recruitment, training and in-competition coaching of representative teams, they have created a new cadre of professional coaches, prepared and evaluated according to national coaching development programs, and have centralized training in permanent national teams, national and provincial training centres, and regular off-shore training camps and tours. To encourage athletes to devote as much time as possible to sport, they have created an ambitious financial incentive scheme. Under the federal Athlete Assistance Plan, an athlete achieving a ranking in the top eight in her/his event in the world earns an "A" card, which pays $650 per month basic stipend plus allowances for special training, day care, special equipment, moving and travel expenses, facility rentals, and university or college tuition, books and instruments. Sport Canada mails the cheques directly to athletes.[4] Federal and provincial plans are integrated to provide five levels of award.

Most of these programs are financed and controlled, if not directly managed, by the state agencies. In Ottawa, Sport Canada provides the national federations with "core funding" to offset the costs of national and international meetings, administration, staff salaries and travel, coaching and officiating development, staging national championships, and conducting a national team. It directly administers the athlete incentives, as well as programs for national training centres, "research which will enhance the results of Canadian athletes in international competition," biomechanical, physiological and psychological athlete testing and counselling, staging international games, and encouraging greater female participation. Within Sport Canada, the High Performance Unit sets and monitors performance targets for each sports body, develops special programs for athletes and coaches, and works with the COA (and other bodies responsible for Canadian participation in multi-sport international games) on preparing the "games missions." In addition, the National Sport and Recreation Centre houses and services the national offices of the sports governing bodies, the Coaching Association of Canda coordinates certification and apprenticeship programs, the Canada Games Council oversees the Canada Games (a quadrenniel multi-sport developmental competition) and the Sport Medicine Council of Canda provides testing and other professional services. The Athlete Information Bureau and the Sport Information Resource Centre provide library, research and public relations services.

14

All are federally created and funded agencies. A similar structure has been created in most provinces.[5]

While the actual athletic activity is carried out by the sports governing bodies, the state exerts tight control. For example, Sport Canada subsidizes the hiring of national coaches (in 1986-7, to a maximum of $42,500 annual salary and $3,900 travel), but demands consultation and the right of veto over the selection process, the successful applicant, the job description and the performance appraisal scheme and "reserves the right to terminate support for any funded position for cause."[6] Athletes receiving incentive awards must sign contracts which obligate them to:

• follow the training and competitive program agreed upon by the athlete, the national coach and where applicable, the regional national coach. "The Athlete shall avoid living in an environment that is not conducive to high performance achievements or taking any deliberate action that involves significant risks for the Athlete's ability to perform or limits the Athlete's performance."
• provide the national coach with an annual training chart, monthly updates, and "any other appropriate information that the national coach may request."
• participate in all mandatory training camps and competitions.
• dress in the required uniform while travelling as a member of the team.
• avoid intoxication at training camps and competitions.
• submit to random doping control testing.
• participate in up to two days of "reasonable non-commercial promotional activities as requested by Sport Canada."
• avoid competitions in which South Africans are competing.
• refrain from airing complaints to the media until all established grievance procedures are exhausted.

Athletes failing to maintain satisfactory training or to honour these commitments may lose their carding benefits.[7] On the whole, governments now provide 65-75 percent of the total cost of the Olympic sports bodies' operations. The federal contribution in 1985-6 amounted to $56 million.[8] The state presence is so great that Canada is sometimes referred to as "the GDR of the Commonwealth."[9]

The Political Economy of High Performance

The inspiration for these programs was the ambition of Olympic leaders and athletes in the 1950s and 1960s to regain the prestige and public influence they had lost to the commercial leagues. To do this, they believed they had to restore Canada's pre-World War II stature in

I. Superiority and Dominance

international competition and to reverse the annual "brain drain" of talented athletes lured away by US "athletic scholarships." They sought public funds to help them and they had precedent and politicians on their side. Governments have been financially contributing to Canadian Olympic Teams since 1920.[10] In 1937, former Olympic hockey captain Hugh Plaxton, then a Liberal backbencher, introduced a bill calling for a ministry of sport and he had been supported by the Conservatives.[11] During and following the war, in response to the widespread demands for better labour and welfare legislation and with revenues buoyed by sustained industrial and urban expansion, the federal government embarked upon a policy of diluted Keynesianism and social intervention, funding not only unemployment insurance, mothers' allowances, universal old age pensions, and hospital insurance, but physical fitness, a national film production agency, higher education, and the arts. In 1957, it created the Canada Council to make the artist and the intellectual "an integral part of the Canadian environment" by subsidizing the visible and performing arts and scholarship in the humanities and social sciences.[12] Olympic leaders began to call for similar assistance for sport.

Few Canadians harboured ideological objection to these new programs, nor would they do so when it came to sport. "Laissez-faire" had never been popular in Canada. The most powerful capitalists have long been accustomed to having the state subsidize and protect their investments and mediate subordinate class pressures through state-administered reforms. In fact, some of the major nationalizations in Canadian history, such as the creation of Ontario Hydro and the Canadian National Railways, were undertaken by Conservative Governments. As Reg Whitaker has written, "the basic engine of development in Canada was to be private enterprise, but it was to be private enterprise at public expense".[13] Upper middle class males, from whom the amateur sports leadership has always been drawn,[14] have frequently sought state assistance for their educational and cultural institutions when private efforts failed.[15] In an earlier period, some amateur leaders would have decried "government interference in sport" and the socialist Workers' Sports Association would have opposed public assistance to the "bourgeois" sports associations, but these views were rarely aired after World War Two. The established sports leaders were prepared to swallow their doubts in the interests of winning teams. Following the Soviet Union's entry into the Olympics, and the repression of the left during the Cold War, the critique of the class-biased nature of amateur sports virtually disappeared.[16]

The first major step was taken by the Conservative Government of John Diefenbaker in response to lobbying by sports leaders such as then COA Vice-President Worrall, public dismay at the decline in Canadian performances in international competition and Diefenbaker's personal belief that successful athletic teams enhanced a nation's image abroad and strengthened capitalist voices in the Cold War.[17] In 1961, it passed the Fitness and Amateur Sport Act to provide $5 million annually for physical fitness research and grants to the voluntary associations and provincial governments for sport, recreation, and professional preparation in physical education. Initially, FAS increased the funding available to amateur sport, giving the established leaders responsibility for policy in a national advisory council. (The first two chairs of this council were COA presidents Ken Farmer and Worrall.) The restructuring of the sports bodies, and their subsequent loss of direct control, did not occur until the early 1970s, under the Liberal Government of Pierre Trudeau. Whereas Diefenbaker was concerned with the ideological impact of national teams abroad, an acute crisis of federal legitimacy led Trudeau to focus on their image at home.

The equation of cultural nationality — in the sense of a single people with a common history, language, and identity — with the federal state has always been contested in Canada. Ever since the Conquest, most French-speaking inhabitants and their leaders have defined themselves as members of a distinct *nation* within Canada and have sought to protect this collective identity through strong representative institutions in Quebec.[18] During the Trudeau years, the federal government's right to speak for all Canadians was not only challenged by a resurgent separatism in Quebec, but by oil-rich western provincial governments demanding a reduction in federal powers, the native peoples seeking self-determination and by organized labour and poor people's groups protesting high unemployment, inflation, and the unequal distribution of power and wealth. At the same time, the acceleration of direct investment by the US-based multinationals eroded Ottawa's ability to plan and coordinate economic development, while the further penetration of American perspectives and preoccupations into education, popular culture and sport undermined the very idea of an independent Canada.[19]

In response to these centrifugal tensions, Trudeau sought to strengthen "pan-Canadian unity" — his own deeply held view, widely shared by most English-speaking Canadians, that Canada is a single nation, made up of individuals with a preponderance of common interests, who happen to speak two official languages and stem from many different cultural traditions.[20] During the 1970s, as labour militancy increased, he began to blend corporatist ideas into this vision of Canada, calling for renewed social "sacrifices" and a new consensus between business and labour in the national interest.[21]

For these goals, the high performance sports project, which recruited athletes from every national and regional group for teams which would march behind a single Canadian flag, compete in identical

I. Superiority and Dominance

red-and-white uniforms, and glorify teamwork and discipline, was ideal. During his successful 1968 election campaign, Trudeau promised more financial support for the Olympic sports, on the grounds that successful teams are "important for the image Canadians have of themselves." Following the disappointing results from Mexico increased lobbying from athletes and officials persuaded him to follow through. He appointed a task force, composed of an oil executive, Olympic giant slalom champion Nancy Greene, and a sports physician, which recommended a much more interventionist approach. In 1970, sport minister John Munro, proclaiming that henceforth the primary goal of Canadian sports policy would be wining medals in international competition, embraced the task force's recommendations and began the creation of the system I have described.[22]

Most Olympic leaders shared these ambitions and actively contributed to the build-up of new programs. Their predecessors had carved out "national" jurisdictions, organized "national" championships, and selected "national" teams long before their activities extended to the boundaries of the federal state. Imbedded in that fraction of the middle class which had cast its lot with the survival of distinctive Canadian institutions, they strived to strengthen them.[23] Certainly they were able to play the strains of pan-Canadian nationalism with telling effect. After the 1976 Olympics were awarded to Montreal, the COA obtained a rapid acceleration of federal and provincial high-performance programs under the code word, "Game Plan," on the grounds that national pride demanded a major effort to win more medals in "Canada's Games."[24] When the US supertanker Manhattan plowed through the North West Passage, raising fears about Canadian sovereignty in the North, a hitherto rejected proposal for an Arctic Winter Games (involving several Euro-Canadian or "southern" sports rather than the life-skill contests and cooperative physical activities of the native Dene and Inuit) was dusted off and presented to Cabinet. It won ready approval.[25] At the same time, provincial governments were encouraged to reproduce the federal pattern of support to help their own athletes and enhance their own prestige. An important stimulus was the quadrennial winter and summer Canada Games, in which athletes competed on a provincial basis.

Needless to say, the pro-active state agencies quickly assumed a stance of autonomy from the COA and other sports bodies, neglecting the national advisory council,[26] reshaping the sports bodies according to their own needs and wishes, and dealing directly with athletes and coaches. While these changes have produced much friction — the sports bodies rightly complain about the number and unilateral nature of state directives — they cannot be viewed as inimicable to the general interests of the male upper middle class nor of patriarchal capital. In the first

18

place, sports leaders have been given the opportunity to pursue their ambitions with public funds and a whole new layer of relatively well-paying and interesting jobs. They may represent different institutions, but sports leaders and government officials come from similar backgrounds.[27] There has been a steady traffic between the leadership positions in the sports bodies and the government agencies. For example, the current COA president, Roger Jackson, has been Sport Canada director-general, while the deputy minister and director-general, Lyle Makosky and Abby Hoffman, have been COA vice-presidents. Secondly, Sport Canada actively contributes to capital accumulation. Federal support for the staging of national and international games has greatly facilitated expansion in the construction industries, while the resulting new facilities have benefitted the commercial sport conglomerates. Montreal's Olympic Stadium, for example, is almost exclusively used by the Seagram-owned Expos and the Carling-O'Keefe-owned Alouettes. In recent years, as supply-side economic theories have gained ascendency in response to the falling rate of profit, and leading capitalists have pressured governments to cut social services and privatize public enterprise, the state has also championed the direct commercialization of the Olympic sports. Threatening wholesale reductions in sport funding, it has urged the sports bodies to sell the good will their athletes and activities generate to advertisers.[28] No one has ever accused Sport Canada of being "socialist." Even the Olympic Trust of Canada, the fund-raising arm of the COA made up of the largest corporations in Canada, both indigenous and multi-national, supports this form of state intervention.[29] Finally, although Sport Canada supports several affirmative action measures for women, and rewards male and female athletes according to identical criteria, it allocates the bulk of its funds according to the Olympic program, which favours males by a ratio of almost three to one. Women are woefully underrepresented in coaching and administration, and even where they hold identical positions, they tend to be paid significantly less. As a result, males still enjoy from 65-75% of the public funds spent on sport in Canada and the patriarchal nature of the activity itself is rarely challenged.[30]

From opportunities to incentives

In the late 1960s and early 1970s, the call to "excellence" was most frequently voiced by advocates of greater state support, in the language of self-development, opportunities and needs: to enable Canadians to develop their talents to the full, went the argument, the state must provide better facilities and be prepared to pay athletes and coaches.[31] However, the COA and the state agencies soon abandoned even the rhetoric of "personal growth," transforming "excellence" into a vocabulary

19

for performance incentives and strict controls. To protect "standards," they said, they could only fund programs which resulted in medals and records[32]. It was not only the athletes who were required to keep winning to maintain funding, but sports governing bodies, coaches and administrators, and even Sport Canada itself. The sports bodies must meet yearly and quadrennial performance targets. In 1983-4, "nearly 75 per cent of the federal expenditures on national sports governing bodies (went to) the 25 sports which have achieved a placing in the 1-12 position in the most recent world championships or the Olympics. (According to Sport Canada) reinforcement of this type of funding strategy (is) essential to Canada's performance prospects."[33] The performance appraisal systems developed by Sport Canada for coaches and administrators emphasize athletic achievement as well. Sport Canada has even risked its own funding on this basis. Early in the 1980s, Sport Canada Director-General Hoffman won Cabinet approval for two new "enrichment" programs — "Best Ever," which has provided $25 million of additional funding in the fiscal years 1983-8 for the winter Olympic sports and "Quadrennial Program Planning," $35 million for 1984-8 for the summer Olympic sports. Although these new programs barely offset inflation and will expire after the Winter and Summer Olympics of 1988, they were justified in terms of additional medals, the implicit bargain being more medals, renewed support.[34]

The message of material incentives has been reinforced by the widespread application of the positivist sports sciences, which naturalize (rather than problematize) the practices of high performance sport, thereby encouraging athletes and coaches to organize their lives around measurable tasks.[35] Official statements, Sport Canada publications, and the state broadcasting network provide a public chorus. Federal officials hold court at major events. On the eve of the 1978 Commonwealth Games in Edmonton, Sports Minister Iona Campagnolo announced medal quotas for athletes in every event and when they surpassed all expectations, she marched with them in the Closing Ceremony parade. The Athlete Information Bureau subsidizes the mass media coverage of Canadians competing outside North America, publishes its own bi-monthly, *Champion*, and distributes it to every carded athlete and national coach. The coverage of major events by the state-owned Canadian Broadcasting Corporation, at least on the English network, tends to validate the same goals: the bulk of air time is devoted to winning Canadian performances and victory celebrations. The COA reinforces this approach by its well-publicized selection criteria, and its own financial incentives for coaches whose athletes are ranked in the top 16 in the world.[36]

Bravo Canada!

Los Angeles was a great triumph for the architects of "excellence." On June 2, 1984, when the deadline for Olympic entries expired without a change in the Soviet bloc's decision to stay away, the COA recalculated the list of likely medal winners and added 113 athletes to the original team of 325. (Of the final squad, 273 were male, 163 female.) In Los Angeles, an experienced and well-prepared "mission" staff, with a contingent of coaches and technical advisors 10-30 percent larger than IOC rules allowed, took every step necessary to ensure the athletes' well-being and competitive edge. Canadians won 44 medals, almost three times as many as other Games. In virtually every sport, they performed more successfully than ever before. Just by themselves, the swimmers and divers won more medals than the entire Canadian team in Montreal. More teams qualified for the final tournaments than ever before. Canada place sixth in the gold medal count, fourth in total medals, and 60 percent of the entire team came home with Olympic Honour Diplomas for finishing in the top eight. The COA could boast: "The biggest Canadian Olympic Team in history was by far the best Canadian team in history, giving an ecstatic Canadian public — by the thousands in Los Angeles and the millions back home in front of their TV sets — the enjoyment of being winners."[37] Sport Canada quickly printed and distributed two large colour posters to schools, universities and sports clubs across the country. One displayed an "honour role" of Canadian medal winners under the bilingual heading "Formidable." The other showed the Canadian team marching behind the flag in the opening ceremonies parade, under the slogan "Bravo Canda." It seemed a great vindication for the strategy of performance incentives. Sport Canada immediately announced that it was "rewarding" Canadian athletes by increasing monthly AAP stipends from $50-100 (to the present $650 for A cards, etc.).

Canadians would draw other lessons from LA. The organizers of the XV Olympic Winter Games in Calgary were so impressed with the public relations triumph of the New York to Los Angeles Torch Relay that they have closely modelled their sponsored coast-to-coast relay on LA's experience. A group of Olympic enthusiasts in Toronto were so taken with LA's private enterprise strategy and the resulting surplus that they are bidding for the 1996 Games on this basis.[38] And the Conservative Government of Brian Mulroney, elected on September 4, 1984, has used the commercial success of the LA Games to justify a radical privatization of the Olympic sports through its Sports Marketing Council, created in February 1986. According to Sports Minister Otto Jelinek, the sports bodies should now be able to obtain sufficient marketing contracts that the public monies lost through cutbacks and the expiration of "Best Ever" will be replaced.[39]

I. Superiority and Dominance

"Sweat-suited philanthropists"

The transformation of the Olympic sports by the programs I have described has radically altered the athlete's experience. It's not only a matter of greatly improved facilities, coaching, technical, medical and financial support, and competitive opportunities. The nature of day-to-day activity and the meanings with which the athlete is encouraged to invest it have been changed *pari passu*. By hiring full-time coaches and technical directors, establishing national training centres and "teams-in-being" (such as the men's and women's volleyball squads stationed at the Universities of Calgary and Regina respectively), and rewarding everyone for better performances, Sport Canada and the sports bodies have created the conditions and incentives for full-time training and they have come to expect it. Most athletes are now encouraged to curtail other activities. Even when they want to pursue education or careers simultaneously, special training camps and major competitions make it all but impossible. In 1982-3, members of the national women's field hockey team were away from home a total of 142 days, while some members of the junior team were away 172 days.[40] In addition, training has become increasingly segmented, routinized, and carried out with mechanical aids such as treadmills and faradic stimulation, planned by the scientist in response to the omnipresent test, and ordered by the coach. The athlete is no longer "subject" of his/her own activity, sharing the planning and conduct of the athletic endeavour with teammates and coach, but the "object" of an elaborate scientific bureaucracy.

In the amateur era, when a coach or official wanted an athlete to devote more time to training, s/he had to employ normative controls and appeal to beliefs that the athlete had internalized, such as loyalty to the team. Such appeals usually were effective, because most athletes shared the coach's ambitions and expectations about behaviour, but if the athlete was not convinced, s/he could have ended the relationship and moved to another club. In an individual sport, s/he could have competed as a self-trained "unattached" athlete. S/he had no material interest in sport and pursued it as a form of leisure. But with state incentives and contracts, the national coach has recourse to the utilitarian and instrumental controls characteristic of wage labour. To be sure, s/he will use normative controls as much as possible, but when all else fails, s/he can enforce behaviour by invoking the contract and the power to penalize the athlete and withdraw benefits. Coaches have used the threat of withdrawal to discourage athletes from taking part-time jobs, travelling and sightseeing after major competitions, and getting married. If the national team has a monopoly on the specialized resources necessary for high performance, including the available living stipends and endorsement fees, the athlete has little choice other than to quit.

Elsewhere, I have argued that the conditions of athletic labour in the Olympic sports in Canada meet the legal test of employment.[41] In effect, most Canadian Athletes have become state professionals. As underpaid professionals — Sport Canada remuneration is less than the minimum wage — Canadian athletes are "sweat-suited philanthropists,"[42] ensuring the careers of hundreds of well-paid coaches, sports scientists and sports administrators, and subsidizing the ambitions of the federal state.

Commercialization has tended to increase these pressures. As National Ski Team Coach Currie Chapman has observed,

> ...all of a sudden it's not just them going down a mountain, but it's also a bank, a drug store, a car parts chain as well. Then comes the phone call or the telex and somewhere there is a little note that says politely 'we'd like to see some results for our money.'[43]

These expectations will intensify as the Conservative Government steps up its privatization campaign. Sport Marketing Council President Lou Lefaive recently said:

> I'm going to get shot for this, but I think we're going to have to look at sports like archery, bobsled and luge, ski jumping, the esoteric sports (which cannot attract a sponsor) and say, should they survive at all? Are they really sponsored by the Canadian people? If they don't prostitute themselves, and become realistic and look at where their position is in the marketplace,...that sport's going to die.[44]

In this situation, athletes are not only competing for the state, the corporation, but the very future of Olympic level participation in their sports. And very, very few of them benefit directly from commercialization, as most contracts are made with their sports bodies.

The ideology of "excellence"

The constant appeal to 'excellence' has muted the voices of resistance and reform. As Dan Thompson, former captain of the national swim team and an athletes' rights advocate, has said,

> The call to 'excellence' in this country is always one of sacrifice and self-denial. You are constantly told, and most of us have come to believe, that if you want to be the very best, you have to be tough at all times, and that means never taking the easy way out. Somehow, the idea of

athletes' rights — being able to appeal bad selection and discipline decisions, having rules slightly more permissive than martial law — sounds like 'the easy way out.' If we ask for our rights, we are told, it will mean that we have lost the will to win.[45]

Immediately following the Los Angeles Games, the senior members of the national women's field hockey team conducted an evaluation of their Olympic preparations, from which they concluded that the national coach could not meet their needs as players and persons. They recommended that her contract not be renewed. But while their recommendation was accepted by the national board, it was overruled by Sport Canada, on the grounds that the incumbent was the only one who could produce a winning team. Sport Canada told the field hockey association that unless it renewed the coach's contract, $400,000 in funding would be cut.[46] Other recent efforts by athletes to assert their own ideas, such as an attempt by track athletes to unionize, have ended in failure. They have been undermined by athletes' relative youth and inexperience, and their lack of genuine spokespersons on national boards and executives. Athlete "representatives" sit on only 17 of 60 national sports bodies recently surveyed by Sport Canada and most of these are appointed by coaches and administrators, not elected. Only a few of the COA's Athlete Advisory Council members are elected by fellow athletes.[47] In 1986, the AAC fully endorsed the COA's selection standards for the 1988 Games. In 1987, its leaders demurred in a new COA drug policy, despite strenuous opposition by some athletes.[48] Most athletes come from the upper middle class so they have grown up with the same assumptions about the importance of self-sacrifice and intense competition as the sports leadership.[49] They can afford to endure the relative deprivation of their years in sport, confident they will find well-paying jobs upon retirement. Outside the Olympic community, there has been even less debate on the merits of "excellence." The North American student movement, whose 1960s critique of secondary and higher education inspired the 1970s "jockraker" criticism of modern sport, is largely silent. In the legislatures, the mass media and other public forums, sport is widely regarded as a "technical," "non-partisan" issue.

Under these circumstances, the "philosophy of excellence" has become a powerful ideology, by which I mean it expresses a world-view that is partial or partisan to the interests of a particular group or groups, clothed in a partial or incomplete description of the complex human reality. C. Wright Mills has defined ideology as those symbols and statements which "justify or oppose the arrangement of power and the positions within the arrangement of the powerful"[50] and I am following

24

his definition here. I also accept the Marxian view that the power of such symbols and statements is magnified by the degree to which they are naturalized as commonsense. As David Harvey observes, "Marx gives a specific meaning to ideology — he regards it as an *unaware* expression of the underlying ideas and beliefs which attach to a particular social situation, in contrast to the *aware* and critical exposition of ideas in their social context which is frequently called ideology in the west."[51] The "philosophy of excellence" effectively blocks out any other view of physical activity, even the humanitarian social philosophy of Olympism. When apprised of the Coubertanian aspirations for personal growth, international understanding, and the association of sport with the visual and performing arts, for example, most Canadian athletes shake their heads in surprise.[52] When they discuss the "doping" and "gender" controls, they usually endorse them (although some doubt their accuracy) in the interests of a fair distribution of the medals, never examining their own preoccupation with the medal hunt.

As others have argued, the unquestioned assumptions of "excellence" reinforce both the hierarchy and the social relations of patriarchal state monopoly capitalism.[53] They may ring true to those who have made it on this basis, but most of those have had advantages of education and income which have enabled them to experience success. "Be the very best you can be," the motto of the COA's Royal Bank-sponsored Junior Olympics program in Canadian schools, is an important message to get across, but without calling attention to the structures of inequality which severely limit the life chances of so many children, such encouragement does little but mystify, especially when tied to the seemingly self-empowering, dramatic, and socially validated activities of sport. When appropriated by governments and corporations, such messages justify the whole neo-conservative project of authoritarian controls, cutbacks in public spending, and the further redistribution of income to the already privileged.[54]

Developing an alternative vision, let alone the programs which would encourage it, will be a difficult task. Much of the scholarly criticism of "excellence," including my own, is rooted in experiences in the days of amateurism, when it was much more possible for athletes to share in the definition and direction of their own activity, and to combine their sport with career and other interests.[55] But this aspect of amateurism has been largely forgotten, while the inequalities it perpetuated are remembered with proper scorn. It will be necessary to tie the hopes for a more self-directed, democratic athletic experience to a more contemporary spirit and adapt them to the realities of state and corporate sponsorship. In the Canadian context, I feel the most promising example is the ongoing attempts by artists — writers, playwrights, painters, and actors — to root their work in their own experiences and

I. Superiority and Dominance

communities rather than the "demands" of the marketplace, to control its distribution, and to influence their dealings with governments, corporations and private patrons through artist-directed associations or unions.[56] There is some athletic precedent for collective action: in the years before the Montreal Games, Canadian athletes pressured the COA into significantly increasing their financial stipends (by threatening strike action) and joined with artists to lobby the organizing committee to a present much more ambitious arts and culture festival than it had planned.[57] Another promising development is the creation of the Olympic Academy of Canada as a forum for the discussion of Olympic issues.[58] But if these examples and opportunities are to contribute to anything other than a faint counterpoint to the full orchestra of "excellence," critical athletes will have to take more responsibility for their own actions and their public interpretations, and be prepared to link up with and mutually support other creative people and communities struggling for self-control. That's a tall order.

Notes

[1] Canadian Olympic Association, "Team Selection Guidelines and Procedures 1981-84 Quadrennial", August 31, 1982; and COA, "The Selection of Canadian Athletes for the Olympic Games," undated information service bulletin. In those events where fewer than 32 entries were expected, a ranking equivalent for the "top half" of the anticipated entry was required; e.g. because only 24 entries were expected in the women's discus and shot, Canadians in those events had to earn a ranking of 12th in the world to be considered. The policy also allowed for the "selection of a very limited number of rapidly improving young newcomers in some events where other Canadians already rank very high internationally. Such selections will be made only in cases where Olympic exposure is deemed...beneficial to that athlete's own future Olympic performance and not detrimental to overall team morale."

[2] "Butler rebuffed in Olympic court bid," *Calgary Herald*, July 18, 1984; and Janet Brooks, "Wrestler wins on mat but loses in courtroom," *The (Montreal) Gazette*, July 25, 1984.

[3] Prior to the 1984 Winter Games, Federal Sports Minister Jacques Olivier threatened financial cutbacks if the COA didn't broaden its selection criteria (Philip King, "Review of grant planned," *The Globe and Mail*, Feb. 1, 1984), but the COA's additions to the Los Angeles team in the wake of the Soviet-led boycott effectively closed the rift. For the 1988 Games, the COA has sought to answer some of the athletes' and Sport Canada's criticism by adding several exceptions to the "top 16/top half" standard. For the Winter Games in Calgary, for example, *"within reason,*

the COA will endeavour to select athletes in every sport." (Emphasis in original). See "Canadian Olympic Association Team Selection Policy 1985-1988," *Olympinfo*, January 1986.

4 Sport Canada, "A Guide to the Athlete Assistance Program...1985-6" (Ottawa, 1985).

5 Eric Broom and Rik Baka, *Canadian Governments and Sport* (Calgary: CAHPER, 1979) and Don Macintosh, N. Franks, and T. Bedecki, *Sport and politics in Canada: federal government involvement since 1961* (Montreal: Queen's-McGill, forthcoming).

6 Fitness and Amateur Sport, *Sport Canada Contributions Program 1986-7* (Ottawa, 1985), p. 19.

7 Sport Canada, "NSO/Carded Athlete Agreement" (Ottawa, 1985).

8 Fitness and Amateur Sport, "Annual Report 1985-6" (Ottawa, 1986), p. 42.

9 This phrase was first coined by British and Australian journalists at the 1978 Commonwealth Games in Edmonton. See Christie Blatchford, "'No apologies' for winning at Games," *Toronto Star*, August 13, 1978.

10 J. Thomas West, "Physical fitness, sport and the federal government 1909-54," *Canadian Journal of History of Sport and Physical Education*, 4(2), 1973, 29.

11 Canada, *House of Commons Debates*, January 20, 1937, 114-26.

12 Robert Bothwell, Ian Crummond, and John English, *Canada since 1945* (Toronto: University of Toronto, 1981). For an analysis of new federal programs in culture, see Robin Endres, "Art and Accumulation: the Canadian State and the Business of Art," in Leo Panitch (Ed.), *The Canadian State* (Toronto: U of T, 1977), 417-445.

13 R. Whitaker, "Images of the state in Canada", in Leo Panitch (Ed.), *The Canadian State*, p. 43; see also, Patricia Marchak, *Ideological perspectives on Canada* (Toronto: McGraw-Hill Ryerson, 1981).

14 Alan Metcalfe, "Organized sport and social stratification in Montreal: 1840-1901," in Richard Gruneau and John Albinson (Eds.), *Canadian Sport Sociological Perspectives* (Don Mills: Addison Wesley, 1976), 77-101; and Gruneau, *Class, Sports and Social Development* (Amherst: University of Massachusetts, 1983), 91-135.

15 E.g., R.D. Gidney and W.P.J. Millar, "From voluntarism to state schooling: the creation of the public school system in Ontario," *Canadian Historical Review*, 66(4), 1985, 443-73.

16 Bruce Kidd, "'We must maintain a proper balance between propaganda and serious athletics': the Workers' Sports Association of Canada 1922-36," *Proceedings of the 5th Canadian Symposium on the History of Sport and Physical Education* (Toronto: School of Physical and Health Education, 1982), 330-39.

I. Superiority and Dominance

[17] Don Macintosh, "Bill C-131 Revisited" and Bill Hallett, "Federal involvement in the development of sport in Canada 1943-79," in *Proceedings of the 5th Canadian Symposium*, 437-462.

[18] Denis Monière, *Ideologies in Quebec* (Toronto: U of T, 1981).

[19] These tensions are best discussed by James Laxer and Robert Laxer, *The Liberal Idea of Canada: Pierre Trudeau and the Question of Canada's Survival* (Toronto: James Lorimer, 1977); see also Ian Lumsden (Ed.), *Close the 49th Parallel, etc.: the Americanization of Canada* (Toronto: U of T, 1970).

[20] Pierre Trudeau, *Federalism and the French Canadians* (Toronto: Macmillan, 1968).

[21] Leo Panitch, "Corporatism in Canada," *Studies in Political Economy*, 1, 1979, 74-5.

[22] The two relevant documents are: *Report of the Task Force on Sport for Canadians* (Ottawa: Fitness and Amateur Sport, 1969), and John Munro, *A Proposed Sports Policy for Canadians* (Ottawa, March 13, 1970).

[23] See, especially, the COA submissions to the 1971 National Conference on Olympic Development and the COA-commissioned study, P.S. Ross, *Improving Canada's Olympic performance: challenges and strategies* (Toronto: Olympic Trust, 1972).

[24] Another fraction of the Canadian middle class has sought managerial positions with the multi-national conglomerates. See Marchak, *Ideological perspectives on Canada*, pp. 160-3.

[25] Interview with Lou Lefaive, March 13, 1982.

[26] Stephen Carroll, "The National Advisory Council on Fitness and Amateur Sport 1961-84," unpub. thesis, Sports Administration Certificate Program, York University, 1985.

[27] R. B. Beamish, "Socioeconomic and demographic characteristics of the national executives of selected amateur sports in Canada (1975)," *Working Papers in the Sociological Study of Sport and Leisure* (Queen's University), 1(1), 1978; and Robert Hollands and Rick Gruneau, "Social class and voluntary activity in the administration of Canadian amateur sport," *WPSSSL*, 2(3), 1979.

[28] "Sport woos business dollars," *Sport Ontario News*, 8(2), March 1979.

[29] The Trust gets about 20 per cent of its revenue in the form of government grants. In the 1980-84 quadrennial, they amounted to $2.3 million. See Canadian Olympic Association, *Quadrennial Report 1980-84* (Montreal: 1985), p. 219.

[30] Ann Hall and Dorothy Richardson, *Fair Ball* (Ottawa: Canadian Advisory Council on the Status of Women, 1982); and Sport Canada, "Women in Sport and Fitness Leadership: Summary of a National Survey" (Ottawa: 1986).

[31] E.g. Bruce Kidd, "A brief to the task force on sports," *Globe and Mail*, November 19-27, 1968.

[32] This transformation is ably documented in Rob Beamish and Jan Borowy, "Canada's High Performance Athletes: From Status to Contract," presented to the Conference on Research into Sports Administration, University of Alberta, October 16, 1986.

[33] Fitness and Amateur Sport, *Annual Report 1983-4*, (Ottawa, 1984), p. 19.

[34] Janet Brooks, "Athletic Excellence: is it worth $45.6 million?," *The Gazette*, June 11, 1984.

[35] David Whitson, "Sociology, Psychology and Canadian Sport," *Canadian Journal of Applied Sport Sciences*, 3(2), 1978, 26-42; and Bruce Kidd, "Athletes' Rights, the Coach, and the Sport Psychologist," in Peter Klavora and Juri Daniel (Eds.), *Coach, Athlete, and the Sport Psychologist* (Toronto: School of Physical and Health Education, 1979), 25-39.

[36] Canadian Olympic Association, *Quadrennial Report 1980-84*, pp. 177-82.

[37] *Ibid.*, p. 14.

[38] Toronto Ontario Olympic Council, "Toronto as Host to the 100th Anniversary of the Olympic Games" (Toronto: TOOC, 1986).

[39] Mathew Fisher, "Jelinek out to tap corporate purse," *Globe and Mail*, May 6, 1985.

[40] Interview with Jan Borowy, March 18, 1986. In a 1985 Sport Canada survey, 46 per cent of carded athletes reported being away for 50 days a year or more and 20 per cent reported absences of 135 days or more; Don Macintosh and John Albinson, "An Evaluation of the Athlete Assistance Program" (Ottawa, 1985).

[41] Bruce Kidd and Mary Eberts, *Athletes' Rights in Canada* (Toronto: Ministry of Tourism and Recreation, 1982), 73-6; Allen Sack and Bruce Kidd, "The Amateur Athlete as Employee" in A.T. Johnson and J.H. Frey (Eds.), *Government and Sport* (Totowa: Rowman and Allenheld, 1985), 41-61; and Kidd, "The Elite Athlete," in Hart Cantelon and Jean Harvey (Eds.), *The Sociology of Canadian Sport* (Ottawa: University of Ottawa, forthcoming).

[42] The term is borrowed from Robert Tressall's classic workingclass novel *Ragged Trousered Philanthropists* (London: G. Richards, 1914).

[43] Quoted in Greg Weston, "Discovering the flipside of success," *Ski Canada*, March 1987, p. 66.

[44] Quoted on Catherine Olsen, "Sports Privatization," Sunday Morning, CBC Radio, February 8, 1987.

[45] Interview with Dan Thompson, July 17, 1981.

[46] James Christie, "Jelinek orders coach's return," *Globe and Mail*, September 28, 1985; and Debbie Fulmore, "National coach rehired despite opposition," *Hockey Pitch*, Fall 1985 Supplement.

I. Superiority and Dominance

[47] Sport Canada, "Athletes' Representation on Boards of Directors," (Ottawa, 1986). In his 1970 White Paper, *A Proposed Sports Policy for Canadians*, John Munro proposed a much greater involvement of athletes "in the operation and policy-making structures of their organizations, at every level — boards of directors, executives, executive committees, advisory staff, everywhere from which the power in the organization emanates" (p. 14). While virtually every other proposal in this paper was quickly implemented, the call for athlete involvement in decision-making has been largely forgotten.

[48] See Athletes' Resource Group, "Proposals for a COA drug policy" (Kingston, 1987), for the alternatives some athletes put forward when the Athletes' Advisory Council refused to contest the COA's new policy on performance-enhancing drugs.

[49] Richard Gruneau, "Class or mass: notes on the democratization of Canadian sport," in Gruneau and Albinson (Eds.), *Canadian Sport Sociological Perspectives*, 108-40; Bob Eynon and Pat Kitchener, "Socio-economic analysis of parents of competitive swimmers in Ontario," unpub. paper, University of Western Ontario, 1977; and Robert J. Rogers and Alan W. Salmoni, "National Alpine Ski Team: Education and Career Survey," unpub. paper, Laurentian University, n.d.

[50] Mills, *The Sociological Imagination* (New York: Oxford, 1976), 37.

[51] Harvey, *Social Justice and the City* (Baltimore: John Hopkins, 1975), 18.

[52] Mike Hamilton, "Learning the Olympic spirit," *St. Catherine's Standard*, June 30, 1983.

[53] E.g. Paul Hoch, *Rip Off the Big Game* (Garden City: Doubleday, 1972); Jean-Marie Brohm, *Sport: a Prison of Measured Time* (London: Ink Links, 1978); and John Hoberman, *Sport and Political Ideology* (Austin: University of Texas, 1984). Of course, each of these authors makes similar points about the ideological role of sport in the socialist countries.

[54] Rick Gruneau, "Commercialism and the modern Olympics" in Alan Tomlinson and Garry Whannel (Eds.), *Five Ring Circus* (London: Pluto, 1984).

[55] Tom West, "Running great remains outspoken," *Champion*, 5(2), 1981, 25-6.

[56] Susan Crean, *Who's afraid of Canadian culture?* (Don Mills: General, 1976); and Independent Artists Union, "The Social and Economic Status of the Artist in English Canada," *FUSE*, Summer 1986, 39-47.

[57] Doug Gilbert, "Canada's Olympians hinting at their own fund drive," "Our Olympic athletes broke and embittered" and "COA votes $1.4 million to athletes," *The Gazette*, June 2, 4, and 13, 1975; and Bruce Kidd, "1976 Cultural Olympics: left at the starting line?" *Performing Arts*, 10, Winter 1973.

[58] See, for example, Olympic Academy of Canada, "Towards a definition of Olympism in Canada: discussion document," March 1986. It should be pointed out that all the COA and government officials mentioned in this paper regularly participate and contribute to the discussions at this annual event.

THE USE OF DRUGS BY ATHLETES

PATRICIA A. LAWSON

The following attempts to present the philosophical arguments on both sides of the debate about the use of performance-enhancing drugs by athletes. The points for and against are stated in very brief form, which is not the usual nature of philosophical arguments. Such a summary may have value in later consideration of more developed arguments dealing with one or a few positions. It may be helpful to have a prior overview of the various factors considered in this debate. While some positions may have been missed or may emerge in future debates it should be possible to add them to this list.

The arguments for and against seem to be centered around four concepts...(1) the potential health hazard, (2) the possibility of creating an unfair advantage between competitors, (3) the nature and expectations of sport, and (4) the ethics of testing for drug use. Under each of these headings the position supporting drugs use as a health hazard, as an unfair advantage, as contrary to the concept of sport and the ethical defence of drug testing are stated first. Then the points for and against are listed under each topic. Those supporting the original position are prefaced with a (+) and the counter arguments are preceded by a (-). The alternative would have been to group all the "pros" and "cons" but it was considered more advantageous to group together points addressing the same topic. The essays from which these arguments are primarily gathered are acknowledged at the end of this paper.

1. Harm

Drug Use is Dangerous To One's Health

(-) Reports on experimental research are mixed and conclude only that risks seem to exceed benefits.

(+) It is reasonable to assume that positive performance effects and negative health effects go beyond the reports of experimental research because dosages and frequency are well beyond the therapeutic doses included in experimental research and allowed in human subjects' research.

(-) There are fewer deaths in sport from drug use than many other sports, from motor racing to deaths on the squash court.

32

(+)   The actual number of deaths is not the issue but rather that drug abuse is so widespread.

(-)   People already use dangerous substances such as alcohol and tobacco. If they are acceptable why not drugs?

(+)   People who drink or smoke are aware of the risks and still choose to do them. In reality athletes have no choice about drugs. If one competitor is suspected of taking drugs the others feel pressure to follow (coercion).

(-)   If pharmacologists were able to develop drugs that were safe and effective then athletes should be free to make use of them.

(+)   Athletes don't know when to stop. Most substances are toxic if taken in large enough amounts.

(+)   In contact sports taking drugs to enhance rage and aggression must be regarded as dangerous to others.

(-)   Banning steroids has increased the use of more dangerous drugs.

2. Fairness

Drug Users have An Unfair Advantage

(-)   Is the use of drugs unfair? Only if some use them and others do not. But why should we outlaw their use? It is also unfair to be born of healthy parents, of a mother who did not smoke, to be well fed, to be encouraged in sport, to train at high altitude.

(-)   Fairness may apply to the structure of the game, but not to participants. The solution to fairness seems to be to provide universal access, not universal prohibition.

(+)   Whatever rules on drugs exist, some will choose to violate them. Such action does not invalidate the moral need for rules any more than violation of traffic laws invalidates them.

(-)   By regulating against drug use athletes are denied the right to choose their training methods. A drug is another tool at the athlete's disposal in addition to equipment, diet, exercise, etc.

I. Superiority and Dominance

(-) The issue is too complex to be resolved. All narcotics, anabolic steroids and stimulants are banned in part yet some anti-asthmatic agents which share certain properties with the stimulants are permitted. Drugs are needed to reduce pain and aid recovery from illness or injury.

(+) The objection is only to drugs taken with the specific intention of augmenting sporting performance.

3. Nature of Sport

The use of performance enhancing drugs by the individual is morally wrong because it changes the nature of the contest without agreement.

(+) Drug use is wrong because it introduces an inappropriate element into the sport contest which is contrary to the ideal of competitive sport. The nonsport element is the differing abilities of athlete's bodies to benefit from drugs.

(+) Outcome (performance) will eventually be determined by chemists with athletes serving merely as pawns. Drug use reduces competition to contests between mechanized bodies rather than total thinking, feeling, willing and acting persons.

(-) No argument against the appropriateness of drug use in sport is feasible on the basis of an accepted single concept of the nature of sport since there is no such conception.

(-) Banning drugs is opting for a conservative attitude toward the human condition which does not give enough weight to personal freedom. Stability, predictability and control are emphasized rather than novelty, change, surprise and creativity which are more liable to meet the value of self actualization.

(-) Individual satisfactions will always be relative: in shoes, on this day, following these workouts and with the aid of whatever substances have become part of my diet, preparation and medication.

(-) If choice is restricted we deny the athlete the values of self reliance, personal achievement and autonomy (paternalism).

34

(-)   The purpose of sport is the pursuit of excellence. Why shouldn't individual athletes be left at liberty to pursue excellence by any means they freely choose?

(-)   Drug use may not radically change the point of athletic competition which is to test the physical and mental qualities of athletes in their sport.

4. Testing

Urinalysis can be defended ethically when it has been clearly established as a procedure for enforcing the rule of a given sport and only when the use of a drug or substance has been determined to be inconsistent with the normal conditions of competition for that sport.

(-)   Privacy rights are denied if testing is done for the purpose of identifying and proving criminal activity, especially when investigative parties are not duly appointed public authorities but persons who derive authority through the regulatory offices of sport or as employers of athletes.

(+)   Team officials have some responsibility for the physical development of athletes.

(-)   Drug testing will help athletes who want to be helped but urinalysis isn't necessary to identify that group. The problem arises with drug abusers who do not wish treatment.

(-)   Even those who are helped are robbed of their autonomy as moral agents.

(-)   Testing is founded on the dubious assumption that all instances of drug use are health problems.

(-)   Sanctions against known offenders might be justified but not against others.

(+)   Individual athletes represent the team, the organization.

(+)   Drug use has a negative affect on camaraderie and team spirit.

(-)   Is there any demonstrable link between drug use and team spirit?

I. Superiority and Dominance

(+)(-) Does a coach or team official have a right or responsibility to insure that an athlete's private conduct does not compromise his/her ability to perform in sports? If so, to what limits?

(+) Professional sports are a different issue. It could be argued that drug testing is in the owners' financial interest (comparable to weight checks). Athletes could agree to checks as a condition of employment.

(-) Anti-drug rules lead to difficulties in effective testing. The disproportionate costs and consistency are major problems associated with testing.

References

Brown, W.M. "Ethics, Drug and Sport." *Journal of the Philosophy of Sport.* VII (1980) 15-23.

Donohoe, T. and Johnson, N. *Foul Play: Drug Abuse in Sports.* New York: Basil Blackwell Inc. 1986.

Fraleigh Warren P. "Performance-Enhancing Drugs in Sport: The Ethical Issue." *Journal of Philosophy of Sport.* XI (1984).

Simon, Robert L. "Good Competition and Drug-Enhanced Performance." *Journal of the Philosophy of Sport.* XI (1984) 6-13.

Simon, Robert L. *Sport and Social Values.* Englewood Cliffs: Prentice-Hall Inc., 1985.

Thomas, Carolyn E. *Sport in a Philosophic Contest.* Philadelphia: Lea & Febiger, 1983.

Thompson, Paul B. "Privacy and the Urinalysis Testing of Athletes." *Journal of the Philosophy of Sport.* IX (1982) 60-65.

PRIVACY AND THE
URINALYSIS TESTING OF ATHLETES

PAUL B. THOMPSON

Under what conditions, if any, is it ethical to require athletes to submit to urinalysis examinations? An answer to this question involves careful consideration as to the purpose of the examination, as well as an understanding of the athlete's right to privacy. The issue of urinalysis provokes serious questions regarding the separation of athletic activity from the athlete's personal life. Does a coach or team official have a right or responsibility to insure that an athlete's private conduct does not compromise his or her ability to perform in sport? If so, are there limits to this authority which would indicate the permissibility of requiring urinalysis examinations?

Urinalysis is a laboratory procedure which identifies the chemical composition of a urine sample. The procedure has become controversial in athletics because urinalysis can reveal the presence of drugs in an athlete's urine. This controversial use of urinalysis should not be confused with the noncontroversial procedure of analyzing a urine sample as a part of a regular physical examination. Controversial uses of urine sampling also break down into two discrete categories. Urinalysis has been required of competitors in track and field events in order to identify the presence of stimulants, pain killers, steroids, and other drugs which are assumed to alter the competitive equilibrium of the sport. Rampant drug use among professional athletes has prompted the suggestion that urinalysis might be used to detect the use of illegal and dangerous substances among athletes. The ethical analysis of these two different uses of urine testing requires differentiation on several key points.

I shall assume without argument that privacy is not a form of property, and hence that privacy rights must not be confused with property rights. An argument for this position is made by Larry May (2). This assumption is important for the discussion of urinalysis testing since, if privacy were merely a form of property, one might argue that privacy rights are surrendered to an employer or official under the contract which a professional athlete signs, or under the implicit contract of amateurism. The point of the assumption is to demand that privacy rights be renounced specifically, and not as part and parcel of a standard employer/employee relationship. There must be some reason specific to the activity of sport which supports the abnegations of privacy. We would not tolerate urinalysis as a matter of course as a condition of employment in a bank, a factory, or a hamburger stand. The fact that it is contemplated as a requirement for participation in sport, needs, therefore, to be justified by some condition or phenomenon which distinguishes sport from other forms of human activity.

The use of urine sampling in the enforcement of a drug ban is largely an issue for the philosophy of competition. Although there may be controversy over *whether* a drug should be banned in a given sport, once the ban has been imposed as a condition of competition there is little question about the ethicality of using urinalysis as a means of enforcement. When entering a competition, an athlete makes an implicit commitment to abide by the rules of the competition, and also to respect the measures required to secure fairness in the enforcement of rules. Clearly, the collection of urine samples provides an objective and impartial means for the enforcement of rules prohibiting the use of certain specific drugs.

It must, of course, be admitted that the decision as to whether a drug ought or ought not to be banned can be tortuous and riddled with philosophical difficulties. It will depend upon our knowledge about the effects of the drug in question, but also upon our conception of sport itself. When does an advance in sports medicine alter the conditions of competition so drastically that, effectively, a *new* sport is defined? How do we define the conditions of competition for a given sport? Do these conditions imply a "natural" or nonenhanced concept of physical fitness? These are questions which will probably be answered on a sport-by-sport and drug-by-drug basis (1). Such questions do not, however, play a role in determining the ethicality of urine sampling once it has been established that the use of a particular substance is inconsistent with the conditions of competition for a sport.

The use of urinalysis to detect banned substances falls within the scope of rule enforcement; hence one might object that urinalysis is inconsistent with philosophies of sport which stress amateurism and voluntary compliance with rules. This is tantamount to suggesting that enforcement of rules is secondary to certain esthetic considerations in the ideal of sportsmanship. It is difficult to imagine a sport so conceived (on an ideal of pure sportsmanship) in which the question of urinalysis could arise at all. Urine testing for banned substances, by its very nature, is a practice applicable only to sports where competition has been formulated in terms of rather precise rules and enforcement procedures.

The more difficult and topical issue involves the use of urinalysis to determine whether an athlete is using illegal or dangerous drugs recreationally. Revelations of drug use made by well-known athletes have brought this issue to prominence in the sports press (cf. 3: pp. 66-82). Urinalysis has been proposed as a means of identifying athletes who use drugs. This proposal has been met with protests citing an athlete's

38

right to privacy as a protection against involuntary testing for drug use (4; 5).

In order to understand the ethical questions involved in such an application of urine testing, several points must be clarified. First, urinalysis for detecting illegal drug use differs from urinalysis for detecting banned drugs in important respects. When a drug is banned, the prohibition of that drug becomes a part of the definition of the sport in question. Banned drugs are drugs used to affect the competitive outcome of a sport. The illegal drugs in question are not ingested in order to affect the outcome of a sport; hence they have no place in defining the conditions of competition for a sport. Since the drugs are not banned on competitive grounds, officials have no referential authority over their use; hence officials have no justification for initiating a procedure designed to detect their use. Athletes are presumed to use these drugs "on their own time," so to speak, and an athlete violates no rules of traditional sports by doing so.

Second, the use of urinalysis specifically to detect illegal substances can be distinguished from urine tests conducted in the course of regular physical examinations. Since the doctors who conduct such examinations will have knowledge of an athlete's drug use, a confidentiality issue arises in regard to the conditions under which this knowledge can and should be disclosed. This is a difficult issue for medical ethics, but it can and should be differentiated from the ethical question of ordering an athlete to undergo urinalysis specifically for the purpose of identifying illicit drug use.

Third, there may be occasions in which coaches or other athletic officials have clear *in loco parentis* responsibility for their athletes. Under such a situation, coaches may be responsible for the moral as well as physical development of their charges. This conception of the coach-athlete relationship is doubtlessly grounded in the philosophical view that a primary goal of athletics is "character development." It is a philosophical view which is probably on the wane in many phases of contemporary sport, and it is clearly inoperative in the professional sports where urinalysis has been proposed. Professional coaches have no responsibility for the moral development of their players. This point is worth mentioning since a coach or team official who did have clear *in loco parentis* authority could quite plausibly construe this to include authority to see that an athlete was not violating any laws. Even in such a case it is difficulty to imagine a situation in which the mutual respect between coach and athlete implied by the *in loco parentis* responsibility could have deteriorated badly enough to make urinalysis justifiable.

Given a situation in which coaches and team officials have no special mandate to watch over an athlete's moral development, are there any sport-related special circumstances which could justify forced

39

I. Superiority and Dominance

urinalysis? There are two relevant possibilities. First, since team officials assume some responsibility for the physical development of athletes, testing for drug use might be interpreted as helping athletes stay in optimal physical condition. Second, a team official might cite a negative impact on team morale or cohesiveness as a justification for the investigation of drug abuse.

The first possibility suggests that, in the long run, urinalysis is in the interest of the athlete himself. It will be argued that a drug user can be given counseling and treatment which will help him or her avoid further abuse. The ethical force of this suggestion is to argue that what at first glance appears to be a clear breach of an athlete's privacy rights can be justified in light of the overriding goodness of its consequences — namely that it helps him or her overcome a drug problem. Cast in this light, the argument is an example of the classic utilitarian problem of forcing someone to do something for their own good; it is a practice which utilitarians have concluded does more harm than good. The weakness of the "helping" argument is shown by examining its probable consequences.

It is clear that a policy of conducting urine tests and referring drug abusers to treatment centres will be helpful indeed for athletes desirous of treatment, but there is no need for urinalysis to identify this group. The problem arises with regard to athletes identified as drug abusers who do not wish treatment. Presumably these athletes will be presented with the alternative of accepting forced treatment or of losing some privilege (probably all opportunities to compete). If there is no penalty for "failing" one's urine test, there is no reason to conduct a test. We may speculate with some degree of assurance that some athletes forced into treatment will later be very grateful and agree that the identification and treatment of their drug use has been helpful. These people are helped at the expense of those who either refuse treatment and suffer for it, or accept the condition of treatment but continue to resent the intrusion into their privacy and claim that the treatment is of little value. Even those who are helped are robbed of their autonomy as moral agents. It is hard to imagine why a coach's responsibility to train and condition players justifies such an abrogation of basic moral respect. The idea of helping athletes by forcing them to undergo urinalysis is also founded on the dubious assumption that all instances of drug use are health problems. Illicit drugs have become an insidious social problem precisely because *some* people have the capacity to resist the debilitating effects of drug use, even over relatively long periods of use.

In the matter of professional team sports, the claim that urinalysis is in the health interests of the player can be taken rather differently. Since the professional team athlete is in the employ of the team owner, and since the team owner derives profits (indirectly) from the athletic performance of such employees, the owner may claim that the health of the athlete is a matter of his (the owner's) financial interest. Such a claim breaks down to two components. One is a general claim regarding employer/employee relations; but this is merely the illegitimate preference of the employer's financial interest over the employee's privacy rights (discussed previously). The more difficult question here is whether the nature of sport itself, the requirement of a physical performance from an employee, alters the basic employer/employee relationship in such a way that an owner can be said to have a legitimate claim.

The strongest argument in favour of such a view is by analogy to other well established sports practices. Current and former training measures have been accepted as more or less legitimate infringements upon the athlete's privacy. At one time, restrictions against sexual intercourse before a game (in extreme cases, throughout an entire season) were widespread. Even more commonly, athletes are subjected to periodic weight checks. Athletes who fail to meet a specified weight can be subject to fines and even firings.

The analogy to restrictions on sexual intercourse is particularly à propos, since this training rule has largely fallen into disuse for reasons directly relevant to the issue at hand. While it is reasonable to suppose that some athletes suffer reduced performance after relatively recent sexual activity it is doubtful that all or even most do. Since the issue is athletic performance, and *not* the underlying moral attitudes toward sex and/or drug use, the athlete should be judged on the basis of performance. Athletes who perform well regardless of sexual activity or occasional drug use would be unjustly restricted by training practices which infringe upon their private life to no apparent purpose. Those who are negatively affected can and should be disciplined or criticized for their reduced performance, and *not* for the private indiscretions which contribute to reduced performance.

The analogy to weighings breaks down for similar reasons. The history of sport is littered with stories of paunchy quarterbacks and outfielders who nevertheless deliver stellar performances. No team owner would have fired Babe Ruth for failing to make a weight limit. The issue, again, is performance. It seems more plausible that an athlete and a trainer might agree on an ideal weight, and that the weight check will be made as a means of monitoring compliance with this explicit contract. By analogy, it seems reasonable to condone an explicit agreement between a trainer and an athlete with a history of drug problems which involves periodic urinalysis as a means of monitoring compliance. The ethics of such agreements are entirely different from those of general and mandatory testing for drug use, since by assenting to the contract, the athlete submits to the test voluntarily, and hence, it is no invasion of privacy. This exception naturally assumes that the athlete has not been coerced into accepting the contract.

The final argument for forced urinalysis appeals to a philosophical concept of team spirit or morale. This justification can itself be broken into two principles. One might claim that individual athletes represent the whole; that is, a team, an organization or institution, or the sport itself. As such, officials of the sport have a "right" to insure that its representatives are of appropriate moral fibre. This form of argument is so patently paternalistic that it deserves little serious analysis. Although it might justify sanctions against known offenders, it can hardly be used to justify the extreme measure of taking urine samples in order to identify individuals who might be potential embarrassments to the whole.

A more serious argument involves the idea that individuals using drugs have a negative effect on the camaraderie and spirit so often noted with respect to team sports. The critical question, which is unresolved, is whether there is any demonstrable link between drug use and team spirit. At the very least, it seems that this argument cannot justify urinalysis as a matter of course. Some confessed drug abusers have played on championship teams. One may also speculate that the ignominy of being subjected to urinalysis might have a worse effect on morale than minor cases of drug abuse, but philosophically, such considerations are beside the point.

The appeal to team spirit assumes a dubious premise with regard to an individual athlete's personal autonomy. It requires an athlete to regard at least some aspects of his or her personal life as subservient to the team concept; furthermore, it gives team officials license to regulate personal affairs in advance of a clear indication that impacts upon the team are involved. While some philosophical visions of the team concept would certainly give credence to the first part of this assumption, the second part is tantamount to a surrender of all privacy rights whatsoever. This totalitarian vision of sport is surely inconsistent with the traditional spirit of athletic competition.

In conclusion, urinalysis can be defended ethically when it has been clearly established as a procedure for enforcing the rules of a given sport. This can be so only when the use of a drug or substance has been determined to be inconsistent with the normal conditions of competition for that sport. There are no special sports-related circumstances which justify the use of urinalysis to identify users of illegal drugs. The normal privacy rights enjoyed by everyone protect athletes from this intrusion into their private lives.

The intentions of the authority conducting a urinalysis are, thus, the critical factor in determining the ethicality of the test. When the purpose of the test is to insure compliance with the regulations of a sport, it poses no threat to privacy. Privacy, in other words, cannot be cited in order to prevent referees from detecting cheating. An individual's decision to participate implies consent to referential authority. Privacy rights, however, can and are cited in restricting the access of officials into the lives of individuals for the purpose of identifying and proving criminal activity. This restriction should apply most strongly when the investigating parties are not duly appointed public authorities, but persons who derive authority through the regulatory offices of sport or as employers of athletes. As such, when the intention of an official conducting a urine test is to identify criminal activity, as opposed to rule violations, the official has usurped the athlete's right to a life beyond sport. The criterion of intention also shows why a medical utilization of urinalysis is acceptable, since the examining physician's intent is to certify the physical well-being of the athlete, and not to ascertain facts about his or her private activities.

The privacy rights of athletes and the possible abridgement of these rights through urinalysis raise philosophical questions about sport and competition which go beyond the scope of the present paper. Given the analysis in terms of intention, the governing bodies of a given sport could technically redefine a sport so as to make the criminal activity of an athlete off the field a violation of the rules of the sport. The purpose for this would not be to justify the expulsion of known criminals; there is strong precedent in sport to establish an official's right to do this already. Rather, the rule change would be to give officials a clear authority to pry into the private activities of athletes by making these activities part and parcel of the sport. Needless to say, such a tactic runs counter to the intuitive concept of sport which, presumably, guides our understanding of rules in sport.

The issue of urinalysis is thus a crucial one in that it could alter the very concept of sport which informs the organization of competitive activity in our society. It is at the cutting edge of issues which ask us to evaluate the distinction between sport and life. Given the current delineation of that distinction, the intention of the official conducting the test determines its moral validity. The ill-considered demand for urinalysis as a way to identify criminal activity is, at best, morally unjustifiable. At worst, it may undermine the philosophical foundations of competitive sports.

I. Superiority and Dominance

Bibliography

1. Brown, W.M. "Ethics, Drugs and Sport." *Journal of the Philosophy of Sport*, 7(1980), 15-23.
2. May, Larry, "Privacy and Property." *Philosophy in Context*, 10(1980), 40-53.
3. Reese, Don, and John Underwood. "I'm Not Worth a Damn." *Sports Illustrated*, June 14, 1982, pp. 66-82.
4. "Schram Favors Exams for Drugs." *The Dallas Morning News*, July 20, 1982, p. B1, B3.
5. "Schram Backs Checks for Drugs." *Houston Chronicle*, July 21, 1982, Section 2, p.4.

COMPETITION:
IS IT WHAT LIFE'S ALL ABOUT?

BIL GILBERT

A basic sci-fi horror scenario involves a crazy but very competent biologist fiddling around with some minor creatures, say, a jar full of pissants. Eventually they turn into major monsters that proliferate and do great mischief. In real life this can happen to words. Commentators and pundits seize on a previously modest little noun or adjective and massage it until it becomes gigantic and ubiquitous. These creations are called buzzwords, and they tend to be inflated until they can mean almost anything a user wants them to. By way of example we have: organic, ecological, all-natural, sensitivity, high tech and, now, competition.

According to traditional usage, *competition* identifies a situation in which two or more people vie for a prize, honor or advantage. However, since it has become a 36-foot-tall pissant of a word, various authorities are suggesting that competition is importantly connected with what should or should not be done about the balance of trade, oil taxes, dependent mothers, Nicaragua, public schools and the Democratic National Convention. John Thompson, the highly successful Georgetown basketball coach, summed up a lot of fashionable thinking when he remarked, "Life is *about* competition."

The fuss over competition is a revival of some older conceits about the survival of the fittest and the laws of the jungle. The idea is that competition is the behavioral equivalent of gravity, a force that makes the world go 'round — the point being that life is shaped by individuals and species continually battling one another for food, space, sex and various luxury items. In the process, goes the theory, the minds and bodies of some individuals or species are greatly improved, and they become winners. The less able or less lucky — the dinosaur, the dusky seaside sparrow — are eliminated like early losers in a tennis tournament. With regard to the human species and its internecine struggles, this is called social Darwinism.

Indeed, it all sounds as if it has a lot to do with the realities of evolution and zoology, but it does not. The trouble with the theory of direct, unrelenting competition as a long-range force in nature is that such a scheme always has fewer winners than losers. Thus the win-or-drop-dead, tennis-tournament model of evolution is at odds with the fact that, through the aeons, life-forms on Earth have become increasingly numerous and various. The multitude of species reflects the evolutionary

45

I. Superiority and Dominance

drive to find a small edge — a niche, zoologists call it — that enables creatures to go about their business without always fighting with others with the same appetites.

Humans have long had a high regard for niches, which allow us to occupy positions in which competition is completely eliminated or greatly reduced. To this end we have invented such things as tariffs, tenure, the American Medical Association and monopolies. A prominent college football coach once explained the attraction of monopolies in relation to the recruiting policies of his school: "We don't want just enough good football players. We want them all. If I have the six best quarterbacks in this great republic tied down at my school, anyone I play against will be going with no better than the seventh best. You follow my meaning?"

Good monopolies, however, are easier to fantasize about than to find. As a practical matter, cooperation is the tactic most commonly used to get what we want. Groups of people agree to divvy up desirable things, just as other species do natural resources and the NFL does draft picks. Individuals may not get everything they yearn for, but few are shut out completely. As a matter of historical record, many of the most notable human accomplishments — cathedrals, constitutions, college athletic departments — are monuments to cooperative behavior. So, while we may in principle praise the virtues and joys of head-on competition, we are much less enthusiastic about it in practice. Getting what we want by taking it from somebody else in an overt contest is usually for us, as for other species, a last resort.

Therefore a good argument can be made that life is mostly about *avoiding* competition. If this is so, then competitive sports jump out not only as a remarkable exception but also as a singular, perhaps definitive, human activity. Here we have something that we have little stomach for in serious, imperative situations but dote on as a leisure pursuit. An obvious question is, Why? Nobody claims to know with certainty, but there are many interesting theories.

Some behaviorists speculate that all creatures are driven by two basic, often incompatible, urges — to be secure and to be stimulated. Much of our energy is devoted to trying to make our lives safe, comfortable and predictable. However, security can bore us, so, as an antidote, we seek challenge, risk and suspense. But stimulation is intrinsically dangerous, and when things get too sticky, we scuttle back to security. Hence we keep bouncing back and forth between these poles of desire.

Some see competitive sports as a marvelously ingenious solution to this dilemma. Sporting contests are stimulating by their very nature, but at the same time, they begin and end by agreement, as struggles over bloody bones seldom do. Moreover, sports lend themselves to handicapping, whereby participants can be mixed and matched on the basis of age, sex, and size, among other factors. This makes competitive games less dangerous and increases the number of winners. Most important, according to this view, the rewards and risks of sport are symbolic — or were, at least, until the recent era of runaway remuneration — and do not threaten our genuine security or survival.

A related theory holds that sports are valuable as easy-to-perform psychodramas. In them we can act out our primeval aggressions and confrontational desires, thus making us less likely in real life to use clubs to obtain meals or mates. This theory, of course, is not universally accepted. Some authorities believe that we learn in competitive games to be more, rather than less, ornery.

Rainer Martens was a college football player, a semipro baseball player and a coach, but he is best known for his research at the University of Illinois concerning children and competitive play. Because of the quality of his work and its influence on others, Martens is sometimes called the father of modern sports psychology.

Martens believes that competitive sports evolve out of what he calls "the process of social evaluation," which can be roughly described as follows: If several three- or four-year olds are playing with balls, they may enjoy one another's company, but each one's attention is centered on how far, straight or high he — not the others — can throw. After good efforts, the children may shout, "I won." They are not using this expression as their elders do; they are simply saying that they have done something excellent and satisfying.

In a couple of years, usually by age five or six, Martens has observed, this changes. Children start paying attention to the prowess of others, making efforts to equal or surpass the throws of their playmates. In due course they learn how to measure the comparative results more precisely, which is to say, they learn to keep score. All the rest — pickup games, Little League, letter sweaters — follows.

Martens thinks this process — their competing and comparing themselves with others — is part of what helps children find out what they can and should be. If not exactly innate, the urge to do this, Martens believes, is almost universal. There are many such standards of comparison — appearance, speech, possessions, knowledge, etc. — but sport is a popular one because it lends itself to objective scorekeeping. Among hundreds of children he has observed, Martens has found none who are not somewhat interested in this kind of evaluation.

Although Martens's work is widely respected, I also sought out about 20 other people who seemed to be authorities on competition either because of their academic work or because of their experiences as successful athletes or coaches. Though their backgrounds, their language and the examples they used were widely divergent, their opinions were strikingly consistent.

I. Superiority and Dominance

Take the question of "the competitive personality." Everyone agreed that while there is probably no such thing as a totally *non*competitive personality, there are, in sports, individuals who are exceptionally eager to enter contests, who usually perform very well and who seem to thrive psychically in them. Yet most of the academics and athletes disagreed with the popular notion that such competitive personalities are equally intent upon succeeding — winning — in all situations, no matter what the contest.

As a swimmer in the 1960s, Don Schollander won five Olympic gold medals and a reputation as one of the fiercest competitors in his sport. But he thinks that because he became a world-class swimmer, he grew much less competitive in other endeavors, particularly football, his first sporting love. On balance, Schollander believes he is now no more than moderately competitive, and he has a theory to explain that. He thinks competitive urges are finite, not insatiable, and that you can get filled up with contests, as he did, and thereafter have less appetite for them.

Another popular notion holds that very competitive people have combative, domineering personalities by which those people can be identified in any circumstances. Again the academics and athletes thought otherwise. John Wooden, an All-America basketball player at Purdue and, given his nine consecutive NCAA titles (and 10 overall) at UCLA, the most successful college basketball coach ever, says "Some of the people I recall as fine competitors were, when not playing, very exuberant and perhaps aggressive. But as many others were rather quiet and withdrawn."

Schollander goes a step further and says that among the world-class swimmers he knew, the most intense competitors tended to be unassertive people once they were out of the pool. He thinks that this may not have been coincidental — that they may have been especially motivated to excel as swimmers and athletes *because* they were awkward and timid in ordinary social situations.

Len Zaichkowsky, a sports psychologist at Boston University, says elite athletes seem to share certain common personality characteristics — "hostility, aggressiveness, vigor, determination, energy" among others. But he quickly points out that these traits usually become apparent after the athletes have succeeded. Though there is a lot of interest among coaches and recruiters in predicting success on the playing field, Zaichkowsky knows of no personality test that can reliably preselect good competitors. Which is simply to say that, for now at least, competitive personalities are generally recognized only after the score is posted.

While it is easy enough to spot great athletes, it is far more difficult to predict who the great competitors will be. Jim McGee is the director of psychology at Sheppard Pratt Hospital in Baltimore and a

48

former consulting psychologist for the baseball Orioles. Of elite athletes he says, "I think that they are wired differently. In a way they are neurological freaks whose bodies almost always do what they want them to do. It is hard for the rest of us to imagine what this must feel like. You can pick them out while they are still kids. Whatever the game, they are the ones doing things quicker, more effectively and more easily than anybody else."

But for psychological reasons many others with exceptional physical gifts never become notable competitors. Former Arizona State and NFL coach Frank Kush tells a story about two tight ends he remembers from his days at Arizona State. The first was big and fast and was signed by ASU in hot competition with other institutions. It turned out to be no coup. "He wasn't lazy, and he wasn't stupid, but he was dogged about repeating the same mistakes over and over," says Kush. "We couldn't show him that he had to develop new skills to get the job done. He came from a small school, and it seemed that being at a big school, in a relatively big city, playing with people who were almost as talented as he was put him into a state of shock. He stayed in shock for four years."

The second tight end was a recruiting afterthought, a roster fill-in. "He went about 190 and wasn't that quick," says Kush. "Don't get me wrong, he had some talent, but not the kind the first kid did. What he had was a great attitude. You never had to tell him twice what he was doing wrong. He was cocky — not about what he was, but because he was certain he was going to get better. He gave us a couple of good, not great, years. He handled some people who had better tools, but couldn't use theirs like he did his. He was a real competitor."

Kush, McGee and others make the point that at the junior levels of sport, prior to high school varsity athletics, physical gifts are often all an athlete needs to succeed. But as he or she moves to levels where everyone is considerably gifted, competitiveness becomes increasingly important, and, paradoxically, having superior physical skills can work to the disadvantage of some athletes — as it apparently did in the case of Kush's catatonic tight end. Early in their careers gifted athletes have few peers and are seldom threatened. They become successful and confident without paying much attention to the management of their talent. When they step up in class and begin meeting others as gifted as they are, the experience can be more traumatic for them than for those less well endowed who long ago learned to operate most efficiently under the stress of competition.

Psychologists, coaches and athletes who have reflected on the subject feel certain that competitiveness can be acquired. The process mostly involves matter over mind rather than the reverse, as is sometimes suggested.

I. Superiority and Dominance

Martens says "People can certainly learn to be more competitive. It is really rather simple. The trick is to concentrate on mastering specific techniques — positioning the feet, gripping the ball, whatever — until the individual is comfortable with them. This obviously helps mechanically, but it is also the best way to reduce stress and the problems it can cause. If people can focus on mastering specific acts that involve things they can control, they will be less inclined to be distracted by things over which they have no control. Being self-centered in this way helps to reduce anxiety about what opponents are doing, which is the source of most of what is threatening about competition."

A great many athletes have arrived through experience at the same conclusions Martens has reached academically. Often they are expressed in hoary clichés — *keep your eye on the ball, play them one at a time* — some of which are highly instructive about the nature of a good competitive attitude and how to get it. George Brett of the Kansas City Royals says he becomes enormously egocentric in the clutch. "I think back to similar instances in the past when I produced," says Brett.

Wooden is known as one of the finest of all teachers of the competitive spirit. He says,

> We had drills aimed at improving individual skills and teamwork, of course. The sole responsibility of the players was to master these things so that they could do in games what they had learned in practice, habitually and quickly. If they did so but were still beaten, this indicated the other team had superior athletes or superior coaching. In either case there was no reason for players to hang their heads, for they had no control over those elements.
>
> It is difficult for young players to learn — because of the great emphasis on records — but, ideally, the joy and frustration of sport should come from performance itself, not the score. While he is playing, the worst thing a player can think about in terms of concentration — and, therefore, of success — is losing. The next worst is winning.

The question comes up frequently, so I asked various authorities whether they thought competitive sports were good or bad for people. Wooden answered succinctly. "You are probably asking about character," he said. "Yes, I think competition can build character. But it can also tear it down."

His response was typical. If my question was not exactly stupid, it certainly was intrinsically unanswerable. Unlike, say, strychnine or tight shoes, the effects of sporting competition are not automatic and universal. Like eating, work or sex, competition can be constructive or

50

corruptive depending on circumstances, individuals and how they behave themselves.

First, the good news. Tara Scanlan, a UCLA sports psychologist, feels that competitive athletics — by their nature and because they are so popular — can be a powerful tool for the general instruction of youth. She says, "Sport can be used to teach a great number of desirable things: how to master skills and the satisfaction that follows; good general work habits and cooperation; how to break down racial and class prejudices; how to build respect for and responsibility toward other people."

Martens tends to agree. "There are 30 million children and probably as many adults who are sometimes involved in competitive sports," he says. "Some may be pushed into them by peer pressure and, thus, may experience more stress than they should and won't get the benefits they might. But it seems plain that most people compete at games voluntarily because it gives them pleasure. Not for all and not all of the time, but often and for many people, sport is a major source of joy and therefore, on balance, is useful to them and to society."

The bad news, at least for those who value sports, comes from sociology professor George Sage of the University of Northern Colorado, who wrote in the *Journal of Physical Education and Recreation* that "organized sport — from youth programs to the pros — has nothing at all to do with playfulness — fun, joy, self-satisfaction — but is, instead, a social agent for the deliberate socialization of people...into the prevailing social structure." In other words, Sage believes that sports tend to pit people against one another, promoting pervasive rivalry rather than cooperation.

While theorists argue about the social and physical benefits of competitive athletics, sport may provide a satisfaction that is more metaphysical — a matter of divine intervention, if you will. Considered in this way, contests are seen as tests of piety as well as athletic ability; winning takes on added importance because it is considered a clear demonstration that the winners are on good terms with important powers above. Victory is a sure sign that the gods are smiling upon you.

In Western civilization such ideas were common among early Olympic athletes, performers in Roman Colosseum contests and medieval jousters, to say nothing of makers of many holy wars. These views are still more prevalent today than is generally believed. Aside from an occasional man of the cloth praying in locker rooms for abundant touchdowns, the supernatural aspects of sport are no longer of much interest to formal theologians. But they are to competitors. In addition to the conspicuous praising of the Lord we invariably see on national TV after important athletic victories, participants in all games talk some and think more about being hot, on a roll, snakebit or victims of bad breaks and bounces. To placate forces that control these things, they chew

51

I. Superiority and Dominance

towels, carry talismans, avoid stepping on baselines. We may not thank or curse Apollo, the bear spirit or local saints, but we certainly do court Lady Luck. If she smiles, it is a sign that we have not done too badly at getting things together — and it feels great. When she frowns, it is because she has caught on to what unworthy wretches we are — and it feels lousy.

When the subject of superstition was brought up, most of the authorities I talked to were understandably annoyed, because their careers are based on the premise that success comes from personal discipline, concentration, anxiety management or blackboards covered with X's and O's. They may well be right that there is no such thing as luck, but a lot of jocks think there is. I have never heard anybody say, "Let's play a round of golf, I want to find out what the gods are thinking about me." But I think that subconsciously something of the sort is at work. Call it primitive irrationality, but the opportunity sport offers for testing luck just might be an abiding attraction of the games we play. It may even be one reason they were invented.

It is not unusual these days to hear reservations and warnings from the experts, not so much about the value of competitive sports but about certain corruptions of that value. To summarize these misgivings: the pleasurable and instructive aspects of sport should derive from the competition itself, not from the final score. Traditionally, and perhaps by ancient design, the tangible awards for victory are of little material worth — symbolic trophies of one sort or another — because the only real and lasting value of a game is what's felt and learned during the contest.

In other words, it is not whether you win or lose but how you play the game. This adage sums up what most authorities think can be the truest value of athletic competition. That it sounds hopelessly old-fashioned reflects what many think has gone wrong with sport.

Nowadays, the rewards are for winning and the costs of losing are becoming more substantial. This is self-evident at the big-money, big-scholarship, big-celebrity level. But even for young children, succeeding at athletics is more and more often a quick, effective means of gaining status, perks and privileges. As the importance of winning is increasingly emphasized, the competitive process — how one plays the game — becomes further de-emphasized. The worth of the inner rewards declines in comparison with the magnificence of the prizes distributed. Raising the material stakes in contests tends to move competition out of the traditional realm of sport — safe excitement and imaginary risk — and into the real world, a world that frequently seems so scary and so stressful that we invented games as a means of escaping it.

Many of the authorities expressed concern about the ills bedeviling elite athletes today — substance abuse, cheating and so on. However, the moral lapses of athletes were generally attributed not to the stresses of

52

competition but to those that accompany fame and fortune, that is, the rewards of winning. McGee thinks that, paradoxically, the superb physical endowments of elite athletes may contribute to their troubles by making them prone to superman delusions, the sense that they are impervious to the pitfalls — carousing, booze, drugs — that strike down lesser men.

The major worry shared by academics and athletes was that the conduct of sports celebrities might unfavorably influence young people. "If you think, as I do, that sports can be a powerful tool in shaping behavior, then you have to be concerned about what children are learning from watching so-called big-time sports," says Scanlan. She is not talking about the impact of the occasional jock junkie, drunk or rapist, but rather of what has become ordinary behavior that, if not officially condoned, is often excused as being more or less unavoidable in big-time sport.

> 'Kids see athletes threatening each other,' Scanlan says, 'and intentionally trying to cause injuries, virtually bragging about cheating and not getting caught. Coaches slug players, intimidate officials, throw chairs, lie about recruiting. The main message is that just about any means you can use is justified by the end of winning. Once, sport encouraged ethical behavior, what used to be called sportsmanship. In many instances it is now teaching violence, greed, selfishness, disrespect for others.'

Glyn Roberts, a University of Illinois professor of sports psychology, is also concerned about the defective role model presented by athletic heroes these days. "Increasingly, the prevailing morality on display in sports is that anything is O.K. if it works and you don't get caught," says Roberts. "There are other things in modern society that teach this, but for kids, sports is now the major activity that drives home the point that being successful, not being good in the conventional moral sense, is what counts."

Besides those who seek success at any price, Roberts is concerned about the much larger group 80 percent, by his reckoning — who try competitive sports and then drop them permanently by age 17. Some quit because of lack of time, some because they find more interesting pursuits. But many leave because they find the pressure to win too great, the agony of losing too painful. It is seldom expressed this way, but they seem to come away with a sense that sports are unhealthy for them. It may well be. Roberts says that some stress in sports and elsewhere is energizing, even pleasurable, but excessive stress can lead to real miseries, including loss of appetite, overeating, insomnia and respiratory disorders.

But perhaps the most destructive competitive experience for a child is one that deprives him of a whole dimension of life by driving him away from future competition.

"Competitive sports can be very good for many children," Roberts says. "Obviously they lose those benefits and pleasures if they drop out. But we are indirectly telling a lot of kids to do just that: If you don't show early promise, competitive sports are not for you. Now we have tournaments and trophies for four-year-old wrestlers. I think the way many children's sports are organized — winners going on, losers going home — is a national disgrace."

Roberts and Scanlan, like almost everyone who has watched children unobtrusively, have noted that, left to their own devices, kids organize their own contests and seem to enjoy them thoroughly. To adults, the games may seem messy and digressive, meandering slowly, if at all, toward a final score. But then kids are kids, not small adults, and they often have different priorities. Scanlan has been struck by the nice, natural touch they have for cooperatively setting up their own competitions that are exciting, but not so exciting as to cause stress, hiccups or hives.

Martens shares the opinion that young children — certainly four-year-old wrestlers — could do with a little more letting alone than many of them get. The main purpose of the American Coaching Effectiveness Program, of which Martens is the founder, is described by its name. In Martens's view, a bad coach is one who gives 14-year-olds powerful pep talks about sucking it up and bearing down so they can close in on the county championship, followed by the states and (who knows?) maybe the nationals. A good coach, in terms of influence and, generally, of won-lost records, too, concentrates on the details of *how* to win rather than on what his charges already are thinking too much about — what happens if they win or lose.

For reasons already noted, focusing on smaller, more solvable technical problems increases physical efficiency and reduces anxiety and stress. Also, these methods increase, in a sense, the number of potential winners. Thus the 12th boy on a junior high basketball squad may play badly by conventional standards. But if skill instead of winning has been made the immediate objective, he can be praised for having thrown two passes better than he ever had.

Taking for granted the need for reform in sports, Martens still thinks the competitive climate for youthful athletes has improved during the last decade. The principal reason is that more coaches, both professional and amateur, not only have learned to teach mastery of sporting skills but also have understood why it is advantageous to do so.

Gilbert: Competition: Is It What Life's All About?

"The national media, understandably, are preoccupied with what is happening with athletes at the highest level of sport," says Martens. "The real story, the most important impact of sports, is occuring at the level where most people compete — in school games, community recreation programs, softball, bowling, golf leagues. At that level there is more and better competition — more useful and pleasant — than ever before."

Bill Harper is a professor in the department of physical education, health and recreation studies at Purdue. Harper is essentially a sports philosopher and the underpinning of his professional creed is his opinion that we are becoming so addicted to competitive games and keeping score that we are forgetting how and why to be playful in ways that can't be scored. Not long ago, Harper told me the story of how he was once pressed into service as the coach of a youth soccer league team in West Lafayette, Ind. He didn't have much expertise in that sport, but he brought to it a conviction that organizers and managers — who should be supernumeraries — have seized control of sports programs from their rightful owners and beneficiaries, the participants.

To counter the influence of such organizers, Harper told his soccer team in the beginning that he had only one basic rule: Everyone was going to have equal playing time. The players themselves would decide tactical and strategic questions. Practices would be optional.

And how did this all-power-to-the-players system work?

"Pretty well, at least superficially," Harper said. "The kids were good about coming to practice, and some of them said it was the best team they'd ever been on. Some of the parents said they acted turned-on about it at home, and all the parents I talked to seemingly liked it."

All right, but what about the "superficially" and "seemingly"?

"Well, it probably wasn't a fair test," he said. "We won a lot. If we'd lost, the kids and parents might have felt a lot differently. In fact," Harper continued, lowering his voice as if he were about to say something shameful, "we won the state championship."

If you badger them enough, you can sometimes squeeze the pith out of philosophers. It worked with Harper. At the end of a long evening of conversation, he finally said, "If competition isn't taken too seriously, it can be important. I mean, what it finally boils down to is, the bigger the trophy the more trivial the contest."

Which seemed as good a place as any to leave large, heavy questions about when and why competitive sport is good or bad.

WINNING AND LOSING IN SPORT: A RADICAL REASSESSMENT

SAUL ROSS

'Winning isn't everything, its the only thing,' as a well-known rallying cry in certain sports circles, leaves no doubt about the value espoused and the forcefulness with which it is held. Acceptance of this viewpoint means that losing is equated with nothing and hence has no value. Benefits only accrue from winning.

Winning in an athletic contest has been equated with excellence by the American philosopher, James Keating (1978, Chapter 2) who asks, "In short, can we, in any meaningful sense of the word, have excellence in a competitive engagement without victory?" (p. 15). Along with philosophical analysis to clarify his position, Keating buttresses his argument by utilizing "expert testimony," in the form of quotations from coaches. Implicit in Keating's position is the employment of one particular standard, one specific criterion with which to measure both success and excellence.

A strong rebuttal to Keating's views comes from a surprising source and will be presented later. That retort will come as part of the line of argument I will develop which calls into question the orientation described above. Two major issues are addressed. In the first instance questions are raised within the confines of sport itself, that is to say, about the contestant qua athlete. A second set of questions will be raised about the contestant as a person, a real, live existential being. These additional questions must be raised because we cannot separate the athlete from the person nor can we divorce participation in sport as an integral part of one's life experience from all other events and activities which count as experience. Although I agree somewhat with the many authors who have expressed concern about the overemphasis placed on winning and also sympathize with those who have urged moderation, my position is somewhat different. Against the view that winning is the only thing and that victory is synonymous with excellence I shall argue a more radical thesis: for the contestant, both as an athlete and as a person, there are times when losing is more important than winning. Furthermore, I shall also argue that excellence in sports can be achieved even in a losing cause.

Procedure and Context

In keeping with the method used by Keating, I, too, shall employ philosophical analysis and utilize expert testimony, in the form of quotations from athletes and coaches, in elaborating my position.

An important insight into the notion of victory in sport is offered by Simon (1985), who maintains that "we should distinguish the conceptual claim that the *goal* of competition is victory from the psychological claim that the competitor's primary *motive* for participating is the desire to win." (p. 45) There are times when the goal and the motive coincide, as we presume they do in professional sport. However, participation for the joy of competition, cameraderie, and involvement with an exciting group practising a wholesome activity are other motivating factors. Where the other factors prompt participation they do not inhibit an athlete from trying to defeat his or her opponent for without this attempt there would not be competition. We can compete in sports for various reasons and gain all the benefits without subscribing to the winning-is-the-only-thing view.

Winning, as a notion, is open to some interpretation. Harper (1982) identifies three distinct nuances: (1) winning as consequence or prize, a view which serves as the foundation for the winning-is-the-only-thing perspective. Here, the emphasis is placed on the outcome or consequence of the contest and is predicated on the notion that *it does matter* whether you win or lose since winning is the primary, indeed, only objective and, therefore, by logical extension, winning is everything; (2) winning as circumstance, which can be regarded as being competitive but, at the same time, takes into account such factors as financial superiority, natural physical advantages, recruitment and tradition which provides a distinct advantage to one side; and (3) winning as experience, which focuses on the quality of the particular performance.

It is the first interpretation, with its focus on winning as consequence or prize that is of direct concern to the topic at hand and will consequently receive the most attention. However, it should be noted that the identification of nuances two and three stands as actual testimony to the view that there is much more to sport participation than only winning. Indeed, nuance three relegates winning to a secondary position, hinting that performance, rather than victory, is a more important criterion for assessing excellence.

Winning is Not the Only Thing

When examined closely considerable difficulty is encountered in attempting to understand what is meant by the slogan, 'winning isn't everything, its the only thing.' If winning is the only thing then all other

I. Superiority and Dominance

benefits derived from sports participation are dismissed out-of-hand since they fall outside the category of the only thing. Health, social and psychological benefits, even financial benefits (think of the enormous salaries paid to athletes and coaches of losing teams) no longer count where a literal interpretation of the phrase, winning is the only thing, transforms everything else into nothing.

Fully subscribing to the view that winning is the only thing brings with it inexorable pressures since by losing the game one loses everything. Given this scenario it is probable that athletes would refuse to participate, and hence forego the sport experience, if they were interested only in winning. To ensure that one does not lose everything, prudence dictates scheduling only weak opponents, but by doing so and winning very little, nothing if anything, is gained. On the other hand, a steady diet of victories may generate excessive self-confidence that would lead to egotistical and obnoxious behaviour which alienates friends. Even where poor behaviour is not the end result, constant victory provides a distorted view of reality since in all aspects of life 'we win some and we lose some.'

Experiencing only victory from the start may be meaningless. Gail Gooderich, a star on the powerhouse UCLA basketball team of the 1960s and later a member of the Jazz of the NBA states, "But you have to experience defeat to really understand victory. The year before, when I was a sophomore, we lost seven games by something like 20 points. Having had that year made the winning experience better." (Deford, 1979, p. 73) Winning is obviously important. After a well-played game which is won there is a feeling of accomplishment, competence and happiness which can be appreciated to a greater extent once one has experienced the disappointment of defeat.

No matter how good the feelings are which accompany victory, an all-out commitment to the view that winning is the only thing creates problems. Real happiness may well become a fleeting phenomenon because each victory provokes worry about what is going to happen the next time. Al McGuire, a very successful major college basketball coach, (when he was still coaching) explains:

> 'I hate everything about this job except the games,' McGuire says, 'Everything. I don't even get affected anymore by the winning, by the ratings, those things. The trouble is, it will sound like an excuse because we've never won the national championship, but winning isn't all that important to me. Maybe it's the fear, the fear of then having to repeat. You win once, then they expect you to win again.' (Deford, 1976, p. 104)

58

Fear of losing the next contest replaces the feeling of elation after victory. In contrast, adoption of a "playful" attitude, one which accepts both victory and defeat while acknowledging the values of each, is incompatible with a total commitment to winning as the only thing.

At this point it is important to make a clear distinction between striving to win and adopting the attitude that winning is the only thing. Striving to win involves total effort, doing one's best, within the rules of the contest. A commitment to that position, which ensures true competition, does not entail the adoption of the winning-is-the-only-thing attitude. Striving to win and regarding victory as the only acceptable thing are two different positions.

Don Shula, the head coach of the Miami Dolphins, has been quoted as saying, "No one ever learns anything by losing." (Nixon, 1984, p. 21) Perhaps, somehow, he has never heard the old adage about learning from experience. If we do learn from experience — I can't see how we could avoid learning from experience — then we also learn by losing since losing is part of our experience. Contra Shula, I would claim that most athletes learn more from losing than from winning. Wayman Tisdale, an Oklahoma basketball All-American, while still an undergraduate, commented, "You grow more from the bad times than the good." (Looney, 1983, p. 52). Tisdale's comment can be applied readily to the contestant as an athlete and to the contestant as a person. An explanation follows.

After a loss, coaches and athletes review their performance with greater care, scrutinizing every move in an attempt to detect the mistakes and flaws. Once they have been identified, concentrated effort is exerted to improve both skill execution and strategy. Seldom, if ever, is the same attention to detail and devotion to improvement manifested after a continuous string of victories. B.M. Swift (1987) describes the situation concisely in his report on the 1987 Canada-Russia hockey series in Quebec City where the Russians lost the first game of the two-game series:

> Here's an important point to remember about the Soviet National Hockey Team: It is seldom pushed to play its very best. When you spend 95% of your time trying not to run up scores on teams, as the Soviets do, you cannot wake up one morning and play at the top of your game. You must first lose, then sleep on it, then spend a practice listening to Tikhonov snap and snarl at the slightest miscue before you begin to dig deep into your belly. (p. 19)

A loss, much more than a win, goads coaches and athletes to improved performance. Since the goal of all athletes is improved performance, here is concrete evidence to support the claim that for the contestant as athlete losing, at times, is more important than winning (see also Looney, 1987, p. 37).

Losing can also have a beneficial effect on a whole league. James Michener (1976, p. 391) maintains that the old AFL, stung by Oakland's 33-14 humiliation at the hands of the NFL's Green Bay Packers, collectively resolved to improve. AFL teams "built better stadiums, attracted superior crowds, and within a few years its brand of football was visibly superior to that played in the NFL." (Michener, 1976, p. 391) Had Oakland, the AFL representative, won then the need for critical self-evaluation and all-out determination to improve would not have been present. Where such resolve and determination do arise following a loss it serves as additional evidence in support of the claim that losing, at times, is more important than winning.

Losing can be beneficial to the contestant as a person. Chris Evert was at the top of her game and of women's tennis early in 1976, beating arch-rival Yvonne Goolagong three of the four times they had met, but she had also lost a first round match the last week in March in Boston to Dianne Fromholtz. It was Evert's first loss in the first round since 1971 when she was 16. The next week in Philadelphia Evert lost again, this time to Goolagong in the final.

> 'Losing in the first round in Boston was a terrible feeling and a great feeling,' says Evert. 'It meant I had the whole week to myself. I was disappointed, but I was relieved too. Losses are always a relief. They take a great burden off me, make me feel more normal. If I win several tournaments in a row I get so confident I'm in a cloud. If I lose, I go back to the dressing room and I'm no better or worse than anyone else. A loss gets me eager again.' (Pileggi, 1976, p. 47)

Experiencing both victory and defeat is normal. A steady diet of winning can distort reality and, as noted above, increase pressure to intolerable levels. A loss can serve to restore normalcy and prevent the undue build-up of pressure. In this way, too, losing becomes more important than winning.

A sentiment that is diametrically opposed to the one embodied in the phrase, 'winning is the only thing,' is expressed by the world-calibre Canadian high jumper, Debbie Brill. Shortly after she unexpectedly won the high jump competition in World Cup II in Montreal's Olympic Stadium in August, 1979, she is reported to have said:

> 'I have never felt so devastated as I do now. I didn't expect to win this. Losing can sometimes bolster you. It gives you energy. You say I can do better. You go to work. But

60

winning...? In a sense I feel a huge letdown.' She looked at Pugh (her coach), 'At the moment I feel there is nowhere to go.' (Moore, 1979, p. 23)

Two points merit attention. First, Brill's comments summarize and confirm the role losing plays in motivating improvement; in that way it is more important than winning. Secondly, it appears that for some athletes the excitement and value of sport is in the preparation and the competition, with winning or losing relegated to a secondary position. In sport, as in many other human activities, the anticipation and participation are far more enjoyable and rewarding than the final outcome. Additional testimony supporting this view follows.

One member of the 1964 UCLA championship basketball team who did not continue his basketball career at the professional level is Doug McIntosh. Winning the 1964 NCAA championship is recalled fondly by him but, he "says that his greatest thrill in basketball was going to the state tournament in high school." (Deford, 1979, p. 74) Keith Erickson, another member of that team, went on to play professionally:

What Erickson remembers most fondly about the pros was the Phoenix team that he played on in 1976, the one that finished the regular season barely above .500 and then went all the way to the finals before losing a magnificent struggle to the Celtics. 'Phoenix was just as good an experience as UCLA,' Erickson says. Just as good? 'Yeah, sure.' (Deford, 1979, p. 74)

Participating, accepting and meeting challenges, doing one's best in a congenial environment appears to be of paramount importance.

Achieving Excellence

Excellence is equated with victory by Keating (1978, Chap. 2), thereby indicating that there is only one criterion to measure both success and excellence. Excellence, as a standard, cannot be regarded in absolute terms; it is a general goal towards which we strive and our efforts are measured by relative standards right from kindergarten. In almost all educational institutions a range exists to recognize the best academic performances. Whether 'Excellent' or 'A+' is used is immaterial because in most places the grade covers the range from 90% to 100%. Applied to sport we have all seen contests where one side has played poorly yet won and other instances where the opposite has occurred, that is an athlete or a team has played very well yet lost.

I. Superiority and Dominance

I readily concede that winning is often, perhaps even most often, an indicator of excellence but it cannot be an invariable criterion. Expert testimony, as additional rebuttal, comes from an unexpected source, an extremely successful basketball coach whose demeanour and being could serve as a symbol of an all-out commitment to winning, Bobby Knight:

> Already he has gone so far that at age 40 winning is no longer the goal. 'Look, I know this,' he says. 'If you're going to play the game, you're going to get more out of winning. I know that, sure. Now, at West Point I made up my mind to win — gotta win. Not at all costs. Never that. But winning was the hub of everything I was doing. And understand, I've never gotten over West Point....I had to win. And, so to some extent I won't ever change.
>
> 'But somewhere I decided I was wrong. You could win and still not succeed, not achieve what you should. And you can lose without really failing at all.' (Deford, 1981, p. 68)

To 'win and not achieve what you should' I interpret to mean winning without performing well. To win without performing well means that excellence has not been attained.

And, equally, if you can lose without failing then it means some measure of excellence can be achieved. Knight's view on this aspect of winning and losing is shared by Keith Erickson:

> But you didn't win at Phoenix, you get beat in the finals. You won at UCLA. 'Well, it was just as good, because we gave the best we could, and that's what you love about it.' (Deford, 1979, p. 74)

Excellence, which can be measured in a variety of ways, appears to have at least two distinct aspects. One measure is an evaluation by others who judge our performances and the other measure is self-evaluation. To improve over previous performances, to extend oneself, to give the best one can is to achieve some degree of excellence even when such performances are not judged as excellent by others.

Participation in sports competition will bring joy and sadness, pleasure and regret, achievement and disappointment. Sport is an activity which allows its participants (and spectators) to experience the full gamut of human emotions. I am certainly not advocating losing. On the contrary, I am convinced that every contestant must strive to win, in accordance with the rules. To do less than that is an abrogation of the tacit agreement entered into before the contest began. What I am positing is the need to accept both winning and losing as part of the range of human experiences we undergo in sport. We gain from both, and at times, as I have shown, both as athletes and as persons, we benefit more from losing. Logically, it then follows that on those occasions losing is more important then winning.

References

Deford, F. "Welcome to His World." *Sports Illustrated*, 1976, 45, 22, 94-108.

Deford, F. "The Team of '64." *Sports Illustrated*, 1979, 50, 13, 70-82.

Deford, F. "The Rabbit Hunter." *Sports Illustrated*, 1981, 54, 4, 56-68.

Harper, W. "Review Essay." *Journal of the Philosophy of Sport*, 9, 69-77.

Keating, J.W. *Competition and Playful Activities*. Washington, D.C.: University Press of America, 1978.

Looney, D.S. "He'd Sooner Be at Home." *Sports Illustrated*, 1983, 59, 18, 50-54.

Looney, D.S. "Stopped Short of The Magix X." *Sports Illustrated*, 1987, 66, 13, 36-37.

Michener, J.A. *Sports In America*. New York: Random House, 1976.

Moore, K. "Give The Girl a Great Big Hand." *Sports Illustrated*, 1979, 51, 10, 18-33.

Nixon, H.L. *Sport and The American Dream*. New York: Leisure Press, 1984.

Pileggi, S. "Sportswoman of the Year — The Court Belongs To Chris." *Sports Illustrated*, 1976, 45, 25, 42-50.

Simson, R.L. *Sports and Social Values*. Englewood Cliffs, N.J.: Prentice-Hall, Inc., 1985.

Swift, B.M. "Detente On Ice." *Sports Illustrated*, 1987, 66, 8, 12-19.

COMPETITION:
A MODEL FOR CONCEPTION

ALICE E. KILDEA

Competition is a very different proposition from one person to another. Debates surrounding the effects of competition on culture and on the individual often lack specific reference; such debates are necessarily problematic. A literature review of definitions of competition revealed great diversity among writers. A model for the conception of competition was offered as a possible solution to some of the confusion and differences surrounding the nature of competition. When examined metaphorically, the constituents of competition take on increased significance. Positive and negative analogies of definitions serve to reaffirm or reconstruct one's understanding of the construct. Congruent articulations between the theoretical framework, the antecedent belief structures, and workable definitions of competition provide the basis of the Model for the Conception of Competition.

Perhaps no issue so typically applied throughout American culture today stirs such a mixture of reverence and anxiety as does competition. Proponents and opponents of competition have bombarded the literature, the convention halls, and the classrooms with irreconcilable differences about the social/psychological effects of competition on the evolving social structure and on the developing human being. Possibly the most significant thing that can be said about competition is that its mention evokes equal degrees of interest, anxiety, and confusion.

Competition is a phenomenon that crosses every sector of life. Philosophers, anthropologists, sociologists, psychologists, and social psychologists all try to explain its effects. Each attempts to prescribe some connection between what is and what ought to be. Athletes, business executives, children in parks, artists, and people in unemployment lines are sensitive to competition from a particular perspective. Each, too, recognizes some connection between what is and what ought to be.

Among others, Gardner has offered a sensitive formula for competitive and noncompetitive emphasis in the socio-cultural context of this country (Gardner, 1961). That task, therefore, is not the focus of this essay. Here a model is offered as a possible solution to the confusion resulting from the array of definitions of competition. Since reference to

64

different constructs within the same argument is necessarily problematic, a model for the conception of competition may have merit.

Basis for Model Development

Diversity in definitions of competition has been apparent throughout the literature (Coakley, 1982; Deutsch, 1949; Fairchild, 1978; Lewis, 1944; Loy, 1968; Maller, 1929; Martens, 1975; Mead, 1937; Orlick, 1980; Triplett, 1897). Beyond linguistic efficiency there appears to be a pervasive, interchangeable use in this culture of the terms "competition" (for "participation") and "competitiveness" (for "competence").

This phenomenon is apparent in the literature as early as 1897 and is supported in more current writings (Allport, 1924; Martens, 1975; Simmel, 1968; Triplett, 1897). The explicit interchange of competition and participation as synonymous functions merits investigation. Further implications suggested in the area of achievement motivation require serious analyses of human morality. That is, when competition and participation are used synonymously, and motivation to task is based primarily upon expectations to succeed (to win in competition), can one infer that the decision not to participate is indicative of incompetence (Scanlan, 1980, p. 59)?

Resolution of these questions rests upon clarity of definition, but clarity of definition requires an appreciation for the underlying theories and assumptions of a definition. A model for the conception of competition is designed to enhance these connections.

Model Structure

Interest in the assumptions underlying many authors' works in the area of competition led to the investigation of supporting psychological thought (Buhler, 1959). Making distinctions of various modes of thought was necessary to the model development. Drawing lines always involves the discomforts of commitment, but survival, mastery, and transcendence were found to provide satisfactory contrasts. These modes provided distinctions conducive to simplicity, coherence, and supporting experimental observations necessary for a model.

The design of the three modes — survival, mastery, and transcendence — was prompted by the philosophical antecedents creating the distinctions. To put it another way, responses to particular issues by individuals of each mode of psychological thought constituted the distinctions. The issues simultaneously derived were Will, Human Relation to the Cosmos, Purpose in Life, and Truth. The model assumes a connection between psychology applied and one's beliefs. A more significant assumption of the model is that definitions applied are not

I. Superiority and Dominance

right or wrong. One's definition of competition is tied to one's beliefs about the whole of life (see Table 1).

A contrast of definitions by Martens, Loy, and Kildea provided adequate foils for the functioning metaphorical model (Loy, 1968; Martens, 1975; Kildea, Note 1). For that reason, the primary focus of definitions exemplifying each mode of the model was limited to those works. As an enduring structure capable of ordering experiences with tentative philosophical claims, the model may provide insight into some of the socio-cultural problems associated with competition.

Model Analysis

Without the capacity for practical application a model has little value. Common questions surrounding the nature of competition, therefore, will be answered differently depending on the psychological mode and the antecedent philosophy. The questions are:

• Do humans compete with nonhumans (deer, bulls)?
• Do humans compete with nonhuman objects of nature (mountains, rapids, wind)?
• Do humans compete with themselves (the clock, personal records, the "historic self")?
• Does a struggle for supremacy imply consciousness of intent?
• When process is obscured by emphasis on product, does competition exist?
• Is the proximity of one competitor to another relevant to the existence of competition?
• Is all coactivity competitive?

Table 1
Model for Conception of Competition

Philosophical question of antecedent of psychology	Modes of psychological thought		
	Survival	Mastery	Transcendence
	Since the individual self is a complex of stimuli and responses and all stimuli lie outside the individual, self-determination is an illusion.	Motivating pressures are needs and hopes. Needs are tensions which tend to seek discharge in motor activity.	Symbol and reason allow for conscious self-relatedness accounting for conscience and freedom.
	All living organisms are governed by the same natural laws.	Hope of satisfaction is based on present opportunity and on memories of previous success. The integrative mechanism stimulates a plan for realizing hope. Hope makes deferment of pleasure possible.	Absence of determinism does not imply indeterminism.
	Freedom from responsibility.	Freedom from disorder.	Freedom of will means freedom of human will, subject to conditions and detriments.
Will	Pushed by drives.	Driven to mastery.	A precondition to health is the acceptance of finiteness. Finiteness and conscience allow humans to make of themselves what they will. Freedom to be. Freedom to be responsible. Moved by drives but pulled by meaning.

Table 1 (Cont.)
Model for Conception of Competition

Philosophical question of antecedent of psychology	Modes of psychological thought		
	Survival	Mastery	Transcendence
Human relationship to the cosmos	Instinctive alienation from other objects of cosmos provides sense of "looking in." Life is education. Product orientation.	Human capacity to adapt and expand provides means for mastery of cosmos. Multiple hurdles of space, time, and matter disrupt the pathway of goals. Product orientation.	Cosmic consciousness, unity and integration of self as member of cosmic family provides simultaneous feelings of insignificance and responsibility. Movement to the periphery of one's attention provides proper awareness of objects beyond the self. Process-product orientation.
Purpose in life — perception of tension in life	Avoidance of pain, attainment of pleasure, upholding internal order, maintaining balance. Overcome tension: establishing homeostasis mechanisms through defense formations.	Coping with deferment of need satisfaction in the process of self-realization. Overcome tension: Integration tasks are somewhat diminished by the enjoyment of power and mastery over material; the self is externalized in the drive for self-esteem.	Meaning: Community with universe — enjoyment is a result of need satisfaction; self-actualization is an effect and cannot be the object of intention. Undergo tension: Integrative tasks are diminished by the delight in struggling with obstacles; character of play is assumed.
Truth	Truth is singular. Purity of truth depends upon value-free, clean, observable data.	Truth is singular. Qualitative and quantitative values are expressed in reference to normative data.	Truth is multiple. Dichotomies between observable data and subjective experience fail to recognize the respective functions and legitimate field of action belonging to each.

The Survival Mode

In order to gain a feeling for the four issues raised in the model (Will, Relation to the Cosmos, Purpose in Life, and Truth), the survival mode of the model will be analyzed vertically. That is to say, all issues will be addressed in the survival mode without contrast. For that reason it will not be feasible to address the aforementioned seven questions in the order presented.

Needs, drives, motives, and goals are common terms of the psychologist. The connotations each of these terms conjures in the mind of the psychologist stem from a philosophical base. Need, from any philosophical base, is a deficiency or lack of an essential element. Needs are recognized as social as well as biological deficiencies. A drive is defined as a tendency to behave in a particular manner to fulfill a need. Though each psychological mode presented subscribes to the notion of drives, the degree of compulsion to act in a particular way is a significant analogy offered in the model. The degree of compulsion to act to fulfill needs (will) that characterize human behavior must be addressed by the philosopher within each psychologist.

Regarding will, proponents of the survival mode would hold that competition is a way of life. The term motive is usually considered as a specific condition contributing to performance and to the general motivational level. A motive is a desire for a specific object or goal, or the desire to escape a particular situation or environment. For the survivalist, motive and drive are frequently used interchangeably (Freud, 1938). Common biological and social drives of humans and other animals predetermine direction and goals. One is free from responsibility rather than free to take responsibility. One becomes much more of a reactor than an actor. Determinism, therefore, is a vital issue in conceptualizing any human endeavor including competition.

The cosmic elements, for the survivalist, lie outside the self. Order is maintained by surviving the parallel growth and extension of other cosmic elements. One "looks in" at the rest of the universe and retains an isolated sense of autonomy. Adjustment to the expressions of other cosmic elements allows one to survive. This view is manifested in sport in "conquering the mountain," "competing with the wind" when running against its force, and "avoiding the consumption of the waves" when surfing their hungry grasp. Regarding purpose in life, balance is foremost for the survivalist. Defense mechanisms and reaction formations provide the basis for the continual struggle for existence. Organisms that make the best adaptation to the environment survive, while the nonadaptive perish (Darwin, 1859). Reich (1971) has portrayed a scenario that will describes the survival mode of psychology:

I. Superiority and Dominance

Each individual would go it alone, refusing to trust his neighbor, seeing another man's advantage as his loss, seeing the world as a rat race with no rewards to losers. Underlying this attitude was the assumption that human nature is fundamentally bad, and that struggle against his fellow man is man's natural condition. (pp. 23-24).

The purity of truth and the simplicity of truth of the survivalist are exemplified daily in newspaper headlines and television sportcasts. The state of affairs in sport often is reduced to ends. Performance is valued or devalued almost exclusively by ordinal position. The API, the UPI, the NFL, and the NBA have been less than subtle, and even less accurate than an old friend, Walter Cronkite, in his closing evening statement, 'and that's the way it is.'

Contrasts of Will

Since model continuity has been established through vertical analysis of one mode, horizontal contrasts can now be effective. Concerning will, the proponent of the mastery mode holds that motivating pressures are needs and hopes. Needs are tensions that tend to seek discharge in motor activity. Hope of satisfaction is based on present opportunity and on memories of previous success. The integrative mechanism stimulates a plan for realizing hope. Hope makes deferment of pleasure possible. Freedom is perceived as the absence of disorder, and one is driven to mastery of cosmic beings and objects.

Contrasting the transcendent mode with the survival and mastery modes on the issue of will allows for increased understanding of competition. Proponents of the transcended mode believe that symbol and reason allow for conscious self-relatedness. This, in turn, accounts for conscience and freedom. Proponents of the transcendent mode hold that the absence of determinism does not imply indeterminism. Freedom of will means freedom of human will subject to conditions and detriments. Freedom in the transcendent mode is freedom to, rather than the freedom from, of the mastery and survival modes. Frankl's (1969) reference to being moved by drives but being pulled by meanings serves as a connection between the contrasting modes of psychology.

Will and death are human issues. A precondition to health is the acceptance of finiteness. Tillich (1952) referred to the courage to be, and the courage to trust one's self despite the fact that one is finite. Kierkegaard pointed out that finiteness and conscience allow humans to make of themselves what they will (Swenson, 1968).

70

The contrast of attitudes on the issue of will provides insight for the question: Is the proximity of one competitor to another relevant to the existence of competition? Proximity of opponents is not the issue of relevance of this argument; the reality of opposition is. Though one could argue that all goals are normative, there are behaviors (perhaps not observable in laboratory rats) independently and simultaneously directed toward upending records of others. It is intention rather than proximity that constitutes the competitive act for one of the transcendent mode. Being driven to mastery and being pushed by drives with little or no distinction between human and nonhuman beings constitutes opposition for persons of other modes of thought. This opposition is often defined as competition.

Contrasts of Relationship to the Cosmos

In examining the relation to the cosmos, persons of the mastery mode hold that the human capacity to adapt and expand provides means for mastery of the cosmos. Multiple hurdles of space, time, and matter disrupt the pathways of goals providing a product orientation.

The mode of transcendence would offer cosmic consciousness. Rather than pain avoidance of the waves' grasp, the surfer of the transcendent mode would feel unity and integration with the waves. The self would be conceived as a member of the cosmic family providing simultaneous feelings of insignificance and responsibility. One would struggle with, but delight in, the wind's interaction. This movement to the periphery of one's attention to self, furthermore, provides awareness of objects beyond the self. There is a process-product orientation.

Fraleigh (Note 2) in "Winning-Losing and Quality of Play in the Good Sports Contest" addressed means and ends in sport. Dewey, too, reminded us that directional order and sequential order do not give a legitimate account of life. Neither the science of being nor the doctrine of natural ends provides an adequate description of reality. As Dewey would put it, the game no more exists for the score than does a mountain exist for its peak (Dewey, 1925). This analogy of the relationship of the process to the product is a significant distinction of the three psychological modes.

The contrast of human relationships to the cosmos allows for better understanding of one's possible dissatisfaction with the proposition that humans can and do compete with other animate and inanimate objects of nature. One may be inclined to ask the question "Why would one want to establish supremacy over a mountain or the wind in one's face?" It seems the "why" is hidden in the very subtle, normative reference implied in the term "inanimate." If animation implies the speed at which molecules move, individuals might be able to conceive of a mountain or a set of rapids as having molecules moving differently from their own. But depending on one's psychological mode, the notion of conquering the mountain or defeating the rapids bears relative appeal. For the survivalist, one has adapted. In the mastery mode, one has achieved human excellence in mastering the elements. For one of the transcendent mode, conquering the elements would be an over-simplified assignment of human beings to a superior reality; for the very obstacles which had served the traveling have been deemed the spoils. Whether one can compete with inanimate objects, then, is much more a matter of belief than it is a matter of fact.

Competing with a bull or a deer is a notion deserving equal consideration. One of the transcendent mode would submit that if animation is relevant, the molecules of a bull move in a fashion more similar to those of humans than those of a mountain. The attempt, however, to equate chance for victory when interacting with a bull (even if the two "sides" shared a common objective) is seldom a consideration. Commonality of objective (will and intention of those in the struggle) is the common denominator of one's conception of competition. Whether competition is a conscious, social encounter or an ongoing, natural phenomenon with all cosmic matter is a question of belief. Depending on one's perspective, then, the delight, the agony, the death, and the exhilaration offered by bulls, mountains, rapids, and winds will find an array of distinctions within and beyond competition.

Contrasts of Purpose in Life

Examining purpose in life or the perception of tension in life from three perspectives gives a basis for analysis of many questions. The mastery mode involves coping with deferment of need satisfaction in the process of self-realization. Tension is overcome for those of the survival and mastery modes. Integrative tasks are somewhat diminished by the enjoyment of power and mastery over material. The self is externalized in the drive for self-esteem.

In contrast, purpose in life is "meaning" for one of the transcendent mode. There is community with the universe. Enjoyment is a result of need satisfaction and can only be experienced as a by-product. Self-actualization, too, is an effect that is often lost when perceived as the object of intention. Rather than overcoming tension, one would undergo tension. Integrative tasks are diminished by the delight in struggling with obstacles. In the struggle there is a balance of means and ends. Product and process diffuse and the character of play is assumed.

To stop playing is to cease living authentically, according to Sadler (1966). In pointing out the differences between love and seduction,

Sadler stated that the latter is an effort to possess the other person, to rob the other of freedom (Sadler, 1966). The "gamesman," the "hustler," the "cheat," and the "wet blanket" described in Ingham and Loy (1973) have provided salient foils to play and authentic living (pp. 21-22).

In its defined character, play is non-productive (Huizinga, 1950). That is to say there is a union of product and process. The "freedom to" of transcendence previously expressed is here employed. Play is free in that its object is that, and that only. One "goes with the flow," and tension exists only in being. On the other hand, to hustle or to cheat requires a loss of the process-product balance. Such an extreme of imbalance in process and product tension in life can result in numerous immoral acts, including a breaking of the competitive act. Though this analogy seems to suggest a taxonomy of morality of the three modes, that is not intended. Competition involves a focus of attention on the object of the struggle and on the means of achieving that end. One who gets lost in the play of the game and does not attempt to win is not playing the game; one who cheats has only displayed different symptoms of the same illness.

Contrasts of Truth

Truth is something very different for each of the three modes. The survivalist retains emphasis on value-free observable data; the transcendent researcher labels any value-free datum a myth (Barbour, 1974). The product orientation and drive for mastery complement the focus on normative data for one of the mastery mode.

Whether truth is singular or multiple is often a point of departure in attempts for understanding. Multiple truth, for some people, signifies no truth or contradiction. This is a complex proposition relevant to the issues, but it deserves attention beyond the scope of this paper.

Proponents of the transcendent mode maintain that dichotomies between observable data and the subjective experience fail to recognize the respective functions and legitimate field of action belonging to each. Sartre (1966) said, "To ski means not only to enable me to make rapid movements and to acquire a technical skill, nor is it merely to play by increasing according to my whim the speed or difficulties of the course; it also enables me to possess this field of snow" (p. 743).

What is true in the matter of competing against oneself? Can one compete against oneself? Are the pursuit of excellence and competition interchangeable phenomena? In answer to these questions two considerations are offered: first, the simple possibility of linguistic inefficiency; second, differences of metaphysics of the three modes.

Failure to recognize distinctions between human activity directed toward personal achievement relatively independent of the performance

I. Superiority and Dominance

of others and activity directed toward establishing supremacy over others is very possibly a matter of linguistic inefficiency. Regardless of what one calls the activities, distinct differences exist. Though it is true that the pursuit of personal excellence is often a struggle, it does not follow that all struggles are competitive.

Attempting to beat the clock or to upend any record previously established by oneself (often referred to as the "historic self") is an attempt toward excellence. It is personal rather than interpersonal activity. The pursuit of excellence is not competitive activity, and regardless of one's beliefs linguistic efficiency needs attention.

Further support for the possibility of linguistic inefficiency can be found in the notion of equating opportunity for victory for each side in any event. Most writers support the notion that each side must share a fairly equal chance for victory in a competitive setting. In keeping with that notion it would appear that competing with oneself would be impossible. With any luck at all in life, the historic self is significantly inferior to the present self in many respects. In other respects, such as physiological aging, the historic self may be significantly superior to the present self. In either case, splitting the self in such a fashion seems at best a misuse of the term competition.

Metaphysically, persons functioning in the survival and mastery modes would be prone to accept the atomistic dichotomies of selfhood (Green, 1875). Individuals of those modes might conceive of the present self as an isolated personality separate from the past self. This conception of consciousness would allow me to compete with the "other self." Splitting up of time or oneself, as the act of competing against oneself would require, would not be possible for one of the transcendent mode. The mental atoms of empiricism so succinctly opposed by James would be exemplified in the notion of competing against oneself. Based upon the continuity of experience in the formation of the self, competition with one's past self would be, in James' quotation, "a purely fictitious product of rationalist fancy" (McDermott, 1977, p. 293).

Application of Definitions to Modes of Model

The Survival Mode

Martens defined competition by making distinctions of competition as a process, as specific behaviors, as behavioral tendencies, and as specific situations. Martens defined the "objective competitive situation" as "a situation in which the comparison of an individual's performance is made with some standard in the presence of at least one other person who is aware of the criterion for comparison and can evaluate the comparison process" (Martens, 1975, p. 69). Competition for Martens is portrayed as a function of social evaluation (Simmel, Hoppe, & Milton, 1968).

Festinger (1954) posed no direct relationship between competition and social evaluation theory. Regarding social facilitation, the framework of Martens' theory, the following quotations provided insight to the psychological model:

> Two processes are accountable for the accelerating effect of the group upon the individual's work. The first of these is social facilitation. The movements made by others performing the same task as ourselves serve as contributing stimuli. The second process is rivalry. Its occurrence is in direct proportion to the competitive setting of the group occupation, though a certain degree of rivalry seems natural to all coactivity. (Allport, 1924, pp. 284-285)

> Many investigators have recognized that the condition of coaction engenders feelings of rivalry and competition. Triplett's theory of dynamogenesis was proposed as a theory of competition. This theory of competition holds that the bodily presence of another rider is a stimulus to the racer in arousing the competitive instinct. (Triplett, 1897, p. 516)

Martens' definition of competition is acceptable if one subscribes to the Survival Mode of Psychology in that: a) social facilitation theory is based upon the general principles of classical conditioning and instrumental learning: b) behavior theory has had considerable success in accounting for the performance of individual animals in simple situations.

The Mastery Mode

Loy (1968) defined competition as a struggle for supremacy between two or more opposing sides. The sides are broadly defined to encompass competitive relationships between man and other objects of nature, both animate and inanimate. Loy's competition relationships include competition between:

1. One individual and another (e.g., a boxing match or a 100-yard dash);
2. One team and another (e.g., a hockey game or a yacht race);
3. An individual or a team and an animate object of nature (e.g., a bullfight or a deer-hunting party);

I. Superiority and Dominance

4. An individual or a team and an inanimate object of nature (e.g., a canoeist running a set of rapids or a mountain-climbing expedition);

5. An individual or a team and an "ideal" standard (e.g., an individual attempting to establish a world land-speed record on the Bonneville flats or a basketball team trying to set an all-time scoring record). Competition against an "ideal" standard might also be conceptualized as man against time or space, or as man against himself (Loy, 1968, pp. 4-5).

Loy's conception of competition is acceptable if one subscribes to the Mastery Mode of Psychology in that: a) distinctions between human, animate, and inanimate beings or objects are nominal. That is to say, the broad interpretation of "sides" leaves only the nominal distinction of interaction between human beings and other objects of nature; b) coping and overcoming the multiple hurdles of environment provide the summit of cosmic consciousness in Loy's definition of competition.

The Transcendent Mode

Kildea (Note 1) defined competition as a struggle for supremacy between two or more sides. Based upon the transcendent mode, the sides were defined with considerable difference from those defined by Loy. In order for a struggle for supremacy to occur, four assumptions require fulfillment. Therefore, competition:

1. Denotes a conscious struggle for a co-identified object culminating in established supremacy of one side;

2. Implies an attempt to equate chance for victory for both sides in order that adversaries may confront one another under "ideal" conditions;

3. Obliges playing according to mutually acceptable and clearly defined rules so that the victor's superiority will be beyond dispute;

4. Implies an effort of all sides to attempt to perform to the limits of their capabilities, and in so doing insures the validity of the struggle and the value of the object.

Kildea's conception is acceptable if one subscribes to the transcendent mode in that: 1) distinctions between human, animate, and inanimate beings and objects of nature are made. Distinctions are not simply

76

nominal nor are they purely ordinal. Human against human or animal against animal may constitute consciousness and intent required in the struggle for supremacy; b) humanistic psychology incorporates a level of cosmic consciousness which transcends coping and overcoming.

Summary

In the normal vein of life an abundance of human effort is necessarily directed toward solving mundane and banal problems. Universal perspective is a condition requiring a sensitivity not easily managed and demanding courage not always affordable. But even a naive understanding of astronomy awakens an appreciation for the awesome issue of human significance. Competition is a construct that permeates every sector of human existence. From the standpoint of human causality, competition encompasses all of life.

Resolutions of the effects of competition on the individual and on evolving social structures have been confusing and conflicting. The literature review clearly indicates a diverse range of meaning associated with the term competition. Since reference to different constructs within the same argument is necessarily problematic, clarity of definition is essential to any resolution.

The purpose of this essay was to provide better understanding of competition as it relates to human life and cosmic interaction. More specifically, the paper attempted to make some critical distinctions between existing definitions of competition and to provide insight into the connotations and ramifications of those definitions. These tasks were attempted through a metaphorical model of competition that provided both positive and negative analogy of varying definitions. Current problems and practical solutions to issues surrounding competition can be traced through the mode. Common flaws in application of theory often result from incongruence of psychology and philosophy. The Model for the Conception of Competition was offered as means to trace congruent articulations of psychology applied, antecedent philosophy, and workable definitions of competition.

Rather than presenting a better or more accurate definition, the Model for the Conception of Competition was offered as a tie between the differences in the way life is conceived and the resulting circumstances. An analysis of the issues of Will, Human Relations to the Cosmos, Purpose in Life, and Truth served as the basis for response by persons of varying modes of psychological thought. The Model for the Conception of Competition was intended to provide understanding of the way one defines competition and, thus, the way one perceives and conceives of life.

I. Superiority and Dominance

Three distinctions in psychological mode were made. The Survival Mode represented the scientific determinism and Social Darwinism vastly held in American culture. Martens' (1975) definition of competition was offered as supporting evidence of that ideology. The Mastery Mode represented a more visible blend of determinism and indeterminism. The distinctions of "sides" offered in Loy's (1968) definition of competition gave rise to critical questions of the formation of consciousness. Nominal distinctions of various cosmic objects and beings within competition issues suggested an evolutionary flavor of Social Darwinism and a base of naturalistic ideology. The Mode of Transcendence represented a position of limited indeterminism. The Kildea (Note 1) definition of competition incorporated subjectivism in knowledge and the responsibility of conscience exercised by existential thought.

Making distinctions between the human condition and the conditions of other cosmic creatures and objects was a critical point in the functioning model. Ecological harmony is a common goal of rational persons of all psychological modes. "Either-or" and "right or wrong" approaches to life's problems often fall short of rational solution. Strindberg (1973) has prompted a question which demands attention to issues posed in the Model for the Conception of Competition:

> It is perhaps this wrong connection of ideas (that the earth is a mere point in the universe) which has led men to the still falser notion that they are not worthy of the Creator's regard. They have believed themselves to be obeying the dictates of humility when they have denied that the earth and all that the universe contains exists on man's account, on the grounds that the admission of such an idea would be only conceit. But they have not been afraid of the laziness and cowardice which are the inevitable results of this affected modesty. The present-day avoidance of the belief that we are the highest in the universe is the reason that we have not the courage to work in order to justify that title, that the duties springing from it seem too laborious, and that we would rather abdicate our position and our rights than realize them in all their consequences. Where is the pilot that will guide us between these hidden reefs of conceit and false humility? (pp. 74-75)

An answer to Strindberg's provocative question will rest on beliefs. Depending on one's beliefs, competition, a paramount construct in the whole of life, will be defined. The Model for the Conception of

Competition was offered to lend insight to solutions of human problems and to provide hope for ecological harmony.

Reference Notes

1. Kildea, A.E. "Competition: A model for conception." In C. Thomas (Chair), *Proceedings of the Philosophic Society for the Study of Sport*, Buffalo, October 1982.

2. Fraleigh, W. "Winning-losing and quality of play in the good sports contest." Paper presented at the meeting of the Philosophic Society for the Study of Sport, October 1977.

References

Allport, F.H. *Social psychology*. New York: Houghton-Mifflin, 1924.

Barbour, I.B. *Myths, models and paradigms: A comparative study in science and religion*. New York: Harper & Row, 1974.

Buhler, C. "Theoretical observations about life's basic tendencies." *American Journal of Psychotherapy*, 1959, 13, 561-581.

Cakley, J.J. *Sport in society*. St. Louis: C.V. Mosby, 1982.

Darwin, C. *Origin of species* 1859. New York: Modern Library, 1936.

Deutsch, M. "An experimental study of the effects of cooperation and competition upon group process." *Human Relations*, 1949, 2, 199-231.

Dewey, J. *Experience and nature*. La Salle, IL: Open Court, 1925.

Fairchild, D. "Man, mind and matter: Toward a philosophy of sport." *Journal of Thought*, 1978, 12, 225-234.

Festinger, L.A. "A theory of social comparison processes." *Human Relations*, 1954, 7, 117-140.

Frankl, V.E. *The will to meaning*. New York: New American Library, 1969.

Freud, S. *The basic writings of Sigmund Freud*. New York: Random House, 1938.

Gardner, J.W. *Excellence*. New York: Harper & Row, 1961.

Green, T.H. *Introduction to Hume*. London: Longman-Green & Co., 1875.

Huizinga, J. *Homo ludens*. Boston: Beacon Press, 1950.

Ingham, A.G., & Loy, J.W., Jr. "The social system of sport: A humanistic perspective." *Quest*, 1973, 19, 3-23.

I. Superiority and Dominance

Lewis, H.B. "An experimental study of the role of ego in work. I. The role of the ego in cooperative work." *Journal of Experimental Psychology*, 1944, 34, 113-127.

Loy, J.W., Jr. "The nature of sport: A definitional effort." *Quest*, 1968, 10, 1-15.

Maller, J.B. "Cooperation and competition: An experimental study in motivation." *Teachers College Contributions to Education*, 1929, 384, 1-176.

Martens, R. *Social psychology and physical activity*. New York: Harper & Row, 1975.

McDermott, J.J. *The writings of William James*. Chicago: The University of Chicago Press, 1977.

Mead, M. *Cooperation and competition among primitive peoples*. New York: McGraw-Hill, 1937.

Orlick, T. *In pursuit of excellence*. Champaign, IL: Human Kinetics, 1980.

Reich, C. *The greening of America*. New York: Bantam Books, 1971.

Sadler, W.A. "Play: A basic human structure involving love and freedom." *Review of Existential Psychology and Psychiatry*, 1966, 6 (Fall), 237-245.

Sartre, J. *Being and Nothingness*. (Hazel E. Barnes, trans.), New York: Washington Square Press, 1966.

Scanlan, T.K. "Antecedents of competitiveness." In R.A. Magill, M. Ash & F. Smoll (Eds.), *Children in sport: A contemporary anthology* (2nd ed.). Champaign, IL: Human Kinetics, 1980, pp. 53-75.

Simmel, E.C., Hoppe, R.A., & Milton, G.A. *Social facilitation and imitative behavior*. Boston: Allyn & Bacon, 1968.

Strindberg, A. *Legends*. New York: Haskell House, 1973.

Swenson, D.F. *Kierkegaard's concluding unscientific postscript*. Princeton: Princeton University Press for American-Scandinavian Foundation, 1968.

Tillich, P. *The courage To Be*. New Haven: Yale University Press, 1952.

Triplett, N. "The dynamogenic factors in pacemaking and competition." *American Journal of Psychology*, 1897, 9, 507-533.

SECTION II.

CONCEPTS
AND
FUNDAMENTALS

INTRODUCTION TO PHILOSOPHIC SELF-EVALUATION IN SPORT AND PHYSICAL EDUCATION

EARLE F. ZEIGLER

What follows is the latest version of a philosophic, professional, self-evaluation checklist that I developed originally in the 1950s. This checklist has been revised and updated regularly over the years to reflect all of the positions, tendencies and stances described above. By employing this instructional device carefully and honestly — while appreciating the subjectivity of an instrument such as this — aspiring professionals will be able to determine quite accurately their philosophy of life (including an ethical position), their philosophy of education, and their philosophy of sport and physical education insofar as their possible meaning and significance in people's lives are concerned. (Additional subsections not included here have been developed for the professions of health and safety education and recreation and recreation education as well.)

Before examining himself or herself, we suggest that each person study briefly the Freedom-Constraint Spectrum below. (You will be asked to do this again after you have completed the professional, self-evaluation, philosophic checklist and evaluated your personal position.) Keep in mind that the *primary* criterion on which this is based is the concept of 'personal freedom' in contrast to 'personal constraint.' Herbert J. Muller's definition of freedom (1954) calls it "the condition of being able to choose and to carry out purposes" in one's personal living pattern.

Within our social environment, the words "progressive" or "liberal" and "conservative" or "traditional" have historically related to policies favouring individual freedom and policies favouring adherence to tradition, respectively. For this reason, the more traditional positions or stances are shown to the right on the spectrum, and the more progressive ones are shown to the left. The analytic approach to doing philosophy is included in the checklist, *but it is not shown on the spectrum* because it has indeed become "philosophy in a new key." The earlier, mainstream positions in educational philosophy are indicated in parentheses on the figure below. Other pertinent definitions of positions on the freedom-constraint spectrum are offered immediately below the figure itself.

II. Concepts and Fundamentals

THE FREEDOM-CONSTRAINT SPECTRUM

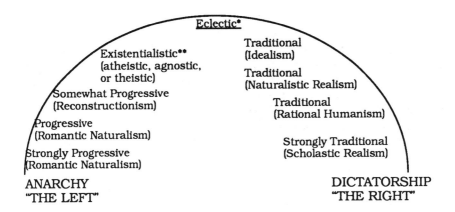

Eclectic*

Traditional
(Idealism)

Existentialistic**
(atheistic, agnostic,
or theistic)

Traditional
(Naturalistic Realism)

Somewhat Progressive
(Reconstructionism)

Traditional
(Rational Humanism)

Progressive
(Romantic Naturalism)

Strongly Traditional
(Scholastic Realism)

Strongly Progressive
(Romantic Naturalism)

ANARCHY
"THE LEFT"

DICTATORSHIP
"THE RIGHT"

Analytic — philosophy "in a new key" — subscribe to a philosophical outlook with ancient origins, but which has moved ahead strongly in the 20th century. The assumption here is that man's ordinary language has many defects that need to be corrected. Another objective is "the rational reconstruction of the language of science" (Abraham Kaplan). Preoccupation with analysis as opposed to philosophical system-building.

The **eclectic** approach is placed in the centre because it assumes that Xs have been placed in several positions on opposite sides of the spectrum. Most would argue that eclecticism is philosophically indefensible, while some believe that "patterned eclecticism" (or "reasoned incoherence") represents a stance which most of us hold.

Existentialistic — a permeating influence rather than a full-blown philosophical position; keep in mind that there are those with either an atheistic, agnostic or theistic orientation. Has been placed to the left of centre because of emphasis on individual freedom of choice.

84

"WHAT DO I BELIEVE?"
(A professional, self-evaluation checklist)

Instructions: Read the statements below carefully, section by section, and indicate by an X the statement in each section **that seems closest to your own personal belief.**

Check your answers only after all *five* sections have been completed. Then complete the summarizing tally on the answer page. Take note of apparent inconsistencies in your overall position. Finally, check yourself out on the freedom-constraint spectrum included at that point to discover your "location" whether you are in the centre or to the right or left.

Note: Many of the words, terms, phrases, etc. have been obtained from the work of philosophers, educational philosophers, and sport and physical education philosophers, living or deceased. I am most grateful for this assistance, but in the final analysis decided to leave them unidentified so as not to prejudice the person taking the test. In this self-evaluation check list, sections relating to the allied professions (e.g., recreation) have been deliberately omitted, but they are available upon request.

Category I
THE NATURE OF REALITY (METAPHYSICS)

A. ____ Experience and nature constitute both the form and also the content of the entire universe. There is no such thing as a pre-established order of affairs in the world. Reality is evolving, and humanity appears to be a most important manifestation of the natural process. The impact of cultural forces upon people is fundamental, and every effort should be made to understand them as we strive to build the best type of a group-centred culture. In other words, the structure of cultural reality should be our foremost concern. Cultural determinants have shaped human history, and a crucial stage has now been reached in the development of life on the planet. Our efforts must now be focused on the building of a world culture.

B. ____ I believe that the metaphysical and normative types of philosophizing have lost their basis for justification in the twentieth century. Their presumed wisdom has not been able to withstand the rigour of careful analysis. Sound theory is available to humankind through the application of scientific method to problem-solving. There,

II. Concepts and Fundamentals

what is the exact nature of philosophy? Who is in a position to answer the ultimate questions about the nature of reality? The scientist is, of course, and the philosopher must become the servant of science through conceptual analysis and the rational reconstruction of language. Accordingly the philosopher must resign himself or herself to dealing with important, but lesser, questions than the origin of the universe and the nature of the human being — and what implications this might have for everyday conduct.

C. ____ The world of men and women is a human one, and it is from the contest of this human world that all the abstractions of science derive their meaning ultimately. There is the world of material objects, of course, that extends in mathematical space with only quantitative and measurable properties, but we humans are first and foremost "concrete involvement" within the world. Existence precedes essence, and it is up to men and women to decide their own fate. This presumably makes the human different from all other creatures on earth. It appears true that people can actually transform life's present condition, and thus the future may well stand open to these unusual beings.

D. ____ Nature is an emergent evolution, and the human's frame of reality is limited to nature as it functions. The world is characterized by activity and change. Rational man and woman have developed through organic evolution over millions of years, and the world is yet incomplete — a reality that is constantly undergoing change because of a theory of emergent novelty that appears to be operating within the universe. People enjoy true freedom of will. This freedom is achieved through continuous and developmental learning from experience.

E. ____ Mind as experience by all people is basic and real. The entire universe is mind essentially. The human is more than just a body; people possess souls, and such possession makes them of a higher order than all other creatures on earth. The order of the world is due to the manifestation in space and time of an eternal and spiritual reality. The individual is simply part of the whole. It is therefore a person's duty to learn as much about the Absolute as possible. Within this position there is divided opinion regarding the problem of monism or pluralism (one force or more than one force). The individual person has freedom to determine which way he or she will go in life. The individual can relate to the moral law in the universe, or else he or she can turn against it.

F. ____ The world exists in itself, apart from our desires and knowledge. There is only one reality — that which we perceive is it. The universe is made up of real substantial entities, existing in themselves and ordered

86

to one another by extra-mental relations. Some feel there is one basic unity present, while others holding this position believe in a non-unified cosmos with two or more substances or processes at work. Things don't just happen; they happen because many interrelated forces make them occur in a particular way. People live within this world of cause and effect. They simply cannot make things happen independent of it.

Category II
ETHICS AND MORALITY (Axiology/Values)

A. ____ The source of all human experience lies in the regularities of the universe. Things don't just happen; they happen because many interrelated forces make them occur in a particular way. Humans in this environment are confronted by one reality only — that which we perceive is it! The "life of reason" is extremely important, a position that emanates originally from Aristotle who placed *intellectual* virtues above *moral* virtues in his hierarchy. Many holding this stance believe that all elements of nature, including people, are inextricably linked together in an endless chain of causes and effects. Thus, they accept a sort of ethical determinism — i.e., what people are morally is determined by response patterns imprinted in their being by both heredity and environment. A large number in the world carry this fundamental position still further by adding a theological component; for them the highest good is ultimate union with God, the Creator, who is responsible for teleological and supernatural reality. As a creature of God, human goodness is reached by the spirituality of the form attained as the individual achieves emancipation from the material (or the corporeal). The belief is that a person's being contains potential energy that may be guided or directed toward God or away from Him; thus, what the individual does in the final analysis determines whether such action will be regarded as right or wrong.

B. ____ There should be no distinction between *moral* goods and *natural* goods. There has been a facts/values dualism in existence, and this should be eradicated as soon as possible by the use of scientific method applied to ethical situations. Thus, we should employ reflective thinking to obtain the ideas that will function as tentative solutions for the solving of life's concrete problems. Those ideas can serve as hypotheses to be tested in life experimentally. If the ideas work in solving problematic situations, they become true. In this way we have empirical verification of hypotheses tending to bring theory and practice into a closer union. When we achieve agreement in factual belief, agreement in attitudes should soon follow. In this way science can ultimately bring about complete agreement on factual belief or knowledge about human behaviour. Thus there will be a continuous adaptation of values to the culture's changing needs that will in turn effect the directed reconstruction of all social institutions.

C. ___ The problems of ethics should be resolved quite differently than they have throughout most of history. Ethics cannot be resolved completely through the application of scientific method, although an ethical dispute must be on a factual level — i.e., factual statements *must* be distinguished from value statements. Ethics should be normative in the sense that we have moral standards. However, this is a difficult task because the term "good" appears to be indefinable. The terms used to define or explain ethical standards or norms should be analyzed logically in a careful manner. Social scientists should be enlisted to help in the determination of the validity of factual statements, as well as in the analysis of conflicting attitudes as progress is determined. Ethical dilemmas in modern life can be resolved through the combined efforts of the philosophical moralist and the scientist. The resultant beliefs may in time change people's attitudes. Basically, the task is to establish a hierarchy of reasons with a moral basis.

D. ____ Good and bad, and rightness and wrongness, are relative and vary according to the situation or culture involved (i.e., the needs of a situation are *there* and *then* in that society or culture). Each ethical decision is highly individual, initially at least, since every situation has its particularity. The free, authentic individual decides to accept responsibility when he or she *responds* to a human situation and seeks to answer the need of an animal, person or group. How does the "witness react to the world"? Guidance in the making of the ethical decision may come either from "outside," from intuition, from one's own conscience, from reason, from empirical investigation, etc. Thus it can be argued that there are *no* absolutely valid ethical principles or universal laws.

E. ____ Ethics and morality are based on cosmic laws, and we are good if we figure out how to share actively in them. If we have problems of moral conduct, we have merely to turn to the Lord's commandments for solutions to all moral problems. Yet there is nothing deterministic here, because the individual himself or herself has an active role to play in determining which ethical actions will bring him or her into closer unity with the supreme Self. However, the fact of the matter is that God is both the source and the goal of the values for which we strive in our everyday lives. In this approach the presence of evil in the world is recognized as a real human experience to be met and conquered. The additional emphasis here is on logical argument to counter the ever-present threat of the philosophy of science. This is countered by the argument that there is unassailable moral law inherent in the Universe that presents people with obligations to duty (e.g., honesty is a good that is universal).

F. ____ Our social environment is inextricably related to the many struggles of peoples for improvement of the quality of life — how to place more *good* in our lives than *bad*, so to speak. We are opposed to any theory that delineates values as absolute and separates them from everyday striving within a social milieu. Actually the truth of values can be determined by established principles of evidence. In an effort to achieve worldwide consensus on any and all values, our stated positions on issues and controversial matters must necessarily be criticized in public forums. Cultural realities that affect values should be re-oriented through the achievement of agreed-upon purposes (i.e., through social consensus and social-self-realization on a worldwide basis). The goal, then, is to move toward a comprehensive pattern of values that provides both flexibility and variety. This should be accompanied by sufficient freedom to allow the individual to achieve individual and social values in his or her life. However, we must not forget that the majority does rule in evolving democracies, and at times wrong decisions are made. Keeping in mind that the concept of 'democracy' will prevail only to the extent that "enlightened" decisions are made, we must guarantee the ever-present role of the critical minority as it seeks to alter any consensus established. A myth of utopian vision should guide our efforts as we strive toward the achievement of truly human ethical values in the life experiences of all our citizens.

Category III
EDUCATIONAL AIMS AND OBJECTIVES

A. ____ Socialization of the child has become equally as important as his or her intellectual development as a key educational aim in this century. There should be concern, however, because many educational philosophers seem to assume the position that children are to be fashioned so that they will conform to a prior notion of what they *should* be. Even the progressivists seem to have failed in their effort to help the learner "posture himself or herself." If it does become possible to get general agreement on a set of fundamental dispositions to be formed, should the criterion employed for such evaluation be a public one (rather than personal and private)? Education should seek to "awaken awareness" in the learner — awareness of the person as a single subjectivity in the world. Increased emphasis is needed on the arts and social sciences, and the student should freely and creatively choose his or her own pattern of education.

B. ____ Social-self-realization is the supreme value in education. The realization of this ideal is most important for the individual in the social setting — a world culture. Positive ideals should be molded toward the evolving democratic ideal by a general education which is group-centered and in which the majority determines the acceptable goals. However, once that majority opinion is determined, all are obligated to conform until such majority opinion can be reversed (the doctrine of "defensible partiality"). Nevertheless, education by means of "hidden coercion" is to be scrupulously avoided. Learning itself is explained by the organismic principle of functional psychology. Social intelligence acquired teaches people to control and direct their urges as they concur with or attempt to modify cultural purposes.

C. ____ The concept of 'education' has become much more complex than was ever realized before. Because of the various meanings of the term "education," talking about educational aims and objectives is almost a hopeless task unless a myriad of qualifications is used for clarification. The term ("education") has now become what is called a "family-resemblance" one in philosophy. Thus we need to qualify our meaning to explain to the listener whether we mean (1) the subject-matter; (2) the activity of education carried on by teachers (3) the process of being educated (or learning) that is occurring; (4) the result, actual aim intended, or #2 and #3 immediately above taking place through the employment of that which comprises #1 above; (5) the discipline, or field of enquiry and investigation; and (6) the professional whose members are involved professionally with all of the aspects of education described above. With this understanding, it is then possible to make some determination about which specific objectives the profession of education should strive for as it moves in the direction of the achievement of long range aims.

D. ____ The general aim of education is more education. Education in the broadest sense can be nothing else than the changes made in human beings by their experience. Participation by students in the formation of aims and objectives is absolutely essential to generate the all-important desired interest required for the finest educational process to occur. Social efficiency (i.e., societal socialization) can well be considered the general aim of education. Pupil growth is a paramount goal. This means that the individual is placed at the center of the educational experience.

E. ____ A philosophy which holds that the aim of education is the acquisition of verified knowledge of the environment; which recognizes the value of content as well as the activities involved; and which takes into account the external determinants of human behaviour. Education is the acquisition of the art of the utilization of knowledge. The primary task of education is to transmit knowledge, knowledge without which civilization could not continue to flourish. Whatever people have discovered to be true because it conforms to reality should be handed down to future generations as the social or cultural tradition. Some holding this philosophy believe that the good life emanates from co-operation with God's grace, and believe further that the development of the Christian virtues is obviously of greater worth than learning or anything else.

F. ____ Through education the developing organism becomes what it latently is. All education may be said to have a religious significance, the meaning of which is that there is a "moral imperative" on education. As the person's mind strives to realize itself, there is the possibility of the Absolute within the individual mind. Education should aid the child to adjust to the basic realities (the spiritual ideals of truth, beauty and goodness) that the history of the race has furnished us. The basic values of human living are health, character, social justice, skill, art, love, knowledge, philosophy and religion.

Category IV
THE EDUCATIVE PROCESS
(Epistemology)

A. ____ Understanding the nature of knowledge will clarify the nature of reality. Nature is the medium by which the Absolute communicates to us. Basically, knowledge comes only from the mind, a mind which must offer and receive ideas. Mind and matter are qualitatively different. A finite mind emanates through heredity from another finite mind. Thought is the standard by which all else in the world is judged. An individual attains truth for himself or herself by examining the wisdom of the past through his or her own mind. Reality, viewed in this way, is a system of logic and order that has been established by the Universal Mind. Experimental testing helps to determine what the truth really is.

B. ____ The child experiences an "awareness of being" in his/her subjective life about the time of puberty — and is never the same thereafter. The young person truly becomes aware of his or her own existence, and the fact that there is now a responsibility for one's own conduct. After this point in life, education must be an "act of discovery" to be truly effective. Somehow the teacher should help the young person to become involved personally with his or her education, and also with the world situation in which such an education is taking place. Objective or subjective knowledge should be personally selected and "appropriated" by the youth unto himself or herself, or else it will be relatively meaningless in that particular life. Thus it matters not whether logic, scientific evidence, sense perception, intuition or revelation is claimed as the basis of knowledge acquisition, no learning will take place for that individual self until the child or young person decides that such learning is "true" for him or her in that person's life. Therefore the young person knows when he or she knows!

C. ____ Knowledge is the result of a process of thought with a useful purpose. Truth is not only to be tested by its correspondence with reality, but also by its practical results. Knowledge is earned through experience and is an instrument of verification. Mind has evolved in the natural order as a more flexible means whereby people adapt themselves to the world. Learning takes place when interest and effort unite to produce the desired result. A psychological order of learning (problem-solving as explained through scientific method) is ultimately more useful (productive?) than a logical arrangement (proceeding from the simple fact to the complex conclusion). However, we shouldn't forget that there is always a social context to learning, and the curriculum itself should be adapted to the particular society for which it is intended.

D. ____ Concern with the educative process should begin with an understanding of the terms that are typically employed for discussion purposes within any educational program. The basic assumption is that these terms are usually employed loosely and often improperly. For example, to be precise we should be explaining that a student is offered educational *experiences* in a classroom and/or laboratory setting. Through the employment of various types and techniques of instructional methodology (e.g., lectures), he or she hears *facts*, increases the scope of information and/or *knowledge*, and learns to comprehend and interpret the material (understanding). Possessing various kinds and amounts of *ability* or *aptitude*, students gradually develop *competencies* and a certain degree or level of *skill*. It is hoped that certain *appreciations* about the worth of the individual student's experiences will be developed, and that he or she will form certain *attitudes* about familial, societal, and professional life that lie ahead. Finally, societal *values* and *norms*, along with other social influences, will help educators, fulfilling role within their collectivities and subcollectivities, determine the best methods (with accompanying experimentation, of course) of achieving socially acceptable educational goals.

E. ____ An organismic approach to the learning process is basic. Thought cannot be independent of certain aspects of the organism. This is because thought is related integrally with emotional and muscular functions. The person's mind enables him or her to cope with the problems of human life in a social environment within a physical world. Social intelligence is actually closely related to scientific method. Certain operational concepts, inseparable from metaphysics and axiology (beliefs about reality and values), focus on the reflective thought, problem-solving, and social consensus necessary for the gradual transformation of the culture.

F. ____ There are two major learning (epistemological) theories of knowledge in this philosophical stance. One states that the aim of knowledge is to bring into awareness the object as it really is. The other emphasizes that objects are "represented" in the human's consciousness, not "presented." Students should develop habits and skills involved with acquiring knowledge, with using knowledge practically to meet life's problems, and with realizing the enjoyment that life offers. A second variation of learning theory (epistemological belief) here indicates that the child develops his or her intellect by employing reason to learn a subject. The principal educational aims proceeding hand in hand with learning theory here would be the same for all people at all times in all places. Others with a more religious orientation holding this position, basically add to this stance that education is the process by which people seek to link themselves ultimately with their Creator.

Category V
VALUES IN SPECIALIZED FIELD
(Sport and Physical Education)

A. ____ I believe in the concept of 'total fitness' which implies an educational design directed toward the individual's self-realization as a social being. In our field there should be an opportunity for selection of a wide variety of useful activities. Instruction in human motor performance relating to sport, exercise, dance and play is necessary to provide a sufficient amount of "physical" fitness activity. The introduction of dance, music and art into physical education can contribute to the person's creative expression. Intramural sports and voluntary physical recreational activities should be stressed. This applies especially to team competitions with particular stress on co-

II. Concepts and Fundamentals

operation and the promotion of friendly competition. Extramural sport competition should be introduced when there is a need. Striving for excellence is important, but it is vital that materialistic influences should be kept out of the educational program. In today's increasingly stressful environment, relaxation techniques should have a place too, as should the concept of 'education or leisure.'

B. _____ I believe that the field of sport and physical education should strive to fulfil a role in the general education pattern of the arts and sciences. The goal is *total* fitness, not only physical fitness, with a balance between activities emphasizing competition and co-operation. The concepts of 'universal man' and 'universal woman' are paramount, but we must allow the individual to choose his or her sport, exercise and dance activities for himself or herself based on knowledge of self and what knowledge and/or skills he or she would like to possess. We should help the child who is "authentically eccentric" feel at home in the sport and physical education program. It is also important that we find ways for youth to commit themselves to values and people. A person should be able (and permitted) to select developmental physical activity according to the values which he or she wishes to derive from it. This is often difficult in our society today because of the extreme overemphasis placed on winning — being "Number #1!" Finally, creative movement activities such as modern dance should be stressed, also.

C. _____ I believe that education "of the physical" should have primary emphasis in our field. I am concerned with the development of physical vigour, and such development should have priority over the recreational aspects of sport and physical education. Many people, who hold the same educational philosophy as I do, recommend that all students in public schools should have a daily period designed to strengthen their muscles and develop their bodily co-ordination and circulo-respiratory endurance. Sport and physical education must, of course, yield precedence to intellectual education. I give qualified approval to interscholastic, intercollegiate, and inter-university athletics, since they do help with the learning of sportsmanship and desirable social conduct if properly carried out. However, all these objectives, with the possible exception of physical training, are definitely extra-curricular and not part of what we call the regular educational curriculum.

D. _____ I am much more interested in promoting the concept of 'total fitness' rather than physical fitness alone. I believe that sport and physical education should be considered an integral subject in the curriculum. Students should have the opportunity to select a wide variety of useful activities, many of which should help to develop "social intelligence." The activities offered should bring what are considered as natural impulses into play. To me, developmental physical activity classes and intramural-recreational sports are much more important to the large majority of students than highly competitive athletics offered at considerable expense for the few. Thus sport and physical education for the "normal" or "special" young man or woman deserves priority if conflict arises over budgetary allotment, staff availability, and facility use. However, I can still give full support to "educational" competitive sport, because such individual, dual, and/or team activities can provide vital educational experiences for young people if properly conducted.

E. _____ I believe that there is a radical, logically fundamental difference between statements of what is the case and statements of what ought to be the case. When people express their beliefs about sport and physical education, their disagreements can be resolved in principle. However, it is logical also that there can be sharing of *beliefs* (facts, knowledge) with radical disagreement in *attitudes*. In a democracy, for example, we can conceivably agree on the fact that jogging (or bicycling, swimming, walking, etc.) brings about certain circulo-respiratory changes, but we can't force people to get actively involved *or even* to hold a favourable attitude toward such activity. We can demonstrate tenable theory about such physical involvement, therefore, but we cannot prove that a certain *attitude* toward such activity is the correct one. Thus I may accept evidence that vigorous sport, dance, exercise and play can bring about certain effects or changes in the organism, but my own *attitude* and subsequent regular involvement — the *values* in it for me — is the result of a commitment rather than a prediction.

F. _____ I am extremely interested in individual personality development. I believe in education "of the physical," and yet I believe in education "through the physical" as well. Accordingly, I see sport and physical education as important, but also occupying a lower rung on the educational ladder. I believe that desirable objectives for sport and physical education would include the development of responsible citizenship and group participation. In competitive sport I believe that the transfer of training theory is in operation in connection with the development of desirable personality traits (or *undersirable* traits if the leadership is poor). Participation in highly competitive sport should always serve as a means to a desirable end.

Note: Appreciation should be expressed at this point to the following people from whose work phrases and very short quotations were taken for inclusion in the checklist. Inclusion of their names at those particular points in the text did not seem advisable, inasmuch as the particular position or stance may have been instantly recognized: John S. Brubacher, Abraham Kaplan, Morton White, William Barrett, E.A. Burtt, Van Cleve Morris, Ralph Harper, Herbert Spencer, J. Donald Butler, George R. Geiger, Theodore Brameld, John Wild, Harry S. Broudy, James Feibleman, Roy W. Sellars, Isaac L. Kandel, Alfred N. Whitehead, Mortimer J. Adler, Wm. McGucken, Pope Pius XII, Herman H. Horne, Theodore M. Greene, Wm. E. Hocking, and, last but not least, Paul Weiss.

Answers: Read only after all *five* questions have been completed. Record your answer to each part of the checklist on the summarizing tally form below.

I. The Nature of Reality (Metaphysics)

a.   Somewhat Progressive (Reconstructionism, Brameld)
b.   Analytic (Analytic Philosophy)
c.   Existentialistic (atheistic, agnostic, or theistic)
d.   Progressive (Pragmatic Naturalism; Ethical Naturalism)
e.   Traditional (Philosophic Idealism)
f.   Traditional (Philosophic Realism, with elements of Naturalistic Realism, Rational Humanism, and positions within Catholic educational philosophy)

II Ethics (Axiology)

a.   Traditional (including elements of Strongly Traditional; Philosophic Realism, plus theology)
b.   Progressive (Pragmatic Naturalism; Ethical Naturalism)
c.   Analytic (Emotive Theory; "Good Reasons" Approach)
d.   Existentialistic (atheistic, agnostic, and some Christians)
e.   Traditional (Philosophic Idealism; Protestant Christian)
f.   Somewhat Progressive (Reconstructionism, Brameld; Ethical Naturalism)

III. Educational Aims and Objectives

a.   Existentialistic
b.   Somewhat Progressive

    c.   Analytic
    d.   Progressive
    e.   Traditional (including elements of Strongly Traditional)
    f.   Traditional

IV. The Educative Process (Epistemology)

    a.   Traditional
    b.   Existentialistic
    c.   Progressive
    d.   Analytic
    e.   Somewhat Progressive
    f.   Traditional (including elements of Strongly Traditional)

V. Sport and Physical Education

    a.   Somewhat Progressive
    b.   Existentialistic
    c.   Traditional (including elements of Strongly Traditional)
    d.   Progressive
    e.   Analytic
    f.   Traditional

Further Instructions: It should now be possible — keeping in mind the *subjectivity* of an instrument such as this — to determine your position *approximately* based on the answers that you have given and then tallied on the form immediately above.

At the very least you should be able to tell if you are progressive, traditional, existentialistic or analytic in your philosophic approach.

If you discover considerable *eclecticism* in your overall position or stance — that is, checks that place you on opposite sides of the Freedom-Constraint Spectrum, or some vacillation with checks in the existentialistic or analytic categories — you may wish then to analyze your positions or stances more closely to see if your overall position is philosophically defensible.

II. Concepts and Fundamentals

Table 5.1
Summarizing Tally Form

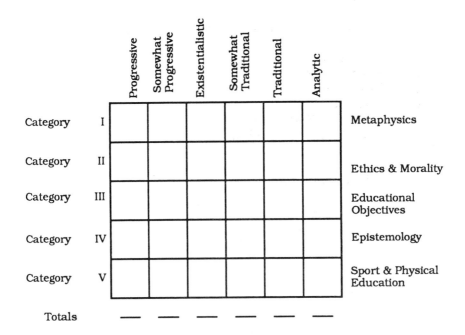

	Progressive	Somewhat Progressive	Existentialistic	Somewhat Traditional	Traditional	Analytic	
Category I							Metaphysics
Category II							Ethics & Morality
Category III							Educational Objectives
Category IV							Epistemology
Category V							Sport & Physical Education
Totals	—	—	—	—	—	—	

Keep in mind that your choices under Category I (Metaphysical or *Nature of Reality*) and Category II (Axiology/*Values*) are basic and in all probability have a strong influence on your subsequent selections.

Now please examine the Freedom-Constraint Spectrum at the beginning of this section again. Keep in mind that "Existentialistic" is not considered a position or stance as the others are (e.g., Traditional or Philosophic Idealism). Also, if you tend to be "Analytic," this means that your pre-occupation is with analysis as opposed to any philosophic/theologic system-building.

Finally, then, after tallying the answers (your "score" above), and keeping in mind that the goal is not to "pigeonhole you forever more," did this self-evaluation checklist show you to be:

(   ) Strongly Progressive — 4 to 5 checks left of centre on the Spectrum?

(   ) Progressive — 3 to 4 checks left of centre?

(   ) Some Progressive — 3 checks left of centre?

(   ) Eclectic — checks in 2 or 3 positions on both the right and left of the Spectrum's centre?

(   ) Somewhat Traditional — 3 checks right of centre?

(   ) Traditional — 3 to 4 checks right of centre?

(   ) Strongly Traditional — 4 to 5 checks right of centre?

(   ) Existentialistic — 4 to 5 checks (including Category I) relating to this stance?

(   ) Analytic — 4 to 5 checks (including Category I) relating to this approach to doing philosophy?

EXISTENTIALISM AND THE ATHLETE

JOSEPH C. MIHALICH

Scholarly studies of the philosophical and humanistic dimensions in sports and athletics should relate the sporting enterprise to commonly recognized philosophical attitudes and approaches wherever the relationship is valid and logical. This is important in the nature of the studies themselves, and in further illustrating the fundamentally philosophical character of sports and athletics in human existence. This chapter is an introduction to the spirit and premises of existentialist philosophy, and an indication and explication of existentialism's unique and significant influences in the world of sports and athletics.

Existentialism is probably the most popular and most pervasive trend or theme in Western philosophy since its inception in the philosophical teachings of Soren Kierkegaard (1813-55) and Friedrich Nietzsche (1844-1900). The universality of the existentialist approach is apparent in contemporary professional philosophical circles, and also in representative schools of contemporary theology and psychology and in many areas and aspects of European and American literature. Possibly some of the professional and popular interest and enthusiasm relating to existentialism has waned somewhat since the peak of its popularity in the two decades immediately after World War II, but the movement is still evident and significant in scholarship and personal allegiance throughout the Western world.

Existentialism is a philosophical attitude (rather than system or doctrine) whose basic tenet is emphasis on the "primacy and dignity of the human reality as an individual." Existentialism rejects abstract speculations and generalizations about reality and human existence, and focuses on the existence and experiences of the individual and the *hard immediacy* of the present decision as the most meaningful context for knowledge and value. The main frame of reference is always the individual's life and actions as the life is lived through the actions. Existentialism emphasizes the concrete rather than the abstract and the individual rather than the universal, and stresses above all the essential and total freedom and personal subjectivity of the individual in being and acting.

Existentialist Philosophy: Spirit and Character

Existentialism is an intensely personal and individual portrayal of reality and human existence and this can create some difficulties in defining and assessing existentialist philosophy. Several avowed and classic existentialist philosophers reject the term *existentialist* as a label or description of their approach, since this common branding suggests a unity or universality of thought which is contrary to their freedom and individuality of expression. The fundamental polarity in existentialist philosophy is the distinction between atheistic or secular existentialism (Jean-Paul Sartre) and Christian existentialism (Gabriel Marcel and Nicolai Berdyaev), with several variations on these basic themes. Both atheistic and Christian existentialism emphasize individual freedom and subjectivity and the importance of personal choice and values, although the world of the Christian existentialist tends to be more hopeful and more ultimately meaningful since it includes the concept of God and the possibility of eternal salvation beyond the temporal satisfaction of a life well-lived.

Despite the diversity and variety in existentialist philosophy, all such versions reflect or manifest certain common characteristics which give existentialist philosophy its unique character and recognizable form. These characteristics are the following: 1) existentialist philosophy is a *living* or *lived* philosophy rather than a formal or academic philosophy; 2) existentialist philosophy distinguishes *authentic* existence from *inauthentic* existence and stresses the importance of authentic existence; 3) existentialist philosophy emphasizes *consciousness-of-self* and *personal subjectivity*; 4) existentialist philosophy opposes *rationalism* and *intellectualism* as ways of explaining reality and ways of explaining human knowledge; 5) existentialist philosophy is a constant *subjective experience* that can be illustrated but never completely communicated; and 6) existentialist philosophy emphasizes the *plight of the individual* in the world.

To say that existentialist philosophy is a *living* or *lived* philosophy means that its precepts and tenets are embodied in the life and actions of the individual as a conscious participant in existence and experience. Existentialist philosophy is primarily the individual's conscious awareness of one's own being and the dimenstions of one's experiences in confronting reality in the world. *Authentic* existence is the individual's conscious recognition (and exploitation) of the definitive aspects of meaningful human existence: absolute freedom and individuality and subjectivity. *Inauthentic* existence is the surrender or the subordination of these aspects to function and utility or to the crowd-mentality and socioreligious and political institutions. *Consciousness-of-self* is an acute and enlightened form of self-consciousness reflected in *subjectivity*, or the awareness of oneself as an original center of free initiative existing in the world as an entity marked with the finitude of death.

Existentialist philosophy opposes *rationalism* and *intellectualism* as modes or ways of knowing because these views conceptualize reality into rigid and abstract patterns, and thus detract from the vibrancy and dynamism and the *hard immediacy* of personal experience in making or creating one's own world. One of the unique aspects of the existentialist approach is its character as a constant *subjective experience* that can be illustrated but never completely communicated. Existentialist philosophy is identified and constituted by the individual's own personal existential experience in being and acting, and thus can never be systematized into principles and premises to be communicated in a pedagogical sense.

The possibility of *illustrating* an existentialist viewpoint or an existentialist experience is the basis of literary existentialism in which life and experience are depicted from an existentialist perspective within the context of fictional or semifictional situations. The *plight of the individual* in existentialist philosophy refers to the frequently awesome awareness of the human condition reflected in our lives as entities "abandoned in the world" with nothing and no one to guide us: we are left to our own personal choices and decisions and the immense responsibility for our own existential destiny. As indicated earlier in the comparison between atheistic and Christian existentialism, the plight of the individual in Christian existentialism is ameliorated somewhat through the consolation of spiritual relationships.

Existentialist philosophy is largely identified in the popular mind with the life and writings of Jean-Paul Sartre (1905-80), and classic formulations are propounded also in the works of Gabriel Marcel (1889-1973) and Martin Heidegger (1889-1976). Other leading existentialist philosophers include Karl Jaspers and Maurice Merleau-Ponty, and the Spaniards Miguel de Unamuno and Jose Ortega y Gassett. Existentialist theology is portrayed in the religious views of Nicolai Berdyaev, Paul Tillich,and Martin Buber. Literary existentialism is reflected in contemporary authors including Albert Camus, Simone de Beauvoir, Fyodor Dostoyevsky, and Herman Hesse. Much interesting and significant pioneer research in existential psychoanalysis is contributed by Rollo May and Victor Frankl.

Scholarly explications and critiques of existentialist philosophy are extensive in number and diversified in character. The definitive expressions of existentialist philosophy are Sartre's *Being and Nothingness* (1956) and Marcel's *The Mystery of Being* (1950), and in certain areas Heidegger's *Being and Time* (1962). Classic secondary sources include W.C. Barrett's *Irrational Man* (1958); H.J. Blackham's *Six Existentialist Thinkers* (1952); F.C. Copleston's *Existentialism and Modern Man* (1948); Wilfred Desan's *The Tragic Finale* (1954); Marjorie Grene's *Dreadful Freedom* (1948); and Jean Wahl's *A Short History of Existentialism* (1949). See also this writer's *Existentialism and Thomism* (1969).[1]

Existentialism and the Athlete

Existentialism in sports and athletics centers on the concept of the athlete as an individual in the world who is acutely aware of the significance of concrete and personal experience, and who is intensely committed to personal values and goals for the moment and for one's athletic lifetime. The athlete reflects an integral unity of consciousness and bodily presence in the world, directed to the achievement of specific purposes "here and now" and apart from speculations and abstractions. The athlete is measured by actions and deeds actually performed now and forever and never by intentions and idealizations that exist only in the realm of the mind. In the philosophically perceptive study *The Philosophic Process in Physical Education*, it is observed that "... There are excellent illustrations in sports of man's long history (pre-Homer) of the human expectation that the individual performer is responsible for what he does. Simonodis and, before him, Hesoid in their poems both point out this same theme. That is, before man expressed the individual's responsibility, he practiced it."[2]

In the unity of consciousness and bodily presence in the lived experience of sports and athletics, the athlete represents the total person experiencing oneself and the world as an authentic and truly committed individual in the existentialist context. Sports and athletics reflect existentialism's rejection of mind-body dualism and its emphasis on our unity and identity as consciousness-in-the-world-with-a-body. Mind-body dualism is an aspect of various philosophical systems and attitudes in the history of philosophy (notably Rene Descartes') radical dualism of *thought* and *extension*), and tends to portray the body as an object distinct from the mind and "out there" in the world. This portrayal of the body as an object somehow distinct from the mind has serious and diverse philosophical and humanistic consequences, and among other things constitutes the basis for various hedonistic and sexist attitudes including our contemporary Playboy (and Playgirl) philosophies. When the body is perceived as an object in the world, one's own body and the bodies of others can be perceived as possessions and instruments to be used for various (pleasure) purposes — usually resulting in the degradation of dignity and virtue. Sports and athletics are directed by their nature and purpose to the achievement of human excellence at the physical level, and thus the athlete is the model of personal consciousness and bodily presence in the world as an integrated entity in being and acting.

In the interests of accuracy and scholarship, it must be noted that the concept of the *body* and bodily presence in the world constitute a serious problem for some existentialist thinkers in their analysis of

II. Concepts and Fundamentals

human existence. This is especially true in Jean-Paul Sartre's definitive version of existentialist philosophy; his attempts to deal with "The Problem of the Body" (and "The Problem of the Other" who perceives my body) are discussed at length throughout the second part of his 722-page *Being and Nothingness*.[3] The problem is that existentialist philosophy (especially Sartre's existentialism) defines the human reality primarily as *consciousness* or conscious subjectivity, perceived as essentially non-hysical in nature and character. One of the basic reasons for this view is to guarantee the ontological freedom of the human reality as a "translucid and non-substantial" entity, totally free and unbounded by physical dimensions and limitations. Obviously the presence of the body as a physically bounded and determined aspect of human existence interferes with this non-physical concept of the human reality and human freedom, and creates ideological anguish and conflict in the existential analysis of mankind.

Despite these theoretical and conceptual difficulites, existentialist philosophers are compelled in various ways to accept the fact of the body, and this is generally expressed in some version of the notion that "consciousness-exists-a-body" and is located in the spatial-temporal world. Gabriel Marcel's Christian existentialism speaks more poetically of the human reality as "incarnated spirit" or spiritual consciousness incarnated in the body, with all the symbolism and significance of the religious Incarnation of Jesus Christ. Thus it is legitimate and realistic to describe the existential human reality as consciousness-in-the-world-with-a-body with all that this entails and portends for sports and athletics and the athletes of the world.

This contention that athletes are existential realities *par excellence* relates especially to one of existentialism's most significant precepts, and this is once again the importance of self-identity and personal integrity achieved through lived experience or the experiential intuition of oneself and reality. The significance of this is that such individual immersion in one's world precludes and eliminates tendencies toward self-alienation and alienation from the world. Self-alienation and alienation from the world result from lack of personal authenticity and probity, and a sense of being somehow separate and apart from the world rather than *creating* one's world through subjective choices and decisions and heroic actions. This separation from oneself and the world brings about a kind of *malaise* in the human condition, and leads to the *bad faith* or personal dishonesty and self-deception so despised in the existential ideal of human existence. The athlete's acute consciousness of self as a functioning bodily presence in the immediate world of personal experience is the source of self-affirmation and the basis for authentic oneness with the world.

One of the subtle paradoxes in analyzing the existential aspects of sports and athletics is that *thinking* about (the athlete's) bodily presence in the world often distorts this presence and detracts from its integrity and validity. This relates in some respects to previous comments to the effect that existentialist philosophy rejects rationalism and intellectualism — primarily because such views conceptualize and idealize reality and human existence, and thus nullify the vibrancy and dynamism of the confrontational experience. The point is that sports and athletics subsume an artistry of consciousness and bodily presence that must be perceived in terms of lived experience rather than conceptual analysis. There is a spontaneity and inventiveness (without arbitrariness) in existential being and acting, and there is a similar spontaneity and inventiveness (without arbitrariness) in sports and athletics and the athlete's being and acting. This is much more than mere instinctive actions and reactions: it is the measure once again of the existential athlete's attunement with the experiential world.

The existential athlete does not *think* about space and time in the world — the athlete *lives* space and time in the world in his or her uniquely acute expression of consciousness-in-the-world-with-a-body. A good example is the anecdote about Yogi Berra used to begin this book. When Yogi contended that "he couldn't think and hit at the same time — it's got to be one or the other," he epitomized the distinction between conceptual analysis and existential action in specific human situations. Conceptual analysis tends to "freeze" reality into static moments of thought and intention, rather than dynamic choices and decisions engendering in successful action. Thinking about hitting is important but only as a kind of prelude destined to be translated into action suited to he hard immediacy of the moment. A more sophisticated and more philosophical explanation of the same phenomenon occurs in John McPhee's *A Sense of Where You Are: A Profile of William Warren Bradley* (1965).[4] Bill Bradley was an All-American basketball player at Princeton, and extended his distinguished scholastic career as a Rhodes Scholar at Cambridge before playing professional basketball and eventually entering politics as a U.S. Senator from New Jersey.

McPhee's thematic interview with Bradley took place on the basketball court during a practice session, and while they talked the player moved through a series of self-devised shooting drills. As McPhee watched Bradley execute a certain shot time after time and seemingly from exactly the same spot on the court, he asked him how he knew when and where to let the shot go to achieve maximum results. Bradley replied that he had previously measured and mapped out the whole maneuver, and knew that he had to be positioned a certain distance from the sideline and a certain distance from the baseline and had to assume a certain angle to the basket. The journalist remarked that during a fast-paced game "you certainly can't stop and decide whether you are a certain number of feet from the sideline and the baseline and so on," and Bradley replied that in (the existential activity of) the game "you have to have *a sense of where you are* and what you can do." In an implicit statement of existentialist attitudes about being and acting, Bradley extends this insight to life in general and our need to be naturally aware without constant analysis of where we are and what we can do in being and acting.

Sports and Zen Philosophies

A different and intriguing approach to the nonconceptual dimensions of sports and athletic participation is reflected in sporadic but enthusiastic accounts of Zen philosophies and other forms of Eastern mysticism applied to the sporting enterprise. The substance of this approach is that properly oriented athletes can achieve surprisingly successful results by eliminating the mind and ego-consciousness from their physical performance, and withdrawing into a mystical state in which the body is "let go" to function as an entity in itself. An interesting and authoritative discussion of these possibilities is contained in "Sport is a Western Yoga" in Adam Smith's *Powers of Mind* (1975).[5] This study suggests that "to groove your game, you have to play without your mind," and quotes a Zen tennis master asserting that...

> The right shot at the right moment does not come because you do not let go of yourself...the right art is purposeless, aimless! What stands in your way is that you have a much too willful will. You think what you do not do yourself does not happen.[6]

The article attributes Jack Nicklaus' legendary golfing success to his immense powers of concentration which enable him "to play in a trance,...he and the club and the ball are all the same thing and there isn't anything else. He can lock right in, real one-pointedness. I think he can influence the flight of the ball even after it's hit."[7] Similar experiences are cited in the athletic career of John Brodie, former star professional football quarterback and now a sports commentator, who contends that...

> The player can't be worrying about the past or the future, or the crowd or some other extraneous event. He must be able to respond in the here and now...At times, I experience a kind of clarity that I've never seen described in any football story; sometimes this seems to slow way down, as if

everyone were moving in slow motion. It seems as if I have all the time in the world to watch the receivers run their patterns, and yet I know the defensive line is coming at me just as fast as ever, and yet the whole thing seems like a movie or a dance in slow motion. It's beautiful.[8]

Existentialism and Sports: Classical Theories

One of the most authoritative existentialist inquiries into the essential nature of play and games (and sports and athletics) is developed at length in Sartre's *Being and Nothingness*, specifically in the section on "Existential Psychoanalysis" which includes "The Problem of the Body." The central theme throughout Sartre's existentialist philosophy is the theme of human freedom, which he perceives as total and absolute: 'To be human is to be free and to be free is to be human." This is the theme that he perceives clearly in play and games and sports and athletics, and this is the measure of the play-world's fundamental reality and authenticity. Mankind committed to the serious work-world is not free; only man at play is free — free to be creative and innovative and free to establish rules and principles for being and doing.

> There remains one type of activity which we willingly admit is entirely gratuitous: the activity of *play* and the 'drives' which relate back to it. Can we discover an appropriate drive in sport? To be sure, it must be noted first that play as contrasted with the spirit of seriousness appears to be the least possessive attitude involves starting from the world and attributing more reality to the world than to oneself; at the very least the serious man confers reality on himself to the degree to which he belongs to the world.... All serious thought is thickened by the world; it coagulates; it is a dismissal of human reality in favor of the world. The serious man is 'of the world' and has no resource in himself. He does not even imagine any longer the possibility of *getting out* of the world, for he has given to himself the type of existence of the rock, the consistency, the inertia, the opacity of being-in-the-midst-of-the-world. It is obvious that the serious man at bottom is hiding from himself the consciousness of his freedoms; he is in *bad faith* and his bad faith aims at presenting himself to his own eyes as a consequence; everything is a consequence for him, and there is never any beginning....
>
> Play, like Kierkegaard's irony, releases subjectivity. What is play indeed if not an activity of which man is the first origin, for which man himself sets the rules, and which has

107

II. Concepts and Fundamentals

no consequence except according to the rules posted? As soon as a man apprehends himself as free and wishes to use his freedom...then his activity is play. The first principle of play is man himself; through it he escapes his natural nature; he himself sets the value and rules for his acts and consents to play only according to the rules which he himself has established and defined....[9]

These remarks identify and summarize Sartre's interpretations of the cardinal human failure, and this is the rejection or the denial of human freedom as the essence of human reality. The absolute character of human freedom is awesome to behold and terrifying to accept for some human realities, primarily because such absolute personal freedom brings with it absolute personal responsibility for being and acting. Some people attempt to flee from this "dreadful freedom" and seek to escape it by taking refuge in the seriousness of the work-world or in the bosom of sociopolitical and religious institutions. This denial of human freedom is perforce the denial of authentic human existence, and thus, such human realities exist inauthentically and in *bad faith* as part of the world of objects and things (*being-in-itself*). Play and games (and sports and athletics) are ennobled because they originate and guarantee human freedom, and provide means and opportunities to avoid the self-alienation that comes with turning away from our freedom and subjectivity.

The fundamental and far-reaching significance of Sartre's existentialist views on play and sport is his contention that the play-world represents the essentially real world — the world of what we *are* and should be as free and conscious existents. In many ways this is the total statement about the nature and destiny of human existence.

The point of these remarks, however, is not to show us that in play the desire to *do* is irreducible. On the contrary we must conclude that the desire to do is here reduced to a certain desire to be. The act is not its own goal for itself; neither does its explicit end represent its goal and its profound meaning; but the function of the act is to make manifest and to present to *itself* the absolute freedom which is the very being of the person. This particular type of project, which has freedom for its foundation and its goals, deserves a special study.... It would be necessary to explain in full detail its relations with the project of being-God, which has appeared to us as the deep-seated structure of human reality. (Such a study) belongs rather to an *Ethics*...and it supposes in addition taking a position which can be *moral* only in the face of values which haunt the For-itself. Nevertheless the fact remains that the desire to play is fundamentally the desire to be.[10]

For a scholarly study of these aspects of Sartre's critical analysis of play and sports, see Ralph Netzky's "Playful Freedom: Sartre's Ontology Reappraised" (Summer 1974).[11]

Earlier existentially oriented views on the relationship of "playful freedom" and the nature of human existence are reflected in the philosophy of Friedrich Nietzsche (1844-1900), who along with Soren Kierkegaard (1813-55) initiates the basic themes and general context for contemporary existentialism. Nietzsche's contention that "God is dead" signifies the demise of the Greco-Christian era with its values and attitudes, and in a similar vein signals the end of the Apollonian tradition and the rebirth of the Dionysian tradition with all that this entails and portends for human civilization (see chapter III). Nietzsche's fundamental premise is that the death of God means that mankind is essentially and absolutely free, and this freedom is perhaps best indicated in the playful and sporting tendencies in human existence.

Nietzsche's "God is dead" thesis is established in a curious way in an episode in his significantly titled and often-quoted *Joyful Wisdom*.[12] The episode depicts a madman running into the market-square of a town shouting to the people that "God is dead!" and then paradoxically the madman goes off to the nearest church and prays. This has led to some confusion and speculation about the real meaning of Nietzsche's dramatic contention about God, but the consensus seems to be that Nietzsche is proclaiming the death of the God of reason, rationality, and metaphysics, the death of the God of the Bible and the entire Greco-Christian and Apollonian tradition. Nietzsche's death of God prepares the way for the emergence of his free and joyful Dionysian society and civilization, in which again forms of play and games and sports and athletics constitute definitive dimensions in human existence.

Along with this theme of joyful freedom leading to true wisdom, other basic themes in Nietzsche's philosophy are the importance of *self-affirmation* and the nature of human life as an unparalleled "tragic celebration." The tragic character or the tragedy of human life is essential because tragedy is the origin of heroism, and the heroic life is the only life in Nietzsche's view (which again relates easily to games and sports and athletics). The heroic conquering of life through "the will to power" is, in turn, cause for joyous celebration as the ultimate expression of the human spirit. This is exemplified in another episode in Nietzche's work, in which he describes the tragic death of a tight-rope walker who falls from the wire and is killed at the feet of the spectators who were watching. One of the spectators is so moved by the performer's courage

109

II. Concepts and Fundamentals

and heroism and the tragic moment that he insists on digging a grave for the fallen hero with his bare hands. Life is the joyful and grateful celebration of heroic attempts to dominate and control the tragic possibilities in human existence.

After the death of God thesis, Nietzsche's most popular philosophical theme is the concept of the "superman or overman or *ubermensch*" — the new breed of philosopher who rises from the death of God and the ashes of the Greco-Christian and Apollonian traditions to lead mankind to the new life of joyful freedom. The superman is superior intellectually and biologically ("blond and blue-eyed and Aryan"), but most importantly he is superior in his recognition and exploitation of the "will to power" as the basis for the radical transformation of society and civilization. The superman is the crux and the symbolic figure in Nietzsche's famous "transvaluation of values" theory, in which the values and morals of the Greco-Christian tradition are totally rejected and replaced by the single standard of power for its own sake. In his *Genealogy of Morals*, Nietzsche proclaims that the insipid "slave-morality and herd-morality" of the Greeks and Christians is inimical and self-defeating, and insists that mankind must go *Beyond Good and Evil* and live according to the single moral precept that "power is always naturally good and weakness is always and naturally evil."[13]

The superman is the human figure with the courage and the strength and the boldness to lead such a moral revolution and to inspire mankind to forsake the fetid darkness of traditional ethics and "to look up at the sun" and bravely rise above the old life of slavish compliance to the new life of joyful freedom. Nietzsche's emphasis on play as the symbol and the context of human freedom and the new life climaxes in the figure of the superman, and suggests that the realm of play and games and sports and athletics is the real domain of the superman and the measure of human perfection and aspirations. In the context of Nietzsche's theories and views on the meaning and purpose of human existence, it is tempting to suggest that the world of joyful freedom and the heroic role of the superman are perhaps best symbolized in the world of sports and athletics and the heroic triumphs of the serious athlete.

Soren Kierkegaard's existentially oriented philosophy is less obviously related to play and games and sports and athletics, but there is one area of his thought that provides an interesting basis for a comparison of athletes and existential attitudes in life and experience. Kierkegaard first originates the existential themes of individuality and subjectivity in the religious context of mankind's search for a meaningful God. Kierkegaard was a religious and God-oriented person in his own right, but he was also a classic foe of organized and institutionalized religious views. He asserted simply but significantly that religion "is a matter of the heart" rather than the mind, and insisted that authentic religious fervor is subjectively and individually experienced in a dogmatically blind "leap of faith" that transcends rational attitudes and institutional boundaries. This reflects the essentially existentialist character of his thought: every human reality must personally choose and decide and act alone and apart from institutions in the religious area and in every area of human experience.

Kierkegaard framatically depicts this fundamental need for personal choice in his *Either/Or*, in which he reduces human existence to everyman's decision *either* to live and function as a freely committed and personally responsible individual *or* to live and function inauthentically in the impersonal façade of institutions and organizations.[14] One of the most popular sequences in this discussion is Kierkegaard's schemata of the "three stages of life" or three ways of living the existential truth. These three stages are: (1) the aesthetic stage; (2) the ethical stage; and (3) the religious stage.

The *aesthetic* way of life represents the existentialist person (committed to individual freedom and personal choices), who exists and acts for given moments and given desires with no intention and no purpose to establish lasting values or standards for oneself or for others. Kierkegaard portrays the aesthetic person (in *Either/Or*) in the character of Don Juan, a sensual young man who freely chooses to seduce a female stranger whom he sees one day walking on a street near his home. He sets up an elaborate and time-consuming plan with the singular purpose and goal of seducing the young woman — simply for the pleasure of the seduction moment with no sense of commitment or responsibility beyond the act itself. After months of carefully planned movements and arrangements, he eventually succeeds and then simply walks away from the act with never a backward glance or thought.

The *ethical* way of life represents the existentialist person (committed to individual freedom and personal choices), who exercises the existentialist spirit *within the system* and through personal involvement in the system. Here there is the sense of lasting values and commitment to oneself and to others, but always within the context and the structure of the system. Kierkegaard portrays the ethical person in the character of Judge Wilhelm, whose philosophy is that "one does what one can" within the system.

The *religious* way of life represents the existentialist person (committed to individual freedom and personal choices) who lives the heroic life and performs heroic actions, and whose life and actions have meaning and significance and lasting value far beyond the man and his times. Few people ever achieve this religious way of life, and Kierkegaard uses as an example the lofty figure of the biblical Abraham ready to sacrifice his beloved son in a high moment of heroic commitment to everlasting truth and value.

II. Concepts and Fundamentals

An intriguing application of these stages to the world of sports and athletics is suggested by John A. Doody, director of the honors program and a member of the philosophy faculty at Villanova University, Villanova, Pa. Doody introduced courses in the philosophy of sports into the university curriculum, and created and hosted a television series on the subject ("Fact or Fiction") originating in 1977 from CBS's Philadelphia affiliate. The application is subject to personal preferences and choices with respect to specific sports figures assigned to the three stages.[15]

Religious figures in sports and athletics past and present are the true champions of the game whose superior ability and dedication and charisma enable them to transcend themselves and their own era to serve as a lasting symbol of the sporting enterprise. Examples in this category might include Knute Rockne, Babe Ruth, Babe Didrikson, Zaharias, Bobby Jones, Bill Tilden, Joe Louis, Joe DiMaggio, Arnold Palmer, Jack Nicklaus, Muhammed Ali, Vince Lombardi, Bobby Orr, Joe Namath, Pele, and Pete Rose. Ethical figures would be gifted but largely unsung heroes whose dedication to the system of "team play" is their greatest strength and finest triumph. Examples in this category might include Lou Gehrig, Bobby Clarke, Bill Russell, Roberto Clemente, Bill Bradley, Robin Roberts, and all the centers and guards in football, and all the members of championship crew teams in the history of the sport.

Aesthetic figures in sports and athletics would be the star performers who are neither existentially religious or ethical, exceptional athletes and prideful individuals whose dedication is turned inward and who lack the last fine measure of charisma and symbolism. Discretion discourages the citing of specific examples.

Notes

1. Sartre, Jean-Paul. *Being and Nothingness*, trans. Hazel Barnes. (New York: Philosophical Library, 1965); Gabriel Marcel. *The Mystery of Being*. (Chicago: Gateway Edition, Henry Regnery Co., 1960); Martin Heidegger, *Existence and Being*, trans. R.F.C. Hull and Alan Crick. (Chicago: Henry Regnery Co., 1949); W.C. Barrett, *Irrational Man*. (New York: Doubleday Co., 1958); H.J. Blackham. *Six Existentialist Thinkers*. (London: Routledge and K. Paul, Ltd., 1952); F.C. Copleston. *Existentialism and Modern Man*. (Oxford: Blackfriars, 1948); Wilfrid Desan. *The Tragic Finale*. (Cambridge, Mass.: Harvard University Press, 1954); Marjorie Grene. *Dreadful Freedom*. (Chicago: University of Chicago Press, 1948); Jean Wahl. *A Short History of Existentialism*. (New York: Philosophical Library, 1949); Joseph C. Mihalich. *Existentialism and Thomism*. (Totowa, N.J.: Littlefield, Adams Co., 1969).

2 Harper-Miller-Park-Davis. *The Philosophic Process in Physical Education*, p. 205.

3Sartre. *Being and Nothingness*, Part 3, "Being-For-Others," especially pp. 221-360.

4. McPhee, John. *A Sense of Where You Are: A Profile of William Warren Bradley*. (New York: Farrar, Straus and Giroux, 1965).

5. Harris, George. "Adam Smith's Invisible 'IT' — An Introduction," *Psychology Today* (October 1975), pp. 45-46; excerpts from Adam Smith's "Sport is a Western Yoga," in *Powers of Mind*. (New York: Random House, 1975). See also Spencer K. Wertz's "Zen, Yoga, and Sports: Eastern Philosophy for Western Athletes," in *Journal of the Philosophy of Sport*, 4, Fall 1977, pp. 68-81.

6. Smith, *Psychology Today*, p. 74.

7. Ibid., p. 48.

8. Ibid., p. 49-50.

9. Sartre. *Being and Nothingness*, p. 580.

10. Ibid., p. 581.

11. Netzky, Ralph. "Playful Freedom: Sartre's Ontology Reappraised," *Philosophy Today*, 18, No. 2/4 (Summer 1974), pp. 125-36; see also Karl Jaspers, *Man in the Modern Age*, trans. Eden and Cedar Paul. (New York: Doubleday Co., 1957). Jaspers is a classical existentialist philosopher who advocates seeking meaningful human freedom in play and games and sports: "Even contemporary human beings wish to express themselves in one way or another, and sport becomes a philosophy. They rise in revolt against being cabined, cribbed, confined; and they seek relief in sport, though it lacks transcendent substantiability. Still, it contains the aforesaid soaring element — unconsciously willed, though without communal content — as a defiance to the petrified present. The human body is demanding its own rights in an epoch when the apparatus is pitilessly annihilating one human being after another."

12. Nietzsche, Friedrich. "Joyful Wisdom," in *The Complete Works of Friedrich Nietzsche*, ed. Oscar Levy. (New York: Russell and Russell, 1964).

13. Nietzsche, Friedrich. "Genealogy of Morals," in *Basic Writings of Nietzsche*, trans. Walter Kaufman. (New York: Random House, 1968); Friedrich Nietzsche, *Beyond Good and Evil*, trans. Walter Kaufman. (New York: Random House, 1966).

14. Kierkegaard, Soren. *Either/Or*, trans. David Swenson and Lillian Marvin Swenson. (Princeton, N.J.: Princeton University Press, 1971).

15. The descriptive language for the sports version of the stages and some of the examples are my own.

WHAT WE KNOW
WHEN WE KNOW A GAME

MARGARET STEEL

Paul Ziff points out in "A Fine Forehand" (7) that there are significant epistemological problems in connection with sports. It is to some of these that I will address myself in this paper. I am asking the basic question: "What kind of knowledge is required to engage in a game or sport?" It is a question that deserves to be answered for itself, and we will find that the answers have implications for other areas of knowledge.

In "The Nature of Sport: a Definitional Effort" (4: pp. 48, 49), John W. Loy, Jr. classified knowledge as one of the technological aspects of games. What he has in mind is our knowledge of the rules and strategies and so on involved in playing the game, or participating in the sport. This is related to the statement that "What we know about a game is how to play it," and "how to play it" is characterized in terms of the rules and strategies. In fact, as I shall show, this is a much too simple view of the matter. A good deal more is involved in knowing a game.

I will begin by characterizing two kinds of learning, both of which are involved in learning how to play a game. This is a good place to begin, as knowledge is what we have learned. This first kind of learning is inductive, which is best described as forming expectations about future experience on the basis of past instances. It is the method by which we acquire many habits. It is also the method by which we make generalizations about the world in our every-day lives, and in science. Clearly, it is an important mode of learning. Much of what we call "factual" or "propositional" knowledge is acquired in this way. The simplest version of this is stimulus-response, but inductive learning can obviously be a good deal more complex than the simple level.

The second mode is one I will call "learning by exemplars." This is most clearly characterized in T. S. Kuhn's (1, 2, 3) writings on the philosophy of science, so I will first give a brief summary of his views. Kuhn's view of science is developed in relation to the notion of a paradigm. He distinguishes two major senses of this term. The first is the paradigm as "disciplinary matrix." The second is the paradigm as "examplar." A disciplinary matrix is a whole world view. It determines what kinds of things there are, what counts as a problem and as a solution, what the values are, what kinds of action and experimentation are acceptable and which are not. That is, it tells us what the world is like, what our relationship with it is and what our attitude to it should be. This notion was intended to explain both the ongoing enterprise of science, "normal science" and to account for scientific revolutions. Normal science is the practice of science within the framework of the accepted disciplinary matrix. When the latter begins to break down and become unsatisfactory, a revolution may occur, and the old disciplinary matrix be replaced by a new one. When the revolution is completed, normal science goes on with a new world view and new problems.

This account of science as a world view is supported and strengthened by Kuhn's account of the paradigm as exemplar. An exemplar, or shared example, is a standard scientific experiment or problem that the student has to work through. The theories of science are merely formal theories until they are given content in experimental situations. By performing the classic experiments, the student begins to see how the theory is realized in the world, in terms of what there is, and what we can do with it. He learns what counts as an entity, and what counts as a legitimate problem, by learning how problems are like each other. This likeness is not in terms of specific criteria, but rather in terms of what Kuhn calls "similarity classes." Kuhn claims that the student acquires a "learned ability to group objects and situations into similarity classes which are primitive in the sense that the grouping is done without an answer to the question 'similar with respect to what'" (2: p. 275). By acquiring this skill, the student can solve new problems in ways analogous to the ways he solved old ones. He can recognize new entities by seeing analogies between them and others. Science thus becomes something that can be extended, rather than a rigid body of fact and procedure.

Kuhn suggests that when we acquire a scientific education, we acquire a disciplinary matrix, and in doing so we enter into a new world and acquire a new language, the language of science, at the same time. A particular way of seeing nature is embedded in the language. The new world and the new language are acquired largely through the exemplars. Now the point is that the student in learning science is learning how to *do* something. In becoming a scientist, he acquires specific skills, and specific ways of perceiving. He learns to see the world in a new way, and this is in itself a skill, acquired by doing. We cannot learn to see the world the way the scientist sees it without trying and practising seeing it in this way. This trying and practising is embodied in the exemplars. In learning science we *do* science by working through the exemplars, the problems and classical experiments. Once the science is learned we can go on to new discoveries.

Note also that in learning science we learn something we cannot say. If we could explain, if we could say exactly what is to be learned, there would be no need for exemplars. As is clear from the quote from Kuhn above, we cannot answer the question "similar with respect to what?", when we recognize that problems are analogous. We do not know how it is that we recognize similarities and dissimilarities because we do not do it in terms of specific criteria. We learn to perceive and to judge in a particular way, yet we do not know precisely how we do it. For some time we are learners, trying to assimilate the unfamiliar. Then at some point the unfamiliar becomes our own world, within which we move easily.

I will now go on to show that this account of the learning of science can be extended to account for the learning of all skills, from simple bodily skills such as an infant's hand-waving, to games such as tennis, and to sophisticated philosophical argumentation. These skills are not equally creative, nor are they equally sophisticated, but I think it will be clear that they are all learned in the same way.

In turning to the learning of games and sports, the first thing to be noticed is that there are two levels of learning involved. There is the level of the game as a whole, involving the rules and the strategies, the moves and the tactics. The other level is that of the particular physical skills that must be acquired; some examples would be such skills as dribbling or heading the ball in soccer, or serving or volleying in tennis. It is clear that if you are unable to dribble or head the ball in soccer, or serve or volley in tennis you will not be able to play these games properly. Even if the word "play" is stretched as far as possible, you will only be, at best, a marginal player. The particular physical skills, therefore, are necessary in order to play the game. It is with this level of learning that I will deal first.

To begin with, learning a physical skill is not an inductive process. We do not learn to play tennis by generalization from past instances. Once the player has "caught on," he knows how it feels to do it right, he knows from past experience that he *is* doing it right, but this is not how he learned. A player may serve incorrectly twenty times, then do it correctly. Those twenty incorrect performances do not teach him how to do it right, nor do they even teach him how to avoid doing it incorrectly. He is not learning a belief or forming an expectation about the future (although I do not deny that these play a part, for instance in estimating the angle and velocity of a tennis return). Rather he is learning how to do something. It is in this sense that what the tennis player knows can be said to be "knowing how" rather than "knowing that."

How *do* we learn a physical skill? First of all we have to know what it is we want to be able to do. We have to be shown the skill by another person, or a picture or diagram. In other words we have to have an exemplar. In order to learn a physical skill we have to try to do it, and practise doing it. To do this we have to know what we want to do, and to want to be able to do it. The instructor demonstrates a serve to a beginner, who attempts to copy him. He tries, by imitating the actions of the instructor, to duplicate the whole physical act, the whole *gestalt* of serving. He must throw the ball up a certain distance, must bring down the racket on it, and direct it to a certain specified area. All this requires a complex and sophisticated muscular control. The beginner can be helped by verbal instructions, such as "Throw the ball higher" or "Bring down the racket at an angle," but these will not tell him what to do. They merely function as clues in his search for the correct performance.

The beginner practises until the instructor says "Now you have it." At this point he has learned something. This is what it *feels like* to perform the serve correctly. He knows how to move his body in order to serve the ball into the opposite side. He knows how much effort to put into his movements, and how to swing and follow through. Of course, he must still practise, and even with practise will not always be successful, but this is because tennis serving is a very complex skill, requiring more muscular control than many others. But the learner now knows how to serve. He can show someone else how to do it. As with science, he has been led through a series of models, and the movements, from being strange and unfamiliar, have become natural and familiar.

Here it is important to consider what the learner does *not* know. He does not as a rule know how his muscles make his body move in the required way. He *does* know what it *feels* like for the muscles to move correctly, but he is not directing this movement, nor is he aware of it. This will be true even when the learner knows physiology, and can give an account of the muscle movements that take place in a tennis serve. Knowing the muscular movements, that is, knowing how the action takes place on the level of anatomy, is not the same as knowing how to perform the action in person. Teaching someone how the muscles move does not teach him how to serve. In fact, thinking about the muscle movements when trying to serve would inhibit, even paralyze action. We are not learning a series of muscle movements, but a whole flowing action. We do not see the forest when we look only at the trees. We do not see the action when we look only at the muscle movements.

There are several important things to notice here. The first is that the student is trying to learn a whole integrated movement. As he cannot "see" himself or what he is doing, he must learn what it *feels* like to do it right. This feeling is in fact a whole bodily *gestalt*. It comprises a new perception of the body's interaction with the world, in terms of balance, sight and so on. There is a particular set of perceptions and sensations that go along with a correct performance, and the student must learn to recognize these. This is learning what it feels like to do it right. This is particularly important, because feelings cannot be described, nor can they be taught. We must learn how to achieve a particular feeling, with out particular body, without knowing in advance what this feeling is. This is why the action must be learned by trial and error, following a model, and why knowledge of anatomy will not substitute.

117

II. Concepts and Fundamentals

Note also, that while the learning must be conscious, that is, we must be aware of what we are trying to do in order to attempt it, what we learn is also, in a certain sense, unconscious. We know how to serve, but we do not know how we do it. Our bodies must learn how to perform the actions, without our minds being aware of the movements on more than a surface level. It is on this point that Polanyi has some important points to make. He says that in the performance of a skill "we are attending *from* these elementary movements *to* the achievement of their joint purpose, and hence are usually unable to specify these elementary acts." (5: p. 10) In "The Logic of Tacit Inference" he says:

> If I know how to ride a bicycle or how to swim, this does not mean that I can tell how I manage to keep my balance on a bicycle, or keep afloat when swimming. I may not have the slightest idea of how I do this, or even an entirely wrong or grossly imperfect idea of it, and yet go on cycling or swimming merrily. Nor can it be said that I know how to bicycle or swim and yet do *not* know how to coordinate the complex pattern of muscular acts by which I do my cycling or swimming. I both know how to carry out these performances as a whole and also know how to carry out the elementary acts which constitute them though I cannot tell what these acts are. (6: p. 223)

It is the whole integrated action that we are aware of in the performance of these physical skills. The individual muscle movements are below the level of awareness. It is for this reason that Polanyi calls the knowledge we have when we know a physical skill "tacit knowing." This of course is not the only kind of tacit knowing, but it is an elementary and indeed important kind. There are a great many things we know how to do with out bodies (walking and talking are two of them) and in all of these the knowing is tacit.

Let us turn now to the other level of learning that is involved in games. The tennis player must not only know how to serve, and how to volley, but must know when and where to perform these actions. He must know when and where he is allowed or forbidden to do them. This involves knowledge of the rules and procedures of the game. Knowledge of this kind is at least initially explicit. We have to memorize the rules, and keep them in mind while playing. However, it is interesting to note that this is the kind of learning that can be "internalized" as moral rules are "internalized." That is, in Polanyi's terms, our knowledge of them becomes tacit rather than explicit, and we follow them in a natural and familiar way, without having to think much about them, rather than in a conscious and forced way. Playing tennis is, however, more than following rules and procedures. The aim of the game is to score points over one's opponent, and this involves strategy and tactics, movements and intelligence.

How does the player learn these? He does not learn every possible strategy in learning the game. He may learn some from his coach, and from watching the play of others. However, the good player develops his own strategies and moves, within the parameters of the rules. The rules do not specify every possible move. The player may invent his own. In this way games are to some extent creative endeavours. The player becomes creative by performing new moves and strategies by analogy to the ones he has seen performed by others. The new moves are similar in unspecifiable ways to the old moves. This skill also cannot be taught. The player must learn by himself to extend his repertoire of moves in terms of similarity criteria. This is clearly analogous to the way in which a scientist extends the field covered by a theory, and discovers new entities to be like old ones.

We should also notice that when playing the game, the player's mind is less on his strokes, but rather on the ball and on his opponent. Here we have another instance of Polanyi's "attending away from something towards something else." The player attends away from his service to the trajectory of the ball. He attends away from his own movements to the attempt to force movements on his opponent. Just as in practising service, the player knows only tacitly his own muscle movements, so in playing the game, he knows tacitly the strokes that he makes. This is perhaps less true of serving than of the other strokes, but even here, the mind is on the effect of the service, rather than on the service itself. The strokes are subsidiary to the game as a whole. One could perfectly execute strokes technically, yet be a poor player, if they are not used to further the game. The player must have in mind the game as a whole as he executes strokes, just as he must have in mind the total action as he performs muscle movements. Clearly, he is more conscious of his strokes than he is of his muscle movements, but the principle is the same.

What I have been claiming is that sports and games are acquired by demonstration, and not by teaching in the sense of being told. But there seems to be a problem with this. What is the role of the coach? Surely he teaches players. And often the best coaches are not good players. For instance some swimming coaches do not even swim. They therefore cannot function as exemplars or models for their students. They surely must be *telling* their students what to do, how to perform better, which would seem to contradict my thesis. This contradiction is only apparent, however, as I shall show.

Let us take two kinds of cases. The first is the one in which the player or athlete already knows how to perform, but he is not proficient,

II. Concepts and Fundamentals

or there is room for improvement. Here the athlete does not need any demonstration. He has had that at an earlier level, and already knows what it feels like to perform reasonably successfully. What he needs is more proficiency. The role of the coach in this case is to tell the student when he is closer to a perfect action and when he is further from it. He then acts as a feedback, or mirror, so that the student knows what and how he is doing. The coach can also give hints. He can make suggestions such as "Raise your elbow higher" or "Follow through with your body." These do not tell the student "how to do it," rather they are ways in which he can adjust his body so that he can discover the most proficient "gestalt." The student, in fact, is being helped to adjust his model, and to come closer to it. This does not mean that he will always be able to attain perfection in the future, but that he has a better idea of how to attain it, and thus a higher chance of succeeding.

The other kind of case is that in which one learns to do something without being shown by the teacher. For instance, I went to swimming lessons where I learned to swim, but the teacher never entered the water. But I knew that what I wanted to do was to float. I had seen objects and other people floating. I had models, exemplars, for what I wanted to do. What the instructor did was to give me clues. She demonstrated and suggested leg and arm movements, and told me when I was performing incorrectly. In this way she acted both as a partial model and as a feedback. But the actual learning to swim, to float on the surface of the water, was something I had to do myself with only demonstrations of floating to help me. Once learned, I could not say how I did it, but could do it any time I wanted to. The instructor could provide a great deal of helpful information, and act as a mirror to record my achievement, but I had to learn the crucial muscle movements myself.

Does this mean that physical instructors and coaches are unnecessary? By no means. But they are not teaching a set of facts. Rather they are leading their students through a series of movements in order to facilitate the student's learning something for himself. The student is not being spoon fed with information. He is being helped to discover for himself. And this discovery is one of how it feels to do certain things, and one of similarities, and how to extend them by analogy to other situations. The coach, by telling the student how he is doing, helps him to see how close he is coming to a perfect execution of the movement, and by making suggestions, helps him to come closer to his idea, or, one might say, to his model. This is why it is easier to improve with a coach than without one. On the level of the game as a whole, the coach helps the student to develop an ability to see how new strategies and moves are permissible, and are likely to be successful. By studying old moves, the student learns to recognize new ones as similar. Coaches thus function as facilitators in the student's own process of discovery.

120

Steel: What We Know When We Know A Game

What I have been claiming is that sports and games are acquired by demonstration, and by the player being "led through" the movements at both levels of the game. He learns what it is like to execute certain physical movements by copying the demonstration, and by being monitored and given feedback by his instructor. He learns strategies and tactics by watching other games, and develops new ones by analogy to those he has observed. This parallels Kuhn's account of learning in science. As we have seen, Kuhn claims that we learn science by being led through a series of classic experiments and problems, and by learning to extend what we have learned to new situations by means of recognizing similarities. Clearly, the kind of learning is the same.

Does this mean that physical educators are doing something different in their teaching from the teachers of other subjects? As I have been arguing, they are at least not doing something so very different from that done by teachers of science. I believe that much of what is called academic learning is in fact of this kind. The so-called "learning of facts" is of relatively minor importance. As a philosophy teacher, I am aware that I teach philosophy as a skill, rather than as a body of propositions to be memorized by the student. I lead my students through the work of a philosopher, explaining and criticizing. I show them how the philosophy is developed and integrated. I show them good arguments and bad arguments. Gradually, by reading, they learn how to read philosophy, and how to recognize important points. By observing, and by trying to argue themselves, they learn how to distinguish good arguments from bad ones. I do not *tell* them how to do these things. I show them, and hope that they will follow, and begin to internalize what they begin to see. This is the same general method as is followed in physical education. In fact, the more advanced the level of the student, the more like a coach a philosophy teacher becomes. This has always been the way in philosophy. A beautiful example is seen in Socrates, who taught philosophy by doing it, and in fact is still teaching philosophers by his example.

I began this paper with the question "What knowledge is required to play a game?" The answer has taken us beyond physical activities to science and philosophy. This is a significant discovery. Knowledge of physical activities is of the same kind as knowledge of those more intellectual areas. This is something we might expect. However, what is interesting is that the kind of knowledge and learning is seen more clearly in connection with physical activities. It may be that a study of learning in this area may be illuminating for the areas of science and philosophy, and many others.

121

II. Concepts and Fundamentals

Bibliography

1. Kuhn, T. S. *The Structure of Scientific Revolution*, Second Edition, Chicago: University of Chicago Press, 1970.
2. Kuhn, T. S. "Reflections on My critics," *Criticism and the Growth of Knowledge*. Edited by I. Lakatos and A. Musgrave. Cambridge: Cambridge University Press, 1970.
3. Kuhn T. S. "Second Thoughts on Paradigms," *The Structure of Scientific Theories*. Edited by F. Suppe. Urbana: University of Illinois Press, 1974.
4. Loy, J. W., Jr. "The Nature of Sport: a Definitional Effort," *Sport and the Body: a Philosophical Symposium*. Edited by Ellen W. Gerber. Philadelphia: Lea and Febiger, 1972.
5. Polanyi, M. *The Tacit Dimension*. Garden City, New York: Doubleday & Company, Inc., 1967.
6. Polanyi, M. "The Logic of Tacit Inference," *Human and Artificial Intelligence*. Edited by Frederick J. Crosson. New York: Appleton Century Crofts, 1970.
7. Ziff, Paul. "A Fine Forehand," *Journal of the Philosophy of Sport*, 1(1974), 92-109.

SKILL EXECUTION:
KNOWLEDGEABLE MOVEMENT

SAUL ROSS

Skill execution is of interest and concern to physical educators, sport coaches, music and art teachers, the military establishment, and vocational instructors. Basically, they are all preoccupied with devising strategies and procedures which will facilitate the acquisition of skill by the learner. Judgements regarding the success or failure of each endeavour can be applied to two basic categories: (1) the learners, who can be examined to determine how quickly and well they have acquired the skill(s) and how well they execute the skill(s) and (2) the methods or procedures employed by the instructor, teacher or coach can be assessed to rate the efficacy of each "teaching style." An empirical approach is needed in these cases to provide us with information required in order to draw conclusions.

On another level of discussion, skill execution is of interest to the psychomotor learning theorist and to the philosopher. Common to both is the desire to explain a unique aspect of our existence but each employs a different approach and each has a clearly delineated different task. A psychomotor learning theorist attempts to give an account of how we learn and how we execute the skill. While the "technical" aspects of how we learn a skill are of some interest to the philosopher, his main focus of attention is directed elsewhere, to the notion of intentional action. As a particular category of human behaviour, intentional action is of interest to the philosopher who is challenged to provide an account which differentiates intentional action from mere bodily movement. Skill execution, as a *prima facie* instance of intentional action, is included in that category since it was obviously the aim of the agent to execute that particular movement. Furthermore, since skill execution can be subsumed under the heading, "knowing how," an explication given of intentional action serves also to increase our epistemic understanding of that particular type of knowledge. By explicating the nature of intentional action in epistemic terms I shall provide insights into the conceptual nature of skill execution.

1. Intentional Action

Intentional human action implies direction, a goal, an end, which is the agent's purpose or intention to bring about or to attain. Intentional

II. Concepts and Fundamentals

action can be described as directed where the behaviour is directed by the agent. Implied in this action is desire or wanting.

> A human being's action is essentially constituted of means toward an end: it is the bringing about of some result with a view to some result. 'With a view to' or 'in order to,' are unavoidable idioms in giving the sense of the notion of an action, the arrow of agency passing through the present and pointing forward in time.[1]

Action is directed behaviour that ends in the result where it was the agent's intention or purpose to achieve this result. For the behaviour to be deemed an intentional action, the agent must not only make the appropriate movements, but it must also be his intention or purpose to do so. That is not to say that intending always (1) brings behaviour about, and (2) that it also achieves the intended goal or aim. There are times when I intend to do something but don't, either because I changed my mind or because circumstances are such as to thwart my behaviour. So also intentional behaviour does not always achieve the goal or aim originally identified. However, even if the goal is not attained, where the behaviour is directed toward it, that behaviour can be regarded as intentional action.

Actions are irreducible to movements, yet the notion of action requires movement, a change of some sort. To act is to move my own body at will in order to attain a desired goal. To move my own body at will implies that I control it when I act. But this should not be interpreted as meaning that all bodily movements are actions, for there are some instances, eg., tics, shudders, times where others move me, that are not instances of intentional action. Moving my body at will, controlling it, is a conscious act, for if it were not a conscious act, then the notion of directed behaviour disappears and the performance becomes mere bodily movement. I know directly, and not on the basis of evidence, when I am raising my arm. And I know it not on the basis of observation, nor do I need to infer it from other observations. I know it simply because it is my intentional action: it has come about as a result of my intention. The characteristic of personal action is that it is the realization of an intention. It is an activity informed and determined by a conscious purpose.

In the view of John Searle there is a need "to distinguish those intentions which are formed prior to actions and those which are not."[2] There are instances where the intention is formed prior to the performance of the action itself; here the agent "knows what he is going to do because he already has an intention to do that thing."[3] However, there are other instances when no prior intention is formed but rather, as

Searle states, the intention is "in the action."[4] He elaborates: "Many of the actions one performs, one performs quite spontaneously, without forming, consciously or unconsciously, any prior intention to do those things."[5] It seems to me that where I form a prior intention, even when I do not carry out the action, I know what I intend, or intended to do since it was my intention. Where the intention is in the action, to use Searle's phrase, I would still know if I am doing the action intentionally or if my body was moved by someone else.

We are conscious of our own intentional actions, of the changes we initiate, of the movements of our bodies. "The most unavoidable feature of our consciousness is the initiation of change at will, the changing of positions and therefore of our relations to other things."[6] I know what I am about to do immediately: I know what I am doing now; and I know what I have just done. In order to know what I am about to do, I must know what I am doing now and in order to make any sense of my present action, I must have known what I was doing when I did it. I know what I am trying to do simply because it is my intention and not anyone else's, and I know what I am doing simply because it is my action and not anyone else's. If a person is doing something without knowing that he is doing it, then it must be true that he is not doing it intentionally.

Most bodily movement is not to be construed as something done deliberately by the person whose body it is, whereas action is a bodily movement made intentionally by the person. Olsen adds that it is not merely a contingent fact that when a person is performing an intentional action he knows what action he is performing: the relationship is much stronger — "there is a necessary, conceptual, connection between a person performing an intentional action and his knowing what it is that he is doing."[7] A person engaged in an intentional action knows what action he is doing since an intentional action is something which a person does knowingly. When I perform an action intentionally, that is, knowingly, it is not that I do something and on the basis of observation know it: in doing it I know what I am doing since I do it knowingly.

Intentional action can then be described as a piece of behaviour which an agent does knowingly. There is a flow of intention into action with the intention governing and directing the action. Preceding the action, and during the action, decision implies concepts, for without concepts there cannot be judgements rendered nor decisions made. Hampshire notes that "while we are awake and fully conscious, we are all the time acting and moving with intent, and for much of the time our thinking is practical thinking, issuing directly in intended action and not formulated in words."[8] An agent executing an intentional action is conscious of what he is doing and although he cannot express the concepts verbally he employs them in the judgements he renders and in the decisions he makes. The thoughts that guide and direct his actions

125

are conceptual in nature even if they cannot be formulated propositionally. These non-verbal, practical concepts are manifested in intentional actions.

Forming and having intentions, rendering judgements and arriving at decisions all involve thought. Intention is necessarily connected with thinking. Thinking, in turn, is necessarily connected with having the means of expressing thought and in that category of intentional behaviour called action, action is the means of expressing thought. Thought and action are intertwined, interwoven; intentional action may be described as thought-impregnated.

Intentional actions are purposive: there is a goal to be attained. Purposiveness implies not only that a selection has been made from amongst a number of options, but it also indicates that motivation and intention are present in action, continuing until such time as the action has been completed. Should the original goal desired not be attained, then the purposiveness and creativity can be seen in the ensuing action(s) which is (are) initiated by the agent in the quest to achieve the objective.

Intentional action is not thoughtless, nor is it devoid of conceptual content. This is readily demonstrated through two very ordinary, everyday acts, walking and sitting down. Ordinarily walking is under the control of habit where the decisions made are implicit and, since they are implicit, we are not consciously aware of making them. However, when we attempt to walk up a slippery incline all of our attention is directed to the placement of each step: each decision is made explicitly and we are fully conscious of "thinking out" each step along the way. A similar scenario prevails with regard to sitting down in most chairs or sofas. However, when it comes to a very low settee or pillows on the floor, we direct our full attention to the act of sitting down and are fully conscious of the explicit decisions made. When we execute intentional actions we have "practised" countless times, we are not self-consciously aware, or reflectively aware, of the decisions we make, nor are the judgements rendered verbal judgements. The judgements made and decisions rendered are tacit judgements, and decisions involved in any physical action, eg., stepping over a barrier or stooping under a rope, are arrived at non-verbally.

Habit and implicit choosing help to explain the absence of self-conscious awareness of the reflection and decision-making processes. This applies equally to action and to what is called thought. Children memorize the times-table as a means of developing habitual responses to certain questions. Once the times-table has been committed to memory, habit takes over and a reply to the question, "How much is 3 x 3?" elicits the correct response without an awareness of the selection and decision-making factors which are always inherent in the process of thought. A similar situation applies when we execute intentional actions as we move about in our usual manner within familiar surroundings: judging, selections and making decisions are inherent in action.

An intentional action is performed by a person who is both a self and an agent at one and the same time. An important insight into the conceptual nature of intentional action is offered by Macmurray:

> The Self that reflects and the Self that acts is the same Self; action and thought are contrasted modes of its activity. But it does not follow that they have equal status in the being of the Self. In thinking, the mind alone is active. In acting the body is indeed active, but also the mind. Action is not blind. When we turn from reflection to action, we do not turn from consciousness to unconsciousness. When we act, sense, perception and judgement are in continuous activity, along with physical movement....Action, then, is a full concrete activity of the self in which all our capacities are employed.[9]

Intentional actions can be appreciated as non-verbal expressions of concepts; they are the embodiment of practical thinking. We know what we are doing when we engage in intentional action. And to "know" does not necessarily imply being able to state correctly.[10] Intentional action involves thinking; it is a form of non-verbal thought which finds its expression in the action. Intentional action, then, is the unity of movement and knowledge; it can justifiably be described as "knowledgeable movement."

2. Epistemological Considerations

Knowledgeable movement, as a descriptor, cannot be applied to all movement in light of the distinction drawn by Hamlyn[11] between knowing how to do something and merely being able to do it. Merely being able to do something, which animals do instinctively, cannot be equated with knowing how to do something because no understanding is involved. Knowing how to do something normally implies some understanding and knowledge of the principles involved in the activity in question; knowing how to do something normally refers to patterns of movement and action (covert and overt) that at some stage require the bringing to bear of attention and directed effort. To speak of knowing how in terms of bringing attention to bear and directed effort is, in effect, to indicate the intentional nature of skill execution.

II. Concepts and Fundamentals

With practice some movements will tend to become routinized habits — but even then some attention and directed effort is present and certainly understanding is readily demonstrated by explaining some of the principles involved. Knowing how to, as distinguished from merely being able, involves the application of judgements and understanding, which presupposes concepts. Where judgements, understanding and concepts are involved, it is reasonable to expect a wide variation in the level and mode of application. Knowing how to is manifested on the plane of human action where practical concepts are employed in those instances when the action is intentional.

Knowing how involves knowledge of principles but does not necessarily involve being able to state or formulate those principles verbally. Each person who modifies and adjusts his or her operations in accordance with previous experience and hypothetical judgements demonstrates the cognitive considerations which must enter inevitably into those acts. That a full theoretical account cannot be given[12] is not surprising, for there are some things about a skill which cannot be stated — such knowledge and understanding is manifested in the execution.

Judging the intelligence or stupidity of an act requires an understanding of the activity in question. Where the act is some form of physical movement the requisite understanding comes about from having experienced the same, or similar, acts. That is the difference between merely witnessing a performance and understanding what is witnessed. An example will illustrate the point. Painting snow is one of the most difficult tasks challenging an artist. When it is done well it is a major achievement and an excellent example of a truly intelligent performance (knowing how). Non-painters observing the end product may appreciate the painting as a fine work of art but unless they have had the experience of attempting to paint snow on their own canvas they cannot fully understand the brilliance of the achievement. That is why musicians are most appreciative of other musicians, artists of other artists, and athletes of other athletes. Each respectively understands, on the basis of his or her own experience, what knowledge is required for a successful performance. Ryle sums up the situation succinctly, "Understanding is a part of knowing how. The knowledge that is required for understanding intelligent performance of a specific kind is some degree of competence in performance of that kind."[13] Understanding is a part of knowing how when executing a skill and it is also a prerequisite for appreciating the execution of the same skill by others.

Understanding, as a prerequisite for appreciating the execution of some skill by others, involves an awareness of what is required of an agent for a successful performance. Often the awareness of the requirements are implicit, particularly in cases where the observer has

128

had experience in executing the same skill but has not had the opportunity to discuss the action with others. Integral to the understanding is an awareness of the criteria involved for a successful performance. In cases of fairly simple acts, such as opening and closing doors, for example, the criteria are obvious but in more complex matters the criteria may need to be articulated beforehand in order that there be a full understanding. Where a person has had experience in executing the action it is reasonable to assume that he or she already knows the criteria. Appreciating the execution of a skill, which involves some knowledge of the criteria, indicates the communicative nature of human action. To speak of understanding, appreciation and communication with regard to human action shows, once again, its conceptual nature.

Ryle's refutation of the intellectualist's legend[14] combined with his proposed conception of intelligence has at least two important consequences for the view I am advancing. In the first place, intentional human physical action is now regarded as a manifestation of intelligence where intelligence earns its consideration from the manner in which the action was carried out and not from the antecedent mental activity. The "thinking" is in the doing. Each action, when it is done intentionally, is thought-impregnated, or conceptual in nature, even though these thoughts and concepts cannot be expressed propositionally.

The second consequence can be expressed in the following way: contrary to the intellectualist's view where knowledge and intelligence are restricted to verbal expressions, propositions, which are the end result of the mental activity we call theorizing, now knowledge and intelligence can be seen in the intentional actions of the agent. A radical shift has been made away from the private domain, the insulated field known as mind where "the Ghost in the Machine"[15] resides, to the public domain of shared concepts. Propositions are no longer the sole means of expressing knowledge; skill execution, as an instance of intentional action, is now understood as a manifestation of knowledge.

To describe intentional action as a piece of behaviour which an agent does knowingly is to ascribe to it, and to skill execution, a conceptual nature. Judging, selecting one course from amongst various options, and making decisions are all integral elements of skill execution. Skill execution involves thinking; it is a form of non-verbal thought which finds its expression in the action. Skill execution, then, is the unity of movement and knowledge; it is "knowledgeable movement."

II. Concepts and Fundamentals

References

1. Hampshire, S. *Thought and Action*, London: Chatto and Windus, 1965, p. 73.
2. Searle, J. R. *Intentionality: An Essay in the Philosophy of Mind.* Cambridge: Cambridge University Press, 1983, p. 84.
3. Idem, p. 84.
4. Idem, p. 84.
5. Idem, p. 84.
6. Hampshire, S. Op. cit., p. 69.
7. Olsen, E.C. "Knowledge of One's Own Intentional Actions," *The Philosophical Quarterly*, Volume 19, Number 27, October 1969, p. 324.
8. Hampshire, S. Op. cit., p. 78.
9. Macmurray, J. *The Self as Agent.* Atlantic Highlands, New Jersey: Humanities Press, 1957, p. 86.
10. Hampshire, S. Op. cit., p. 131.
11. Hamlyn, D.W. *The Theory of Knowledge.* Garden City, New York: Doubleday and Company, Inc. 1970, pp. 103-104.
12. Polanyi, M. *The Tacit Dimension.* Garden City, New York: Doubleday, 1961, p. 4.
13. Ryle, G. *The Concept of Mind.* New York: Barnes and Noble Books, 1949, p. 54.
14. Ibid., pp. 11-32.
15. Ibid., p. 15.

EPISTEMOLOGY, INTENTIONAL ACTION AND PHYSICAL EDUCATION

SAUL ROSS

Traditional western epistemology traces its roots back to Ancient Greece, to the writings of Plato. In the *Meno* (98 b) Plato has Socrates reaffirm that one of the few things of which he is certain that knowledge and right or true opinion (belief) are different. One can have a true belief or a false belief and one can have knowledge but one cannot have false knowledge. Since belief or opinion can be either true or false but knowledge can only be true — false knowledge is an obvious contradiction — there must be a difference between the two. Since the time of Plato, if not even earlier, one of the fundamental assumptions, if not *the* basic assumption, in traditional epistemology, is that there is a distinction between knowledge and belief. Johnson (p. 6) observes that "with few exceptions, philosophers have accepted the view that knowledge is justified true belief." His comment applies equally to the rationalist and empiricist tradition (Hamlyn, p. 29-36) since both epistemologies are committed to the search for undubitable and infallible truths.

A basic, unstated assumption of this epistemological approach is the view of a person who has knowledge of facts and who is able to state these facts in propositional form so that each statement can be tested for truth. Approaching what is to count as knowledge within the conceptual framework of knowledge as justified true belief demands that all knowledge be stated propositionally. The importance attached to the propositional statements as the vehicle for expressing knowledge is reflected in the comment made by Pears (p. 13), who states,

> Pieces of knowledge are made out of words, or at least out of symbols, and they must be meaningful. That is to say, they must either be, or be like, statements. Furthermore, they must be true and they must not be guesswork.

'Symbols' are taken to mean mathematical or chemical signs which replace words in our everyday speech but act in the very same way as words.

II. Concepts and Fundamentals

Knowledge, defined as justified true belief, demands success in justifying the truth of our belief and the veracity of our knowledge claim. One way to express this definition of knowledge is the following formulation:

> x knows that Q
> if and only if
> (i) x believes that Q
> (ii) x has adequate evidence that Q
> and (iii) Q

Three conditions need to be met for 'knowing that.' First there is the belief condition, that is that x must believe that Q. Implicit here is the assumption that the belief is true since false belief cannot be a basis for knowledge (Lehrer, p. 497). Second is the evidence condition, that is, there must be sufficient justification for the propositional statement to count as knowledge; and third, the actual condition, Q, must prevail, that is, it must reflect or mirror reality accurately. Failure to meet the third condition disqualifies the claim for there cannot be false or untrue knowledge.

While the procedure just described may be satisfactory for knowledge which can be formulated in propositional statements, insurmountable difficulties are encountered when attempts are made to this approach to procedural or practical knowledge which is subsumed under the category of 'knowing how.' Instances of knowing how, procedural or practical knowledge, cannot be transposed into propositional statements. In these cases the knowledge is expressed in the action itself. Truth, which is the criterion for propositional knowledge, is inapplicable to knowledge expressed in intentional acts. Knowing how, practical knowledge, cannot be formulated propositionally and, as a consequence, this type of knowledge appears to fall outside the conceptual framework of the knowledge-as-justified-true-belief approach.

Tacit, uncritical acceptance of the traditional epistemological formulation by physical educators have prompted some, such as Henry (1964), and those who followed his lead and developed the sub-discipline approach (Ross, p. 9-10), to look at other disciplines as the source of physical education's body of knowledge. Academic disciplinary status is claimed for physical education by Henry: his rationale for this assertion is rooted in what he describes as the scholarly field of knowledge basic to physical education. "It is constituted of certain portions of such diverse fields as anatomy, physics and physiology, cultural anthropology, history and sociology, as well as psychology" (Henry, p. 33). These are the "cognate" fields from which physical education draws its knowledge and the physical education disciplinarians working in their respective fields would devote themselves to the study and transmission of knowledge as an adequate and worthy objective. As a result of the efforts of these disciplinarians physical education would then have its own body of knowledge.

Propositional statements arrogated from such diverse sources as physiology, biomechanics, sociology and history can be tested for truth. While these propositional statements may somehow constitute a "body of knowledge" at least two damaging consequences ensue for physical education. First, the impression clearly given is that physical education, as a subject area, does not have its own endogenous knowledge. Unlike other subject areas, physical education stands apart, with a status that differs from all the other subject areas which have their own endogenous knowledge. Physiology has its own endogenous knowledge, just as biomechanics, sociology and history do. True, each discipline "borrows" some knowledge from those related to it (e.g., physiology arrogates some knowledge from biology) but, at the very same time, each can point to a set of interrelated propositions which constitutes its own, unique conceptual structure.

More damaging is the second consequence: tacit confirmation is given to the view that knowledge is confined to propositional statements. Physical education is placed in an untenable position under such an epistemological approach. Arrogating a wide and diverse range of propositional statements from a variety of disciplines may provide, in a very loose sense, a body of knowledge but that, by itself, does not describe or define physical education. What is omitted is the very element which distinguishes physical education from all the other subject areas, namely, people moving about intentionally executing the various skills which comprise the program. Where the view of knowledge is limited to propositional statements, intentional human action, which cannot be transposed into propositional form, is not considered a source, nor an expression, of knowledge.

Contemporary advances in epistemology based, in part, on the teachings of Wittgenstein (1953) and Hamlyn (1970) have recognized different types of knowledge and it now becomes the task of philosophers to give a full and comprehensive account of each type of knowledge. In place of an essentialist approach, where an attempt is made to explain the very essence of the concept, Aspin (1976, p. 106 ff) argues that since knowledge can be 'cut' many ways another approach is required, one which takes into account how words are employed, by whom and in what institutional contexts. A view of knowledge, such as the one propounded by Aspin, Hamlyn and Wittgenstein, argues in favour of different types of knowledge. Implicit in this new conception is an acceptance of forms other than words for the expression of knowledge. This advance is to be welcomed by physical education since it places skill acquisition and skill execution in a new epistemological light.

Skill execution can be categorized as an instance of intentional action since it is an act carried out deliberately by an agent. Human action, which presupposes intention, needs to be differentiated from mere bodily movement where there is no intention present. Action can be defined in a preliminary and minimal way as a detectable change in the external world but such a definition creates problems for the observer for whom action appears to be the same as a happening. To resolve this matter, action is further defined as that which is done by an agent, hence confining the notion of action to that which is done by a human being.

A preliminary statement of the essential features of an intentional act is provided by Hampshire (p. 154) who notes "(a) that it is something done at will and (b) at some particular time, (c) that it constitutes some recognizable change in the world." To do something at will presupposes both intention and the selection of one course of action from amongst a number of possibilities. In turn, selection of one course of action from a number of other possibilities presupposes that certain judgements were rendered and that a decision was made. Forming and having intentions, rendering judgements and arriving at decisions all involve thought. Thought encompasses our intentions, beliefs, judgements, and decisions and so serves as the base from which actions flow. This description of the relationship of thought and action may be amenable to a two-step, sequential event (first thought, then action) interpretation. To do so is to err. Human action, as a form of behaviour, is not detachable or separable from the thought which motivates and directs it. An explanation follows.

Action can be described as a piece of intentional behaviour. Intention, in Hampshire's view (p. 170) is necessarily connected with thinking. Thinking, in turn, is necessarily connected with having the means of expressing thought and in the category of behaviour called action, action is the means of expressing thought. Thought and action are intertwined, interwoven. Hampshire (p. 165) explains:

> When I am fully engaged in some intelligent activity, including the activities of writing and talking, I cannot easily single out from within the whole activity a purely mental component, except by arresting my physical movements and utterances.

In other words, action may be described as thought-impregnated. An example will elucidate. A surgeon operating on a patient, moving his scalpel, is engaged in a form of behaviour which is both theoretical and practical at the very same time. Each thrust of the scalpel, a movement which is done intentionally, is one wherein thought and action work

134

together, not as to separate additive components nor as two consecutive events, one mental and the other material, but as one where the mental and material components are interwoven. An action is a piece of overt behaviour that cannot be detached or separated from the thought which motivates and directs it.

An action cannot consist of a sequential set of events, one mental and the other material, with a *de facto* relation between them. If it were a two-step affair then the first event, thought, would become an action which would, itself, require a preceding action, thus involving us in an infinite regress. Thought cannot be separated out from the physical movement in action; action is a form of activity involving the whole self.

When I am engaged in action I am doing something knowingly and I know what I am doing. I know it because it was my intention to do so. If it can be said that I have done something without knowing it then I must have brought it about by accident, without intending to do it. Where I intend to do something I know of my intention and I also know that I am engaging in action. Olsen (p. 324) is more emphatic, noting that it is not merely a contingent fact that when a person is performing an intentional action he knows what action he is performing; the connection is much stronger — "there is a necessary, conceptual, connection between a person performing an intentional action and his knowing what it is that he is doing." A person engaged in an intentional action knows what action he is doing since, by definition, an action is something which a person does knowingly. When I am engaging in action I cannot, according to Olsen (1969), not know.

Explicating the conceptual nature of intentional human action clarifies certain ontological issues and represents the first step in moving toward an alternate epistemology, one which does not demand that all knowledge be expressed propositionally. Intentional action, as an expression of intelligence, need not be transposed into propositional form to be regarded as knowledge. In this type of human activity the knowledge is in the doing. Additional insights into the conceptual nature of human action are found in the writings of Piaget and Ryle and their teachings form the basis for an alternate epistemology, one that appreciates skill execution as an expression of knowledge.

Piaget (1970, a; 1970, b), as part of this Theory of Genetic Epistemology, offers a detailed ontogenetic and epistemic account of Sensorimotor Intelligence which he views as a type of non-verbal intelligence. An appreciation of Piaget's theory starts by understanding that his original training as a biologist had a profound and lasting influence on his subsequent endeavours in psychology and philosophy. Genetic epistemology, which encompasses biology, psychology, and philosophy, springs from a single unifying principle: all adaptively useful knowledge has a biological origin and grows according to biological laws.

II. Concepts and Fundamentals

Envisioning knowledge as a form of adaptation frees Piaget from the conception of knowledge as something confined only to propositional statements and allows him to see knowledge and intelligence in other forms of human behaviour.

Envisioning prelinguistic behaviour, physical action, as intelligent and acknowledging the complex intellectual processes which occur in children long before they can speak or understand language presents no difficulty for Piaget. Language, for him, is not equated with thought, "nor is it the source or the sufficient condition of thought. The root of thought must thus be sought in action" (Piaget, 1971, p. 181). Action is the base for the development of thought, and it is also the base for development of all subsequent stages of intelligence (Piaget, 1970, b, p. 23). Where action is deemed as the base for thought intentional human action is to be regarded as thought-impregnated rather than devoid of thought.

Sensorimotor Intelligence is the name given by Piaget to the first stage of development in the child; it spans approximately the first two years of life. Sensorimotor intelligence is regarded by Piaget (1952, p. 359) as a 'practical' intelligence, an intelligence employed to solve practical problems, one which has as its criterion success or failure. Rational, or reflective intelligence, is seen by Piaget (*Idem*) as leading to knowledge as such and therefore yields to norms of truth. A delineation is made of one of the differences between the two types of intelligence, but yet, at the very same time the similarities are pointed out:

> By virtue of the very fact that the child cannot translate his observations into a system of verbal judgements and reflexive concepts but can simply register them by means of sensorimotor schemata...there can be no question of attributing to him the capacity of arriving at pure proofs or judgements properly so called, but it must be said that these judgements, if they were expressed in words, would be the equivalent to something like, 'one can do this with this object', 'one could achieve this result,' etc.
>
> (*Idem*)

Similarities between the two types of intelligence are found throughout Piaget's (1952) discussion devoted to this matter. Piaget treats intelligence from a structural and from a functional perspective and in both categories sensorimotor intelligence is the same as rational intelligence.

Even if there were differences the very fact that Piaget chose to describe the behaviour of the infant in terms of 'intelligence' proclaims the conceptual, thought-impregnated nature of intentional human action. Although Piaget, in his description of both types of intelligence, finds little difference between them I deem it important to draw attention to two discernable differences, one relating to the plane of activity and the other relating to one particular feature of 'rational' thought. 'Practical' concepts emerge and are utilized on the plane of human action where they are employed to solve a certain class of problems, those relating to moving about in the world in order to attain certain concrete material objectives. In these cases, the use of propositional statements, 'rational' concepts would be a misadaptation and hence non-intelligent. In contrast, 'rational' concepts emerge and are utilized on the plane of human activity where physical action (other than verbal expression) is not needed.

With reference to the second difference, 'rational' concepts are manifested in speech and can be formulated propositionally. 'Practical' concepts are manifested in intentional action and cannot be transposed into propositional statements. Although they cannot be formulated into propositional statements, and hence tested for veracity, that should not prevent us from recognizing and acknowledging the conceptual nature of this type of intelligence.

A comparison of the two types of intelligence described by Piaget is, in effect, a comparison of two types of knowledge, one practical and the other propositional. For propositional knowledge the appropriate criterion is truth; for practical knowledge the appropriate criterion is success. Piaget's efforts in delineating sensorimotor intelligence results in an epistemology which recognizes various types of knowledge. One type of knowledge is sensorimotor intelligence. To speak of knowledge and intelligence is to imply concepts for without concepts there can be no thought or intelligence. With regard specifically to sensorimotor intelligence the concepts are non-verbal and the knowledge is expressed in the action.

Ryle's avowed purpose in *The Concept of Mind* is to discredit the "intellectualist legend" by debunking the rather widespread and pervasively held belief that all knowledge is fundamentally of a verbal or symbolic nature. Under that view to know something is to be able to make appropriate statements about what is known. All knowing how can be assimilated to knowing that. By pointing out that we commonly refer to people knowing *how* to do things, and noting that this is different from their being able to describe such performances verbally, Ryle, in effect, identifies two types of knowledge. Mental features — intelligent, clever, sensible, inventive, dull, silly, careless — can be seen in each and every act of the individual. Intelligence is not confined to the inner mental process called thinking which is usually associated only with the activity called theorizing; intelligence needs to be judged by the *quality* of the action.

137

II. Concepts and Fundamentals

Intelligent action is not a two-step operation, first a bit of theory followed by a bit of practice, which is the process Ryle attributes to the intellectualist legend. That is not to say that we do not often reflect before we act for often we reflect in order to act properly. What is being refuted is the general assertion that all intelligent performances require to be prefaced by the consideration of appropriate propositions — someone performing a skill which demands intelligence must first recite the theory in his head before he puts it into practice. If that were the case then the prior act of theorizing would itself be an action for which a still-prior act of theorizing would be required, resulting in a vicious regress (Ryle, p. 30). 'Intelligent,' when applied to an act, describes the procedure followed, in effect, the quality of the act and not the prior intellectual operation.

Knowing how is equated with intelligent performance, with careful skillful performance, where the agent could be described as "thinking" what he is doing while he is doing it. This thinking is manifested in the manner in which the action adheres to the rules, the ease with which it was carried out, the propriety of the application of that particular act in the specific circumstance. Ryle (p. 50-51) cautions us not to misinterpret the notion of the thinking in the doing. "He is bodily active and he is mentally active, but he is not being synchronously active in two different 'places' or with two different 'engines.' There is only one activity, but it is one susceptible of and requiring more than one kind of explanatory description." A parallel or synchronous dualism is ruled out. The knowledge is in the action; the knowing is in the doing.

Hamlyn (p. 103-104) believes that a further distinction needs to be drawn between knowing how to do something and merely being able to do it. Merely being able to do something, which animals do instinctively, cannot be equated with knowing how to do something because no understanding is involved. Knowing how to do something normally implies some understanding and knowledge of the principles involved in the activity in question; knowing how to do something normally refers to patterns of movement and action (covert and overt) that at some stage require the bringing to bear of attention and directed effort. Knowing how to, as distinguished from merely being able, involves the application of judgements and understanding, which presupposes concepts; and in executing a skill a non-verbal concept is employed and judged by the manner in which the act was carried out.

Knowing how, executing the wide range of skills which are the concern of physical education, is now understood and judged epistemically in a different light. Learning of all skills, even the most unsophisticated knacks, requires some intelligent capacity. To speak of learning is to speak of the acquisition of concepts and so skill acquisition and execution is now seen as conceptual in nature even though these concepts are non-verbal. Executing skills in accordance with instructions, performing according to rules, and applying the skills in standard and unique situations are clear indicators of intelligence. A radical epistemic shift has been made away from the private domain, the insulated field known as mind where "the Ghost in the Machine" (Ryle p. 15) resides to the public domain of shared concepts. Propositional statements are no longer the sole means of expressing knowledge.

Skill execution, as a form of behaviour subsumed under the heading of intentional human action, is appreciated as a type of knowledge, one which is non-verbal but conceptual nonetheless. Each attempt is to be judged by the manner in which it is executed. It receives its recognition as knowledge from the quality of the act and not from the supposed antecedent theoretical internal bit of behaviour. For physical education this means that we can point to our own domain, skill acquisition and skill execution, as the source of our own unique non-verbal, conceptual body of knowledge.

Bibliography

Aspin, D. "'Knowing How' and 'Knowing That' and Physical Education," *Journal of the Philosophy of Sport*, III, 1976, p. 97-117.

Hamlyn, D.W. *The Theory of Knowledge*. Garden City, N.Y.: Doubleday and Company, Inc., 1970.

Hampshire, S. *Thought and Action*. London: Chattos and Windus, 1965.

Henry, F. "Physical Education: An Academic Discipline," *Journal of Health, Physical Education and Recreation*, 35 (7), September 1964, p. 32-33, 69.

Johnson A.O. *The Problem of Knowledge*. The Hague: Martinus Nijhoff, 1974.

Lehrer. K. "Belief and Knowledge," *The Philosophical Review*, LXXVII, 1968, p. 491-499.

Olsen. E.C. "Knowledge of One's Own International Actions," *The Philosophical Quarterly*, XIX (77), October 1969, p. 324-336.

Pears. D. *What Is Knowledge?* New York: Harper and Row, 1971.

Piaget. J. *Biology and Knowledge*. Translated into English by Beatrix Walsh. Chicago and London: The University of Chicago Press, 1971.

Piaget. J. *Genetic Epistemology*. Translated by Eleanor Duckworth. New York: Columbia University Press, 1970(a).

Piaget. J. *The Origins of Intelligence in Children*. Translated by Margaret Cook. New York: International Universities Press, Inc., 1952.

Piaget. J. *The Principles of Genetic Epistemology*. Translated by Wolfe Mays. London: Routeledge and Kegan Paul, 1970(b).

II. Concepts and Fundamentals

Plato. *The Collected Dialogues*. Edited by E. Hamilton and H. Cairns. Princeton, N.J.: Princeton University Press, 1973.

Ross, S. "Physical Education: A Pre-Discipline in Search of a Paradigm," *International Journal of Physical Education*, XV (2), 1978, p. 9-15.

Ryle, G. *The Concept of Mind*. New York: Barnes and Noble Books, 1949.

Wittgenstein. L. *Philosophical Investigations*. Translated by G.E.M. Anscombe. Oxford: Basil Blackwell, 1953.

SPORT, ART AND PARTICULARITY:
THE BEST EQUIVOCATION

TERENCE J. ROBERTS

David Best (1; 3; 4; 5; 6) has mounted a consistently strong attack against too closely associating most sports with the aesthetic or any sport with art. His position consists of two main arguments: first, that the aesthetic cannot be central to most sports because, unlike art wherein the aesthetic is central, most sports have an aim or purpose which can be identified independently of the way that aim or purpose is accomplished; and second, that, unlike all art forms, no sports have the capacity to express a conception of life situations. While there are important ways the two arguments interrelate, this paper attempts to overcome the obstacle posed by the first by demonstrating that it rests upon a fundamental equivocation.[1]

Before that argument can proceed, it is necessary to outline Best's position.[2] In the chapter entitled "The Aesthetic in Sport" in *Philosophy and Human Movement* (3), Best begins by asking whether all sports can be considered from the aesthetic point of view. He affirmatively responds, "any object or activity can be considered aesthetically — cars, mountains, even mathematical proofs and philosophical arguments" (3: p. 99). The affirmation does nothing to advance the case of an intimacy between sport and the aesthetic: it's true, but trivial, that sport is aesthetic in this sense. With respect to the nontrivial claim, Best argues that an examination of the respective natures of the aesthetic and most sports reveals that an intimacy between them is impossible. Employing works of art, specifically paintings, as paradigms of that which is primarily of aesthetic interest, Best contrasts the aesthetic way of looking with the functional, purposive way:

> To take a central example again, when we are considering a work of art from the aesthetic point of view we are not considering it in relation to some external function or purpose it serves. It cannot be evaluated aesthetically according to its degree of success in achieving some such extrinsic end. By contrast, when a painting is considered as an investment, then it is assessed in relation to an extrinisic end, namely that of maximum appreciation in financial value. (3: p. 101)

It is the nonpurposive, nonfunctional character of the aesthetic that Best thinks precludes the possibility of a close relationship between sport and

141

II. Concepts and Fundamentals

the aesthetic[3] because most sports are assessed in terms of an extrinsic end:

> there are many sports, indeed the great majority, which are like the painting considered as an investment in that there is an aim or purpose which can be identified independently of the way it is accomplished. That is, the manner of achievement is of little or no significance as long as it comes within the rules. For example, it is normally far more important for a football or hockey team *that* a goal is scored than *how* it is scored. In very many sports of this kind the over-riding factor is the achievement of some such independently specifiable end, since that is the mark of success. (3: p. 101)

Art, and more generally the aesthetic, Best argues, are much different:

> The end cannot be identified apart from the manner of achieving it, and that is another way of saying that the presupposition encapsulated in the question, of explanation in terms of purposive action is directed onto an external end, is unintelligible in the sphere of aesthetics. In short, in an important sense the answer to 'What is the purpose of that novel?' will amount to a rejection of the question. (3: p. 103)

That is, an understanding and an appreciation of the so-called "purpose" of an art work cannot be separated from an understanding and an appreciation of the art work itself. The means are the end, and consequently any change in the means will change the so-called end. As Best puts it,

> there is a peculiarly intimate connection between the form of an object of aesthetic appreciation, i.e., the particular medium of expression, and its content, i.e., what is expressed in it. So that in art there cannot be a change of form of expression without a corresponding change in what is expressed. (3: p. 102)

Whereas on the other hand, he argues, something (e.g., most sports and paintings considered as investments) is appreciated primarily as a means to an end, the means employed become relatively unimportant and can be altered without affecting the nature of the end attained. For instance, Best points out, if a painting is valued exclusively as a means of attaining maximum appreciation in financial value, what sort of painting

142

it is matters little. Similarly, in most sports there are many ways of achieving the end (i.e., scoring); how it is achieved is relatively unimportant.

Notice that Best restricts his comments to "most" sports. He does admit of another class of sports (i.e., the "aesthetic" sports) whose purpose, unlike that of the "purposive" sports just described, "cannot be specified apart from the aesthetic manner of achieving it" (1: p. 157). Similar to the arts, these sports (e.g., gymnastics, diving, figure skating, synchronized swimming) have "an intrinsic end which cannot be identified apart from the mean" (3: p. 104). Consequently, in these aesthetic sports,[4] as contrasted with the purposive ones,[5] "the way in which the appropriate movements are performed is not incidental but central" (3: p. 104). He argues that while "it would make perfectly good sense to urge a football team to score goals without caring how they scored them" (3: p. 104), it would make no sense to urge a gymnast to perform a vault without caring *how* he or she did it. Not *any* way of getting over the box could count as even a bad vault, whereas "*any* way of getting the ball between the opponents' posts, as long as it is within the rules, would count as a goal, albeit a very clumsy or lucky one" (3: p. 105).

At first glance Best's argument appears sound: sport and art do seem to differ radically with respect to their means-end relationships. Goals in sport are identifiable apart from how they are accomplished. This is borne out by the frequency with which participants in and observers of sport appear to be more concerned with the fact *that* goals are scored rather than with *how* goals are scored. Alternatively, the "sadness" of a painting is indissolubly linked to the way it is expressed; not only can it not be expressed in a better or even a different way, it cannot be understood or even identified apart from that way.

On closer inspection, however, I think it can be shown that the veracity of Best's argument is more apparent than actual. The "fundamental" differences between sport and art are not fundamental at all. Rather, they are simply and trivially a function of the equivocal way Best characterizes sport and art. If that can be demonstrated, groundless will be his claim that the aesthetic can be only incidental to most sports.

The plan is to first outline Best's "particularity theses,"[6] a device he uses to demonstrate the particularity of response appropriate to works of art. Employing the same thesis, it will then be shown that many of Best's statements about sport and art are equivocal or misleading or both. More specifically, it will be demonstrated,

1. That under certain descriptions, art too can be characterized as "having an aim or purpose which can be identified independently of the way in which it is accomplished";

2. That Best's argument inappropriately equates "having an aim or purpose which can be identified independently of the way in which it is accomplished" with "having an external aim or purpose which it serves";
3. That Best understands goals only in the trivial sense and that this way of understanding is no more inappropriate for art than it is for sport;
4. That the claim "there are many ways to score a goal" is correct only in certain respects and that in those same respects similar claims can be made of art;
5. That Best's failure to realize all of the above is a function of his exclusive viewing of art in particular terms while equivocally viewing sport exclusively in general terms.

In the chapter "The Particularity of Feeling" in *Feeling and Reason in the Arts* (1), Best discusses a "general-particular" spectrum within which can be placed emotional responses to works of art and, for that matter, many other aspects of life:

> Emotions can be seen as forming a spectrum with at one extreme those feelings which are relatively undifferentiated and at the other those which are highly particular. Placing on the spectrum depends upon the variety of intentional objects, that is, the possible objects on to which typical behavior may be directed, and by which each such emotion is identified. (1: p. 141)

Best explains that feelings at the undifferentiated or general extreme of the spectrum may be identified in widely different ways because there are many different objects onto which the fear of, say, people or reptiles would be directed. In the middle of the spectrum the feelings are more particularized. That is, there are fewer possible objects of, for instance, the fears of aggressive people and snakes than the previous, more general, fears of people and reptiles (1: p. 141). At the most particular extreme of the spectrum, Best argues, the intentional object of the feeling can be but one:

> At the other extreme of the spectrum are those highly particularized feelings each of which can be experienced and identified in only one way. In the case of such a feeling it would make no sense to suggest that there could be another intentional object since, apart from its relation to *this particular object*, the emotion could not intelligibly be said to exist. An example might be fear of a particular person with a peculiarly sneering and sarcastic manner, or,

more obviously, love or friendship for a particular person. In these cases the emotion is directed on to and is identified by only one object. (1: p. 141)

It is clear that Best wishes to place works of art at the most particular end of the spectrum. The sadness of Mozart's 40th Symphony, he argues, can be identified only by that piece of music: "to change the particular form of the expression, whether within the same artistic medium or into another, would be to change the object of the emotion, and consequently the emotion itself " (1: p. 142). Best makes similar claims elsewhere. For instance, he argues that the impossibility of expressing *King Lear* emotions in another play is a logical one, not a practical one: "it simply does not *make sense* to speak of expressing *King Lear* emotions in another play, since it is the language of that play which identified the emotions" (2: pp. 315-316). Elsewhere he claims,

> if anyone thought that the purpose of Picasso's Guernica could be expressed as 'man's inhumanity to man,' or the 'the horrors of war,' or any such trite phrase, he or she would thereby reveal a failure to understand it. Such phrases *are* trite and commonplace. The work is not. (5: p. 36)

Yet virtually whenever Best advances this particularity claim with respect to art and what it expresses, he makes what I take to be a very important qualification which suggests that what is expressed in a work *can* be identified and understood (albeit generally) independently of the particular. For instance, in countering Boxill's (7) position and arguing against the possibility of different works expressing the same thing, Best admits,

> In a very trivial sense, of course, that may be true. One could say that Tolstoy's *Father Sergius*, and Shakespeare's *King Lear* are expressing the same idea, namely that renunciation is not a form of self-interest. (5: p. 36)

While Best is careful to point out that such a characterization is decidedly inadequate, it is, as will be explained later, nevertheless *an* understanding of them, albeit a very general one. The qualification is made yet more forcibly:

> clearly the response to a work of art could be specified in a general way, for example as 'sad,' or, according to the theme of the work, it could be specified with varying degrees of particularity. It could be placed at any point on the

spectrum according to the way in which it is specified. That is, it will always be possible to redescribe a 'particular' response in more general terms. (1: p. 142)

Best argues that such an admission does not damage his thesis since, unlike many emotions characterized in general terms, such as the fear of snakes, responses to works of art will always be capable of specification at the particular extreme. Yet once again, that a work can be described as sad generally implies that what is expressed can be understood, albeit generally, apart from the work. And neither are such general descriptions as trivial, trite, commonplace and heretical as Best makes out. If so, Best himself is guilty of a heresy of the highest order when he describes, in fairly general terms, an aspect of Beckett's play, *Not I*:

> The character in this play, of whom it is significant that only her mouth can be seen, pours out a stream of incidents which have happened to her during her life. She appears to be engaged in a desperate but vain search for the essence of what she is, or at least for some essential aspect of her life. Yet each of the incidents she recounts seems to be only *contingently* related to what she is, since it might not have happened to her, or it might have happened differently. This seems to leave her with nothing that is essential, and therefore with the despairing feeling that she has no identity. Thus she finds it confusing, abhorrent and terrifying to refer to herself in the first person. (2: p. 309)

But the heresy of heresies comes with Best's next statement: "Francis Bacon is, I think, making a similar point in his painting *An Accidental Being*." Both "heresies" are tacit admissions of precisely what Best denies! The first is a description of the meaning of a work, or at least part of that meaning, apart from the work itself. The second demonstrates that what is expressed (at the level of generality in which Best has described it) in one work *can* be expressed in another. It is clear that what has been described has been identified independently of both works. Having seen neither (to admit my ignorance), I nevertheless can understand the description to be a correct statement about the meaning of both. Of course it still could be argued that the description is trite, commonplace and trivial, and so, consequently, must be my understanding of them. While I would argue to the contrary, such a claim is really beside the point. Of both works I now have *an* understanding — an understanding of their meaning which has been identified and described independently of them.

Best has consistently argued that complete identification of means and end is an important distinguishing feature of the concept of art. That claim can now be seen in a different light. While complete identification of means and end is necessary to a complete understanding of works of art, less particular characterizations become more general, so that which is described as expressed (e.g., sadness) becomes more independently identifiable from the work, that is, from how it is expressed peculiarly by the work. So whether the aim, purpose or meaning of a work of art can be identified independently of the way it is accomplished is not a function of the nature of an art work itself, as Best would argue, but rather is a function of the *way* it is described, particularly or generally. Described particularly, the sadness of the work cannot be understood nor even identified independently of the work. But under other levels of description, that is, general ones, the sadness can be identified independently of the work.

Best has been blinded by his *way* of looking. His overriding reluctance to view art in other than exclusively particular ways blinds him to the realization that under more general modes of description which, depending on our interest, are equally legitimate, what is expressed by a work can be identified and understood (albeit generally) apart from the work. This reluctance is only the first side of the two-sided fundamental equivocation to which I earlier alluded. Before that second facet is revealed, however, I would like to suggest how the reluctance just described may be the hidden cause behind Best's misconception that an object's "having an aim or purpose which can be identified independently of the way in which it is accomplished" is equivalent to the object's "having an external function or purpose it serves."

An examination of several statements by Best reveals he does assume such an entailment. For instance, he claims that "there are many sports, indeed the great majority, which are like the painting considered as an investment in that there is an aim or purpose which can be identified independently of the way it is accomplished" (3: p. 101).

Earlier, however, Best has made it quite clear that a painting considered as an investment is a paradigm case of considering something "in relation to some external function or purpose it serves" and of assessing it "in relation to an extrinsic end" (3: p. 101). Later when contrasting aesthetic and purposive sports, he implies the entailment by arguing that because aesthetic sports have means-end identity, they, unlike purpose sports, have an *intrinsic* end (3: p. 104). Absence of means-end identity in an object or event must then mean for Best that the object or event serves an extrinsic purpose.

Although it may be correct to claim that both paintings considered as investments and most sports (under certain descriptions — more on this later) have an aim or purpose which can be identified independently

II. Concepts and Fundamentals

of the way it is accomplished, that does not necessarily mean that therefore both have or serve external aims or purposes. That can be true only if all instances of independently identifiable ends are instances of external ends. To be sure, many of the former are instances of the latter, as exemplified by the painting considered as an investment. But many are not, and I argue that sport (and art under certain descriptions) is just such a case.

My argument that the scoring of goals is not an external purpose of sport but rather an internal purpose within sport is virtually identical to Joseph Kupfer's (9; 10), and I am indebted to his precise formulation of it. Kupfer argues that the common overemphasis on scoring/winning as something somehow apart from the game is a result of a mistaken understanding of scoring/winning as *the purpose* of playing. The consequence of this mistake, he argues, is that the playing of games is devalued to the point at which it is viewed as merely a means to the attainment of the dominant end of scoring/winning. In an effort to explain this mistake, Kupfer employs the Kantian distinction between purpose and purposivity. Kupfer admits that art, purely purposive, may contain within it aims or purposes, and as such appear to have something in common with purposeful objects such as telephones and cars. But the critical difference is that in contrast to such purposeful objects, the purely purposive serves no external purpose. He concludes,

> The purely purposive then may include purposes within it without as a whole being subservient to any extrinsic purpose or end. Sport is like art in being purposive but without external purpose. (9: p. 204)

So, for Kupfer, scoring/winning are purposes to be sure, but purposes within sport and akin to such other internal purposes as "'taking tricks' in bridge; singing a harmonic in a barbershop quartet; or achieving validity in an argument" (9: p. 121).

Such internal purposes abound in art. Instances can be taken from Best's work itself. For example, in his attempt to distinguish between the aesthetic and the artistic, Best argues that a critical appreciation of a work such as Shakespeare's *Measure for Measure* might consider a number of questions relating to the characters of Angello and Isabella. For our purposes, principal among these are,

> whether their learning from their experiences is central to the play, or whether the intention is rather that those reading or watching it should learn from the inability of the characters to recognize their own weaknesses. (1: p. 162)

148

Admittedly, the answer to the question of whether the intention is to have the readers learn from the inabilities of Angello and Isabella can be resolved only in terms of the play itself. But that is beside the point because it only shows the purpose as an internal one. The fact remains that such in intention, such a meaning, such a purpose, *can*, in an important sense and as Best has done, be identified apart from the way it is accomplished.

Best's failure to recognize the above can be seen as a result of his penchant to characterize art exclusively under the particular level of description which precludes the possibility of discovering an important counterexample to the common but facile conclusion that all instances of independently identifiable ends are instances of external ones.[7] In the absence of any important counterexamples, it is understandable to conclude that a newly discovered object or event (e.g., sport) that has an independently identifiable purpose (under certain descriptions) must be like all those other objects or events that also have independently identifiable purposes which are *external* to the object or event (e.g., paintings viewed as investments and social surveys). That is, if all known cases of X are also cases of Y, there is no good reason to believe that a newly discovered X is not simply just another instance of Y. But art, under certain descriptions, is the counterexample that renders suspect all such facile "X, therefore Y" judgments. Viewing it exclusively in particular terms blinds one to that discovery.

Of course, to show up the incorrectness of Best's apparent assumption that all independently identifiable purposes are external ones does not yet get sport off the hook. It has to be proven, not just claimed, that scoring/winning is not external. Once again Kupfer's work is helpful. He argues that sport is unlike common purposeful activities, such as shingling our roofs or taking medicine, which came into existence for the sake of keeping homes dry and restoring health, respectively. Without those prior desires there would be little reason to shingle or to take medicine. But it is ludicrous to suggest that the scoring of goals was the previously desired purpose for which the playing of sport was brought into existence. Prior to sport no one ever needed goals. Prior to basketball no one ever needed balls passing through netted hoops. Yet, not only can the scoring of goals not be the *raison d'être* of competitive sport but, unlike the purposes of shingling and taking medicine, it cannot be achieved by any other means:

> Practical purposes in the everyday, however, are independent of their means and are rightly said to be the purposes *of* their activities since they are attainable by some other means. The practical activity is itself subordinated to the goal as its instrument. There are other

ways besides shingling of keeping homes dry, other ways of restoring health besides taking medicine. These just seem the best, given our circumstances, resources, and know-how. (9: p. 120)

But there are no ways of accomplishing the so-called "purpose" of basketball or baseball other than by playing basketball or baseball. We are always on the lookout for more effective, less costly ways of keeping homes dry and restoring health. But no one is thinking, "Basketball, as a means of getting balls through hoops, is decidedly ineffective. It is imperative that a more cost-effective strategy of getting more balls through hoops be devised." The reason for this is clear:

> Scoring is not an end which could be accomplished by some other avenue because what it *means* 'to score' depends upon the particular game being played. Obviously, scoring in tennis is defined by the structure of the game of tennis, and so on for the other sports. (9: p. 120)

It is now clear that scoring/winning is not a purpose external to sport. Whereas under certain descriptions scoring/winning can be identified independently of its means, it, unlike the externality of the appreciation in value of a painting considered as an investment, is not external to sport. But even if Best were to concede this along with the concession that under certain descriptions at least some works of art have independently identifiable but not external purposes, he might still wish to claim that the main thrust of his argument remains intact. That is, even if he does admit that scoring is not external to, say, hockey, because the rules of hockey define what it *means* to score, he may still wish to argue that within those rules there are many ways to score.[8] In other words, it might still be maintained that even if scoring can be viewed as an end or purpose within purposive sports, unlike art there remains an undeniable gap between the achievement of the internal end and the way in which it is achieved. Such a view is highly misleading, entails a trivial view of goals, and is generated by the following equivocation; viewing sport in exclusively general terms while viewing art in exclusively particular ones. We have already exposed the latter facet of that equivocation. We can expose the former by examining Best's trivial conception of goals.

Although it is possible to view goals in hockey or soccer as simply the event that occurs precisely at the moment when the ball or puck passes into the net or over the crease, or a run in baseball as simply the event that occurs precisely at the moment when the runner's foot hits home plate, such an understanding of goals is trivial. Yet if Best's view of the place of goals in sport is correct, it is to this trivial understanding of them that we are restricted.

Obviously we do not often view goals in such an empty way. We know and wish to know so much more. Imagine what the video highlights of any game in any sport would be like if such a trivial understanding of goals were operative. We would see only so many pucks passing over creases, feet hitting plates, balls passing through hoops, falling into little holes, or landing in back of nets. Such "highlights" would be decidedly uninteresting and over in seconds. We would feel cheated; we demand much more. Luckily, normal video highlights cater to those demands — they detail precisely *how* the goals were achieved. Admittedly there is no necessary connection between what is included in video highlights and the nature and place of goals in sport. Yet they do suggest an alternative, at least as legitimate, understanding of goals that includes much more than the trivial view depicted above. The passing of the puck over the crease or the ball through the hoop marks only the completion of a goal. In an important sense they begin much earlier and cannot be distinguished from all those elements directly and indirectly contributing to that completing moment.

How far back we go and how much we include is a function of our interest and the nature of the sport and goal in question. For instance, contrast a gridiron touchdown that is a dazzling runback of the opening kickoff with a ninth-inning, game-winning run in baseball that is the culmination of a full-count base-on balls, three close but unsuccessful attempted pickoffs, a full-count strikeout, another unsuccessful attempted pickoff, a stolen second base, a full-count sacrifice fly to left field with a missed tag at third, and a two-out-full-count ground ball single just beyond the outstretched glove of a diving second baseman. And contrast both of the above with that sort of goal characteristic of such fluid games as hockey, soccer, basketball and Australian Rules football, in which the scoring play seems to imperceptibly flow out of the play itself such that where and when we choose to pinpoint its beginning is fairly arbitrary.

Such nontrivial complete understandings of goals are examples of the inseparability of scoring and the play itself as explained by Kupfer:

> As the culmination of play scoring helps determine its form and completeness. The scoring aspect of a play is not detachable from it in that the play is partially defined in terms of the success or failure in scoring.... The complete description of the play includes whether or not it issues in scoring. But just as the play cannot be completely specified independent of scoring, neither can scoring be specified or identified independent of the play. (10: p. 356)

II. Concepts and Fundamentals

While Kupfer admits that the score, understood in a numerical sense, can be separated from the means employed, its independent specifiability is merely an abstraction from the way in which the goals were achieved. Scoring is not so independently identifiable (10: pp. 356-357).

To attempt to understand a goal as somehow separate from the way it is scored is no less inappropriate than is the attempt to understand the sadness of a work apart from the way that sadness is expressed. The description "that a goal was scored" tells us no more about *the* goal scored than does the description "sadness is expressed" tell us about *the* sadness expressed. Though useful in some situations depending on our interest, such descriptions are no more than trite, trivial and commonplace understandings of *the* goal and *the* sadness, respectively. By describing art in exclusively particular terms, Best seeks to avoid those general and trivial accounts of the meaning of art works, the implication of which is the supposition that what is expressed in one work could be expressed in another. Such a supposition, Best argues, in an important sense reveals a failure to understand the nature of art. But the implication of Best's exclusively trivial account of goals is to suppose that one goal scored is the same as another goal scored. In that same important sense, such a supposition reveals a failure to understand the nature of sport.

We have at last come face to face with the second facet of Best's fundamental equivocation. He refuses, or at least fails, to describe goals in other than exclusively general terms. That refusal either entails or is entailed by his failure to recognize that goals can be particularly described and must be so described if our understanding of them is to be anything more than trivial. The equivocation can be clearly seen: Best describes art in exclusively particular terms, while he equivocally describes sport in exclusively general terms. With such an equivocation operative, it is little wonder that he sees radical differences between them. But *what* he sees has been determined by the *way* he looks and in that sense is not there.

I would now like to discuss yet another manifestation of that equivocation, and in the process demonstrate further that the differences Best sees between sport and art are not so much a function of their radically different natures as he assumes but a function of the radically different ways he respectively views them. The manifestation in question is Best's (3: p. 103) claim that, "in contrast to a work of art,...there are many ways of achieving the end, i.e., of scoring a goal, in hockey." Although the assertion that there are many ways to score a goal is true in certain respects, in those same respects similar and no less legitimate claims can be made of what is expressed in art.

Viewed particularly, there is only one way to paint the painting painted or express the sadness expressed: the constitutive way it was painted, the constitutive way it was expressed. Any change to any relevant aspect of the way the painting was painted or the sadness was expressed would produce a different painting, a different sadness. Yet because Best fails to apply this particular level of description to sport, he fails to realize that virtually the same can be said of goals scored. Viewed particularly in that nontrivial sense depicted above, there is only one way to score the goal scored: the constitutive way it was scored. Any change to any relevant aspect of the way the goal was scored would result in a correspondingly different goal.

To view goals generally is to separate them from the particulars that constitute them. So separated goals lose what makes them peculiar. One becomes the same as another. Viewed this way, it makes sense to claim there are many ways to score *a* goal. And so it is with art. To view expressions of sadness generally is to separate them from the particulars that constitute them. Separated expressions of sadness lose what makes them peculiar. One becomes the same as another. Thus, it also makes sense to claim there are many ways to express sadness, represent Churchill, man's inhumanity to man and the horrors of war. The protest that such generalized accounts fail to capture the sadness expressed can be mounted just as legitimately on behalf of sport: such generalized accounts fail to capture *the*[9] goal scored. To deny that is to equivocate.

Therefore, Best's claim that there are many ways to score a goal in the purposive sports[10] but only one way to paint the painting can be seen as nothing more than an unfortunate manifestation of a fundamental equivocation. Viewed generally, there are just as many ways to express sadness as there are ways of scoring a goal; viewed particularly, there is only one way to express *the* sadness expressed or score *the* goal scored. Once the equivocation is righted, the differences vanish.

One loose end remains. It might be objected that while the above particularized account of goals may be a legitimate way of viewing them, its occurrence is rare; most players and fans don't really care how goals are scored as long as they are scored. In contrast, the argument would claim, the parallel generalized account "that sadness is expressed" is relatively unimportant to most artists and viewers of art. For the sake of simplification, this objection will be discussed in two parts: the comparison of the relationships fans and observers of art have to sport and art works, respectively, followed by a similar comparison of athletes and artists.

II. Concepts and Fundamentals

The claim that most fans don't really care how goals are scored but rather that goals are scored not only belies the fact of our interest in the detailed depiction of scoring plays as catered to in video highlights, but is more of sociological than philosophical interest. Even if such a claim is correct, and it certainly is not clear that it is, there is no necessary connection between the way something is most often viewed and the nature of the thing itself. Kupfer argues that it may be the case that most observers of sport are as jaded in their appreciation of it as are art dealers who evaluate works of art exclusively in terms of their market value. Nevertheless, we should not "appeal to the priorities of...typical audiences to determine the place of scoring or winning within the logic of sport" (10: p. 357).

We need not go to the extreme of jaded art dealers to find parallels in art. They — like those who view works exclusively in such terms as a hedge against inflation, as a means of tying together the disparate colors within a room, or as a means of filling blank or ugly walls — miss or ignore the meaning of those works altogether. I would like to demonstrate that parallels to the common importance of "*that* a goal is scored" in sport can be found in art but which, unlike the examples given above, involve an understanding of the meaning of the work in such a way that, due to the interest operative, the meaning is appreciated at a high level of generality such that, for instance, "*that* sadness is expressed" is more important than how it is expressed. Novels, poems, plays and movies, for instance, are often employed as aids in the teaching and discussion of moral issues. If the issue to be discussed, for instance, is "man's inhumanity to man," those responsible for selecting the works to be employed may be much more interested in *that* the issue is expressed by the works than in *how* it is expressed. Or, to choose an example from Best, if the issue to be discussed is "why people should be cognizant of their own weaknesses," one might choose, among others, Shakespeare's *Measure for Measure*, being more concerned with that it expresses the idea than with how it does it. Similarly, the principle concern of those in libraries and museums who classify works on the basis of subject matter is whether "such and such" is expressed, represented or discussed and not the intricacies of how that is done.

In all these cases the interest in the works' meanings is at a more general level. Admittedly, if the interest remains at that level we might think it unfortunate because so much will be missed. And just as we should not let the jaded interest of so-called "typical" fans determine the place of scoring within the logic of sport, we would not let such generalized, and in that sense trivial, accounts determine the place of meaning within the arts. There is so much more to be seen, known, and appreciated.

Turning now to the producers of those goals and works, I argue that, similar to those athletes who sometimes value "that a goal is scored" more than how it is scored, some artists, at least sometimes, are more concerned with, for example, *that* a painting is painted or sadness or beauty expressed rather than with how it is accomplished. Ironically, Best provides the backdrop for an example of such:

> It has been said, with some justification, that beauty is what the bourgeoisie pays the artist for, that is, that he or she has to take time off from serious art in order to produce beauty for a living. (5: p. 35)

Faced with the threat of eviction from an irate landlord for his failure to pay the last two-months' rent, a down-and-out painter who normally prides himself in not pandering to the common taste may come to the grim realization that he'd better paint something that sells. Knowing that beautiful (but dreary!) "works" recently have been selling like hotcakes down at the local flea market, he might exhort himself thus: "Look, I don't care how you do it, you've just got to get in that damn studio and paint some paintings that are beautiful." Viewed from that perspective, once they are painted, *that* they are beautiful will be their mark of success.

Such sacrifices of "how" for "that," I would argue, are fairly typical in the arts. Yet I would not want to argue, as Best has done with sport, that such sacrifices reflect the true nature of art even though it would be no less legitimate to do so. Certainly there are times when many, perhaps most, athletes will take any goal they can get and show little concern for how it is achieved. But just as our proud artist above could take little pride in his beautiful paintings, little pride can be taken in the scoring of such goals. Most artists and athletes most of the time care very much for the *how* of it, for it is only through such a concern that their true prowess can be realized and displayed.

In summary, it has been shown that under an unequivocal application of the general mode of description, both sport and art can be characterized as having respective aims or purposes that can be identified independently of the way they are accomplished without it being entailed that those ends or purposes are external. Concomitantly, the claim "there are many ways to score a goal" is correct, but no more correct than the claim "there are many ways to express sadness." It was also revealed that this general mode can produce nothing but equally trivial, trite and commonplace accounts of goals and that which is expressed or represented by a work of art. Since Best's view of goals is restricted to this level, it was shown to be a trivial one.

II. Concepts and Fundamentals

An unequivocal application of the particular mode or level of description to both sport and art revealed that just as *the* sadness expressed by a work cannot be identified or understood apart from the way it is expressed, neither can *the* goal scored be identified or understood apart from the particular way it was scored. It was shown that, in that important sense, not only is there only one way to paint *the* painting painted or express *the* sadness expressed, but only one way to score *the* goal — *the* way they were painted, expressed or scored. And just as it was accepted that under the particular mode of description a failure to understand the above reveals a failure to understand the nature of art, it was argued that Best fails to understand the nature of goals as constituted by and unidentifiable apart from the particulars.

Best has told the truth, but only half of it. What he says of art is correct but misleading in that its correctness is a function of the application of a certain mode of description: the particular mode. The application of the general mode of art reveals a much different picture — a picture Best fails to see and is unable to describe. Most of what he says of sport is also correct but, once again, correct only within the context of a limited way of looking: the general way. His failure to view them particularly has blinded him to their other side, a side that is not dissimilar to art particularly described.

Best has strongly and consistently maintained that the differences between sport and art with respect to their relationship with the aesthetic is a consequence of their fundamentally different natures in terms of form-content, means-end identity. It has been shown, however, that those "fundamental" means-end identify differences are simply and trivially the result of an equivocal application of radically different modes of description to sport and art. Once the equivocation is righted, the "differences" evaporate.

In conclusion, although there still may be substantial differences between sport and art in their relationship to the aesthetic, they cannot be for the reasons Best gives us. Although this paper contributes little to the advancement of a systematic theory of the sport aesthetic, it at least removes a major obstacle to the successful advancement of any such theory.

Notes

1   A subsequent paper will attempt to counter Best's second argument that, unlike all art forms, no sport forms have the capacity to express a conception of life situations.

2   Since nowhere is there any indication to the contrary, I have assumed that Best understands the position he advances in all his works discussed here (1; 3; 4; 5; 6) to be a consistent whole.

Consequently, my discussion of his position frequently jumps from one work to another.

3   While it is sometimes referred to by Best as a difference between sport and the aesthetic, I think the difference he advocates is more fundamentally and properly a difference between sport and art.

4   Best argues that the gap between means and end is never completely closed in the aesthetic sports because they have an externally identifiable aim (e.g., in gymnastics, the requirements set by each particular movement) to which the performances must conform if they are to be successful.

5   Since my argument is with Best's position, and since the "aesthetic" sports are immune to that position, unless otherwise indicated all future uses of "sport" or "sports" are references to the "purposive" sports.

6   Although Best employs this term only in "Logic, Particularity and Art" (2), where he discusses it fully, it is operative in a less detailed way in his other works.

7   It is difficult to guess which came first. Either his exclusively particular treatment of sport has blinded him to the realization that art, under the general level of description, provides an important counterexample to the claim that all independently identifiable purposes are external ones, *or*, for fear that otherwise art could be characterized as having an external purpose, his assumption that all independently identifiable purposes are external ones has led him to describe art in exclusively particular terms. Either way, the result is the same.

8   While he has never admitted that scoring is internal to sport, he has always maintained that those many ways in which a goal can be scored must be understood as within the rules (e.g., 3: pp. 101, 103).

9   Note the importance of the definite article here. While there are many ways to score *a* goal, there's only one way to score *the* goal. Best (1: p. 144) makes a similar point elsewhere.

10   With respect to this issue, the purposive sports may have a closer affiinity with the arts than do the aesthetic sports. Just as "the poet may take liberties with the sonnet form without necessarily detracting from the quality of the sonnet" (3: p. 106), athletes in most "purposive" sports may take liberties with established conventions of style and strategy without necessarily detracting from the quality of performance. Contrastingly, as Best points out, "if the gymnast deviates from the requirements of, for instance, a vault, however gracefully, then that inevitably does detract from the standard of performance" (3: p. 106). So while the ways to score goals, express sadness and perform a particular vault are infinite, the range of infinity of the last is more restricted. Related to this is the "aesthetic"

II. Concepts and Fundamentals

sports' peculiarity of having a built-in standard of perfection such that a performed dive or vault can be said to be perfect. The same sense of perfect doesn't seem to operate in art or the "purposive" sports; in that sense there are no perfect expressions of sadness or perfect goals. These issues need further examination.

Bibliography

1. Best, David. *Feeling and Reason in the Arts*. London: George Allen and Unwin, 1985.
2. Best, David. "Logic, Particularity and Art." *British Journal of Aesthetics*, 23 (1983), 306-318.
3. Best, David. *Philosophy and Human Movement*. London: George Allen and Unwin, 1978.
4. Best, David. "The Aesthetic in Sport." *British Journal of Aesthetics* (1974), 197-221.
5. Best, David. "Sport is Not Art." *Journal of the Philosophy of Sport*, XII (1985), 25-40.
6. Best, David. "Sport is Not Art: Professor Wertz's Aunt Sally." *Journal of Aesthetic Education*, 20 (1986), 95-98.
7. Boxill, J.M. "Beauty, Sport and Gender." *Journal of the Philosophy of Sport*, XI (1984), 36-47.
8. Goodman, Nelson. *Ways of Worldmaking*. Indianapolis: Hackett Publ., 1978.
9. Kupfer, Joseph H. *Experience as Art*. Albany: State University of New York Press, 1983.
10. Kupfer, Joseph H. "Purpose and Beauty in Sport." *Sport and the Body: A Philosophical Symposium*. Second Edition. Edited by Ellen W. Gerber and William J. Mogan. Philadelphia: Lea & Febiger, 1979.

TO EARN YOUR NEIGHBOUR'S LOVE

HANS SELYE, M.D.

" Thou Shalt Love Thy Neighbour As Thyself "

Thus it is written in the Old Testament and re-emphasized by St. Matthew (Ch. 19, v. 19) and St. Mark (Ch. 12, v. 31); indeed, with certain variations, the same command can be found in the most diverse religions and philosophies. In fact, the golden rule, "Do unto others as you would have them do unto you," is only a modification of this command, but it still means you have to obey an unquestionable authority who orders you to love and be kind. Zoroaster taught it to the fire worshipers in Persia three thousand years ago. Confucius, Lao-Tse, and Buddha incorporated it in their doctrines, and it reappears in Judaism and Christianity. It seems to have been formulated quite independently by numerous thinkers throughout the ages and throughout the world; hence, it undoubtedly has its roots deeply embedded in the human mind.

It is the earliest historic guideline designed to maintain equanimity and peace among men. If everyone loved his neighbour as himself, how could there be any war, crime, aggression, or even tension among people? In Biblical times, there was no better way of convincing the multitudes to be nice to each other than to issue this command. However, to follow it, one had to be unshakably convinced that it was the wish of some divine master whose authority and wisdom were unquestionable.

The various religions which encouraged us to accept this command differed in many ways; in some respects, they even held strictly opposite views. Yet, the existence and authority of one divine master was accepted on faith by the adherents of every group, although each vehemently denied the existence of all other gods. Fortunately, the devotees of any one god usually knew very little about the teachings of other religions; hence, such contradictions and uncertainties did not unduly disturb them. As long as faith was strong enough, I think the basic idea of keeping peace among men could not have been expressed any better. The effort to "love they neighbour as thyself " probably has done more good, and more to make life pleasant, than any other guideline.

The only trouble is that strict adherence to such behaviour is incompatible with the laws of biology. As I have said previously, whether we like it or not, egotism is an essential feature of all living beings, and, if we are honest with ourselves, we must admit that none of us actually

159

II. Concepts and Fundamentals

loves all our fellow men as much as ourselves. When interests clash, I cannot expect others to take my interests as much to heart as their own.

Far be it from me to condemn the dictum "Thou shalt love thy neighbour as thyself," especially since I am convinced that it has long been most useful to humanity as a personal goal to strive for. But as the philosophical outlook and knowledge of man have developed since Biblical times, more and more of us have asked ourselves: How do we know who formulated this command, and is it really possible to follow it?

Frankly, I for one cannot abide it. When I was younger I really tried hard, but I soon found that, try as I might, I could not love my neighbour as much as myself...even if success had not depended so much on the nature of my neighbour. With some of them — very few — I can come quite close to following the command, but I would be lying if I tried to convince myself that with more effort I might succeed in following it as a general law. When it comes to an obnoxious aggressive enemy who makes every effort to destroy me and all the things I believe in, and when I think of the lazy drunkard who lives as a parasite off the efforts of others, or of an incorrigible criminal and corrupter of youth, I feel it would be most unnatural for me to love him as much as myself or even as much as some of my truly lovable relatives or friends. Actually, I cannot succeed in loving even my most lovable neighbour as much as myself. In the extremely remote eventuality that I would have to decide whether my neighbour's or my life should be saved, I would choose my own. There are exceptions to this (a parent may not hesitate to die in order to save a child from a burning building), but — let us admit it — they are rare and cannot justify this type of behaviour as a general guideline for conduct.

So why go on with this pretense? The self-deception leads only to feelings of inferiority; it gives us a bad conscience for not acting according to our avowed principles. And it is no satisfactory solution to say *mea culpa* and admit (even though with an undertone of righteous honesty) that you are an unworthy miserable sinner. Besides, I do not consider myself an unworthy miserable sinner. I think that, on the contrary, within the limits of my innate gifts, I have spared no effort to become a respected physician and scientist. I had to work hard for this all my life, and I continue to do so. I have tried to earn the satisfaction of being able to hold my head high in the conviction that I am doing my utmost to give meaning to my life through useful work. I refuse to lie about this. If I thought I were a despicable miserable sinner, I would get no satisfaction from merely confessing it; instead, I would immediately change my ways and try to deserve the respect and love of my neighbours.

I am convinced that without rejecting the principle "Love thy neighbour" we can adapt it to conform with biological laws discovered in our time and still be compatible with, yet independent of, any particular religion or political creed. As adapted, it neither presupposes nor excludes the existence of an infallible commander whose orders must be blindly followed. And, most important, it does not deny the essentially egotistic nature of living creatures. All that is needed is a simple rewording of the dictum.

"Earn Thy Neighbour's Love"

Thus expressed, we need not offer love on command to people who are truly unlovable; we need not love others as much as ourselves, which would be contrary to the laws of biology. Now success is up to us! Not all of us will be equally good at it, but, even so, the effort to follow the principle will give us a purpose for work; as we have seen the human body is so constructed that, to maintain its physical and mental health, it must work for a purpose which can be accepted as worth the effort.

But in order to understand fully the dictum "Earn thy neighbour's love" — whether interpreted as a divine command reworded or as a sound biological law (and indeed the two interpretations are not mutually exclusive, for the laws of Nature are divine creations) — we must first come to grips with three questions:

1. What is love?
2. Who is your neighbour?
3. How can you earn love?

As mentioned earlier, I think that, according to the spirit of the Biblical command, the term "love" includes all positive feelings towards a person — certainly not only the almost instinctive love between man and woman or parents and children, but also the feeling of gratitude, friendship, admiration, compassion, and respect — in other words, goodwill. In any event, it is in this broad meaning that I am using the term here.

By "neighbour" I mean anyone close to me, including not only geographic but also genetic and — mainly — spiritual and intellectual proximity. In this general sense, the terms neighbour and brother are often used interchangeably, and I have tried to emphasize my view of this relationship in my book *From Dream to Discovery* by the question: "For who is my brother? The man of my blood, even if we have nothing else in common — or the man of my mind to whom I am bound only by the warmth of mutual understanding and common ideals?"

To make the motto "Earn thy neighbour's love" valuable, the goodwill of those who are physically or intellectually closest to us is most important, but the greater our contribution, the broader will be the neighbourhood whose goodwill we can earn. An accomplishment like

II. Concepts and Fundamentals

Einstein's theory of relativity won him the goodwill of nearly the entire human race.

But in order to earn your neighbour's love, you do not have to be an Einstein. For anybody, the best and simplest guide to accomplish this aim is to make himself as useful as possible. Of course, nobody is completely indispensable — but there are degrees. The sudden disappearance of some people would pass unnoticed, whereas the loss of others would be a serious blow to many. I think that the security and the feeling of fulfillment that we can earn, by becoming increasingly more necessary to our neighbours, are directly proportionate to the degree of our success. Although indispensability is never complete, working towards approximating it gives us a feeling of purpose, and represents the best way of earning love.

By helping them, you not only earn your neighbours' love, but also earn more neighbours. Isn't this why people adopt children? The main gratification of adopting children is that it furnishes us with the purpose of earning their love.

A charming true-life story illustrates how even very simple people can have the wisdom to realize that the love of your neighbours is much more likely to bring happiness than efficiency in your work. It was brought to my attention by Professor U. S. von Euler, who was awarded the Nobel Prize for his outstanding work on adrenalin and similar hormones which participate in stress reactions. In a letter commenting on a preliminary draft of this book, he wrote:

> On the train over the Andes, between Mendoza and Santiago, I sat talking to a Bolivian farmer, and asked him whether he utilized modern fertilizers to increase his harvests. 'Oh, no,' he said, 'that would only create dissatisfaction in my neighbours. I prefer a modest harvest to be on good terms with them.' You may say he earned the love of his neighbours by not trying to be too efficient.

I admire this farmer's wisdom because, in all honesty, I seriously doubt that I would have the strength to imitate him in my own field. If I knew a simple answer to something that puzzled a young graduate student, I often allowed him the satisfaction of proving that he could work it out himself, but when it came to my peers, I am afraid my desire to show off my superiority always got the better of me.

Finally, never forget that the only treasure that is yours forever is your ability to earn the love of your neighbours. Unpredictable social changes can suddenly deprive you of all the money, real estate, or political power that you were able to accumulate, but what you have learned is yours for life and is your safest investment. Work on that. Lost wars, social upheavals, and political changes have deprived — and continue to deprive — some of the mightiest of all their possessions overnight. History has shown us again and again that thousands of powerful aristocrats, eminent members of religious, political, or racial groups have suddenly become destitute after an unpredictable event made their privileges worthless. Among them, only those escaped this fate who had always invested in themselves, in their own ability to earn their neighbour's love.

I have always advised my children and students not to worry so much about saving money or about climbing up to the next rung on the ladder of their career, an attitude which seems to be an obsession with highly motivated people, concerned about economic security. It is much more important to work at perfecting yourself and thereby ensure your usefulness no matter what fate does to you. A great economist, artist, or scientist, or a first-rate machinist or plumber rarely has difficulty finding a job if some political or religious persecution drives him out of his country penniless. Remember that no matter what your degree or title, your highest rank is the reputation of your name. You are as valuable and secure as past accomplishments and present capabilities have helped to make you; in other words, you are worth as much as your ability to earn your neighbour's love.

CARTESIAN DUALISM AND PHYSICAL EDUCATION: EPISTEMOLOGICAL INCOMPATIBILITY

SAUL ROSS

The "New" Physical Education

Late in the 19th and early in the 20th centuries, major changes in thinking encompassing philosophy, politics and education, amongst many others, pervaded the American social scene. Under the influence and urging of such seminal thinkers as G. Stanley Hall, Edward Thorndike, John Dewey, and William Heard Kilpatrick, the progressive movement emerged, advanced and flourished, extending its ideas into many aspects of life. Their teachings and ideals also had an impact on the leaders in physical education — men such as Thomas Wood, Clark Hetherington, and Luther Halsey Gulick, who are generally credited with formulating the conceptual framework upon which "the new physical education" would be elaborated (Weston, 1962, p. 51).

These leaders shifted the focus of physical education away from the European (Swedish and German) formal schools of gymnastics with their medical and biological orientation by moving it squarely into the domain of education. Physical education's new educational orientation was championed in the 1920 to 1940 era by authors such as Jay B. Nash and J.F. Williams. They not only carried the banner of "the new physical education," but vigorously attacked the previous conception of physical education (which may be more accurately described as physical culture or as physical training) with its narrow concern for bodily development and physical health.

J.F. Williams, the man credited with coining the term *physical education* as education through the physical, fired the first salvo in what has become known in the physical education literature as "The Great Debate." He juxtaposed the two rival notions: "No one can examine earnestly the implications of physical education without facing two questions. These are: Is physical education an education *of* the physical? Is physical education an education *through* the physical?" (Williams, 1930b, p. 279). Some concomitant learning takes place in the education of the physical and, as well, an education through the physical would produce some distinct physical gains. However, it is important to realize that in these two questions there are (a) two distinct points of view, (b) two radically different ways of looking at physical education, (c) two different ways of understanding the meaning, scope and aim of

164

education, (d) two conceptions of man, and (e) two implicit epistemological theories.

Supporters of the education-of-the-physical school of thought identify strong muscles and firm ligaments as the main outcome, a position staunchly defended by McCloy (1936) in his "How About Some Muscle?" rebuttal to the original attack launched by Williams (1930a, b). Williams rejected the education-of-the-physical notion, which implies that the body can be educated as a thing apart from the mind, on a number of grounds. These are (a) its focus on the cult of muscles and motor or skill learning was too narrow and limited; (b) its general orientation was incompatible with the progressivist ideal of education for complete living; and (c) its dualistic conception of man where mind and body can be regarded as distinct and separate entities. Defending his own position by contrasting it with the notion implicit in the education-of-the-physical view, Williams (1930b) asserted that "modern physical education with its emphasis upon education through the physical is based upon the biologic unity of mind and body" (p. 279). Its goals extend to total education accomplished through the medium of physical activity. Basic to this concept is the belief that education of the *mind* may, indeed, does occur *through* the education of the body.

Williams gives no explanation for his notion of "the biologic unity of mind and body" save for a passing reference to the then emerging philosophy of behaviorism. No further consideration of the mind-body problem in relation to physical education in his writings is made beyond pointing out that a dualistic conception of man allows for the notion of a cult of muscles where the body can be "educated" as a thing apart from the mind and beyond asserting the unity of mind and body in his own conception of physical education. Neither is any such discussion found in McCloy's views in defending his position. Indeed, the entire corpus of literature devoted to the philosophy of physical education is marked by a paucity of attention to this important topic; it is a subject which has not attracted the attention of scholars in the field either from a metaphysical or an epistemological perspective.

I regard this lack of scholarly attention as a major omission because the very notion of physical education — be it as education *of* or as education *through* the physical — involves persons. Unless we clearly understand what a person is, we cannot be very effective as educators. In part to remedy this oversight, and in part to augment and develop what Williams barely started, there is a need to examine and analyze what most philosophers regard as the clearest articulation of the dualistic conception of man — the thesis posited by Descartes, the father of modern philosophy. An analysis of his position will show that there cannot be such a thing as physical education whether it is interpreted as education *of* the physical or as education *through* the physical.

II. Concepts and Fundamentals

Furthermore, the analysis will also show that under the Cartesian thesis, the common notion of education as a process and as an institution generally understood to involve teachers and students cannot be.

Descartes' Dualistic Conception of Man

Descartes insisted that epistemology is the proper starting point of all philosophy. His basic philosophical question is, "What do I know?" He hopes to be able to answer that query by reflection on the beliefs he finds himself disposed to hold. Posing the question in this manner shifts the problem from a general approach to knowledge to an emphasis on the *individual* thinking man. Before attempting to answer questions about what *men* may know, Descartes saw the primary task as attempting to determine what *a man* may know. Changing the focus from the general to the individual carries with it a shift in the locus of the problem of knowledge from the external, communal world to the "internal" world of the mind. All replies now become individualistic.

In addition, such a shift in locus involves certain consequences that have been extremely detrimental to physical education in its quest to be recognized as an integral part of education. This will become clearer from the discussion in the succeeding sections. For now it is sufficient to note where knowledge is restricted to the individual's internal thought processes, human physical action, executed by the "body," cannot be regarded as a manifestation of knowledge. For Descartes, knowledge must be indubitable, but undubitability cannot be achieved through sense perception; thus, bodily activity cannot yield knowledge nor can human physical action be regarded as an expression of knowledge. Under this thesis, physical education is confronted with insurmountable obstacles in regard to its proper place in the educational spectrum.

Method of Deducing Knowledge

In common with many other philosophers who confront the problem of knowledge, Descartes deals with the issue of scepticism. However, unlike other philosophers who devote their efforts to the refutation of scepticism while elaborating their own epistemology, Descartes adopts what might best be described as a methodological scepticism. His procedure is quite simple and direct: he rejects as being absolutely false everything, all beliefs which he should have the slightest cause to doubt, and then sees if he can eventually find anything which is entirely indubitable (Descartes, 1637/1968, p. 53; 1642/1951, p. 23). The tone and underlying optimism indicate confidence in finding some truth which is indubitable and certain to serve as the base upon which to build the edifice of knowledge.

Such a system of knowledge — the ideal of knowledge — is a systematic, ordered body of propositions dependent one on the other.

Although Descartes is not a sceptic, his initial epistemological position does not include taking any instance of human knowledge for granted. His efforts are devoted to proving that there are examples of human knowledge; for Descartes, knowledge is restricted to what is certain and indubitable. To achieve this goal, his method is to prove to himself that he knows something with a certainty that is able to withstand any conceivable criticism. Success in this endeavour demands careful consideration of the manner in which the proof is obtained and presented should anyone doubt the validity of the claim. Influenced by his training in mathematics, particularly geometry, Descartes believed that if he could find a set of certain statements that could serve as axioms for a deductive system, both consistent and complete, the theorems which could be developed from them would build an irrefutable and uncontestable system of knowledge. The notion of a deductive system is very important, for it eliminates the possibility of error; rational, logical thinking is the only certain way to proceed.

Argument Against Empirical Knowledge

Our senses often deceive us, and so they cannot be trusted as a source of knowledge nor as an avenue through which knowledge is discovered. Descartes' argument against empirical knowledge rests on two grounds. First, it is well known that we sometimes see things which do not exist and that, conversely, we sometimes overlook things which are right in front of us. Equally well known is the fact that our senses deceive us at times; a straight stick will appear bent when part of it is submerged in water. Secondly, we are unable always to tell with absolute certainty whether we are awake or dreaming. There is always room for doubt, and where there is doubt, there is also the possibility of confusion. Impressions from dreams are mixed with reality. If dreams and states of waking are at times confused, how can it ever be known by someone with certainty that he or she is awake, or dreaming, at any given moment? Because there is no way to tell, the result is that no sense experience can serve as the source of knowledge. We can always be wrong about sense experience, meaning that our senses cannot provide the conclusive, irrefutable evidence needed for knowledge.

Proof of Existence

Everything based on sense perception can be doubted, even the existence of one's own body. Descartes is therefore compelled to turn away from sense perception in his search for certainty, but at the very same time, he must still deal with the problem of his existence, both bodily and nonbodily. Denial of the existence of his body is not necessarily the denial of his own existence. The body and the senses are not needed to confirm his own existence; it is confirmed whenever he thinks about the problem. For every time Descartes ponders his existence, he knows for certain that he exists. "I think, therefore I am" is a necessary truth every time the statement is uttered. Where the existence of material things is acknowledged, the existence of a thinking substance, mind, presents no problem. Even if Descartes is deceived into believing that all material things exist, he still must exist, for there must be some existent being which is deceived. He (Descartes, 1642/1951) states,

> There can be no slightest doubt that I exist, since he deceives me; and let him deceive me as much as he will, he can never make me be nothing as long as I think that I am something. Thus, after having thought well on this matter and after examining all things with care, I must finally conclude and maintain that this proposition: *I am, I exist*, is necessarily true every time that I pronounce it or conceive it in my mind. (p. 23)

Under any and all circumstances, as long as Descartes thinks, he exists.

For Descartes, the act of doubting is part of the act of thinking, so every time he doubts, it is further confirmation of his existence. It is also, in a paradoxical way, further proof for the certain and indubitable status of his knowledge claim, "I think, therefore I am," which is the end product of his method of doubt. Certain knowledge of one's existence is the first principle, or axiom, but what Descartes then needs to decide is what precisely the "I" is that exists. "But I do not yet know sufficiently clearly what I am, I who am sure that I exist" (Descartes, 1642/1951, p. 24). In pondering this question, Descartes cannot deviate from his established principle of accepting only that which is entirely certain and indubitable; the only certain and indubitable thing he knows is that he is "a thing which thinks. And what more?...I am not this assemblage which is called a human body" (p. 26). The "I" that exists is not a bodily person but a thinking person who knows through pure "intellection" and not through sensation. To leave no doubt about what the "I" is, Descartes (p. 42) adds, "I understand perfectly that I am a being that thinks and that is not extended."

Differences Between Mind and Body

Mind is defined by Descartes as an unextended substance, an immaterial, thinking thing which does not exist in space but does exist in time. In contrast, *body* is defined as a bounded figure which can be located in some place, occupying space in such a way that every other body is excluded from it; it can be perceived by the five senses. Body is a material, nonthinking, extended substance. Two additional differences distinguish mind from body: (a) mind is known with certainty, for it is a necessary truth that it exists every time I think, but body, which is known through sense perception, is open to doubt — therefore, knowledge of the body cannot be a necessary truth; and (b) body is divisible while mind is indivisible.

Descartes is very clear about mind and body as separate and distinct entities: "And certainly my idea of the human mind, in so far as it is a thinking being, not extended in length, breadth, and depth, and participating in none of the qualities of body, is incomparably more distinct than my idea of anything corporeal" (p. 51). Conversely, it can be stated that the body, as an extended substance, cannot participate in any of the qualities of the mind because the major quality of mind is intellection. It should be noted that the last phrase in the quotation just cited further underscores Descartes' view that the only thing which cannot be doubted is the existence of his own mind.

Minds are characterized by predicates that do not apply to bodies, while bodies are characterized by predicates that do not apply to minds. The distinction is radical: minds and bodies are ontologically different types which are mutually exclusive so much so that Ryle (1949, p. 11) describes a Cartesian person as living through two collateral histories — one consisting of what happens in and to his body, the other consisting of what happens in and to his mind. Events of the body are public because it is an extended, material substance, but events of the mind are private because it is an unextended, immaterial substance. A Cartesian person can be regarded as a composite of two essentially distinct substances, and when we refer in any way to such a person, we are actually referring to one, and sometimes to both, of the separate substances. Strictly speaking, under the Cartesian thesis, whenever I use the personal pronouns "I" or "you" to refer to a person, only one substance — mind — is indicated. But a strict interpretation is possible only on a very abstract level, for in reality, we cannot identify another mind, we can only identify another body. This "unique" situation yields two uses of the term *person*: one sees the person as mind only, and the other more commonly accepted usage sees the person as a combination of mind and body.

According to Descartes two things, mind and body, can be made to exist separately by God.

> From this very fact that I know with certainty that I exist,
> and I find that absolutely nothing else belongs (necessarily)
> to my nature or essence except that I am a thinking being, I

readily conclude that my essense consists solely in being a body which thinks (or a substance) whose whole essence or nature is only to think). And although perhaps, or rather certainly, as I will soon show, I have a body with which I am very closely united, nevertheless, since on the one hand I have a clear and distinct idea of myself so far as *I am only a thinking and not an extended being, and since on the other hand I have a distinct idea of a body in so far as it is only an extended being which does not think, it is certain that this "I" (that is to say, my soul, by virtue of which I am what I am) is entirely (and truly) distinct from my body and that it can (be or) exist without it.* [italics added] (Descartes, 1642/1951, p. 74)

Virtually the same passage appears in the *Discourse on Method* (1637/1968, p. 54) leaving no doubt that for Descartes the "I" is confined to the thinking substance, mind, and that mind and body are separate and distinct entities. If mind can exist without the body, then it is only a contingent fact that I have the body I do have now.

One of the central doctrines of the *Meditations*, if not *the* most important, is the real distinction between mind and body. This is shown by the full title of the work: *Meditations on First Philosophy, in which the Existence of God and the Real Distinction between Mind and Body are Demonstrated.*

Such a radical division and separation of mind and body creates problems with regard to any account for ordinary, everyday bodily occurrences. Descartes (1642/1951, p. 76) feels compelled to modify his stance.

Nature also teaches me by these feelings of pain, hunger, thirst, and so on that I am not only residing in my body as a pilot in his ship, but furthermore, that I am intimately connected with it, and that (the mixture is) so blended, as it were, that (something like) a single whole is produced.

Where Descartes had insisted that mind and body were separate and distinct entities, he now claims that they are intimately connected. At first, he maintains that he is a being whose sole essence is thinking and that the substance which thinks is ontologically different and exclusive from bodily substance. But now it appears that he is modifying his dualistic thesis when he argues that sensations and images can only arise in the mind through its union with a material body. While it is reasonable to believe that sensations do arise in the body, serious, insurmountable problems still remain regarding how two such disparate substances, mind and body, which are irreducible to each other, can become intimately connected.

Even on the assumption that answers to the problem just cited can be provided — and to date this has not happened — from the epistemological perspective of physical education and education, nothing changes. According to Descartes, the pure intellect of the mind gains knowledge by reflection upon itself in the case of intellectual imagination to add to its store of knowledge. Descartes' epistemological position is that there is no conceptual connection between any thought, or mental occurrence, and any physical occurrence. Even if there were some conceptual connection, no knowledge would be produced because bodily sensations can always be doubted, and imagination can surely conjure up inexistent or false images. Only the intellect, reflecting upon itself in its close association with God, can produce knowledge. For Descartes, it is the business of the mind alone, and not of the mind and body, to decide the truth of all matters where there may be some doubt.

Three specific features of the Cartesian view are identified by Langford (1977, p. 66): (a) mind and body are exclusive kinds of things; (b) being a mind or body is a yes/no kind of thing; and (c) the mind, as characterized by privacy, is thought of in highly individualistic, nonsocial terms. These features provide the specific context for the analysis which will show that holding a Cartesian view of man is inimical to both the notion of physical education as well as to the notion of education.

The Incompatibility of Physical Education and Education With Cartesian Philosophy

Education of the Physical

Physical education, as education of the physical with its emphasis on the training and development of the body, including the acquisition of motor skills, gives the impression that no thinking is needed, that there is no mental involvement. The very claim that there can be such a thing as education of the physical is open to the charge of being unintelligible when discussed within a Cartesian conception of man. Under that thesis, physical is contrasted with mental to show the difference between the two and it is only the mental, the thinking component, which can be educated. Physical substances, by their very nature, are not the sorts of things which can think, and so it follows that a Cartesian body, a physical substance, cannot be educated. True, the muscles of the body can be strengthened to delay the onset of fatigue and enhance health and can be trained to perform a myriad of tasks more efficiently, such as the most complex motor skills; but that training cannot be construed as education because truths are not transmitted. Minds, thinking things, can be educated, but nonthinking things, such as bodies, cannot.

What may, at first sight, appear to be physical education turns out to be something which cannot be called education because that which is to be educated is an uneducable physical substance. Or, if one insists on calling it education, it would have to be under a special definition of that term, one devoid of epistemological connotation. Our ordinary understanding of the term *education* includes the transmission of knowledge; but that understanding is inappropriate when applied to a Cartesian body, for the body is a substance which cannot incorporate into itself such a thing as knowledge. The conception of physical education as education *of* the physical is, therefore, completely incompatible with a Cartesian conception of man because the very idea of knowledge is ruled out.

Education Through the Physical

Replacing the conception of physical education as education of the physical with its successor, physical education as education through the physical appears to eliminate the problems encountered by the former conception. Implicit in the latter view is the belief that physical education contributes to the social, psychological, physical, and intellectual development of the individual. In effect, it is the mind that is educated through the education of the body during vigorous physical activity. Claiming that it is the mind that is being educated appears to be perfectly compatible with Descartes' theory, but even this claim encounters a number of very serious difficulties.

In the Cartesian view, what is essential to the mind is its ability to reflect on its own activity in thinking; therefore, it needs no stimulation or input from external sources. Thus, it can be a mind and know that it is and what it is without knowing anything at all about the physical world or other minds. Knowledge is developed deductively from the first axioms or principles which were discovered without resorting to sensory experiences or information garnered from the external world. True knowledge comes about as a result of developing further theorems from the initial axioms. Consequently, external events in the form of instruction, whether in reference to physical activity or mental activity are both superfluous and redundant.

Difficulties in Mentally Educating the Cartesian Mind

Another consequence arises from the notion that the Cartesian mind is essentially complete as a mind. Acquiring a new or improved body, improving various motor skills, gaining knowledge of the external world,

172

or entering into social relationships makes no essential difference to the mind. These experiences may affect the modes of consciousness or perhaps even the content of the mind, but logically, they cannot alter the essence of the mind which is essentially complete at all times. One cannot even state that the mind was complete at birth because it could well have existed as a complete mind well before birth. A Cartesian mind can exist in the bodies of various and sundry other people, past and present. Wherever and whenever a Cartesian mind exists, it is essentially complete as a mind. Our concept of education, however, always implies changes of a fundamental or nontrivial kind. Education changes the kind of person one is, making one, in a sense, a different person. One is simply not the very same person about whom certain things happen to be true; the Cartesian view of mind is not amenable to change of this kind. It is not, therefore, possible to educate the person (here person is used in the strict Cartesian sense as referring only to the mind) because the person, in being a mind, is a complete whole from the start.

A further difficulty confounds the idea of educating a Cartesian mind which stems from the view that the concept of education is above all a social process involving teachers and students. No matter how narrowly or how broadly education is defined, one basic, essential element must be present: there must be a "meeting of minds." According to Descartes' description and definition of mind, mental happenings (which would be the process and products of education) occur in insulated fields known as minds. Ryle (1977) notes the consequences:

> There is, apart maybe from telepathy, no direct causal connection between what happens in one mind and what happens in another. Only through the medium of the public physical world can the mind of one person make a difference to the mind of another. The mind is its own place and in his inner life each of us lives the life of a ghostly Robinson Crusoe. People can see, hear and jolt one another's bodies, but they are irremediably blind and deaf to the workings of one another's mind and inoperative upon them. (p. 13)

By describing mind as an immaterial, unextended substance, Descartes created a situation where there is no way to identify mind. Intersubjectivity becomes impossible. We have no way of knowing that other minds exist, and so it follows that no "meeting of minds" is possible. Without this meeting, we must conclude that even the Cartesian mind cannot be educated.

II. Concepts and Fundamentals

From an epistemological perspective, one additional issue needs to be raised regarding the Cartesian mind and its source of knowledge. Epistemological analysis is not only concerned with analyzing the nature and validity of our present knowledge, but is also concerned with examining our sources of knowledge. Frequently, the analysis of our present knowledge cannot be undertaken without first exploring the source.

A Cartesian mind is complete in itself; it learns all it needs to know about itself from itself, or from God, and confirms its knowledge either on the basis of rational logic or on an appeal to the infallibility and honesty of God. While such knowledge may be valid, its source is forever hidden behind an impenetrable wall. By placing the source of our knowledge beyond the reach of ordinary mortal epistemological analysis, Descartes compels us to accept on the basis of pure faith. Acceptance on the basis of pure faith either precludes the need for epistemological analysis, or else limits the scope so severely that very few philosophers would be attracted to such an enterprise.

Conclusion

Our analysis has shown that a Cartesian person cannot be educated physically nor can such a person be educated mentally. A Cartesian mind, in being complete as a mind right from the start, does not require external stimuli for its intellectual development, nor can it trust bodily sensations as a source of knowledge because there always exists the possibility that our senses will deceive us. Knowledge cannot be gained through or from physical activity. Acceptance of a Cartesian conception of man renders the term *physical education* under both the education of and education through the physical interpretations, meaningless. Further, acceptance of a Cartesian conception of man also precludes the possibility of elaborating an epistemology of human action, where such an epistemology would explicate the knowledge that an agent has in performing the action. Such knowledge cannot be transformed into propositional statements. We can point to the knowledge and tell many things about it, but the exact, specific knowledge is only demonstrated in the action itself. This form of knowledge is of direct interest to physical education, but to date, it has not commanded the attention of physical education philosophers who, almost totally, have neglected epistemology.

Neither has much effort been devoted in the physical education literature to the mind-body problem and the theory of persons. One interpretation of the Cartesian thesis sees a person as a composite of two distinct entities, a mind and a body. By positing the existence of these two distinct and different sorts of entities, Descartes provides the ingredients for the concept of a person, but this does not, by itself,

174

provide an account of the concept of a person as such. The ingredients are there but the problem of the relationships between such disparate components still has not been solved. If we keep the components separate, we could then go on to say that a person consists of two parts, a mind and a body, and so education of the whole person would simply require educating both parts. Success in this educational venture would result in, as the familiar saying has it, a sound mind in a healthy body. But we have just seen that the Cartesian body is not the sort of thing which can be educated and, for various other reasons, neither can the Cartesian mind be educated. Because both components of the Cartesian conception of man do not appear to be educable, the concept of education of the whole man is inapplicable to a Cartesian conception of man.

For physical education to merit consideration as an educational endeavour, an alternate model of man is required. Within the theory of persons there are four possible options: (a) a combination of two separate entities, mind and body, such as described by Descartes; (b) mind only, such as described by Berkeley (Armstrong, 1710/1965); (c) body only, such as described by materialist and physicalist theories; and (d) an integrated, unified entity. We have seen that the first option is not viable for physical education (nor for education) from both an epistemological and educational perspective. The second option is a philosophical position no longer seriously considered, but if it were a viable option, the notion of physical education would obviously be unintelligible.

While the third option appears to be very attractive for physical education, it has great difficulties in accounting for the "self," and without a self, we have no way of distinguishing mere bodily movement from action. Of greater consequence is the fact that without a self there can be no learning, hence no knowing and so, once again, the notion of education is destroyed. We are left with one final possibility — man as an integrated, unified entity, a model that is consonant with the notion that education is of the whole man. Enunciating and elaborating a theory of an integrated, unified person is a challenge that should rank as a very high priority with philosophers of physical education.

Under an integrated, unified model of man, physical education is not education *of* the physical nor is it education (of the mind) *through* the physical: It is education of the person. Whenever such a person engages in action, both decisions and judgments are involved. Decisions made and judgments rendered presuppose concepts; hence, a person's actions are always conceptual in nature, or thought-impregnated. This is the knowledge that is of concern to physical education, a wide-ranging, infinite variety of nonpropositional concepts, knowledge that is in the action. Because epistemologists have devoted almost all of their efforts to describing and analyzing propositional knowledge, it now becomes the task of philosophers of physical education to render an account of the

175

II. Concepts and Fundamentals

knowledge that is pertinent to their domain — physical action knowledge.

References

Armstrong, D.M. (1965). "Introduction." In G. Berkeley (Ed.), *Berkeley's Philosophical Writings*. (pp. 7-34) New York, NY: Collier Books. (Original work published 1710)

Descartes, R. (1968). *Discourse on method and the meditations*. Translated with an introduction by F.E. Sutcliffe, Penguin Books. (Original work published 1637)

Descartes, R. (1951). *Meditations on first philosophy*. Translated with an introduction by L.J. Lafleur. Indianapolis, IN: Bobbs-Merrill. (Original work published 1642)

Langford, G. (1977). "Education is of the whole man." *Journal of Philosophy of Education*, 13, 65-72.

McCloy, C.H. (1936). "How about some muscle?" *The Journal of Health and Physical Education*, 7(5), 302-303, 355.

Ryle, G. (1949). *The concept of mind*. New York: Barnes & Noble Books.

Weston, A. (1962). *The making of American physical education*. New York: Appleton-Century-Crofts.

Williams, J.F. (1930a). "A fundamental point of view in physical education." *The Journal of Health and Physical Education*, 1(1), 10-11, 60.

Williams, J.F. (1930b). "Education through the physical." *Journal of Higher Education*, 1(5), 279-282.

COLLEGE SPORTS REFORM:
WHERE ARE THE FACULTY?

JOHN C. WEISTART

Many surprising things have been revealed in the recent college sports scandals. But one of the most surprising is the historical absence of effective faculty oversight of the educational experiences of student athletes in big-time college programs. Among the revelations that point to a failure of faculty governance in these matters, the most embarrassing must surely be the dismal graduation rates of athletes in several basketball and football programs. Reports in the popular press indicate that four percent of black basketball players graduated at the University of Georgia in a recent period. At one Big Ten school, the graduation rate for all basketball players was nine percent. At Memphis State, the NAACP — and not the faculty, it might be noted — discovered that in a ten-year period, no black basketball player graduated. The list goes on and covers twenty or more schools that should have been embarrassed.

The troublesome question remains: where were the faculties? In almost all instances, the low graduation rates were accumulated over a period of time. While each individual campus yields a different story, available evidence suggests a common and consistent failure on the part of faculties to pick up available signals that things were awry in their revenue-producing sports programs.

A significant commentary on the present state of athletics and higher education can be found in the manner in which improprieties are revealed. The moving force is much more likely to be a newspaper reporter than a concerned faculty member. Indeed, in two of the past three years, Pulitzer Prizes were awarded to reporters who in effect told university communities how their athletic programs were being run.

The faculty, of course, is not the only entity on campus that should be concerned about serious misdirections in the athletic program. The president and, as we have recently seen, the board of trustees often share responsibility. But faculties have a particularly important role to play in shaping a school's academic program and, most importantly, in ensuring its integrity. In most universities, the faculty's responsibility for defining the institution's educational mission is explicit. Faculties frequently are quick to indicate the primacy of their role in preserving the rigour and legitimacy of the school's other academic pursuits. Moreover, because it is relatively unaffected by the pragmatic demands of day-to-day administration, the faculty properly serves as the conscience of the university, especially in matters that affect an issue as basic as the institution's academic reputation. As a number of universities have learned, the misdeeds of the athletic department can have a great effect in shaping public perceptions on such matters. Hence, the question remains: where were the faculties?

The recent sports scandals suggest at least two significant issues relating to the faculty's role in athletics. First, why did not faculties assume a greater oversight role over the deteriorating conditions of big-time sports? And second, can we expect a better faculty performance in the future? Virtually every school that has experienced a significant sports controversy has subsequently undertaken a major internal review. Typically, the resulting report promises more careful control for the future, often with significant input from the faculty. But we must ask whether, once the warm winds of scandal have passed, faculties will do better than they historically have.

One view of the role of faculty governance in athletics offers little reason for optimism over the long term. A variety of factors, including the highly commercial nature of athletics, work against an effective governance function by faculty members. There is little evidence that universities are prepared to change this business orientation in athletics. Thus, the persistent tension with the university's educational goals is likely to continue. This raises the prospect of a regulatory role for the faculty that is extremely time consuming and that holds limited prospects of success.

A more fruitful alternative for faculties would be to urge that the basic structure of college sports be reoriented to reduce its conflict with the university's educational goals. Two changes offer particular promise. One involves eliminating the present university monopoly on preprofessional training in football and basketball. By providing the exclusive training for aspiring athletes, universities assume a social role that inevitably places great downward pressures on academic standards. A second change would end the Athletics Arms Race, as Harry Edwards aptly calls it. At present, college athletics operates according to an arrangement in which the rewards of athletic success go to those who spend the most and demand the least academically.

Faculties interested in ending this economic and academic pressure would seek to implement changes that rewarded the athletically successful with recognition, but broadly disbursed the revenues from broadcasting, tournaments, and bowl games.

The fact of the faculty's limited oversight of the academic performance of the athletic department is not much in doubt. Less clear are the reasons why faculties choose not to be involved in matters that have turned out to hold such a great capacity for institutional embarrassment.

Faculties at many universities can properly argue that their athletic departments have been organized purposely to operate at great distance from the normal channels of faculty governance. In some instances — the University of Georgia, for example — the athletic association is a legally distinct entity and the faculty has no juridical claim to regulate its affairs. Even when the athletic department is "part of the university," autonomy may be *de facto*. Not infrequently this happens when a powerful coach insists, and a less forceful president agrees, that the supervision of athletes will remain with athletic personnel. Thus, unlike many other issues of academic policy, the special problems of athletes would not normally come before the faculty.

Ultimately, though, explanations based on internal governance structure are only partial ones. It is often unclear whether the autonomy of an athletic program is the cause or the effect of limited faculty oversight. As many of the recent in-house reform efforts confirm, when faculty assert a strong interest in the treatment and achievement of student athletics, structures can be found to accommodate this concern. Thus, it is likely that there are other, more substantive reasons why faculties have tolerated the considerable distance that many athletic programs have put between themselves and their universities' core academic function.

A search for alternative explanations suggests several points that warrant attention.

The different nature of a major athletics enterprise. Big-time athletics — again mainly football and basketball — have taken on a distinctive characteristic in recent years. At many schools, the athletic department operates as the entertainment division of the university. Largely as a result of the impact of television, big-time programs now produce events that compete with a variety of other offerings in the entertainment market. Increasingly, decisions are made with a view to ensuring the suitability of the end product for broadcast purposes.

Most of the large football and basketball programs operate at a substantial profit, largely due to the impact of television. A trip to the Final Four in the National Collegiate Athletic Association basketball tournament pays each participating school over one million dollars, an amount greatly in excess of the operating expenses of the typical program. When revenues from the conference television package, national telecasts, and ticket sales are added, a three to one ratio of revenues to expenses is not uncommon in basketball. In football, with postseason bowls paying out a total of more than fifty-six million dollars, profits of two to four million dollars in a single program are often attained.

Such levels of profitability are not assured, of course, and continued success requires very astute, very pragmatic decisions about a variety of entertainment-related issues, including how to increase the size of the regular season television audience and how to select opponents so as to attract the attention of the bowls with the most lucrative broadcast contracts. Not surprisingly the entire orientation of the athletic department adjusts to accommodate the demands of producing a successful — that is, profitable — entertainment product. For the people who run the division, a strong business orientation is a necessity. Increasingly success within the profession of athletic administration is judged primarily, although not exclusively, by the dollar results an individual produces.

This athletics-entertainment venture is carried on in an environment that is unusually competitive. College athletics stands in sharp contrast to professional sports in this regard. Revenue-sharing and financial support for weak competitors are the hallmarks of successful sports leagues. The worst NFL team gets as much from the league's lucrative national television contract as does the best. Quite the opposite situation is found at the college level. The greatest rewards from television go only to the most successful programs. These are typically the programs prepared to pay the most for recruiting, facilities, coaches' salaries, and promotion. And the most successful teams have the most to spend. The operative principle seems to be that a school must spend to win and must win to spend. Each new lucrative broadcast arrangement ups the ante and invites an expensive response.

The values important in these ventures are quite different from those that typically come into play in faculty governance decisions. Faculties are not terribly "bottom-line" oriented and have little experience in ensuring commercial success in highly competitive markets. Indeed, the best of faculty values — deliberateness, a liberal concern for the treatment of individuals, and an openness that encourages the accommodation of differences — are antithetical to the common ingredients of profitable business ventures.

Athletic personnel may thus come to feel that faculties have little to say about athletic policy that will be useful. For their part, faculties may have a natural reluctance to venture into areas where they will be neither welcome nor particularly effective. In the same vein, the trustees and presidents who determine organizational structure often take account of the lack of synergy in this match and develop lines of authority that ensure that it does not occur. There is little to suggest to them that the success of the entertainment product will be enhanced by the opposite arrangement.

The risk of being co-opted. A second problem is that faculties involved in athletic policy making appear to run a particular risk of being co-opted into a lenient, if not overly favourable, view of the demands of the athletic department. While this is hardly inevitable, it does occur with sufficient regularity to suggest that a truly independent faculty governance role in athletics may be very difficult to achieve.

Various devices presently in use are intended to preserve a role for the faculty in athletics matters. Each NCAA school has a "faculty representative," for example. Rarely, though, is this position reflective of carefully gauged faculty sentiment. Direct election of the "faculty representative" by the faculty is rare if not nonexistent in big-time programs. More typical is the situation in which the person is designated by the university president after informal approval by the athletic department. Seldom are NCAA votes subject to systematic faculty review. For all of these reasons the faculty voice in NCAA matters has historically been neither loud nor distinctive.

Many schools have an athletic committee or similar entity that provides the occasion for faculty involvement in deliberations on athletically related issues. Again, at big-time schools, the faculty participation on these bodies has not been noted for its independence. Indeed, such bodies existed at most of the schools that have experienced major scandals in recent years.

The loss of independence by faculty members involved in athletic oversight is difficult to avoid. As already noted, "ensuring athletic success" is often the stated goal of committees involved in this work and in the modern environment that means heeding the demands of an external marketplace. Athletic department personnel will consistently speak more authoritatively on these matters.

Other features of work on athletic committees present temptations not found elsewhere in university service. Offers of favourable seating at popular events, school-paid trips to postseason contests, and the opportunity to rub elbows with celebrity coaches and players will inevitably have the effect of reducing criticism and encouraging accommodation. This will be true even when these special rewards for committee service are wholly benign. Combining this bit of human nature with a selection process that favours candidates who have a sympathetic orientation to the athletic department, the mildness of the regulation undertaken by university athletic committees is not surprising.

The modest professional rewards for effective oversight. Few incentives encourage a faculty member to engage in rigorous examination of athletic department policy. A promising career in English, physics, or geology is not likely to be advanced by correcting the defects of a big-time sports program that enjoys wide support on and off campus. Moreover, the task will seldom be either easy or abbreviated. In short, the absence of professional rewards for university service in the oversight of athletics, the athletic department's coolness to such a role, and the strong incentives to mind one's own business in academia combine to discourage vigorous faculty involvement in reviewing athletic department policy. Indeed, for those who are most promising in their academic endeavors, probing the athletic department may be among the least appealing of administrative assignments.

Almost all of the schools beset by major scandals in recent years have undertaken elaborate self-studies. The end result is typically a thorough report and a list of recommendations addressing a variety of reforms. Increased academic standards for athletes and closer institutional oversight of the athletic policy are commonly urged. The question can reasonably be asked whether these reform efforts provide reason for optimism about the future, either in terms of more effective faculty involvement in athletic matters or in terms of other institutional controls to prevent a recurrence of the problems of the past.

There will certainly be some short-term improvements. Almost every school that has looked at its athletic problems has agreed that standards should be raised for the admission of athletes and that the embarrassing graduation rates of the past should not continue. Moreover, in several schools, the individuals responsible for prior academic misdirections were unmasked and their associations with the university ended. And, in almost all cases, the mechanisms for institutional control were strengthened.

But serious problems are likely to remain. A review of the recent internal reform efforts will reveal that, despite the wide array of matters subjected to reconsideration, little or nothing has been done to address the fundamental cause of the recent scandals — the competitive pressures created by commercialization. Virtually every school that has endured severe academic embarrassment has emerged from its self-study continuing to embrace implicitly, if not explicitly, the notion that its athletic programs will be "competitive." In the present environment, this means that the cycle of spending to win and winning to spend will continue.

If the evidence of the recent past is taken as a guide, such an orientation will present a considerable threat to the goals of academic rigor and integrity. Even where academic standards for the athletic department have been raised, the new standards are likely to be subjected to considerable downward pressures. As several schools have already learned, there will almost always be competitors willing to admit less-qualified athletes. Thus, a pledge to remain competitive commits a school to a course in which the determinants of success are frequently being influenced by the preferences of the lowest common denominator.

The decision to stay in the athletics arms race also means that the basic entertainment orientation of the athletic department is not likely to change. It can be hoped that personnel antagonistic to the academic function of the university will be eliminated and that more attention will be given to the athletes' classroom endeavors. But at the bottom line is a bottom line. Even allowing for the many good athletic directors who will execute their functions as their universities dictate, we should not be surprised to find that difficulties of the past reappear. With two-million-dollar bowl games and one-million-dollar basketball tournaments at stake, there will be great pressure to shave off the subtle edges of academic preparedness and substantive achievement. Again, over time some athletic departments will likely conclude that academic minimalism enhances their ability to compete.

Just as the basic orientation of the athletic department is unlikely to change, so are incentives for faculties to become involved in a sustained effort at oversight unlikely to increase. The faculty will continue to be ill-equipped to evaluate claims of necessity in a profit-oriented venture. As in the past, the faculty is apt to find itself deferring to the judgments of those who are more knowledgeable and who have more at stake. In addition, the occasions for reducing faculty independence will persist. And ultimately, the same low level of professional reward that has been evident in the past will attend future efforts at oversight, particularly as recent embarrassments fade. Thus, while things have changed, they have in many respects remained the same.

The time has come to reconsider the agenda for college sports reform. To date, the prevailing assumption has been that what is needed is mainly a tightening of the rules. By and large, the basic structure of big-time sports is left unaffected. These features seem inevitably to lead to a more time-consuming regulatory role.

A more positive approach would seek to modify the structural features of big-time sports that create undue pressures for the academic program. Rather than seeking to increase the degree of control that has to be exercised by faculties and others, this different agenda would undertake to reduce the need for intense oversight. Reform would be undertaken with the specific intention of introducing economic forces more naturally complementary to the university's goals.

In redirecting the present debate, attention should be given not only to the substance of proposals for change but also to the matter of how change will be achieved. Any internal, single-campus reform is destined to be ineffective in stemming the influences of commercialization in college sports. For a school that plans to operate a visible program, unilateral disarmament simply will not work. As noted, the intensity of the economic competition and the tools necessary to engage in it will in large measure be dictated by forces beyond the individual campus. Thus, if truly effective reform is to occur, it must be in a different forum, specifically one that has authority to impose collective controls. Several alternatives are available.

The NCAA is the logical group to provide the necessary legislative response. However, despite four years of repeated scandals, the NCAA has taken little action. The movement of this body has been so halting as to raise doubts about its basic resolves. While there is no particular reason to assume that the NCAA will take a new direction, the matter of resolve is one that can be affected by the actions of the constituent members. Thus, an appropriate first step for a concerned faculty would be to assert a more active interest in how their institution's votes on NCAA matters are cast.

But the NCAA is not the only forum available. In the event of continued inaction by that group, other outlets for concern will become increasingly attractive. An enhanced role for education accrediting organizations is properly explored. Most of these groups presently have authority to review the academic performance of any component of the university, including the athletic department. Much could be done to increase their role. A clear statement of academic standards, meaningful reporting of academic statistics, and the threat of suspension of accreditation offer the promise of an alternative that avoids the limitations of unilateral action.

Perhaps the ultimate forum for collective action is Congress. While college sports have historically enjoyed something approaching legislative immunity, this situation may be changing. In recent years, various bills have been introduced to address the ills of college sports. A continued failure of self-regulation by the NCAA increases the plausibility of this type of response. And the antimonopoly fervor in Congress in recent years suggests that such legislation might well take a different view of the economic ground rules of preprofessional sports than does the NCAA.

The issue of where further deliberation should occur is a procedural one. On the substantive side, the focus should shift from debates about merely tightening existing rules to a discussion of changing the basic structure of college sports. Two areas in particular offer the prospect of relieving the university's educational venture from much of the pressure that athletics presently creates.

First, the athletics arms race is not inevitable. A range of choices is in fact available that will ameliorate or eliminate it. Revenue sharing would offer the most complete tempering of the inclination toward commercial excess in individual programs, a lesson well learned by professional sports leagues. Schools would still receive the public recognition that attends success in championship events. But there would be no disproportionate financial bonanza for that outcome. Television rights, fees, and the like would be distributed among a wide

184

group of participants, perhaps all who participate at a particular level of play.

The basic objective of a revenue-sharing arrangement would be to eliminate the pressures for bending academic and athletic rules that arise in the present environment. As occasional ups and downs in programs would carry no particular toll, most of the recent by-words — "win at any cost," "eligibility rather than real education," and the like — would lose their justification. Winning would, of course, still be important. But other values would become much more ready competitors because financial outcomes would have been made independent.

While revenue sharing is an anathema to many athletic administrators, those who take a broader view of university budgets may find it quite attractive. The vast majority of schools offering major sports programs would be better off under such an arrangement, for it offers the unavoidably attractive prospect of both enhancing revenues and reducing expenses. In addition, it promises a stability for the future that cannot be assured in the present environment, in which only winners are rewarded.

If control is not exercised over revenues, then the next logical step is the control of expenditures. In this area, further reform could simply involve an undertaking to execute more effectively a regulatory effort that presently receives only half-hearted attention. The NCAA has a number of rules ostensibly intended to equalize the competitive positions of a large range of schools. Thus, there are limits on the size of team rosters, the size of coaching staffs, and the permissible number of athletic scholarships. But to legislate parity only on these matters is almost certain to be ineffective as a control on competition. No spending controls presently exist for many other items that contribute to a school's competitive position. These include training and playing facilities, promotional expenses, salaries, student housing, and a long list of other items. Not surprisingly, with only a part of the expenditure budget subjected to regulation, the pursuit of competitive advantage finds ample alternative avenues through which to express itself. The incompleteness of the present economic regulation invites a corrective response in the form of more extensive budgetary controls.

A second structural issue warrants attention. At the present, a rather unnatural link exists between academics and athletics at the post-high-school level. A promising high school basketball or football player who wishes to secure further training effectively has no choice but to aspire to a four-year degree program. Moreover, the athlete must be a full-time student; part-time status is insufficient for eligibility. Other program options — community college, technical school, corporate sponsored teams, and minor leagues — are unavailable. In what must surely be one of the great non sequiturs of our society, we tell promising athletes in the two most popular high school sports that to get further

II. Concepts and Fundamentals

physical training they must also embrace our most advanced form of post-high-school degree.

Thus, 100 percent of football and basketball players are required to choose an arrangement that only roughly 30 percent of their nonathlete peers select. Moreover, this limitation is not imposed on other aspiring athletes. Those interested in baseball, hockey, golf, and tennis all enjoy sports options not tied to education, let alone a full-time four-year education.

The contrived nature of the present structure should be a particular concern of faculties. A good deal of available evidence — including the experience of baseball players who can choose between college and minor leagues — suggests that perhaps as many as one-half of present college athletes in football and basketball would not choose the collegiate option if good alternatives were available. Thus, educationally it appears that we may be forcing square pegs into round holes. At the minimum, many of the athletes are likely to have their attention focused elsewhere.

Colleges, of course, cannot be expected to bear the full burden of establishing noncollegiate options. But that does not mean that universities and their faculties are powerless to influence the present monopoly. In fact, universities have done much to perpetuate the existing arrangement. Faculties that wished to be relieved of the tensions created by the present compulsory relationships would seek to modify the NCAA rules that sustain them.

A variety of changes could be considered. The mildest alternatives would change existing rules on eligibility. At present, the NCAA embraces an extremely narrow view of amateurism. For the mere receipt of fifty dollars in compensation money, even for an appearance in a perfectly legitimate competition, a young athlete can be denied collegiate eligibility. In a world in which educational values come first, the goal would be quite different: athletes would be encouraged to test their semiprofessional and minor league opportunities before deciding on whether to go to college. An exploratory period of perhaps two years would be allowed. Those who later enrolled in a university presumably would have a more focused interest in the educational opportunity that was available. By the same token, since the university would no longer be the exclusive vehicle for post-high-school athletic training, it could reasonably demand that its athletes approximate the educational achievement of other students.

This article can end where it began, with a reference to the shockingly low graduation rates achieved in several big-time athletic programs. It is difficult to imagine that a faculty at a serious university would tolerate the continuation of an academic program in which, for every student who graduated, nine others did not. Yet, in several athletic programs these levels of failure, and some even worse, were endured.

We would be reassured if we could believe that these institutional lapses were only inadvertent or temporary. However, the frequency of their occurrence and the presence of very powerful economic forces that reward low academic aspiration suggest that the causes are much more basic. Something other than a mere lack of attentiveness appears to be involved. This awareness counsels in favour of a greater boldness in the debate on college athletics than we have seen to date.

Specifically, the time has come to ask whether it is athletic success that is valued or the large dollars that increasingly attend it. The former has a role that can be comfortably accommodated at a university. Profit making, particularly as a part of an intense competitive market, fits much less well. The opportunity to separate athletics from excess does exist. Whether it is pursued is a matter over which the entities with the most at stake — the universities themselves — have considerable control.

SEMI-PROFESSIONALISM IN SPORT: WHY NOT?

EARLE F. ZEIGLER

In North America over the years we have developed anywhere from 35 to 100 different definitions of an amateur — but none of a semi-professional! This is why any attempt to define an amateur in sport correctly will soon bring you to a state where you begin to wonder why you ever got involved. Traditionally our brethren in the amateur organizations have described the amateur — this "vanishing Canadian" — as follows:

> An amateur sportsperson is one who engages in sport solely for the pleasure and physical, mental, or moral benefits to be derived therefrom and to whom sport is nothing more than an avocation.

(Try telling that definition to some of today's Olympic athletes!)

Even a dictionary's innocuous statement that "an amateur is one who is not rated as a professional" leaves you high and dry. It helps a bit if you read further and learn that "a professional is one, generally, who has competed in athletics for a stake or purse, or gate money, or with a professional for a prize, or who has taught or trained in athletics for pay."

Finally — in desperation — you may agree that Paul Gallico had good insight when he stated many years ago, "An amateur is a guy (gal?) who won't take a check!" Nowadays, however, even this formerly sage remark is a bit outdated. The international athlete may simply reply, "Please make it out to my trust fund."

Just What Is an Amateur?

Some go as far as to say that there are no more amateurs — at any level. This is not true. There are — and I hope there always will be — amateurs as defined in the traditional Amateur Athletic Union definition above. However, it is my hope that people like us will bring pressure to bear so that all will agree that the amateur is the *beginner* in *any* sphere of activity — including sport. For example, when a young man or woman just learning the game of golf turns in a score of 125 for eighteen holes, he or she is indeed *an amateur* — a beginner or duffer in the game of golf.

This agrees with the original meaning of the term "amateur" as "one who cultivates any art or pursuit for the enjoyment of it...sometimes implying desultory action or crude results." The amateur simply lacks the talent or polish of the semi-professional or the professional

From Amateurism to Semi-professionalism

If we think of the amateur as the beginner, the novice, the duffer (if you will), we might therefore argue that only high school or middle school athletes are still amateur — and some college or university performers too. It would not be wrong to state, however, that semi-professionalism of a type is creeping into many programs at this level. For certain overly emphasized high school programs, this statement holds true in the U.S., whereas we have relatively recently begun to see the development of this mentality at some universities in Canada.

It is true that today's highly competitive sport demands long, hard practice to reach the level of perfection necessary for winning records. Thus, we must continually ask ourselves how far we should let this trend go — this pursuit of excellence — especially in educational circles where boys and girls, and young men and women, are there to get an education and need so many other valuable experiences as well (like learning to read, write and cipher).

Let me say quickly that I have no quarrel with a young person striving for excellence in competitive sport on a semi-professional or professional basis. Why should anyone? After all, sport is a legitimate aspect of our culture. What I do get upset about, however, is what we permit to happen to a lot of boys and young men in Canadian hockey, for example, or what has happened to a very large extent with young men (and now young women too) in U.S. university sport — and so often for underprivileged youngsters too. This is why I am so worried that this "cancer" will continue to spread north of the border.

Canada has Done Quite Well Until Now

High school teacher/coaches in Canada can, by and large, take a bow for preserving athletics of an educational nature in their programs for both young men and women. Undoubtedly there has been much support from principals and superintendents too. Now I trust that university and college presidents and deans will show as much sense — that they won't be unduly swayed by a federal government determined to use the universities as training grounds for international elite sport. In the final analysis, it will take wise judgment on the part of enlightened parents, alumni and community leaders — and those who are administering and

189

coaching — to help athletics serve the best and highest educational purpose.

The Concept of the 'Semi-professional'

It would help further if much of the sham and hypocrisy could be removed from competitive sport. In other fields, the field of music for example, the problem of amateurism, semi-professionalism, and professionalism has been resolved quite nicely. The person who plays the trumpet in the high school band is an *amateur*. If he or she is good enough to play with some group regularly on weekends for fifty dollars a night, then we can agree that *semi-professionalism* has been achieved. Who would be critical of this? Finally, this person might eventually choose to become a professional musician or music teacher as a lifetime occupation. At this point the individual really is a *professional* because his or her entire living will come from this source.

Such a graduated scheme has been viewed for a long time as quite acceptable in our society for musicians, artists, sculptors, actors and many others — but not for athletes! Why are athletes so different when it comes to involvement either within education circles or on national- and international-level teams? Granted there have been several break-throughs in isolated instances (e.g., trust funds for downhill skiers), but this has been accompanied by a lot of smirking and/or grimacing by die-hard purists.

A young athlete who takes money, or something else of intrinsic worth, may find that he or she is barred from so-called amateur athletics (although there are instances regularly where some "dirty pros" achieve "pure" amateur status again). There are still a great many people who believe that men and women athletes should not be permitted to accept *any* monetary return to support their efforts — but they wouldn't think of insisting upon this for young people in other areas of cultural endeavour. (Horrors! I am suggesting that sport is indeed an area of *cultural* endeavour!)

How Sport Became Singled Out

How did all of this come about historically? I am referring to the idea that an amateur athlete who takes anything other than a varsity letter sweater for playing a favorite sport is a *professional*. Somehow in our background, the snobbish elitists in the late 1800s didn't want the "butcher boy from the other side of the tracks" imported to make a stronger team for the annual sporting competition of some upper-class group of sportsmen. This attitude has resulted in what is now a hoary tradition in Olympic competition, and it is akin to moving heaven and earth to (oh so) slowly bring about any significant change.

Even well-intentioned provincial and state athletic associations tend to go overboard on this subject. However, we have finally outgrown the castigations and imposition of penalties that used to be meted out to university varsity swimmers who got paid during the summer for coaching younger swimmers at country clubs or municipal pools. Further, college baseball players have typically had to be careful as to which league they played in over the summer holidays. Finally, the ghost of Jim Thorpe is able to rest because Jim's withdrawn Olympic medals have now been returned to the bosom of the Thorpe clan. (You remember those gold medals that were stripped from Jim because he accepted money for playing summer baseball.)

Let's Make 'Semi-professional' Official

One answer to this long-standing impasse would be the official creation of a category designated as the *semi-professional*. To be a bit facetious, I suppose we could argue that the National Collegiate Athletic Association in the States did just that a number of years ago. Only they called it the *scholar-athlete*, and with certain carefully defined — but often broken — stipulations they allow such a person to receive an athletic tender or scholarship. Of course, they can now take it away at the end of a semester (for example) if the athlete "looks cross-eyed" at the coach or is injured. (And now — woe is us! — Canada is flirting with this idea too. However, we think that we can learn from the mistakes of the States and do it right — ha! ha!).

Technically, if the officials enforced the law and the spirit of the Olympic oath that the athletes all take, a great many young men and women would be barred from participating. I suppose the same thing could be said for our carded athletes in Canada. Recently, however, even professional hockey players are "released" so that they can now play in Olympic competition. ("Avery Brundage, please stop turning so rapidly in your grave!") However, the various Olympic officials have come to understand that they would be "torn from limb to limb" if they didn't look the other way. Then to save face, they and their international colleagues gradually alter the outmoded rules and regulations to conform to prevailing practice — to a degree at any rate.

It's all part of the sham and hypocrisy that has built up around highly competitive sport — a most sordid mess to put it bluntly. Is it any wonder that our young people think us hypocrites when this topic arises, take their expenses and other "goodies" under the table, and then rush off offering their wares to the highest bidder when the next occasion arises?

II. Concepts and Fundamentals

One of the biggest laughs of all is when our Canadian professional hockey all-stars blithely play the Russian "amateurs" for the world championship — and lose as often as not. In the meantime our semi-professional Olympic hockey team takes on these same "amateurs" in the Winter Olympics — and then heads for the nearest exit to sign as many professional contracts as might be available the minute the Olympic Games have been concluded.

I am not criticizing the young people here; they are simply "playing the game" that has been created by their elder hypocrites who seem so unwilling to adjust with the times. (Here I am referring to those men who have control of international "amateur" competition, and who quite willingly accept the many perquisites that go along with this involvement.)

Highly competitive sport today demands long, hard practice over a period of years. Most of our athletes simply could not afford to participate if they didn't receive such financial help. If highly competitive sport is worthwhile — and I realize this is a moot point under conditions that prevail all too often today — then in our society we must give every boy and girl equal opportunity to take part regardless of family background. If this person (1) has the talent and (2) is truly prepared to sacrifice to become a great athlete, we should not hesitate to help him or her to the best of our ability to do so.

There Is One Major Caution

Further, if this deserving individual can be helped to work his or her way through college or university — even by virtue of athletic proficiency during the long summer break — we should still make this opportunity available. However, we must control overemphasis during the time when the athlete is officially registered in a university and taking classes. No other approach should be acceptable in Canada. The individual must be a bonafide student progressing toward a degree — even if it takes a bit longer. This is where Canada should continue to part company with the United States. There is no other acceptable way.

Sport As a Socially Useful Servant

Finally, then, I have argued here that competitive athletics can hold great personal value for young men and women. Through their efforts these young people can make a significant social contribution as well. If we can't continue to work out ways that highly competitive sport and athletics will be a socially useful servant for Canada, we should eliminate it.

We have made mistakes in the past, and we are still making them. Hockey is the cross that we have to bear, but that is probably largely out of our hands (and resultantly out of control).

However, we still have it within our power to keep educational athletics in its proper perspective. By all means let's pledge ourselves to do it, and we can hope that the coming generation might then rectify any mistakes that have been made in the past.

SECTION III.

WOMEN, SPORTSMANSHIP AND RELATIONSHIPS

HOW URGENT IS THE NEED FOR IMPROVED ETHICAL BEHAVIOUR AND DECISION-MAKING IN SPORT?

PATRICIA A. LAWSON

The Ethical Decision

A decision may be defined as making a judgement in relation to what one ought to do in a certain situation after having deliberated on some alternative courses of action. It implies that there are a number of choices that we could make and that we are free to decide upon our own choice.

We make decisions about which car to buy, where to go on our holidays, what to cook for dinner. In sport, we make decisions about what strategy to use, what players to put into the game, what equipment to buy.

Decisions of this type may be based on any number of reasons. We decide to buy the car which is the most economical in terms of mileage. We select a holiday site on the recommendation of friends. We decide on the dinner menus on the basis of the likes and dislikes of our family. In sport, our strategy decisions are determined by our knowledge of the game, the opponents and the abilities of our players.

But these decisions, like the majority of the decisions we make everyday, are not necessarily involved with ethics. An *ethical* decision is one which involves the lives or welfare of people. They are decisions which we voluntarily make after weighing a variety of values — deciding what is best for an individual or group or society. Ethical decisions about what kinds of acts are right or wrong, good or bad, ought or ought not to be done, are being made by individuals in our society today concerning abortion, euthanasia, decriminalizing marijuana, premarital sex, capital punishment, and many others.

In sport, the ethical issues might include: sportsmanship or lack of it, as demonstrated by the behavior of players, coaches and fans; the attitudes of coaches toward their players; practices employed by coaches in recruiting athletes; use of drugs; practices related to academic eligibility provisions; etc.

I think the important point in distinguishing ethical decisions is that they *ought* to be based upon the welfare of people. Too often they are made for other reasons. A large number of those other reasons are involved with the emphasis on winning and the entertainment value of sport. If these become the overriding purpose of an athletic program decisions are made which will promote winning and entertainment rather than the welfare of the individual athlete.

In the recent exposé of athletics in *Sports Illustrated* (May 1980), an educator is quoted as saying, "The problem is not educational, not economic or fiscal, not social — but moral. And what is morally wrong can never be educationally right."

So I think the title of this panel discussion could be reworded to read, "How urgent is the need for decision-making in sport which is based upon the welfare of individuals or groups?" My response is obviously that in order to preserve sport and athletics in the form we consider desirable we must continue (or begin) to base our decisions on the welfare and self-realization of the individual rather than on winning, entertainment, finances, past practices, what others are doing, etc. We must avoid decision-making that is based upon gut feelings or emotions or hunches. We must try to influence the decision-makers to base their decisions on ethical principles.

Another way of viewing this is to say that decisions about sport are, by definition, ethical decisions because they do involve the welfare of individuals or groups.

One feature of many moral decisions is worth noting because it is particularly prevalent in decision-making in sport. It is the fact that an individual often stands in some degree of conflict between his/her personal needs or convictions and the needs or values of others. We experience conflicts because our needs or the needs of our team are so important to us that we give less emphasis to the needs of all players, all teams in the league or conference or all athletes, coaches and administrators in the realm of sport.

I do not pretend to be a philosopher or to be an expert on Emmanual Kant, but I think we can extract from his philosophy a simple rule of thumb which can be of help with many of the ethical issues we face in sport. He said, in part, that we should act on the maxim, and that maxim only, which you could will to become by your act a universal law of nature — or — I ought never to act except in such a way that I can also will that my act should become a universal law. He would not say, for example, do unto others as you would have them do unto you, because that could be interpreted to be a self-preserving motive. He would say, rather, do unto others as you would want all people to do unto all other people (because that will result in the greatest good to the greatest number).

If I can be presumptuous, let me try to interpret Kant in terms of sport and the aspect of breaking or bending rules. These could be the rules of the game or conference regulations. My decision to abide by the rules ought to be based on the premise that I will decide to do so because I think the game will be better if all people do abide by the rules. This implies a preconceived idea about what is good about sport. Let us say for the sake of simplicity that the purpose of rules is to create an equality of competitive opportunities between the players or teams. And this is necessary to preserve the essence of sport which is the opportunity of an individual or team to test its physical abilities against some standard or opponent. The rules (both written and unwritten) are designed to define the conditions under which the competition must take place and to control the factors which would make the contest anything other than a pure test of physical abilities.

According to Kant, if we bend the rules to gain an advantage for our team, we are saying by that act that we think all other teams should bend the rules. But if that line of reasoning is followed to its conclusion, it would lead to something other than the concept of the game that was originally structured. On the other hand, if there is some agreement about what the value or essence of sport is, we decide to abide by the rules because we believe that everyone ought to do so in order to preserve the essence of the game.

At an athletic conference level, the rationale for regulations is to create the conditions which best provide for equality of competitive opportunity between the member institutions. Each institution ought to abide by the conference regulations because they understand the need for preserving the equality of competitive opportunity.

But, as in many cases of ethical or moral decision-making, there is conflict between personal needs and the needs of others. It is apparent that to some individuals, the win-loss record of their team is more important than the preservation of equality of competition, the welfare of athletes, or even the essence of sport.

Equality Between Men's and Women's Programs

Having discussed briefly some of the characteristics of ethical decisions, I would like now to turn to the issue of equality between men's and women's programs. My remarks will be directed mainly at intercollegiate athletic programs but may be appropriate for programs at other age levels.

I will be attempting to show that the decision to provide equal programs for males and females is an ethical decision.

In developing this argument, it must first be established that inequalities in the opportunities of males and females to participate, coach and administrate sport do exist. I have chosen not to review all the statistics that have been collected but to assume that we are all aware that there are fewer minor sport programs for girls than for boys; that there are fewer interschool and intercollegiate sport programs for girls than for boys; that there are fewer female coaches and administrators at all levels of sport; that at the universities, females have less representation than males as graduate students, faculty members and in administrative positions.

I am assuming then that it has been established that inequality exists in the sense that fewer women than men are actively involved in sport. If we can start with that assumption the next step would be to ask why this state of inequality exists.

Again, a vast amount of literature is now available which has examined the reasons why and I do not propose to explore them in great detail here. Research studies have examined beliefs and facts about the physical differences between men and women; societal attitudes toward sport and sexuality; the self image of participants; and much, much more. I think the important point to make here is that the number of people asking why the situation exists has increased and is increasing. And the evidence they are gathering is making it more and more difficult to defend such a position of inequality on a factual or scientific basis.

The next step then is to ask the ethical question — should or ought we be striving toward the attainment of equality between the sexes in sport? Is it the morally right thing to do? Is the sport experience valuable for both boys and girls? My previous description of the essence of sport as being an opportunity for an individual or team to test its physical capabilities implies that some values accrue from this experience. I contend further that those values are desirable for all individuals — males and females.

If a state of inequality exists and we ought to rectify it, how can this be accomplished? My answer is that we must regulate it to happen. Just as we have in many other areas of sport and society, we have a goal which is seen to benefit the most people and the individual recognizes the need to submerge individual needs to the needs of a larger or different group. Individual players choose to support the rules of the game because it is necessary in order to preserve the game and it is important that the game continues to exist. Similarly, member institutions of a conference place the value of a good competitive league above individual aspirations which might enhance the immediate success of one team but might destroy the competitive equality which is viewed as important to the value of a conference.

We create special rules and regulations for minor league sport because we have decided that they will result in better sporting experiences for more children. The Canadian Intercollegiate Athletics Union regulates the number of American players that can be used on a university basketball team because they value or give high priority to the opportunity of Canadian players to participate. The same type of regulation exists in Canadian professional football in order to insure the participation of Canadians.

There are also many examples in society at large where decisions about what ought to be done are based upon decisions about what is right/wrong, good/bad. These decisions must then be defined by legislation or regulations or rules, because individuals have to be encouraged to subjugate their individual needs to the greater needs of particular groups of people.

Debra Shogan (1) has cited as an analogy, the recording industry in Canada. She writes,

> A few years ago there was no recording industry to speak of in Canada. The occasional individual succeeded in producing a record which could compete with the very successful music industry in the United States, but because of the years' head start and the sheer numbers of American musicians, Canadians could not compete even in their own country. Then, the Canadian Radio and Television Commission legislated that a certain percentage of time on Canadian air waves had to be devoted to Canadian music. From that difficult decision, Canadian artists are now very successful both in Canada and around the world. Whereas before the regulations, Canadians with potential could not possibly hope to infiltrate the music industry, Canadians are now among the world's best. It is not realistic to think this result could have occurred naturally; a definite action was required to ensure the result.

Debra was making the point that we must institute regulations which will give priority to the training of females to assume positions as athletic coaches and administrators. Her specific suggestion was that in order to ensure that women learn to coach, the Coaches Association of Canada should institute a program designed specifically for women to allow them to gain the confidence and expertise they need to compete with men for coaching positions. This idea could be expanded to include the setting of regulations by universities to increase the number of female graduate students, the number of faculty positions and the number of administrative positions.

The argument for actively taking steps to correct the imbalance of females in positions of authority is that it is required to provide role models for young people. The young female athlete needs to know that she can have a future in sport after her playing days are over. More role models will encourage more girls to participate and the number of females involved at all levels will continue to increase until there are as many females as males involved.

III. Women, Sportsmanship and Relationships

Regulations are needed at all levels of sport. Communities need to take active steps to increase the number of opportunities for females to participate. Schools and universities must create and support girls' teams until they are equal in number to the boy's and until there is equitable sharing of facilities, time and leadership.

Many other examples could be given but in all cases the action taken must be a positive action and may well involve special subsidization, scholarships, etc.

Without going into any more detail about the specific situations which are in need of control or regulation, the need at this time is to convince people that it is the morally right thing to do. At a time when athletic programs are becoming more expensive and funds are becoming scarcer and at a time when athletic programs seem to be moving toward a "big time" philosophy, decisions about increasing female involvement are liable to be made on other than ethical considerations. The tendency to promote the more visible sports like hockey, football and basketball could result in the elimination or decrease in both minor sports and women's sports.

In summary, decision makers must be convinced:

(1) that for whatever reason, inequalities do exist in the number of male and female participants, coaches and administrators in sport.

(2) that the ethical, morally right thing to do is to eliminate this inequality.

(3) that changes will not just happen. Active steps must be taken in the form of regulations, rules or legislation, plus subsidization, in many cases to increase the number of female participants, coaches and administrators.

The Results of Legislation in the United States

If we can agree that active steps in the form of regulations of some type are required to rectify the imbalance between male and female involvement in sport, it would be interesting to speculate about some of the practical results such moves would have. Fortunately, such a forecast does not have to be entirely based upon speculation. Our neighbors to the south have undergone and are continuing to undergo the enactment of legislation entitled Title IX, and a commentary on its results is available to Canadian readers.

The Canadian situation involving the imbalance between male and female involvement in sport is not exactly the same as the situation in the United States. Generally speaking, boys' and girls' programs in Canada have developed in a somewhat parallel fashion — albeit in uneven numbers. On the other hand, women's interschool and intercollegiate programs in the United States were almost non-existent for 50 years prior to 1972 — years in which men's programs grew in number and size at a very rapid rate.

So it is recognized that the situation in the two countries is somewhat different. But it is possible that the differences are a matter of degree only and that we might be forewarned about the successes and problems which might accompany regulatory actions in Canada.

Title IX and the AIAW

History

Title IX was a 37-word law passed in 1972 as an Educational Amendments Act prohibiting educational programs and institutions who receive federal funds from discriminating on the basis of sex.

In July 1975, three years later, regulations were published explaining how the law should be implemented. This rather lengthy document was distributed to all institutions receiving federal funds. July 1978 was the initial deadline set by which time institutions were expected to be in compliance with the rules and regulations of Title IX.

In December 1979, H.E.W. (the federal department of Health, Education and Welfare) issued a policy interpretation of the intercollegiate athletic provisions of the law and its implementing regulations. This document was published to explain the regulations in more detail and to supply a framework for resolving the problems.

The AIAW (Association for Intercollegiate Athletics for Women) was established in 1971. It was originally associated with AAHPER (American Association for Health, Physical Education and Recreation) and NAGWS (National Association for Girls' and Women's Sport) and was structured to provide an educational basis for women's intercollegiate programs.

As recently as 1978 the AIAW reiterated its commitment to (1) achieving balanced competition, (2) a concern for the welfare of the student, and (3) a belief in the principle of institutional autonomy.

Successes

(1) The AIAW in 1979-80 had (from a beginning of 200 schools in 1971) 972 member colleges and universities, serving 125,000 student athletes, in 3 divisions. Thirty national championships were held in 14 sports plus 150 regional and 750 state events; and the association had received a one million dollar television contract.

III. Women, Sportsmanship and Relationships

(2) Colleges offering grants-in-aid increased from 60 to 460. In 1979-80, one journal listed 448 colleges and universities offering a total of 19 million dollars in scholarships for women.

(3) The number of girls participating in high school athletics increased 460% from 1971 to 1977.

(4) The female athlete now receives financial aid; a coach whose primary responsibility is coaching not teaching; access to better facilities (often the men's); uniforms; quality of equipment; athletic trainers and sports information directors.

Issues

(1) The AIAW has had difficulty in retaining its original concept of intercollegiate athletics for women as being different from the men's programs.

(a) In the very beginning, a position was taken to prohibit athletic scholarships for women. Very quickly this was taken to the courts by some female athletes; the courts ruled that it would be an infringement of human rights; and so it was rescinded. In 1978, the AIAW reorganized its competitive divisions to be based upon the amount of financial aid offered to student-athletes. Division 1 schools are permitted to award full financial aid to athletes. The athletic scholarship is not to exceed tuition, fees, room and board. Division II schools are limited to 50% of the maximum financial aid allowed and Division III Institutions are limited to 10% of the maximum financial aid allowed.

(b) The AIAW's original position on transfer rules was that the student should be free to change schools and not have to sit out a year. It was felt that the female athlete should be able to select the institution she wished to attend. However, this has become a very controversial issue, probably due at least in part to the fact that the institution winning the women's national basketball championship has made liberal use of transfer students. It is quite possible that the women's regulations will soon be similar to those of the National College Athletic Association.

(c) The growing similarity between the men's and women's programs has resulted in many criticisms of both programs. For example, the agenda of a recent AIAW general assembly meeting included the following items for discussion: illegal recruiting practices; coaches who are not respected because of their coaching style; athletes shopping for more than scholarships; and kidnapping of players by other teams.

(d) The AIAW's original concern that the intercollegiate athletic program have an educational base was demonstrated by its affiliation with AAHPER and NAGWS. In January 1979, this affiliation was severed and the AIAW is now an autonomous entity.

(e) One of the reasons for the change in philosophy of direction that the AIAW has taken has been a change in the voting members. The original members were women who had lived through the years when competition for women was almost non-existent. In the view of one of those original members, there is now in the AIAW a "strong and determined group of ardent feminists who are convinced that what the males have, the females should have — even if it is not entirely desirable. These strident feminists continue to sponsor discord within the AIAW. There are numbers of them who see the role of the AIAW as an important cog in the women's movement, and they are willing and ready to use sport organization as one more lever to assure women of eventual equality with their more privileged brothers — and equality means an athletic program for women that is based upon the business model — i.e. an enterprise where players are bought, where coaches are held job accountable for their win-loss records, and where athletic foundations harbor untaxed funds for the entertainment or enhancement of the university's public image."

(2) There has been a great reticence or the part of the men to comply with the Title IX Legislation. The NCAA has challenged the legislation every step of the way in Congress, in the courts and in individual institutions. This reticence can probably be explained but not justified, in terms of tradition. The resistance to compliance has centred around the sensitive areas of finance and administrative authority.

(a) Finance

(i) The men argued that if an institution was required to allocate more money to a women's program, it would diminish the quality of the men's program. The argument that football produces revenue for minor sports and that if women had to be given funds the whole program would suffer, was investigated and the results published in the *New York Times* in 1978.

This report stated that of the 475 NCAA member institutions which had varsity football programs, only 92 (19%) achieved revenue from football at least equal to the team's operating expenses. Eighty-one percent did not even break even. In Division II and III schools, 92-96% did not pay their way. In Division I or "big time football" schools, 43 out of 81 respondents reported making money. One of those which did not, reported a loss of 1.2 million dollars.

III. Women, Sportsmanship and Relationships

(ii) Additional evidence against the argument that the men's programs would suffer with the inauguration of women's programs is provided by the fact (8 years after the passing of Title IX), that firstly, in 1979, in Division 1 schools, the average men's athletic budget was $1,656,000 and the average women's budget was $276,000. Secondly, in salaries, the average in Division 1 schools was $427,000 for men and $68,000 for women. The increase in men's salaries from 1973 to 1979 was twice as much as the total amount paid to women in 1979. Women currently represent 14% of the total athletic budget and 15% of salaries and wages.

It appears then that while men might be expected to argue against any change in the funding of athletic programs, the facts are that (a) their programs are not as financially successful as they would have us believe and (b) that the gains in women's programs, to date at least, have not slowed the rate of increases in men's budgets.

(b) Administrative Authority

The second major bone of contention in the debates between men and women and between the NCAA and AIAW has been the administrative control of the women's programs.

One might expect that the increase in the number of women participants and competitions would be accompanied by an increase in the number of female coaches and administrators, the thought of which posed a threat to the men. But in fact, this has not happened. A study by the AIAW of women in athletic administration positions showed a decline in control by women over their own programs since Title IX became law. In 1973, 79% of the administrators of women's athletic programs were women and 21% were men. In 1976 (only 3 years later), 55.7% were female and 44.3% were male.

This has come about largely by interpreting the legislation as recommending merging of the men's and women's athletic departments into a single department with the result that the single athletic director is invariable male and the former women's athletic director becomes his assistant or is relegated to some other subordinate position. The male athletic director then has the final say about the conduct and financing of women's programs. If the woman is critical or pushes for change, her job may be in jeopardy or, as has actually happened, she may be fired, demoted or forced to resign.

The increase in the number of female coaches has not materialized as expected either. Where the salaries of coaches of women's teams are made equal to the salaries of coaches of men's teams, the decision is often made to hire men to coach women's teams. It is argued that there are more males qualified to coach than females.

The men have decided that if Title IX legislation is here to stay, they would be wise to have control of the finances and direction of both men's and women's programs. Merging of departments is one step toward this end. Another has been the proposal to merge the AIAW with the NCAA or the sponsoring of women's competitions by the NCAA in opposition to those conducted by the AIAW. This is currently being debated by the two groups — one seeking to retain control of women's competitions and the other seeking to take it over and make it conform to the male model.

Conclusion

Legislation such as Title IX in the United States was designed to remove the discrepancies between men and women, boys and girls, in terms of athletic programs in educational institutions. It has been successful to a degree but not to the extent one might have expected. Some of the reasons for this seem to be:

(1) There has been no sign from the legislating agency that the regulation will be enforced. Many cases of non-compliance have been reported but they have not been acted upon and federal funds have not been withheld from any institution as yet.

(2) Title IX legislates equal opportunity for women in school sports but it is up to the women to take advantage of the opportunity — to gain access to it. This is often a very painful process. Women have been cast in an adversary role and are expected to battle for budgets and Title IX compliance.

(3) Legislation such as this prohibits overt discrimination but cannot eliminate the inhibiting effects of covert bias. The stigma attached to those women who speak out and try to effect change is a very real one. The women on a university faculty or school staff are best able to recognize discrimination but are often the least able to speak out for fear of reprisal. Those reprisals may be very visible ones in terms of promotion and salary but they may also be very subtle in terms of respect, friendship and cooperation from other members of the faculty or staff. The latter can be as personally devastating as the former.

(4) The bottom line, of course, is that there has been great opposition by the men. They view the legislation as a threat to the status of men's programs and this view is the result of a history of societal attitudes toward sport and the masculine image. What changes the men have made, they have made grudgingly because it has been forced upon them. They have not been made from a sense of fairness. It is not viewed as the ethically, morally right thing to do.

III. Women, Sportsmanship and Relationships

I think we in Canada can learn a great deal from the experience of our neighbors to the south. One practical suggestion might be to specify the regulations in much more detail initially.

But the real problem is to strive for acceptance of the equality of men's and women's programs as an ethical issue. This is a process which is necessary prior to, during and after the enactment of any regulations. It is an educating process which must be taken at every opportunity from individual one-on-one conversations to open forums such as this.

The enactment of regulations requires the acceptance by decision makers that insuring equality is the ethically right thing to do. The successful attainment of that equality is dependent upon the acceptance of that principle by everyone involved in sport. And finally, there is a need for scholarly development of the conceptual and ethical issues involved in womens' relation to sport.

Iris Marion Young (2) has made a significant contribution in this regard. In her essay she develops the arguments: (1) that insofar as our culture defines woman's body as object, the culture necessarily excludes women from its concept of sport; (2) that institutions and practices exclude women from sport in our society; (3) that insofar as our culture excludes women from both the idea and reality of sport it excludes them from full participation in humanity itself. Hence inclusion of women in both the idea and institution of sport is a fundamental condition of women's liberation; and (4) that the cultural exclusion of women from the idea and reality of sport has given sport a masculinist bias which prevents sport itself from exhibiting its potential humanity. Hence the inclusion of women in the idea and institutions of sport is a fundamental condition for the humanization of sport.

I would like to conclude with a quotation from this essay by Iris Young.

> From several points of view, then, the call for full inclusion of women in the symbols and institutions of sport may represent a demand more fundamental and far reaching than demands for simple justice, like equal pay for equal work, or shared housework, despite the importance of these other demands. If the exclusion of women from the concept of sport symbolizes our exclusion from humanity itself and if our exclusion from the institutions of sport contributes in a basic way to a sense of weakness, body-objectification and physical timidity among women, then the inclusion of women in the symbols and institutions of sport is a basic aspect of our full participation in humanity.

NOTE: The comments on Title IX included in this paper are based on the writings of people directly involved with women's athletics in the United States. The primary source of this information was the journal *Coaching: Women's Athletics* — 12 issues from March/April 1978 to May/June 1980.

References

1. Shogan, Debra A. "The Case for Ensuring Women's Involvement as Leaders in Sport." Unpublished paper, University of Alberta.
2. Young, Iris Marion. "The Exclusion of Women from Sport: Conceptual and Existential Dimensions." *Philosophy in Context*, Vol. 9, 1979, pp. 44-53. Cleveland State University.

THE PARADOX OF PHYSICAL ACTIVITY IN THE WILDERNESS[1]

DEBRA SHOGAN

Too often physical educators limit their understanding of physical activity experiences to games of sport — those activities which are rule bound and which take place within the boundaries of a circumscribed playing surface. Although outdoor educators have long extolled the virtues of physical activity in natural environments, most people are physically active in gymnasia, in swimming pools, and on playing fields.

In this paper I am interested in the possible effects of a shift in emphasis from sport-based physical activity programs to outdoor physical activity programs and particularly what the effects might be if a shift is made to physical activity in wilderness areas. I want to suggest that educating people about the virtues of physical activity in the wilderness might paradoxically contribute to the eventual demise of wilderness. Two other paradoxes emerge as I develop this position: the first of these is the paradox of the commons in which acting to maximize one's benefits leads to destruction of both one's own and others' benefits. The second paradox concerns the relationship of human beings to the wilderness. This paradox suggests that human beings are at one and the same time separate and part of wilderness and consequently that human culture is both the potential destroyer of wilderness and the only possible way to preserve it.

Wilderness as a Tragic Commons

In his article, "The Tragedy of the Commons," Garrett Hardin describes the evolution of an area of land which is open to all to graze their cattle as self-interest dictates.[2] This commons functions without difficulty for many centuries with herders keeping as many cattle as each possibly can on the commons. Eventually stability is reached because the commons cannot be utilized beyond its fixed "carrying capacity." The herders do not exercise restraint, however, because to do so would be to be eliminated from competing for the now scarce resources of the commons. Each herder calculates what the utility of adding one more animal to one's own herd will be. This utility has two components. The positive component is a function of the increment of having another animal in one's herd. The negative component is a function of the overgrazing created by another animal added to the herd. Since, however, the herder will share the effects of the overgrazing with all the other herders, the herder adds another animal and several more. Meanwhile every other herder does the same. Each herder realizes that to refrain from adding cattle while others do not would be to suffer the effects of more cattle on the land without experiencing any benefits of having more cattle grazing. Each herder adds cattle without limit in a world that has limits on what it can carry. And, of course, therein lies the tragedy. The herders are caught in a paradox. In a rational attempt to maximize personal benefits, each is left in a situation which is neither personally beneficial nor beneficial for others.

The entire Earth is a commons with a fixed carrying capacity. With an ever-increasing population (in 1987 the human population passed the 5 billion mark), the Earth's resources can no longer be regarded as "a 'free good' or 'commons' which any person is entitled to use as self-interest dictates."[3] I am particularly interested in the *wilderness* as a commons with a maximum human carrying capacity and I am interested in whether education about physical activity in the wilderness might in fact contribute to reaching this carrying capacity. It is not my purpose to attempt to sort out what *is* the maximum number of human beings wilderness can carry. Some would argue that any is too many because, by definition, wilderness is wilderness by virtue of having no human inhabitants. Others would argue that human beings must also be considered to be an important part of the ecosystem and, consequently, any notion of wilderness can and should accomodate human beings. The latter would have to admit, however, that wilderness is distinguishable from, for example, urban environments and too many people in the wilderness put these distinguishing features in jeopardy. Too many people, however many that may be, creates a tragedy for the wilderness. As Dustin and McAvoy report in their paper, "The Decline and Fall of Quality Recreation Opportunities and Environments," "not only do people appear to be growing less sensitive to crowding in recreation settings, they appear to be growing less sensitive to the environmental deterioration that inevitably accompanies crowding."[4]

It might be argued that, although rapidly expanding human population may put *some* resource systems in jeopardy, there is no real threat to the wilderness by those who want to be active in the wilderness since most people will continue to be interested in urban physical activities. However, even if the proportion of the population interested in wilderness experiences remains constant, total numbers will continue to increase as the population increases. And, if outdoor educators are successful at what they do, the *proportion* of people interested in wilderness experiences is likely to increase as well. As more and more people enjoy wilderness experiences, the maximum human carrying capacity of wilderness comes closer to being reached. If the logic of the commons persists, the wilderness as a commons will be tragically and

211

inevitably destroyed just as the grazing grounds as a commons is inevitably destroyed.

Being aware of the effects of a large number of people accessing a wilderness area is not sufficient to stop overuse since what compels someone to go back to the wilderness, even after it is endangered, is the realization that others may not be curtailing their wilderness experiences. The utility of whether to have another wilderness experience, once again, has two components. The positive component is a function of the increment of another personal wilderness experience while the negative component is the function of the overuse created by this additional experience. The effects of this additional experience are not born alone, however — they are shared with other users. Each individual realizes that to stop having wilderness experiences while others do not stop will mean that he or she must bear the effects of the overuse of the wilderness while getting no benefits.

The Role of Outdoor Educators

What role does outdoor education play in the resolution of this dilemma? I want to suggest that, despite valuing wilderness more than most, outdoor educators may paradoxically contribute to the creation of the wilderness as a tragic commons.

To be educated about an enterprise, as contrasted to being trained, conditioned or indoctrinated, is to come to see what is important about the enterprise and to believe that it is worth doing. An educator of literature, for example, is successful if a learner values the literature experience and comes to think that it is worth engaging in literature. If an enterprise is valuable, it is generally desirable that human beings come to see its value and think it is worth doing. Physical activity in the wilderness, paradoxically, seems to be an exception to the general case that it is desirable to come to see the point of and engage in valuable activities or enterprises. Unlike the education of literature experiences in which arguably the more who have these experiences, the better, the more people who are educated to see the value of wilderness *experiences* as something in which to engage, the closer we are to wilderness becoming a tragic commons. To educate people about the value of physical activity in the wilderness is to interest at least some of them in actually having these experiences. As outdoor educators do this job well, wilderness becomes jeopardized. An alternative is to be circumspect about educating people about the virtues of wilderness experience by limiting this information to a few. This would solve the problem of the wilderness as a commons because wilderness would no longer be a 'free good' available to all. Wilderness would be limited to a few knowledgeable people. The goal of outdoor education would be to teach everyone else to respect wilderness but without also interesting these people in actually having wilderness experiences.

Certainly an essential component of education of physical activity in the wilderness is that people learn respect for the wilderness. It may be that reducing the focus of outdoor education to having people come to see the value of wilderness without also having them want to have wilderness experiences is a solution to a possible tragedy of the wilderness as a commons. It is, however, debatable whether someone can come to value wilderness without having at least some wilderness experiences. Arguably, understanding the wilderness does not come from studying about wilderness from a book. But even a minimum number of experiences puts wilderness that much closer to its carrying capacity. Moreover, if physical activity in the wilderness is the goal and not just education about the value of wilderness, there is necessarily an involvement in the wilderness.

Educating only some people about the joys of wilderness experiences creates other problems. It raises questions, for example, about who is to receive education about wilderness experiences. Who are to be the privileged few who are to have these experiences; who will decide this; and how will this be decided? Even though we must realize that the Earth is a commons which cannot carry an infinite number of people, such a realization does not suggest easy answers about how we are to deal with large numbers of people on the Earth. As Wendell Berry rightly says, "There is great danger in the perception that 'there are too many people,' whatever truth may be in it, for this is a premise from which it is too likely that somebody, sooner or later, will proceed to a determination of *who* are the surplus."[5]

Are There Solutions to These Paradoxes?

Garrett Hardin's solution to the tragedy of the commons is "mutual coercion, mutually agreed upon". In other words, since the logic of the commons makes it impossible to appeal to people to use constraint because they fear that others will not use constraint, we must agree to legislation which will force us to control our behaviours. Meanwhile, says Hardin, an educational program must be put into place which will allow people to see that they must give up certain freedoms in a world with finite resources. Hardin fails to see, however, that unless everyone either accepts the legislation or comes to see the point of relinquishing certain freedoms, some will continue to benefit from short term gain at the expense of others. Being educated to look long term or accepting legislation that forces one to do so, while others ignore legislation and education, is not a remedy for the tragedy of the commons. This is because those who look short term will continue to gain short term

213

advantages. It is just this kind of dilemma which convinces many that they also must look out for their own short term interests.

Education about appropriate use of the wilderness, to be effective, must convince all that they must look long term. It is highly unlikely, however, that *all* could be educated to do this and consequently legislation with effective penalties *is* necessary. It is doubtful, however, whether education or legislation of wilderness areas will be sufficient in solving the tragedy of the wilderness as commons. A fundamental change in all parts of our culture, including our economy is required. As Wendell Berry writes: "It is not only the number of people inhabiting a landscape that determines its future — it is the way people divide the landscape and use it."[6] "Conservation is going to prove increasingly futile and increasingly meaningless if its proscriptions are not answered positively by an economy that rewards and enforces good use."[7]

This introduces the third paradox — that human culture and wilderness are different but inseparable. Humanity cannot survive unless the natural world is preserved but the preservation of the natural world also now depends on human culture. We require nothing less than a radical shift in our thinking about the ways in which human beings can live in harmony with wilderness. Living in harmony with wilderness likely requires that people live in harmony with each other. If we cannot recognize and develop connection rather than separation among human beings, it is highly unlikely that we will see the connections we have with wilderness. What is required is recognition that the lives of people and other living things are interconnected instead of continuing to function as if moral communities are comprised of autonomous, separate individuals acting from self-interest and who must contract with one another for protection against the self-interest of others. In this latter type of community, trust is rare and individuals manoeuvre to take advantage of others before they are taken advantage of. An interconnected community, on the other hand, has the best features of a family or a group of friends in which lives have meaning within the context of the group and in which it would be unthinkable to subvert those who depend on you and on whom you depend. And, as unthinkable, would be the sacrifice of the very physical environment in which the community lives and acts. The boundaries of this moral community extend to include not only people but the living Earth.[8]

I have introduced three paradoxes that must be understood if we are to contend with real and ongoing threats to the wilderness. The first of these paradoxes is that, as long as people attempt to optimize personal gain with respect to finite resources, the inevitable result is loss of personal gain. The second of the paradoxes is that the very people who value wilderness more than most, outdoor educators, may contribute to its demise if those they educate live in a community of competing self-interested individuals. The third paradox is that human cultural enterprises, including education, have both the potential to destroy wilderness and to save it. Outdoor educators must be clear about their role in this complex endeavour if they are to protect wilderness and not be culpable in its demise.

Notes

1. This is a revised copy of a paper I presented at the World Leisure Congress in Lake Louise, Alberta on May 20, 1988. I would like to thank Catherine Bray for her helpful comments.
2. Garrett Hardin, "The Tragedy of the Commons," *Science* 162 (1968): 1243-48.
3. Daniel Lehocky, "Review of Garrett Hardin, *The Limits of Altruism: Ecologist's View of Survival.*" *Environmental Ethics* 1 (1979): 83.
4. Daniel Dustin and Leo McAvoy, "The Decline and Fall of Quality Recreation Opportunities and Environments." *Environmental Ethics* 4 (1982): 52.
5. Wendell Berry, "Preserving Wildness," *Resurgence* 121 (1987): 9.
6. Berry, p. 10.
7. Berry, p. 7.
8. For work on a "contextualized" view of persons within an interconnected moral community see, for example, Lorraine Code, "Second Persons," *Canadian Journal of Philosophy*, Supp. 13 (1987): 357-82 and Virginia Held, "NonContractual Society: A Feminist View," *Canadian Journal of Philosophy*, Supp. 13 (1987): 111-37.

PATERNALISM AND SOVEREIGNTY IN ATHLETICS: LIMITS AND JUSTIFICATIONS OF THE COACH'S EXERCISE OF AUTHORITY OVER THE ADULT ATHLETE[1]

KENNETH RAVIZZA
KATHY DARUTY

The training and performance of athletes presents numerous ethical challenges. We have particular interest in the questions of the individual's sovereignty over his/her own body and person in the pursuit of athletic excellence, and the appropriate role of the coach as mentor in the competitive setting. Sometimes an athlete cannot appreciate the importance of what a coach requires, and other times the coach is expected to urge the athlete beyond what he/she is initially willing to do. Often the coach seems to have gone beyond what might be considered the propriety of the unique situation presented in athletics and has used means that many would deem unethical in eliciting good performance from the athlete. This line between justifiable and unjustifiable exercise of the coach's authority is notoriously difficult to define: Conduct that some would deem necessary to the achievement of athletic excellence may be regarded by others as unjustified coercion.

Questions of the coach's responsibility to protect athletes from becoming unjured also arise. When, if ever, does a coach have the right, even the obligation, to forbid an athlete to attempt activities that are patently dangerous? A recent case illustrates this point. In July 1983, Soviet diver Sergei Chalibasvili, involved in the World University Games in Edmonton, Canada, died after attempting a dive that many felt he was too inexperienced to make. American coach Bob Rydze refused to even watch the attempt because he feared an accident was likely, based on the athlete's prior performance. Rydze said, "It is the coach's responsibility to make sure his divers are not attempting dives they're not capable of doing. I firmly believe the responsibility is on the coach" (4: p. III-1).

The purpose of this paper is to clarify the conditions that must be fulfilled to ensure that authority exercised by coaches is appropriate, and that the athlete's rights and integrity are preserved. We will begin by considering what individual sovereignty means, and under what specific conditions the coach oversteps the limits of legitimate authority as mentor to the athletes he or she is responsible for. The concept of "informed consent" as developed in medical practice will be examined,

216

and the potential of developing a similar guideline in athletics will be presented.[2]

Individual sovereignty is no insignificant ideal — in fact it is the very basis on which a free society is built. In a free society, those who would limit individual liberty must be able to show justifiable reason for so doing or face legal sanction. This policy is pursued in the belief that the environment that protects individual sovereignty is the same environment that enhances opportunities for individual growth and achievement, and ensures that sacrifices made for the good of others are undertaken willingly. Likewise, when we speak of athletic excellence, we will mean achieving one's optimal level of performance, the end result of which is personal fulfillment. This definition provides for a broader interpretation of excellence than just winning. The social motivations for sport participation such as playing for fun, exercise, and/or the health benefits or the diverse social values obtained are excluded from consideration because these aspects are not directly relevant to the topic of this paper.

Although winning and excellence have a strong correlation, many athletes derive great satisfaction and fulfillment from performing to their potential, even though this level of performance may be insufficient to win. This view of athletic excellence has been more widely adopted than some might admit. The official position of the National College Athletic Association is that it is organized for the promotion of "amateur student athletes" who participate in sports "for the education, physical, mental and social benefits derived therefrom" (10: p. 9). A 1974 Association of Intercollegiate Athletics for Women position paper further supports our preferred definition of athletic excellence by stating that, "The enrichment of life and of the participant is the focus and reason for the existence of any athletic program. All decisions should be made with this fact in mind" (1: p. 87). An excellent personal performance remains just that, whether the team wins or loses; that is, athletic excellence is measured by far more than the final score. Yet, most observers of intercollegiate athletics agree that in high-level NCAA athletics, the sheer joy of participation and the pluralistic ends of participation that Keenan (6), for one, addresses, are not primary rationale for participation. For this reason, optimal performance has been selected because it mediates the goals of winning and development of the person.

In other words, we live in a free society and it is unacceptable for the athlete to be treated as a sacrificial animal to the goals of winning. The American athlete is fundamentally a member of a free society and individual sovereignty should be reasonably protected within the athletic environment. Further, when individual sovereignty is to be mediated in the name of athletic excellence, strong justification is needed.

217

III. Women, Sportsmanship and Relationships

I

Let us begin, then, with the well known and widely accepted definition of individual sovereignty presented by John Stuart Mill in his landmark work *On Liberty*. Mill argues that,

> There is one fundamental principle which governs absolutely the dealings of society with the individual in the way of compulsion and control.... That principle is that the sole end for which mankind is warranted, individually or collectively, in interfering with the liberty of action of any of their number is self-protection. That the only purpose for which power can be rightfully exercised over any member of a civilized community, against his will, is to prevent harm to others. His own good, either physical or moral, is not sufficient warrant. He cannot rightfully be compelled to do or forbear because it will be better for him to do so, because it will make him happier, because, in the opinions of others, to do so would be wise or even right. These are good reasons for remonstrating with him or reasoning with him, or persuading him, or entreating him, but not for compelling him or visiting him with any evil in case he do otherwise.... Over himself, over his own body and mind, the individual is sovereign. (9: p. 13)

In the further explication of this principle, Mill (9: p. 13) adds the obvious condition that sovereignty as he has defined it is "meant to apply only to human beings in the maturity of their faculties," that is, to adults.

At this point we will confine ourselves to the adult person in American inter-collegiate athletics, where the age of adulthood is specified by state statute. State laws arbitrarily define the age of adulthood and courts presume that the individual who has reached this age has achieved sovereignty over body and development of personal character. We may question whether this reflects reality, either for the general population or the athletes in particular, but it is a public policy that is not susceptible to individual differences.

The application of Mill's principle on sovereignty to athletics would appear to constrain the coach's right to compel the athlete to act or forbear in any given way unless the athlete's behavior would actually bring harm to others. Let us be clear on what is meant here by harm: We do not mean that the athlete's behavior might be disliked or even offensive to others, but that some actual physical harm would be visited on others by the behavior in question. What will count as harm to others, particularly in team sport where the athlete's performance may affect the

218

success of teammates, it is a difficult and complicated issue that goes beyond the scope of our present inquiry. Let us simply say that where real harm to others can be demonstrated, some limitation on the individual's behavior will be justified.[3]

But will there be no other condition, outside of harm to others, in which individual sovereignty might be set aside justifiably in athletics? Certainly, even Mill is forced to mediate his absolute principle somewhat, particularly in the now famous proscription against an individual's selling himself into slavery. It has been argued (2; 3: pp. 104-125) that Mill's principle of individual sovereignty as stated will not permit this injunction against slavery on the grounds that Mill invokes, and that he must either amend his principle to allow for some additional infringement on sovereignty, or admit that the principle cannot be applied on so absolute a basis as he would like.

Mill's problem, of course, centers on the question of whether paternalism can be justified in a free society, that is, whether an individual can be justifiably compelled to do or forbear in his/her own interests. In the case of children, we normally do not argue that individual rights are unjustly abridged when the parent compels the child to do or forbear when the child's maturity and knowledge are insufficient to allow the child to make an informed choice. In fact, we would probably agree that any parent who failed to protect a child in this way would be remiss in parental responsibility. Concerning adults, however, it is not so simple, since individual sovereignty for the adult usually means precisely that the adult is entitled to decide for him/herself what is in his/her own best interests.

In order to pursue the question of the justifiability of paternalism in a free society, an essential distinction must be made. When speaking of paternalism let us understand that we mean the exercise of authority *in the interests of the person whose sovereignty is at stake.* This is to be clearly distinguished from what might be termed "authoritarianism," where power is exercised to satisfy the desires of the person in power, without regard for the person over whom power is exercised. It should be clear from our previous discussion of a free society that simple authoritarianism will never be an acceptable justification for limiting individual freedom. Compelling another to act or forbear on mere authoritarian grounds is the supreme denial of individual sovereignty, and is rightfully sanctioned both by the general ethical sense of free people and by the laws of our society.

II

To this point we have established the importance of individual sovereignty both in terms of what it means to be a member of a free society and what it means to achieve athletic excellence. We have agreed that preventing harm to others is justifiable ground for limiting individual sovereignty, while simple authoritarianism is not. The question now becomes, "When, if ever, will a coach be justified in applying pressure to extract performance from the athlete on paternalistic grounds?"

In general, we presuppose that as adults we are better able to see and pursue our own best interests than is some third party, and that therefore no one should compel us to behave one way or another. As Mill has pointed out, if we did not make this supposition, the maxim of individual sovereignty which is so vital to a free society would be reduced to folly. If we were to habitually allow others to dictate to us what is in our best interest, or what would make us happier, we would eliminate our fundamental freedoms.

However, we sometimes do seek outside help from experts when making decisions about what course of action we should pursue to maximize our interests. In the medical setting the courts have mandated the duty of physicians to disclose information to the patient who faces a complicated medical procedure to preserve health or arrest the advance of disease. Laypersons are usually quite clear on the goals they hope to achieve, but need information when deciding whether the risks and consequences associated with the procedure are worth the anticipated benefits. The parallel to athletics is similar in several important respects. The coach's expertise from years of study and experience can benefit the athlete. The good coach knows the physiological and biomechanical aspects of the sport and understands the technical aspects of optimizing the athlete's potential. Further, the coaching staff has an in-depth understanding of the emotional makeup of team members and makes judgments about the most appropriate mental preparation for the athlete.

If the athlete's goal is to reach optimal performance, the coach's expertise and guidance are essential. Hence, it is usually in the athlete's best interests to follow the experienced coach's advice. For example, in gymnastics the coach will know what the best skill progressions are to execute the complex and often dangerous moves required of this sport. In distance running, the coach's expertise extends to advice about the best workout schedule to follow to meet the needs of the individual. In both instances, it is not authoritarianism but the expertise the coach brings to the athlete that justifies the coach's role. But does the coach's expertise then justify applying pressure upon the athlete to do or forbear against his/her will, for his/her own good? In other words, does the expertise of the coach override individual sovereignty and justify paternalism?

In order to answer this question, it may be helpful to consider different categories of cases (3: pp. 104-124). The first group of cases would involve situations that, in the opinion of the coach, an athlete's conduct would surely impair ability rather than simply create a *risk of* impaired performance, for example, if the athlete's refusal to perform a given workout simply creates a risk that performance will be impaired, it would seem that this is for the athlete to decide, given our earlier definitions of sovereignty and athletic excellence. The athlete participates to reach optimal performance, and if he/she is willing to take the risk that doing or forbearing will hamper the ability to perform, perhaps even in being cut from the team, it would seem that this must be the athlete's choice. It is the athlete's right to know the sacrifice that must be made and the possible consequences, and at this point it is that individual's choice.

However, what about situations in which the athlete's possible behavior will *surely* impair his/her ability to perform? Suppose that in the best professional opinion of the coach, doing or forbearing will make it impossible for the athlete to achieve full performance potential, and yet the athlete objects to the training routine. For example, the coach knows that the athlete must push to his/her fullest limits in preseason conditioning drills. The coach knows that the endurance skills are essential for this athlete. If the athlete doesn't have a certain level of conditioning, performance at the full potential cannot be achieved. Another example is an athlete who does well in practice but "chokes" in pressure situations. The coach knows it is essential for this athlete to learn specific ways to relax so that he/she can more effectively manage the stress of competition. Given that the athlete's objective is to reach optimal performance level, the expertise of the coach will normally be reason enough for the athlete to acquiesce.

But even under these circumstances, the coach has no right to compel the athlete. If the coach has explained that in his or her best professional opinion it is impossible for the athlete to attain Y unless the athlete performs X, and still the athlete refuses, that athlete is well within his/her rights. We may consider the athlete's decision foolish, even arrogant, but if the only harm done is to the athlete's own performance, the coach would not be justified in using further coercion. This becomes a complex issue in relation to team sports and reflects a pitfall in the application of Mill's principle to sport. It may be added that the coach's responsibility as mentor has been fulfilled when a full disclosure of his/her expert opinion has been made to the athlete.

The second group of cases concerns an athlete's desire to take an unreasonable risk that performance will be impaired. If an athlete simply wants to assume what would be regarded as a reasonable risk, the doctrine of individual sovereignty would clearly call for allowing the athlete to make the choice. However, if the athlete's desire is to accept a patently foolish risk of harm, the coach is responsible for using his/her expertise and influence to ensure the athlete's safety and well being. Consider the athlete who has a serious injury but who wants to play in the championship game. The team doctor and coach both explain the likelihood that harm would result, but the athlete wants to participate anyway and thus insists on undertaking an unreasonable risk. Now the unreasonable risk will not in itself be sufficient grounds for the coach to interfere further. However, the threats of liability suits against the coach of the facility where the supervised athlete is participating make it necessary for the coach to think of self-protection. Here, if intervention is justified, it will rest not on paternalism, but on the principle of harm to others.

A third group of cases arises in connection with the principle of Roman law known as the *volenti maxim*, which states, "To he who consents, no wrong is done." If we were to apply this maxim to athletics, it would seem that if the athlete agrees to abide by the wishes of the coach or to submit to the pressure of his/her peers, and is subsequently harmed, that still no wrong has been committed since the athlete gave free consent to abide by the wishes of these specified other people.[4] Once again, however, since the athlete cannot know ahead of time what behavior will be required, we cannot say that the criteria of voluntary action has been preserved, and hence we would argue that the athlete can be wronged in this instance since he/she did not understand to what he/she had consented. The case is complicated because of the intense socialization process that occurs. For example, a player may not want to be "shot up" for a game, but if he doesn't take the injection he is not a "man," and the coaches and peers may view that athlete as lacking the "proper" attitude.

Many collegiate athletes do incredible things because they fear losing the scholarship that supports their college education. Often in team sports, the intense dedication to the team encourages the athlete to be unconcerned about him/herself and to make personal sacrifices for the good of the team. Individual choices and asking questions is often discouraged in these situations: *Esprit de corps* is often considered justification enough to do whatever is asked. The willingness to go along is often bolstered by public pressure for the athlete to acquiesce. For example, when Frank Kush, then a coach at Arizona State, was sued for hitting a player, the community supported Kush. ASU social psychologist Bob Cialdini believed that Kush's reputation as a disciplinarian was at the focus of this support. Cialdini (5) stated that "Many have a sense that people are getting away with things these days, especially students and athletes. They believe that the crucible of white-hot fire Kush subjects his players to, makes better people of them." It is clear in all these examples that outside influences are being used to pressure the athlete. Since the athlete could not have known what pressures he/she would face when joining the team, it cannot be maintained that the athlete gave consent in the first place.[5]

The fourth group of cases where paternalism might appear to be justified involves situations in which the athlete does not understand the risk he or she is taking, and therefore does not assume the risk in a fully voluntary way. For example, the gymnast who wants to learn the double back flip may not be aware of its potential risk. The coach must educate the athlete to the potential risks and explain the progressions that should be followed to minimize those risks. If an athlete clearly is about to undertake a risk he/she is not aware of, the coach has the responsibility as mentor to stop the athlete long enough to make him or her aware of the risk being taken. Those with specialized skill and knowledge have a duty in law and convention to protect the less knowledgeable from risking harm to themselves involuntarily. Again, the justification here is strictly not based on paternalism but rather on protecting the individual's right to base his/her action on a freely chosen alternative. We base our position here on the Aristotelian sense of voluntariness of action, in which an action is chosen involuntarily if ignorance of relevant facts is the basis of the action. Hence, if the coach interferes in this case, it is to ensure that individual sovereignty is preserved by giving the athlete the information necessary to make a free, informed choice.

It is our belief that the criteria of informed consent as developed in medicine may clarify the limits of a coach's authority as the athlete is encouraged to achieve athletic excellence. The following section will provide an analysis of the development of informed consent in medicine and develop a similar model for intercollegiate athletics.

III

The development of the legal doctrine of informed consent in medicine has logical parallels that deserve to be explored and adapted to athletics. Historically, medical consent involved a patient's grant of permission to an assault and battery. In other words, the patient expressly agreed to be touched and treated by a physician for a specific purpose. In a now classic statement of the underpinnings of the informed consent doctrine, Justice Cardozo proclaimed the following in the early part of the 20th Century:

> Every human being of adult years and sound mind has a right to determine what shall be done with his own body; and a surgeon who performs an operation without his patient's consent commits an assault for which he is liable in damages. (20)

III. Women, Sportsmanship and Relationships

Yet, many abuses of this basic principle resulted in judicial rulings that a patient's visit to a physician's office does not necessarily constitute conclusive proof of a consent to simple touching. As a result, doctors and hospitals began to require a written signature, often with no explanation of what was to occur. As a result, signing of broadly worded consent forms, often with no explanation, became routine practice in hospitals and doctors' offices. Although the medical world has now accepted the doctrine of informed consent as a part of everyday practice, the world of athletics today is generally expected only to have on file a broadly written consent or release from liability. These forms are usually signed by athletes with little knowledge of the contents of the rights being waived.

As medicine became more complex, the number of alternatives and potential dangers of various forms of therapy became far greater. During the 1960's federal and state courts began to fashion the informed consent doctrine which gave the individual a legally enforceable right to sue a physician who failed to disclose information sufficient for the patient to make an intelligent choice between alternative forms of treatment. This new legal right was based on principles of negligence, rather than the more difficult standard of proof required in the traditional assault and battery tort. Although initial reaction in the medical community was negative, informed consent statutes or court decisions in 37 states now give the individual the right to recover when informed consent has not been provided (14: p. 98). Medical practitioners who actively follow informed consent guidelines generally report that they are under less psychological pressure when their patients are involved and participate in the decision making process.

Before proposing application of informed consent principles to athletics, a brief summary of the essential elements is in order. Although some variations exist between states, the California rule represents a standard followed by many states. Briefly, informed consent focuses on the informational needs of the patient and requires the physician to provide all material information (16;21).

This overall statement of principle has been difficult to fully implement because most patients do not understand the complexities and technology associated with medical procedures. Similarly, in athletics, many training procedures are extremely complex and beyond the understanding of the average athlete. Yet, the medical and legal world has further defined the level of disclosure that must occur. Four major rules give a practical depth to the principle of informed consent:

1. The patient is entitled to information about the nature of the medical problem in nontechnical terms and including diagnosis.

2. The patient must be informed about known risks and complications associated with the proposed treatment.
3. The patient should understand the benefits associated with the proposed procedure.
4. The patient must be made aware of feasible treatment alternatives (14).

The purpose of these general legal rules is to provide the patient with information sufficient to decide whether to proceed with the proposed procedure in the consent of the fullest possible understanding of available options. Even in life-and-death situations, alternatives may be rejected. No physician has the right to compel a patient to undergo a given procedure or course of treatment.

IV

The principles of informed consent can be used to clarify the limits of a coach's authority so that the athlete is encouraged to achieve excellence. The application of these rules is no more difficult in athletics than it is in medicine. Clearly, an experienced coaching staff has a great deal more expertise is all aspects of a particular sport than the athlete starting out on the college level. A truly informed disclosure has many advantages, not the least of which is a reduction of the coach's stress, as responsibility for the athlete's performance is placed upon both the athlete and coach.

It is important to recognize that informed consent provides the athlete with an understanding of the parameters of what is likely to be experienced. This involves a process, not a disruption on the practice field, that requires a detailed explanation. The coach's focus should be that all team members are aware of the range of possibilities that may occur, rather than simply a written piece of paper that must be signed whenever a new skill is being practiced.

In an effort to develop the structure of a realistic and practical informed consent for athletics, full disclosure should be made to athletes in three basic areas:

1. The nature of the coach's philosophy or attitude related to coaching a particular sport;
2. Current information about the risks, complications, and benefits associated with specific aspects of participation in that sport;
3. Recognition that feasible alternatives may exist to the coach's position in certain situations and the athlete is responsible for communicating reasons for a change in the team plan or individual strategy as it relates to training and performance.

225

III. Women, Sportsmanship and Relationships

The coach's attitude about his/her particular sport provides the athlete an understanding of what to expect on a regular basis. In a sense, this aspect of informed consent encourages the coach to disclose coaching priorities and idiosyncracies. When the coach explains at the beginning that screaming and yelling are used as a technique to reach optimal performance, the athlete has at least a general understanding of what to expect. At the same time, the individual who responds poorly to criticism from coaches would do well to play somewhere else if this kind of coaching behavior is offensive.

This overview of the coach's approach should include such specifics as the importance attached to fundamentals, training and conditioning, how skill develoment progressions are handled, and the degree to which the athlete will be held responsible for performance. It is probably fair to say that full disclosure has taken place if the athlete finishes the season without having experienced any major surprises from the coach. For example, when a team qualifies for a national championship, it cannot be assumed that the athlete will be able to participate in extra practices, especially if the practices are scheduled during academic class periods. The athlete has the right to know in advance if there will be additional responsibilities so that he/she has time to make the necessary arrangements.

Of course, this general disclosure to the team may have to be modified for individual team members based upon the coach's assessment that a modified strategy will be needed for a particular athlete to reach optimal performance. Most coaches probably make these types of adjustments anyway, but generally they do not inform the athlete as to why there has been a deviation from the usual rules. In some cases, with the athlete's permission, it may be appropriate to discuss with the entire team why exceptions are being made from the usual process. Team members often recognize deviations instinctively, and a clearly stated rationale makes good sense.

Information about risks, complications, and benefits associated with a sport are self-evident, in many respects, by the time the athlete has reached the college level. Generally, in this area we are talking about interactions with the individual athlete related either to skill and training progressions or to the disadvantages of playing with a particular injury.

The practicalities of disclosure in this area require that the coaching staff function as educators throughout the season. College athletics today comprise a coaching staff of specialists or a coach who has access to a wide range of support staff. The coach has overall responsibility for making sure that team members understand the types of injuries that occur in the sport, how they can be avoided, and the long-term prognosis once the injury has occurred. The athlete with this understanding is in a much better position to make decisions and take risks that may have a lifelong impact. There is no justification for failing to provide the athlete with adequate information about risks and complications associated with the sport. The athlete who plays under the effect of a painkilling drug and does not recognize the possible harmful effects should have grounds for a suit against those responsible for failure to disclose necessary information.[6]

The athlete who knows the types of injury to expect in the sport is better able to make realistic informed decisions in the event that injury or its risk is at issue. The informed athlete may often make decisions similar to the uninformed athlete but at least is not surprised when the worst-case scenario occurs.

We have pointed out that the goals of intercollegiate athletics place primary emphasis on individual fulfillment of the athlete, even at the expense of winning. The idea of an athlete pursuing a course different from that recommended by the coach is extremely threatening to most coaches. Yet, the reality is that most coaches grant athletes discretionary judgment when a situation arises that has not been anticipated. The broken play is a useful, if minor, example of a situation in which the athlete is expected to use his or her best judgment.

It is not a very significant extension to permit the athlete the right to choose an alternative course of action when the situation merits. The critical aspect here is that the athlete learns to communicate to the coach a rationale to support a possible change in game plan. For example, during premeet warmups, a gymnast who previously had sustained a pulled hamstring may determine that a double back flip dismount does not feel right. The athlete is responsible for listening to his or her body and being certain that this feeling is not just a fear response to the situation. If the athlete has previously informed the coach of the hamstring problem, then it will not be a surprise to the coach that the athlete only wants to do a single back flip dismount for this particular meet. However, if the gymnast has failed to inform the coach about the situation, the jolt to the coach is significant and may be interpreted as a challenge to his or her authority.

The point here is that the coach and the athlete share a responsibility to communicate regularly. Flexibility is the nature of competitive situations, but most coaches are unwilling to allow last-minute changes in a tried and tested game plan unless there is good reason. We have argued that the essence of informed consent in athletics is the coach's responsibility to ensure that there are no big surprises during the season; however, the corollary is that athletes cannot expect last-minute flexibility in the absence of a regular ongoing communication with the coach. This continuing communication builds a bond between athlete and coach that ultimately results in mutual respect. Where this has occurred, the coach will generally give the athlete the benefit of the doubt in an ambiguous situation.

College athletes essentially train to learn the subtleties of a higher level of play. In some sports, athletes strive to achieve professional status, while in other sports they merely reach for a more sophisticated level of play. Great attention is placed upon physical skills but very little is placed upon developing communication skills. Athletes can learn that certain interactions may be appropriate in public whereas other communications must be handled privately with the coach.

Thus, we are calling for an attitude on the part of coaches that encourages discussion of the rationale for directives to athletes. In collegiate athletics, coaching staffs are generally large enough to allow an athlete to talk with a coach when questions arise. Untimely questions would only make sense when the athlete perceives a blatant infringement of rights or a great risk to self or others. The point is that the athlete's questioning of a procedure is acceptable, and this ability to assert one's sovereignty should be encouraged.

V

Our conclusion, then, is that simple paternalism cannot be justified in the case of the adult athlete: The coach cannot pressure an athlete to do anything by offering the rationale that it is in the athlete's interests to do so. The coach can compel an athlete when his or her behavior is likely to hurt others, or when it is clear that the athlete does not understand the risks being taken, but not simply because the coach thinks that it is "best" for the athlete to do what is asked. In promoting this objective, coaches should encourage questions from athletes and make certain that the athletes are making an informed choice to participate.[7]

Now, it may be objected that our conclusion takes the teeth out of the coach's ability to mentor the athlete in a meaningful fashion; that is, by requiring the coach to tolerate and even encourage questions from athletes, we have undercut the traditional authority coaches use to encourage athletes to athletic excellence. Our response is simply that in a free society, individual choice means taking a risk, in this case, that by their own choices, athletes may find that they are not able to perform at their full potential. In other words, by leaving the choice to athletes and by refusing to allow the coach to utilize coercion, athletes assume more of the responsibility for their own achievement.

The advantages to be gained from requiring these limits on a coach's authority should not be underestimated. First, when the athlete follows the directives of a coach, it will be because of the trust and confidence placed in the coach's expertise and not merely because of the coach's power over the individual. In this way, we greatly reduce the potential that the coach will abuse an individual's sovereignty and increase the athlete's sense of self-discipline and personal achievement. Second, when the athlete acts or forbears, he/she will have full responsibility for so doing. If we do not insist on informed consent on the part of the athlete, we cannot be sure that these risks are undertaken willingly.

Notes

1. This essay was developed from a paper presented at the 1981 Philosophic Society for the Study of Sport Conference held at Trinity College in Hartford, CT. The authors wish to acknowledge the expertise of James Tehan, J.D., regarding the legal issues that the paper addresses.

2. The reader is advised to review Thomas' (12) 1980 presentation which addresses the issue of athlete's rights from the perspective of informed consent and the problems that arise from the sport environment specifically. Thomas' major point is that socialization of athletes must be clearly understood because of the way that it may interfere with informed consent. In addition, Kidd's (7) article discusses the athlete's rights when psychological interventions are introduced to maximize sports performance.

3. The recent emergence of the field of applied sport psychology has clearly demonstrated the significant impact of psychology on sport performance. At the same time, judgments on the causes of psychological injury have a great deal more subjectivity attached to them. Generally, there is broad acceptance of what constitutes physical injury; psychology has not yet advanced to the point where broad acceptance exists for what constitutes psychological injury and this paper therefore excludes this topic from detailed discussion.

4. Zeigler (13) provides a discussion of the coach's sources of power, love, fear, and inter-personal power that can be used in the athletic setting. Also, Lenk (8) discusses "acceptable" and "unacceptable" uses of manipulation of the athlete by the coach.

5. Alan Sack, (11, p. 94) the director for the Center for Athlete's Rights, encourages paternalism by advocating the establishment of an outside organization to protect the rights of the athletes: "There is a crying need, therefore, for an organization to defend the rights of athletes. Such an organization would provide high school and college athletes with the information and resources they need in order to gain control over their education."

6. To date, most courts have not been particularly receptive to this argument. Particularly in contact sports, the weight of legal decisions has gone against players, finding that such injuries have been

III. Women, Sportsmanship and Relationships

unforseeable, unavoidable, or that the athlete assumed the risk (19; 21). However, when the facts of a particular case indicated intentional conduct, lack of good faith, or coercion, courts will ignore the traditional rule and allow the injured player to recover monetary damages (15; 17; 18).

7. Lenk (8: pp. 116-117) refers to this as "A Program of Enlightment." "Not enough has been done and taken care of the 'enlightment' and the critical capacities of the athlete to think over his role and the importance and significance of his successes or defeats as well as his athletic activity in general." Further, he asserts that, "coaches and officials should be convinced of the value of the guiding idea that sportsmen and athletes should be able to critically think over their training, possibly to participate in shaping programs and strategies, and linguistically to articulate their ideas in order to no longer be a 'speechless product and object.'"

Bibliography

1. *Association for Intercollegiate Athletics for Women Handbook.* (1974). AIAW Publications, Washington, DC.
2. Dworkin, Gerald. (1971). "Paternalism." In R.A. Wasserstrom (Ed.), *Morality and the Law.* Belmont, CA: Wadsworth.
3. Feinberg, Joel. (1971). "Legal Paternalism." *Canadian Journal of Philosophy*, I, pp. 104-125.
4. Edes, Gordon. (1983, July 11). "U.S. Coach Raps Soviet Officials." *The Los Angeles Times*, III, p. 1.
5. "Frank Kush Report." (1979, Nov. 2). *The Los Angeles Times*, III. p. 13.
6. Keenan, F.W. (1975). "Justice and Sport." *Journal of the Philosophy of Sport*, II, pp. 111-123.
7. Kidd, Bruce. (1979). "Athletes' Rights, the Coach and the Sport Psychologist." In P. Klavora and J. Daniel (Eds.), *Coach, Athlete and the Sport Psychologist.* Toronto: University of Toronto.
8. Lenk, Hans. (1978). *Social Philosophy of Athletics.* Champain, IL: Stipes Publ.
9. Mill, John Stuart. (1859). *On Liberty.* New York: Bobbs-Merrill.
10. *National College Athletic Association Manual, 1979-1980.* (1979). Shawnee Mission, KS: NCAA Publication.
11. Sack, Allen. (1981). "A Proposal for a Center for Athletes' Rights." *Proceedings of the National Association for Physical Education in Higher Education. Volume II* (pp. 91-97). Champaign, IL: Human Kinetics.
12. Thomas, Carolyn. (1981). "The Golden Girl Syndrome: Thoughts on a Training Ethic." *Proceedings of the National Association for Physical*

Education in Higher Education. Volume I (pp. 136-146). Champaign, IL: Human Kinetics.

13. Zeigler, Earle. (1980). "Coach and Athlete-In Each Other's Power." *Proceedings of the 1979 National Association for Physical Education in Higher Education.* Volume I (pp. 56-65). Champaign, IL: Human Kinetics.

14. United States President's Commission. (1983). "Informed Consent as Active Shared Decision Making." *President's Commission for the Study of Ethical Problems in Medicine & Biomedical & Behavioral Research.* Washington, DC: Government Printing Office.

Legal References

15. *Carabba v. Anacortes School District.* 72 Wn.2d 939, 435 P2d 677 (1967).

16. *Cobbs v. Grant.* 8 Cal 3d 229,502 P2dl (1972).

17. *Mogabob v. Orleans Parish.* 239 So. 2d 456 (La.App 1970).

18. *Morris v. Union District A.* 160 Washington 121,294 p988 (1931).

19. *Oswald v. Township High School.* No. 24 84 Ill. App3d 326,406 N.E. 2d 157 (1980).

20. *Scholendorff v. Society of New York Hospital.* 211 N.Y. 125,105 N.E. 92,95 (1914).

21. *Truman v. Thomas.* 27 Cal 3d 285,291 (1981).

22. *Vandrell v. School District.* 233 Ore. 1, 376, P2d 406 (1962).

EATING DISORDERS, PHYSICAL FITNESS, PERSONS AND PHYSICAL EDUCATION

SAUL ROSS

Observers of the contemporary social scene are well aware of the major increase in physical activity on the part of many Canadians in the past few years. This change in lifestyle has become apparent in Canada as well as in many Western industrialized nations as governments have funded organizations to promote exercise amongst the general population. ParticipACTION, created by the Federal government, was charged with the responsibility of getting Canadians moving through a mass advertising campaign aimed to encourage sports and physical fitness (Ross, 1984). ParticipACTION's emergence coincided, more or less, with the publication of Cooper's book, Aerobics and the jogging craze was launched. Vigorous exercise programs, in a variety of packages, became the rage, justified by the health-related benefits to be derived. Obesity was out, replaced by thinness as the desired physical appearance. ParticipACTION's campaign to improve physical fitness has been actively abetted by many physical educators both within the schools and in the general population as well.

At the very same time as the physical fitness boom was expanding, involving children and adults of all ages, incidents of bulimia and anorexia nervosa have been increasing sharply (Eppling, Pierce and Stefan, p. 40). Part of the reported increase may be due to better diagnosis by health care workers and more efficient reporting but "most authors believe that the disorder is actually increasing" (*Idem.*). Bulimia, in its mildest form, leads to uneven nutrition as a few meals are skipped deliberately to compensate for small splurges in eating. At its worst it can be a deadly binge-and-purge syndrome as excessively large quantities of food are consumed at one sitting to be followed by self-induced vomiting and excessive use of laxatives. Anorexia nervosa is a disorder characterized by a voluntary refusal to eat, extreme loss of weight, and in some cases, death. While it is most prevalent amongst adolescent females, recently it has been reported in males, children and adults.

An increase in self-starvation occurring contemporaneously with a major campaign to promote better health by raising the level of physical fitness is a strange paradox. For physical educators it represents a development which demands their serious consideration. Greater participation in exercise usually signifies a desire to upgrade the level of physical fitness which we generally equate with an enhancement of

232

health but self-starvation, which is carried on at the very same time, and often under the misguided guise of promoting health, is a complete negation of all interpretations of better health. For physical educators what is most alarming is the growing clinical evidence that excessive activity may be an integral part of a causal chain which can result in extreme weight loss and death (Eppling, Pierce and Stefan, p. 21, p. 40-41). These authors claim that 75% of anorectics are physically active, participating strenuously in activities such as jogging and swimming. This syndrome applies to a condition they call "activity-based anorexia" which may be identified as a specific subset of the more general diagnostic category, anorexia nervosa.

Due to the complexity of the condition many diverse attempts will be needed in order to provide a reasonably satisfactory answer. At least two categories of explanation for this conundrum are available, one scientific and the other sociocultural/philosophical. What follows is the beginning of an attempt to account for this seemingly strange development. Both lines of explanation have important consequences and implications for physical education at the macro level (general education aimed at the entire population via the mass media) as well as at the micro level (individual classes, in schools, at the "Y"s, community centres, and private health clubs).

I. Biological Factor

Current scientific thinking regards the relationship between physical activity and food intake as a reciprocal arrangement. Psychologists, such as Levitsky (1974), who have studied the matter, have demonstrated in animals what physical educators have long known — physical activity before mealtime suppresses appetite and hence there is a reduction of food intake in both animals and human beings. At first the idea of a reduction in food intake occurring when energy expenditure is increasing appears to contradict common sense but an explanation based on evolutionary biology theory resolves the matter. Where food supply is scarce and widely dispersed the organism, in order to survive, must increase energy expenditure while reducing food intake in order to travel the distances needed to obtain food. In human beings, particularly for those who inhabit a culture that has recently placed even greater value on slimness, excessive exercise can readily become a positive reinforcer of behaviour which, in this case, means reduced food intake.

Exercise is an important factor in reducing body weight. A clear link between exercise and suppressed appetite is quickly discovered by the person engaging in exercise when vigorous activity before a meal reduces the desire to eat. This phenomenon serves as a positive reinforcer and so anyone seeking to reduce weight comes to regard exercise as doubly effective. First, through increased activity more energy is expended, thereby engendering weight loss and, secondly, where appetite is depressed lesser food intake — the goal of most diets — results in further weight loss. Operant conditioning is in effect here and repeated use, with the attendant positive reinforcement, serves to entrench the behaviour.

II. Sociocultural/Philosophical Factors

Three interrelated factors can be identified: (i) the role of the media; (ii) the notion of health; and (iii) the conceptual understanding of persons. Each is discussed separately but it is important to emphasize that they are interconnected, influencing the thoughts and behaviour of all of us to varying degrees.

(i) The Role of the Media

Our aesthetic tastes are determined, in part, by the culture we inhabit. Implicit in this insight is the role played by various media in reflecting and transmitting the culture. In contemporary times television appears to have the greatest impact with newspapers, radio, movies, magazines and books exerting varying degrees of influence depending upon availability and readership. Years ago, before the advent of the modern media, art, as a medium, not only reflected the culture but also exerted a greater influence on many people. An examination of 16th, 17th and 18th century paintings by the Italian, Dutch, and Flemish masters shows well-endowed women, whom we would consider "chubby" at the very least, as models of beauty. In recent times, post World War I, Hollywood stars possessed full figures. Marilyn Monroe and Betty Grable serve as examples.

Shortly thereafter Twiggy, a toothpick-thin waif, became the female ideal, and slender, androgynous figures of both sexes were celebrated. Thinness became the lauded and desired "look"; the lean and bony figure was promoted by people who were in a position to influence the masses. Jane Fonda, the new "guru" of exercise and physical fitness, sold countless record albums and television cassettes. Her gaunt, lean look was the goal to strive for. Psychologist David Garner, director of psychiatric research at Toronto General Hospital, voices grave concern about Jane Fonda's influence, noting in particular that her "thinly veiled pursuit of thinness is causing women to crave anorexia nervosa" (B. McAndrew, p. A5). He regards the media treatment of anorexia nervosa as trivializing the disorder and by promoting the lean, gaunt look "helps convince young women that anorexia nervosa is something that is a healthy part of growing up" (*Idem*). Women face immense pressures from society; these are intensified and exacerbated by media presentations of extremely thin, almost emaciated-looking women as the models of beauty.

The influence of the media on anorectics needs to be appreciated in light of the following considerations. Those who suffer from anorexia nervosa see themselves as much heavier than they are, and maintain unrealistically low, sometimes dangerous weight levels. Perhaps of greater concern is the personality composition of the anorectic. Those afflicted are generally high achievers and possessors of a very strong sense of morality. Once they embark on a path which they deem to be appropriate and correct, one which does not infringe upon the rights of others, they are very persistent. Messages of diet encouragement, whether from physical educators on a person-to-person basis or from stars such as Jane Fonda through the visual and print media, serve to reinforce the anorectic's resolve. Garner's comments are more cogent when the self-perception and personality configuration of anorectics are taken into account. Although others see them as underweight, gaunt, drawn-out, even emaciated they still regard themselves as much too heavy.

Jane Fonda has publicly admitted that she has had serious eating disorders and many exercise physiologists have raised important questions about the validity of some of the advice she offers. Instead of focusing on these points the media have accorded her a degree of quasi-respectability and, as a famous movie and T.V. star, she is believable. Advertising bombards women with images glorifying thinness, encouraging them to have bodies which are psychologically and biologically destructive. Lack of knowledge about exercise physiology and the medical aspects of eating disorders prevents the general population from criticizing Fonda's exercise program. Large sums of money are involved in the production, promotion and sale of her products and that, almost by itself, creates a juggernaut effect. Knowledgeable physical educators have not spoken out publicly on these matters and if they have, their voices have not been amplified by the media. One result has been to equate the lean, emaciated look and near-starvation regime with beauty and health.

(ii) Health

The World Health Organization defines health as "a state of complete physical, mental and social well-being, and not merely the absence of disease or infirmity." As a beginning definition this may be satisfactory but as a definitive statement it appears to be inadequate in at least two ways. First, it lacks an emphasis on the dynamic quality of wellness, the feeling a truly healthy person has of being able to achieve, to accomplish, to do. Absent is an intimation of a zest for living, and an appetite for engaging in healthful activities and satisfying social interactions. Secondly, and perhaps more importantly, the definition does not go far enough; there is no comment regarding the interrelated nature of physical health, mental health, and social well-being. In the absence of such discussion the impression given is that each of the three — physical health, mental health, and social well-being — can be achieved independently and discretely. That assumption merits analysis since, on one level of understanding, it invokes the notion of what we believe constitutes a person.

Health and wellness are difficult concepts to define precisely even though most people would readily assert that they know what is meant by these words. However, when the concept of the whole person is brought to the fore certain questions emerge which challenge our thinking. Can we consider a person to be healthy if there is a deficiency in any one of the three components listed in the WHO's definition? What can "physical health" mean for the "whole person" if there is a mental disorder or if there is an absence of social well-being? What does "mental health" mean if there is physical illness? Can a person who is "mentally" healthy but "physically" ill be called healthy? Most important, is it possible, or sensible, to even attempt to subdivide the notion, "health," or is it an indivisible concept, one that can only be described in terms of varying degrees? These questions have great importance for physical education when emphasis is placed on physical fitness which, in turn, becomes equated with health and wellness.

An increase in physical activity is generally regarded as an improvement in physical health. Under the WHO's definition this may be an acceptable view but when the notion of the whole person is invoked judgment must be withheld until other factors are considered. For instance, what effect does a higher level of physical fitness have on the health of an individual if that gain has been achieved at the expense of "mental health" or a reduction in "social well-being"? These are issues physical educators need to address when the matter of health/wellness is raised. Its importance is magnified when we come to realize that certain people are using massive doses of exercise in the name of improvement in their health but they are actually accomplishing the diametrically opposite goal. This is the very behaviour pattern of the person Eppling, Pierce and Stefan have identified as the activity-based anorectic.

(iii) Theory of Persons

Our philosophical heritage has descended from the ancient Greeks whose aesthetic beliefs inclined them to adopt a position of favour of symmetry and symmetrical development. "A sound mind in a healthy body" is a reflection of the belief in symmetrical development but, on one level of interpretation, this is a misleading way of describing a person. To speak of symmetrical development between mind and body implies that there are two separate and isolatable entities here, mind and body, and that each can be developed independently of the other. Where mind and body are regarded as separate entities a dualism exists. Elsewhere (1986) I have pointed out some of the epistemological consequences which arise from a dualistic conception of a person. Here it is important to note that a dualistic conception allows for the notion of bodily health as something separate from mental health and vice versa.

Descartes, the father of modern philosophy, has articulated a dualistic theory of persons, one where mind and body are deemed to be separate entities. Malcolm, a contemporary philosopher, observes that the "belief in the essential separateness of mind and body, is a common assumption of the most articulate and influential philosophers in the past three centuries" (p. 12). Separation of mind and body has a long and deep tradition in Western thought and has strongly influenced developments in many fields, medicine, education and physical education included. With regard to medicine, the body, from the neck down, is assigned to the physician; the part of the body above the neck is delegated to the care of the psychiatrist and psychologist. A similar split is discernable in education. Matters pertaining to the "mind" are assigned to the care of classroom teachers with the care of the body given over to physical educators.

Philosophers whose professional interest and education qualify them to examine such matters critically have, in the view of Malcolm, implicitly accepted a dualistic thesis. Gerber and Morgan describe the situation as it pertains to physical education.

> Strangely, those who have been interested in sport and/or physical education, have shown little interest in the philosophy of the body. They have treated the body as an object to be trained, trimmed, studied in a laboratory, or made a cause célèbre. In the first quarter of the twentieth century when the physical educators became satisfied with the idea of unity of mind and body, they ceased to speculate about it in any meaningful way (p. 146).

Without philosophical discussion and analysis, and without wide spread dissemination of these findings in the physical education and popular literature the influence of Cartesian dualism remains pervasive. Where dualism is accepted uncritically the notion of training the body as something apart from the mind is a reasonable view to hold. Under such a view one can speak of bodily health as something separate and apart from mental health. The idea of an integrated whole person is replaced by a view which sees a person as a fragmented entity composed of two component parts, mind and body.

Physical education's recent emphasis on physical fitness as the goal serves to reinforce the notion that body and mind are separate entitites. This interpretation is feasible in a culture which has a lengthy tradition of belief in dualism. Inadvertently, the stress on physical fitness may be a contributing factor in the increase in anorexia nervosa since, as discussed above, those who suffer from this disorder must have a distorted view of health. A wholesome view of health, one which applies to the total, integrated being of the person does not allow for self-starvation under the guise of improving physical health. Under an integrated view of persons health, as a concept, is only applicable to the person; it cannot be applied to only one "component" or the other.

A theory of a person as an integrated, monistic being has been elaborated by P. F. Strawson, the contemporary philosopher, in his book, *Individuals: An Essay in Descriptive Metaphysics* (1959), where chapter 3 is entitled "Persons." Cartesian dualism (subjective idealism) with its notion that states of consciousness are ascribed to mental substances (minds) which are distinct from, but somehow connected to, bodies and materialism behaviourism ("no-ownership" theory) which holds that states of consciousness are not, strictly speaking, ascribed to anything at all, are shown to be ultimately incoherent. In their place Strawson presents his own concept of a person, one which he claims comes closest to coinciding with what we ordinarily think of as a person. He states that "the concept of a person is the concept of a type of entity such that both predicates ascribing states of consciousness and predicates ascribing corporeal characteristics, a physical situation, etc. are equally applicable to a single individual of that single type" (Strawson, p. 101).

To better comprehend what the quotation just cited means it is important to add that Strawson is adamant, insisting that the concept of a person is a primitive (indivisible) concept which "is not to be analyzed as that of an animated body or of an embodied anima" (p. 103). Starting from either of these two positions, an animated body or an embodied anima, leads to insurmountable obstacles which Strawson wishes to preclude. Under Strawson's thesis the concept of mind is derivative from the primitive (basic, indivisible) concept of person and the concept "person" cannot be constructed from the two component parts, mind and body, as Descartes attempted to do. An important implication arises from this view — we cannot speak of a mind as a thing separate and apart from a person nor can we speak of a body as a thing separate and apart from a person. Every time we speak of mind and body we must be referring to some particular person's mind or body. As a result, whatever happens to that particular person's mind and/or body affects that person

238

as an integrated monistic entity. Health, under this thesis, can have only one understanding and only one application: whatever happens to any part of a person affects the health status of *the whole person*.

Under a dualistic thesis, where mind and body are envisaged as separate, isolatable entities it is logical, and possible, to speak of mental health and physical health as discrete, unrelated conditions. Within this frame of reference physical fitness and physical health can be considered without reference to mental health or the "whole person" since a dualistic person consists of two parts, mind and body. Where a dualistic thesis is replaced by a monistic theory, mental health and physical health cannot be separated logically since every health status refers to the particular *person* being described. Health, as suggested earlier, appears to be an indivisible concept we apply in terms of degree — poor, good, excellent — to a particular person.

Where dualism is the prevalently accepted belief an emphasis on physical fitness may serve to strengthen the mistaken view of separation of mind and body. To speak of physical fitness under these conditions is to imply that the body can be trained and developed as a separate entity and health can be misinterpreted as a status attributable to one component part of a person. Such mistaken beliefs can lead to a situation where self-starvation occurs at the very same time as good health is being promoted through an increase in physical activity.

In light of the emphasis placed on increasing physical activity coupled with the influence of the mass media, in particular the prominent coverage given to diets, physical educators concerned for the health of the population are advised to note carefully the comment made by Eppling, Pierce and Stefan.

> While strenuous physical activity or severe food restriction may have independent effects on the development of anorexia, the animal research on self-starvation suggests that the combined effects of these variables are multiplicative rather than additive. Thus, activity anorexia is most likely to occur in families, social groups, or organizations that encourage both high-rate activity and dieting practices (p. 41).

Physical education is dedicated to the improvement and enhancement of health and is primarily interested in prevention rather than cure. Physical educators who give advice to students in school and to the general population regarding exercise and diet must take the quotation just cited into serious account. We must be extremely careful to avoid contributing anything which may induce anorexia or bulimia. That is a minimal position for our role ought to be more prominent. Due

III. Women, Sportsmanship and Relationships

to the close relationship physical educators have with their students they are in a privileged position to raise questions about all aspects of good health, including what constitutes good health practices. By helping students gain greater insights into what a person is, along with a better appreciation of the notion of health, we could well prevent some from starting down the wrong path.

Anorexia nervosa and bulimia are characterized by many psychological symptoms. Eppling, Pierce and Stefan offer a thought-provoking observation, "While these symptoms may have importance for the etiology, diagnosis, and treatment of many anorexias, they may just as plausibly be by-products of activity-induced self-starvation" (p. 43). To be forewarned is to be forearmed. Physical educators must guard against setting anyone on the path of activity-induced self-starvation. To guard against such eventualities a return to the basic principle of our field is recommended but with some modification. Physical education's basic aim is the social, emotional, mental, moral and physical development of the person. It is the total development of the whole person which is now to be understood as an integrated, non-divisible concept. Just as health cannot be divided so also is the notion of human development indivisible. We can emphasize one specific aspect but that does not detract from the fact that it is the whole person who is involved always. Dynamic good health is the status sought for all but now it is to be understood as meaning total health for each person in the integrated, monistic sense given to the term by Strawson.

References

Cooper, K. *Aerobics*, New York: Bantam Books, 1968.

Descartes, R. *The Philosophical Works of Descartes*. Rendered Into English by E.S. Haldane & G.R.T. Ross, Cambridge: University Press, 1967.

Eppling, W.F., Pierce, W.D., and Stefan, I. "A Theory of Activity Based Anorexia," *International Journal of Eating Disorders*. Vol. 3, No. 1, 1983, p. 27-46.

Gerber, E.W. and Morgan, W.J. Editors. *Sport and the Body: A Philosophical Symposium*, Second edition, Philadelphia: Lea & Febiger, 1979.

Levitsky, D. "Feeding Conditions and Intermeal Relationships," *Physiology and Behavior*, Vol. 12, 1974, p. 779-787.

Malcolm, N. *Problems of Mind: Descartes to Wittgenstein*, New York: Harper & Row Publishers, 1971.

McAndrew, B. "Jane Fonda driving women to anorexia researcher says," *Toronto Sunday Star*, August 26, 1984, p. A5.

Ross, S. "Political and Philosophical Implications Arising From a Public Education Campaign: The Canadian Experience," in *Leisure: Toward a Theory and a Policy*, edited by H. Ruskin, Cranbury, N.H.: Associated University Presses, 1984, p. 80-102.

Ross, S. "Cartesian Dualism and Physical Education: Epistemological Incompatibility," in *Mind and Body: East Meets West*, edited by S. Kleinman, Champaign, Ill.: Human Kinetics Publishers, Inc., 1986, pp. 15-24.

Strawson, P.F. *Individuals: An Essay in Descriptive Metaphysics*, London: Methuen & Company, Limited, 1959.

COACH AND ATHLETE:
IN EACH OTHER'S POWER

EARLE F. ZEIGLER

Walt Kelly's Pogo once said, "We have faults which we have hardly used yet." This wise creature seems to be describing the situation in the United States in which "a typical roll call of contemporary villains: shoplifters, trashers, time-clock cheaters, expense-account padders, tax evaders, political bribe takers, perjurers, economic exploiters...and those responsible for violent crime" (Marty, 1975, p. 64) affects the quality of life both directly and indirectly. With such a situation prevailing, one could hardly expect that competitive sport would be free from society's influence or that, in turn, the growing influence of sport would not affect societal practices.

Such problems take us into the realm of ethics and morality, a topic that is receiving a greater amount of attention in professional preparation in many fields today. We are discovering, however, that the entire matter is quite thoroughly tangled; we are tied into knots from which we are only feebly seeking to extricate ourselves. Nowhere do we seem to find weaker efforts to escape from our ethical dilemma than in the realm of highly competitive sport. We hope that the "good guys" will win, but we are haunted by the slogan that "nice guys finish last" — and who wants to be a "good loser"?

Part of our problem stems from the fact "we have reached a stage in our civilization where many different strands of ethical tradition have been woven together" (Miller, 1960, p. 51). This has resulted in our society's being faced with a variety of distinctive ethical patterns from which to choose — actually an almost impossible task. Thus, we have been influenced by (a) the Hebraic culture based on the Ten Commandments, (b) the Christian system based on the Beatitudes, (c) the Medieval way of life based on penance, (d) the Renaissance culture based on individual development along with freedom, (e) the Industrial Revolution based on the application of science to technology, and (f) the scientific approach based on empirical method and its influence on the determination of truth (Miller, 1960). Our dilemma today (rather than continuing along, seemingly hopelessly mired in the sludge that characterizes the welter of conflicting value systems with which we are confronted) is to seek to make sense out of a situation that demands serious attention as we approach the 21st century.

Concomitants of the Demand for Improved Levels of Performance

One of the aspects of highly competitive sport where sense is needed is the use of stimulants, painkillers, and/or body-building agents by the athlete. This often develops through the advice and encouragement of the coach and/or athletic therapist to improve the level of performance required for success in an increasingly competitive environment. The question has a direct relationship to what has been identified as the need for ethic in a sports world of cheating and violence. Frenchman Jean Borotra, a former world class tennis player, spoke out as chairman of the International Fair Play Committee in an article which decried the ever-increasing departure from the true "sporting spirit" (Borotra, 1975).

This appeal for "fair play" has been expanded and clarified in Peter McIntosh's excellent new volume *Fair Play*, in which he speaks of the "industrial transformation of sport [because] the level of performance necessary for success [has been causing an upgrading that] has recently been accelerating curvilinearly" (McIntosh, 1979, p., 136). As a result, the highly intensive training required for success in competition today "has led to the adoption of methods which may permanently injure the athlete, such as the taking of anabolic steroids to increase muscular bulk" (McIntosh, 1979, p. 136).

The entire problem of drugs and performance demands continuing investigation. This is only part of a still greater societal issue — the use of marijuana, LSD, heroin, alcohol, tobacco, and the variety of related major and minor drugs being used. It is true, of course, that many different natural and synthetic chemical substances and preparations have been used since ancient times in efforts to improve both physical performance and endurance. At the present time, however, the International Olympic Committee has declared the following doping substances to be unacceptable and cause for disqualification from further participation — when their use can be detected: (a) stimulants used to increase performance and ward off fatigue — such as the psychomotor stimulants — (e.g., amphetamines and sympathomimetic amines such as ephedrine and related compounds); (b) painkillers used to help the athlete continue with top performance despite sprain and injury with varying levels of pain — such as the narcotic and synthetic narcotic analgesics — (e.g., morphine and novocaine); (c) so-called body builders used to promote growth and weight gain — such as anabolic steroids. The large majority of the drugs in the stimulant and painkilling groups are addictive in nature. Further, when they are used to disguise fatigue, the over-exertion and heat buildup may precipitate circulatory failure. The body-building agents have been shown to have damaging side — and after effects.

243

III. Women, Sportsmanship and Relationships

Even though many of us are parents, and all of us consider ourselves professionals in the field of sport and physical education, we may know little more than the average parent about drugs. The average pusher would probably regard the large majority of us as being "out of it" in regard to overall knowledge of the subject of drugs. We may know generally that drugs are classified typically as opiates, stimulants, psychedelics, and depressants. But, for example, did you know that heroin is *prepared* from morphine, which is *extracted* from opium? Further, did you know that a stimulant like amphetamine is *not* physically addictive like an opiate, but that is does produce a psychological dependence? Did you know that mescaline is a drug *derived* from the peyote itself and produces more vivid visual impressions than the cactus from which it is derived? Finally, moving from the psychedelic category to the depressants, did you know that *more people die* in the United States from an overdose of barbiturates (addictives taken in capsule form) than any other single substance? (I'll omit the inhalants, such as glue-sniffers, from our present discussion.)

Level of Consumption

Just how many people of all ages have been, and are presently, involved with the consumption of some type of stimulants, painkillers, and body-builders as part of their efforts toward high-level achievement and winning in competitive sport? Who knows? One can't help but believe, however, that what we see, hear, and read about drugs represents merely the tip of the iceberg. This problem has already assumed large proportions, and its severity is increasing almost daily.

We can get some indications about the matter from Shinnick's (Note 1) "Testimony to the U.S. Senate Subcommittee on Juvenile Delinquency" in 1973 in which he discussed his earlier experiences and observations in the 1960's. He concluded that "there seems to be evidence that drug usage is on the rise, especially among highly specialized competitive teams with management structures that insulate them from close interaction with the team members" (p. 20). In a study completed about the same time, O'Shea (1970) states that "while there seems to be no serious side effects associated with short term treatment (3 to 6 weeks) of anabolic steroids, long term usage must be viewed with extreme caution" (p. 13). Of course, who is there to control the individual who experiments with such body-building agents?

The number of articles on this topic seems to be increasing. Recently, for example, Renate Neufeld, the former East German female sprinter, claimed that she was forced to take performance enhancing drugs in the form of hormone tablets ("It's Not Nice," 1979). This was followed by Steve Riddick's innocuous admission that he was taking pills made of bee's pollen enriched with Vitamin E as an essential part of his diet ("Sprinter Credits Pill," 1979). A few weeks later we learned that Ken Stabler, the football quarterback, was still under investigation in an incident in which a cocaine plant was evidently made on the car of a California sports writer, although Stabler denies any connection with the incident (*Times*, Raines, 1979). Janice Kaplan stated that drugtaking by women to turn them "into men or keep them in suspended childhood" (Kaplan, 1979, p. 2) is really not as widespread as the gossip would lead us to believe. Her concern is that we eliminate the idea that the "nymphet syndrome" is desirable for women because it leads them to greater success in any sport.

It is apparent that we are going to hear more, rather than less, about this perplexing problem in the months and years ahead. We will undoubtedly end up with ever more stringent regulations and accompanying testing to determine rule infractions. Of course, we will typically face the question of whether coaches and athletes are living up to the letter and/or the spirit of the various rules and regulations. One of the latest practices to plague us is blood doping. Even though Webb (1978) states that "reported research is inconclusive and inconsistent regarding the benefits to be expected," (p. 189) a recent Canadian Association of Sports Sciences *Newsletter* explains that "British Army tests over the past year have shown conclusively that blood doping can improve athletic performance substantially" (1978, p. 4). Can we tell the coach and the athletes that their own blood can't be used in this manner? Further, how can we detect it by testing if such a practice is routinely followed?

Coach and Athlete — In Each Other's Power

The Scenario has now been outlined. We have a hypothesized chain of events in which one person may be exploited or used by another. It could be argued that it usually is the coach who exploits the athlete, but one can also imagine situations in which the opposite is the case. (In this paper we will largely avoid discussion of the extent to which athletes are presumably exploiting themselves for benefits that are considered to be more important than the possible harm imposed upon self, relatives, and close friends by the improper use of stimulants, painkillers, and body-building agents.)

Consider first the situation in which the athlete may be exploited by the coach. We are all familiar with the situation in California in which a number of athletes recently sued the coach and a university because they had presumably been used. They had been brought to the university with the lure of athletic scholarships, university degrees, and perhaps an opportunity to receive a contract to play "pro ball." It is being argued that certain academic programs were recommended so that continuing eligibility would be maintained and that a trust may have been broken because the desired educational knowledge, competency, and skill were not acquired. In some cases not even the academic degree was obtained, and the athlete was "cast adrift" because eligibility was used up after 4 years of play. Finally, to make the case even stronger, imagine that during the time of active participation the athletes were often encouraged to take certain stimulants, painkillers, and/or body-building agents. Certainly this last stipulation is well within the realm of possibility and is probably occurring regularly in the case of many athletes in a variety of sports.

We are now definitely faced with a philosophical question to which we may seek appropriate and just answers. Fortunately, there have been several recent attempts to look at some of these questions in the philosophical literature, although the treatments are not based on problems of this nature that arise in highly competitive sport. For example, Flemming has asked the question, "Are we morally forbidden to treat a man entirely as a means to some other end?" (1978, p. 283). The "greatest good for the greatest number" argument of the utilitarians seemingly gives us the opportunity to use a person to some extent for the good of the whole. Further, Nozick (1974) has argued that a Kantian must pursue the greatest good while only viewing the welfare of an individual involved as a "side constraint," to be considered while in active pursuit of a higher goal or greater good (p. 32).

Blum (1973) approaches the subject from a different perspective. He argues that it can be wrong to use a person even though the individual involved doesn't believe that he or she has been wronged and, in fact, is not the least bit unhappy about his or her involvement. Blum sees deception as using a person, and deception is wrong no matter how it is viewed. He also argues that people often know they are being used, and thus the fact that deception is being used is indeed separate from the wrong use of a person.

One of the most helpful philosophical treatments of this topic has been made available by Wilson (1978), who further examines Blum's example of the love relationship between man and woman. Obviously, we will need to transpose some of the questions raised into the realm of competitive sport and the relationship that may exist between coach and athlete (and vice versa). Wilson refers initially to the terms "entrapment" and "exploitation" and seeks to define them as accurately as possible. Entrapment is defined as an action that lures another into danger, difficulty, or self-incrimination. Exploitation, which usually accompanies entrapment, is the utilization of another for selfish purposes. (The latter, Wilson believes, can be active or passive in nature — passive when no deception is involved or necessary.)

Wilson argues further that entrapment "is thus a form of treachery, an abuse of trust, very akin, as the metaphors suggest, to the treachery of the soldier who abuses the conventions for instituting a truce" (p. 303). Further, "if entrapment is the treacherous acquisition of power over a person, exploitation is the exercise of such power for selfish ends" (p. 303). Obviously, there are general questions of a moral nature that arise when any form of official or unofficial power is used for either selfish or benevolent ends. Why is this so? It is true because "any source of power provides a kind of lever with which one person can move another, a means of influencing the other to act or to refrain from acting in a certain way, a means neither rational nor straightforwardly coercive" (p. 304). It has now become clear to us as teachers and coaches what a tremendous ethical responsibility we have in our everyday dealings with student-athletes — a responsibility that often appears to be assumed in an almost unbelievably light manner.

The Sources of This Interpersonal Power

Power is defined as the ability or official capacity to exercise control or influence over others. Politicians have such power or influence, bureaucrats have it, parents have it, and coaches most certainly have such power to influence their eager charges. Fine distinctions among the concepts power, authority, influence, control, etc., will not be drawn here. Our basic concern in this context is the power that the coaches exert — i.e., the leverage that they can apply regarding the athlete's use of stimulants, pain-killers, or body-building agents in order to improve performance and thereby achieve success in sport. What are the elements or sources of interpersonal power, then, which coaches can bring to bear on aspiring athletes, elements that must be used very carefully and with foresight because of the great impact they may have on young athletes striving for success?

First, Wilson introduces the concept of *love* as perhaps the major one of a number of such feelings that one person might have for another. Other terms used to describe such a feeling are affection, friendship, sympathy, trust, respect, awe, and admiration. If athletes have any or all of these feelings for their coach, then the coach is continually faced with an assessment of what constitutes a reasonable request that might be made of the athlete, and what might actually be an imposition. If the coach were to make too great a demand of the athlete based on the amount of love or similar emotion felt, the reaping of excess benefit from such an excessive demand could well constitute exploitation to a greater or lesser extent. Additionally, in the case of the athlete, other feelings that might accompany those indicated above would be gratitude, indebtedness, obligation, and desire for approval (see Wilson, 1978, pp. 304-307).

Second, a frequent source of power over another which is held by coaches is that of fear — fear that can be overt, subtle, and often irrational. Herein coaches have a lever that can be used if and when they deem it necessary in dealing with their athletes. The athlete may be afraid of losing his/her scholarship, education, place on the team, status as an athlete (and possible future employment), and even status as a person.

A third source of interpersonal power that could well place the coach in too strong a position vis-a-vis the athlete, is that the athlete may have too strong a desire, or too pressing a need, to make the grade athletically. If this were to be the case, the coach would not have to be exceptionally bright to realize this and to be tempted occasionally to use such a desire or need for his or her own end — even if such use were against the best interests of the athlete concerned. Many athletes come from so-called lower-middle and lower socioeconomic classes, and there may well be an urgent need, and therefore a stronger desire, to "make it" both financially and socially in our society.

A fourth way open to an unscrupulous or selfish person in our society is to take advantage of another individual through the exploitation of that person's virtues or qualities of character. In the case of the athlete, such qualities as goodness of nature, tolerance, good manners, gentleness, usefulness, and sense of responsibility can often be exploited by the ill-natured, greedy coach.

Turning the "virtue coin" over, we can immediately find a fifth mechanism — that of character defects — which may be used by person A to gain power over person B. The athlete may be gullible, susceptible to flattery, foolhardy, vain, or indeed may be subject to feelings of dislike and hatred of a rival university or particular opponent ("I'd die for dear old Yale if it meant we could beat those Harvard bastards!"). Such emotions are often very easily triggered by an unthinking or possibly unethical coach.

Flipping our virtue-vice coin back on the other side again, we note that through the ages youth has been especially prone to idealistic, unselfish commitments to causes. Such willingness to pledge allegiance may take the form of love of, or pride in, or concern for another. This sixth mechanism that might be used by the coach appeals to such elements as loyalty, idealism, patriotism, etc. For athletes, this involves a commitment, often irrational, to someone or something outside of themselves.

A seventh mechanism often exercised to gain power over another person is that of knowledge. How often have you heard the phrase "knowledge is power" in recent years? We are told almost daily that the ignorant, naive, and inexperienced person is practically powerless in our society in relation to those people who have the facts and know how to put them to work. In athletics, the coaches and their associates both individually and collectively usually know a great deal more than the young athlete. Typically, in fact, a disproportionate mystique is built around knowledge often lacking in a scientific base. Nevertheless, young athletes usually put their trust in the coach and typically follow the coach's directions in almost all matters. Coaches should ask themselves what responsibilities accompany such knowledge and resultant power.

An eighth consideration for the coach, or any person in society relating to another for that matter, is the situation in which A finds B rendered relatively powerless because of some temporary or permanent handicap or incapacity. Such a condition may be exploited by coaches presumably in possession of all their faculties (in fact, coaches could be more intelligent, more facile in thought and verbal capacity, and more self-confident). Thus, the athlete could well be dominated in this regard by a coach who was either unscrupulous or thoughtless because the athlete might be injured, might be worried about status as a student or might even lack self-confidence for one of a variety of reasons.

Finally, then, we can agree that there will always be opportunities to exert power over others in a society, because we will probably always find greater or lesser dependency existing in human relationships in any society which can be conceived. This is true with the status of the child, the aged, the infirm, the poor, the ignorant, the mentally handicapped, etc. In the case of the athlete, we typically find a strong dependency on the coach and the establishment in the United States because of the Athletic scholarship system that has developed. This dependency is present until graduation, until eligibility is used up, or until a pro contract becomes available. (I should state parenthetically that I am in favor of the practice of striving for excellence in intercollegiate sport, and I see no problem — except the question of how long we can afford it — in the granting of financial assistance to bona-fide student athletes where there is proven need.)

Summary and Conclusion

We began by stating that there is some evidence pointing toward a conclusion that an increasing number of men and women in various countries in the world are consuming stimulants, painkillers, and body-building agents in increasing amounts as part of their efforts toward winning and high-level achievement in competitive sport. We know further, through the media, that the International Olympic Committee has declared these substances to be unacceptable and cause for disqualification from further participation — if discovered. Still further,

III. Women, Sportsmanship and Relationships

evidence is accumulating that great care should be exercised in the use of these materials because of temporary and/or permanent damage that may result in the human organism. Thus, we have a situation where athletes and their coaches are faced with ethical decisions in regard to both the letter and the spirit of the rules.

The question of being in another person's power was then applied specifically to the relationship between the coach and the athlete. Nine different ways were presented in which the coach may have both official and unofficial power over the athlete. This power undoubtedly gives rise to certain general ethical or moral questions. The coach is therefore continually faced with ethical decisions as to when it is right to exercise certain levels of power over an athlete. If we combine these two problems, we can readily see that the athletes may well need guidance as to *when* and *if* they should consider taking stimulants, painkillers, and/or body-building agents.

Power over another may be exercised for one or more different reasons: for one's own benefit, for the benefit of the other, for the shared benefit of oneself and the other, etc. We are forced to the conclusion that the coach truly faces an awesome responsibility in the world today. A coach may well rationalize using his or her power over an athlete for the coach's benefit by arguing that it is all right so long as the other is not hurt or made unhappy thereby. One final question: Where in our programs of professional preparation for coaching do we help the prospective coach learn what's right?

Reference Note

1. Shinnick, P.K. Testimony to the United States Senate Subcommittee on Juvenile Delinquency. Unpublished statement obtained from the author, 1973.

References

Blum, L. "Deceiving, hurting and using." In A. Montefiore (Ed.), *Philosophy and personal relations.* London: Routledge & Kegan Paul, 1973.

Boratra, J. "The need for ethics in a sports world of cheating and violence." *The New York Times*, Oct. 26, 1975.

Canadian Association of Sports Sciences. *Newsletter*, December, 1978, X (4), 4.

Flemming, A. "Using a man as a means." *Ethics*, 1978, 88, 283-298.

"It's not nice to fool mother nature." *Maclean's* (Canada), January 8, 1979, p. 39.

Kaplan, J. "Women athletes are women too." *The New York Times*, March 4, 1979.

"Sprinter credits pill with giving him pep." *The London Free Press*, February 21, 1979.

Marty, M.E. "Vice and virtue: Our moral condition." *Time*, October 27, 1975, pp. 64-66.

McIntosh, P. *Fair play*. London: Heinemann, 1979.

Miller, S.H. "The tangle of ethics." *Harvard Business Review*, 1960, 38(1), 59-62.

Nozick, R. *Anarchy, state, and utopia*. New York: Basic Books, 1974.

O'Shea, J.P. *The effects of anabolic steroid on blood chemistry profile, oxygen uptake, static strength and performance in competitive swimmers*. Unpublished dissertation, University of Utah, 1970.

Raines, H. "Drug case continues to trouble Stabler." *The New York Times*, March 4, 1979.

Webb, J.L. "Blood doping: Help or hindrance." *The Physical Educator*, 1978, 35, 187-190.

Wilson, J.R.S. "In one another's power." *Ethics*. 1978, 88, 299-315.

SPORTSMANSHIP

PATRICIA A. LAWSON

My presentation is based on a recent book by Warren Fraleigh (1984). This might appear to be somewhat lacking in originality but I hope it is justified.

My contention is that in order to make any progress in the understanding and teaching of the concept(s) of sportsmanship we require a framework for our discussions. Much of what has been written and debated to date is either too specific, concerning itself with individual incidents in sport, or too general and theoretical and not having direct application to the process of influencing behaviour. What is required is a structured debate that (1) examines the principles that are essential to the concept of sportsmanship and (2) tests the applicability of those principles to actual sport situations. Philosophical truths can only be arrived at through debate and logic — we can't test them out on a treadmill or force platform.

If everyone interested could concentrate their efforts in the same direction we would have a better chance of producing a "theory" of sportsmanship that stands up to scrutiny at both the theoretical and the practical level. So in order to make any progress we need first to define the parameters of the subject we wish to examine and to agree upon what it is we are talking about.

Warren Fraleigh has, I believe, taken the first step in this direction. He has produced very specific "guides to right action" — guides which he believes can be applied to all sports contests and all situations within all sports contests. He has also given us the framework that is necessary for further investigation of what we mean when we talk about good sportsmanship. While his book is one of the first to make such an attempt he admits that its primary value will be in focussing future discussions. He has said:

> Indeed, this entire book has been an attempt to develop a normative ethic for the good sports contest which is a rational exposition of what kinds of guides for action are necessary. The arguments presented here attempt to explicate what ought to guide our sports actions and why those guides are morally mature. Only time and considerable debate can tell whether this normative ethic is totally deficient, or totally correct, or whether it is correct in certain respects but incorrect in others. As a reasonably comprehensive ethic of the sports contest, it represents one

252

contribution to the development of the moral maturity of sports participants. As author, I assure you that completing this task has contributed to the ongoing development of my own moral maturity in sport.

In my case I have found his work provides an excellent outline around which to structure discussions by students in my Sport Philosophy class. Not all of you may be teachers of a philosophy class but I suspect nearly all of you are in a position to influence others (particularly young people). At the very least it may be helpful in formulating definitive statements about your own beliefs.

The outline provided by Fraleigh isolates the questions which must be answered if we are to progress logically to a list of statements which we believe represent the "essentials" of sportsmanship.

The first question asks about the "rightness" of our reasons for saying an action is one that we ought to do or ought not to do. If there are two or more reasons given for why a certain action is right or wrong how do we evaluate between those reasons?

Fraleigh, Kohlberg and others have suggested that there are three types of reasons or three levels of moral development. The first is self-interest. We decide what we ought to do on the basis of whether it will benefit us, in the short term or the long term. In other words the "right" thing to do is what is in the participant's self-interest. The problem with this justification for our actions, is that it will often happen that people's interests conflict. How would we then decide upon the right thing to do?

The second type of reason we may give for our actions is known as convention or custom which suggests that an action is right because that is what is commonly done. It is very common and is a frequent comment in discussions of sport incidents. The "intentional foul" for example may be seen as undesirable by students but they say that it is now ingrained in the "strategy" of the game of basketball and is accepted as part of the game and a team would be disadvantaged if they didn't use it. The problem with this justification is that an action based on what is done conventionally is not "right" because it is consistent with what is done by a group. The ethical convictions of the group may be wrong.

The third and most defensible justification of our actions is called the moral point of view by Fraleigh and post conventional level by Kohlberg. It is also illustrated by Kant's Categorical Imperative which may be paraphrased as "do unto others as you would have everyone do unto all others." Fraleigh suggests that this view has two characteristics: firstly, that it is universalizable, that it can apply to everybody, equally, in all situations, and secondly, that it is reversible, which means that what I consider right when I am the acting agent, I must be able, rationally, to consider right when I am the recipient of another's act under the same circumstances. If I am in favour of capital punishment I must be equally in favour of it if I am the one to be put to death. The "moral" basis of decision making is superior because it provides for the best possible world, in which everyone is better off if everyone follows moral rules rather than rules of self interest.

In order to make these decisions we must have an idea of what we consider to be the "best possible world." In our case we need to decide what we consider to be the ideal sport world.

Even before thinking about the ideal sport world it is probably necessary to give a definition of sport. In explaining our own definitions, the nature, purpose and value of sport must be shown to be logically interrelated. If, for example, I was trying to explain the game of golf to someone who had never seen it before I would talk about the layout of a course, the clubs, the objective of putting the ball in the hole, and perhaps a bit about the rules under which I was able to do that. The reaction of the person unfamiliar with the game would probably be to ask why I would want to do that. What is the point of seeing how many times you have to hit the ball to get it in the hole? What is it that you find enjoyable about that? What do you get out of it? What value does it have? My response would have to explain why attempting to put the ball in the hole was something I liked to do.

Generalizing this to all types of sport, we must arrive at a definition of sport which makes it obvious what its purpose and value is. Fraleigh has done this very succinctly. I would refer you to his book for the complete definition but the main points are that the *definition* of the sports contest is an event in which participants seek the mutual appraisal of their relative abilities: the *purpose* of the sport contest is to provide equitable opportunity for participants to seek the mutual appraisal of their abilities: and the *value* of the sport contest is the accurate and complete knowledge of the participant's relative abilities. In other words people play sport because they enjoy it and what they enjoy is finding out how well they perform, and so sport is structured to provide for a true evaluation of one's performance. You may arrive at different descriptions of sport or the sport contest but it is necessary to show logically, as Fraleigh has done, how the inherent characteristics of sport are the source of the value participants receive. Other values have been claimed for sport such as fitness, sociability, entertainment, etc., but these are not *necessarily* attributable to the essence of what all sport is.

We have now suggested the first two steps in formulating a personal philosophy of sportsmanship. (1) To identify moral or ethical reasons for justifying actions as being superior to reasons based on self-interest or custom. (2) To articulate descriptions of the nature, purpose and value of sport. Next, we need to describe the ideal or "good" sport contest because, as we said earlier, we must have a vision of the state of sport we are trying to achieve when we make recommendations about how participants ought to act.

People often say, "That was a really good game." It was widely said about the 1987 Grey Cup game or the Canada-Russia hockey series of the same year. What made them good games? What are the characteristics of all the sports contests that we consider to be good? Again, to be logical, we must keep in mind our stated purpose of sport, which in Fraleigh's case is *"to provide equitable opportunity for mutual contesting of the relative abilities of participants."* If that is what sport is intended to do, what conditions are necessary to ensure that participants have this equal opportunity to test their abilities?

Fraleigh's response to this question will be briefly reviewed here but others may wish to suggest alternatives since his main objective is to stimulate discussion and debate.

1. Participants in the good sports contest must be aware of and committed to the true purpose of the sports contest. To appreciate that equal opportunity is necessary in order for all participants to realize the potential value of sport, must take precedence over personal intentions such as making money, entertaining spectators, winning at all costs, etc. When people agree to play a game there is an unspoken agreement that everyone is going to play by the written and unwritten rules of the game, because they understand that those rules are designed to provide the most equitable opportunity for all participants to test their abilities.

2. The good sport contest is also characterized by the highest quality of play of which each performer is capable. The good game is the well played game in which participants play at, or close to, all performers' previous best performance. When all contestants play well it assures (a) the best possible contest, (b) the determination of the true relative abilities of all, and (c) the maximum positive satisfaction of all.

3. Closely associated with the above is the connotation of "winning" in the good sport contest. Winning or trying to win, as "contesting" is essential. This is an important distinction to make because critics of sport often suggest that the purpose of sport is to annihilate the opponent rather than to play one's best in order to measure one's abilities. The terms "winning" and "losing" are also used to signify the end result of the contest — the indication that the contest has ended and that one participant performed better or worse than the other.

III. Women, Sportsmanship and Relationships

4. Participants in the good sport contest adhere to the letter and spirit of the rules because they understand that their intent is to yield the value of sport to the greatest number of people. That value, once again, is a complete and accurate evaluation of each participant's performance. Sport inherently yields that information and participants intrinsically value it.

5. Competition is understood by the competitors to be an attempt to perform the same skillful actions better than an opponent in order to express and develop competence. Excellence is a qualitative concept concerned with how well the contest is played. Therefore in the good sports contests opponents regard one another as facilitators or partners who strive together to produce excellence. They recognize that the hindrance provided each other is necessary to develop and express excellence and therefore a mutual regard and respect is evident.

I have a theory that most elite athletes understand and agree with this view of sport. When the Eastern Bloc countries announced that they would not be attending the 1984 Olympics the American athletes, when interviewed, did not say they were happy because it improved their chances for medals. Rather, they expressed disappointment that they would not have a chance to test themselves against the best in the world. Similarly, in the April 4, 1988 issue of *Sports Illustrated*, the Olympic and world champion figure skater Brian Boitano is quoted as saying about his long rivalry with Brian Orser: "I hope that we have set an example — that people who want the same goal can push each other as friends. Not in a feuding way, but as sportsmen who can raise each other's level of performance."

To this point my presentation has been limited to an interpretation of the work of Fraleigh and to suggest how it might be used as an outline for the expression of one's personal beliefs about sportsmanship. The culmination of Fraleigh's work is the formulation of a list of "guides to the right action." He requests that this list be reviewed by others to see if there are any guides there which should not be included or if there are other guides that ought to be added.

I have used the guides to solicit the opinions of others. In 1986-87 the students in my class took each "principle" cited by Fraleigh and illustrated it in the form of a specific sport situation. These situations were given to 200 university students who were asked to indicate the degree to which they agreed or disagreed with the action described. In 1987-88 I reworded the list of guides in a manner which I hoped retained the intent of Fraleigh but would be easily understood by the students.

Rather than being sport specific the statements were "principles" which would apply to all sports. The respondents were asked to indicate the extent to which they agreed/disagreed that the actions described were necessary to ensure a good contest in any sport, in any situation. These students were also asked to evaluate the items and on the basis of their comments a few revisions were made and the same students completed the questionnaire again which gave at least some indication of reliability. Assigning values of 1. (strongly agree), 2. (agree), 3. (disagree), and 4. (strongly disagree), the means of the individual averages were 2.00 on the first test and 2.02 on the retest one week later.

A copy of the most recent version is included at the end of this paper. I would invite the reader to complete the questionnaire, and would appreciate receiving comments about any of its features.

One way that I have used the guides is to stimulate and structure class discussion. In general there has been a high degree of agreement with the guides. By selecting for review those which didn't receive total acceptance the students are led to a consideration of the relative merit of different justifications for the action and eventually to their beliefs about the nature and value of sport. Some examples of "problem" guides are:

1. When the good sports contests is sought, schedule makers will attempt to schedule contests between equally competent participants. There are many examples of this in sport such as seeding, the reverse draft, conference affiliation, etc. The respondents pointed to the exceptions such as league play in which some teams may be weaker, or the advantage of playing a stronger team, or the fact that the opponent should not matter as long as the team's goals are met. In this case the basic intent needs to be clearly identified and then opinions sought.

2. Athletes and coaches should seek oppositional superiority in the sport contest continuously. This means playing to the best of one's ability at all times. The main objections here seemed to be: in the situation where one team has a big lead; that coaching methods may dictate otherwise; or that in some cases playing for a tie is acceptable. This seems to be one of the more controversial guides.

3. Athletes and coaches should not use prohibited actions to negate an advantage gained skillfully and legally by an opponent (i.e., should avoid intentional fouls). This received one of the lowest ratings of all the items. It is a clear example of the reason of "what is done" having priority over what is best for the most people and what the good contest ought to be.

257

III. Women, Sportsmanship and Relationships

4.   In sports contests where there are no contest officials, a participant should withdraw from the contest if that person perceives him/herself to be the recipient of acts that intend injury or unnecessary physical danger. An example would be a racquetball player with a dangerous backswing or follow through. There was very little agreement with this concept and the main objection was that the person leaving a game would look like a "wimp."

5.   Athletes and coaches should actively attempt to halt the actions of their home fans which are intended to negatively affect the performance of players on visiting teams. Fan control is a very current issue, in many sports. Some people view the fans as part of the home field advantage. Others would argue that the principle of equal opportunity should make such actions unacceptable.

One group of items, all of which received little support, dealt with the concept of "voluntary assessment" — the suggestion that players and coaches have an obligation to volunteer the information that they committed a violation that the official missed, or that they benefited from an incorrect call. While most students would agree that in the absence of officials the players must be honest in making judgements, they seem to think that players are absolved of any responsibility when officials are present.

Another small group of questions received a surprisingly high degree of support. They are what Fraleigh calls supererogatory. They are not actions which *must* be done by all participants in order to ensure a good sports contests but rather it would be nice if they were done. They include the concepts of mutual respect, courtesy, politeness, sympathy. While Fraleigh does not think they are essential to the good sport contest perhaps others view them as symbolic of the attitudes of participants and therefore important.

As you have probably guessed I am enthused about the potential of Fraleigh's work and I am anxious to solicit other opinions. The guides I have distributed are a first attempt at delineating the actions that comprise sportsmanship. I welcome your comments.

Lawson: Sportsmanship
Questionnaire

Your help in defining the parameters of "Sportsmanship" is very much appreciated. You are invited to complete the attached questionnaire and give me your reactions to it. An answer form is provided below. You may wish to write your comments on the back of it, or on the questionnaire beside specific items, or on a separate sheet(s).

After you have completed the questionnaire I would be interested in your responses to all or some of the following questions. Is the intent of each item clear? Are there elements missing, actions that you consider important to fair play? Are there items that should not be included, that you do not consider essential to good sportsmanship? Do you think the questionnaire could be adapted to specific sports by replacing the words "good sport contest" with the name of a sport (basketball, for instance)? Any and all reactions will be most welcome.

You may wish to record your responses to the questionnaire here. Remember that #1 = strongly agree; #2 = agree; #3 = disagree; and #4 = strongly disagree.

1._____	10._____	19._____	28._____
2._____	11._____	20._____	29._____
3._____	12._____	21._____	30._____
4._____	13._____	22._____	31._____
5._____	14._____	23._____	32._____
6._____	15._____	24._____	33._____
7._____	16._____	25._____	34._____
8._____	17._____	26._____	35._____
9._____	18._____	27._____	36._____
			37._____

Sportsmanship

The following have been identified by Warren P. Fraleigh (1984) as actions that are required to insure a "good" game or a "good" sports contest. Together they might be considered the elements of good sportsmanship.

The actions are intended to apply to all sports and all situations. You are asked to indicate whether you agree or disagree that each of the following actions is necessary to insure a good sports contest.

III. Women, Sportsmanship and Relationships

Do this by marking one of the following numbers on the response sheet:

1. Strongly agree
2. Agree
3. Disagree
4. Strongly disagree

1. All sport participants should abide strictly by the letter and spirit of the rules in order to provide equal opportunity for opponents and themselves to perform to the best of their ability.

2. In order to have equal opportunity for optimal performance, participants and their opponents should have *equal access* to effective coaching, adequate facilities and equipment, effective sports medicine services, and sufficient practice time.

3. Athletes and coaches should avoid acts, or the encouragement of acts, that *intend physical injury* to another person or unnecessarily increase the possibility of injury.

4. Athletes and coaches should avoid acts, or the encouragement of acts, that are known to be *detrimental* or possibly detrimental *to the health of participants* (e.g., drugs with known harmful side effects).

5. Athletes and coaches should never intentionally perform acts that unnecessarily increase the possibility of injury by *physical intimidation* or other interference of a kind not prescribed by the rules.

6. *Athletes* should avoid *harassing actions* that are intended to insult or derogate the character, intelligence, physical abilities, ancestory or the motor abilities of others in the sports contest.

7. *Coaches* should avoid *harassing actions* that are intended to insult or derogate the character, intelligence, physical abilities, ancestory or the motor abilities of others in the sports contest.

8. All sport participants should *prepare as fully as possible* for scheduled sports contests in order to be able to play their best. The amount and complexity of the preparation required will differ markedly between professionals/amateurs, experts/novices; but all contestants should be appropriately prepared for their level of competition.

9. While participants should be as fully prepared as possible, (#8), they should not violate league or conference rules during their preparation; such as rules of eligibility, the date for starting practices, etc.

10. Those agents responsible for scheduling sports contests should aim *to provide an equal contest.* To the best of their ability, and barring unusual circumstances, they should schedule contests between opponents whose experience and preparation are equal.

11. Athletes and coaches should *seek oppositional superiority continuously* in the sport contest. This means trying to perform always to the best of one's ability in executing the skills of the sport, exerting the required effort, and choosing tactics and strategy.

12. When opponents have gained an advantage skillfully and legally, athletes and coaches should not intentionally use prohibited actions to negate that advantage. (*should avoid intentional fouls*).

13. Athletes and coaches *should acknowledge* voluntarily and in a positive manner the skilled and effective actions of other participants including opponents and officials. This may be by comment, gesture, shaking hands, etc.

14. Athletes and coaches *should instruct* other sports participants, voluntarily and in a positive manner, in sports actions that improve performance. This may be informal teaching or more formal seminars, demonstrations, video tapes, etc.

15. Athletes, coaches and officials *should act* toward other sport participants *with respect* for their competence to discharge the duties and obligations of their roles in the sport contest. This display of *trust and confidence* should occur between athlete and coach, athlete and opponent, official and athlete, official and coach, etc.

16. Athletes, coaches and officials should exhibit ordinary *politeness and courtesy* to other participants in the sport contest.

17. Athletes, coaches and other sports participants should act toward other participants in ways that *exhibit sympathy* for their unwarranted misfortunes — such as illness or injury, environmental factors, equipment failure, spectator interference, etc. This sympathy may be expressed as a word, gesture, etc.

III. Women, Sportsmanship and Relationships

In games or sports contests an advantage or disadvantage is often given to a player or team as a result of an illegal action by a participant. The violation/infraction may have been intentional or accidental.

Each of the remaining items (#18 to #37) recommends the action that ought to be followed to make the contest equal again. Do you 1. *Strongly agree*, 2. *Agree*, 3. *Disagree*, or 4. *Strongly disagree*, that the stated sanction is necessary to discourage sport participants from cheating, being violent, or breaking the rules?

The next six items (#18 to #23) deal exclusively with situations in which (a) the action is *intentionally done* and (b) the intent is to *injure* another participant.

18. By word or action, coaches, athletes and officials should give a *clear message of social disapproval* to show that acts intending injury are not condoned by other participants.

19. Contest officials should *expel* from the contest any participant who, in the judgement of officials, intentionally attempts to injure another even if he/she is unsuccessful in such an attempt.

20. If contest officials (item #19) fail to expel from the contest any participant who unsuccessfully attempts to injure another then the *coach* of the offending player should do so.

21. In sports contests in which there are *no contest officials* a participant should *withdraw* from the contest if that person perceives him/herself to be the recipient of acts that intend injury or unnecessary physical danger. The withdrawing player should accompany the withdrawal with a brief, courteous and dignified statement of his/her reason(s) to the offending player.

22. *Contests*, in which successful intentional injury would clearly influence the eventual winners, should be *suspended* by the contest officials. This sanction is required so that offending contestants cannot win or finish higher in a contest as a result of intentional injury to opponents.

23. Officials of appropriate sport organizations should *exclude from* a significant number of *future contests* any participant who has performed actions intended to injure another participant in *two or more contests*. (The exact number of future contests would depend on the particular circumstances).

The next eleven items (#24 to #34) do not involve injury or the intent to injure but are still concerned with:

(a) acts which are *intentionally* done, and

(b) the intended consequence of these acts is either wrongful reduction of an opponent's performance effectiveness or wrongful increase of the acting agent's performance effectiveness.

These wrongful or inappropriate acts which might be called "cheating" include: intentional acts that are against the rules, such as holding in football or basketball, and intentional acts which are not stated in the rules but which are against the spirit of the rules (unauthorized modifications to equipment, for example).

24. Contest officials or sport organization officials should provide *appropriate compensation* for participants who are disadvantaged by the intentional, wrongful acts of opponents. This statement is very general because the specific appropriate compensation will differ between sports and in relation to situational factors. The appropriate compensation may or may not be included in the sport rules.

25. *Athletes and coaches* should actively attempt to halt actions of their home fans which are intended to negatively affect the performance of players on visiting teams.

26. Athletes, coaches and contest officials should clearly *demonstrate disapproval* of intentional, wrongful acts that inappropriately intend to decrease the performance effectiveness of another or to increase one's own performance effectiveness. This social disapproval may be formal or informal, verbal or nonverbal.

27. Contest officials should officially and publicly *threaten to expel* from the contest any participant whose intentional, wrongful acts inappropriately attempt to decrease an opponents' performance effectiveness or to increase his/her own. This formal warning notifies the offending agent (and others) that further such acts will invoke additional penalties.

28. If contest officials fail to officially and publicly threaten to expel the above offender (item #27) then the offending player's own *coach* should *warn* the player that he/she will be taken out of the contest if another offence occurs.

29. Contest officials shall *expel* from the remainder of the contest any participant whose intentional, wrongful acts inappropriately attempt to

decrease an opponent's performance effectiveness or to increase his/her own *more than once in a contest.*

30. If the contest officials fail to expel from the remainder of the contest the above offender (item #29) who intentionally acts inappropriately more than once in a contest then the player's own *coach* should do so.

31. In a sport contest *not governed by contest officials*, a participant who feels certain that an opponent has performed two or more wrongful acts, intended to inappropriately decrease the participant's effectiveness or increase the offending participant's effectiveness, should *withdraw* from the contest. In such instances the withdrawing participant should accompany the withdrawal with a brief, courteous and dignified statement of his/her reason(s) to the offending participant.

32. Officials of appropriate sports organizations shall *exclude from a significant number of future contests* any participant(s) who, in their judgement, inappropriately acted intentionally and wrongfully in *two or more contests* to decrease another's performance effectiveness or to increase their own.

33. If intentional wrongful acts result in an offender winning, tying or placing in a scoring position, then the contest officials should *disqualify* the offender. This would apply when expulsion is not possible, such as during a race.

The remaining situations are still concerned with instances of inappropriate actions (violations/fouls). However in the following five items (#34 to #38) the wrongful act was done *unintentionally or inadvertently.* The action may have been accidental, due to lack of skill, or because the rules were not known.

A common theme in these situations is *"voluntary assessment"* which means the erring participant takes responsibility for correcting the unfair situation that has occurred. The voluntary and correct assessment assumes that (a) the inadvertent negative result of the participant's action is recognized by the responsible participant and (b) the responsible participant's perception is accurate.

34. Athletes, coaches or contest officials whose acts inadvertently result in denial of equal opportunity for optimal performance by a contestant, should *volunteer the correct assessment* of the situation to allow the necessary compensation for the negatively affected participant(s).

35. When the athletes, coaches or the contest officials — whose acts inadvertently break the fairness of the sports contest — do not offer the correct assessment of the situation, then their *teammates, coaches or colleagues* should voluntarily offer the correct assessment of the situation to allow the necessary compensation for the negatively affected participant(s).

36. An *athlete or coach* who perceives an advantage has been bestowed upon him/her or the team inappropriately, either by an *official's error* or inability to assess the situation correctly, should *volunteer the correct assessment* of the situation if such assessment would help eliminate the inappropriate advantage.

37. Athletes, coaches and contest officials, when able, should provide *appropriate compensation* when participants have been inadvertently denied equal opportunity for optimal performance. The voluntary compensation considered appropriate will vary with the situation but the intent of the statement is everyone, not just contest officials, should be responsible for providing appropriate compensation.

Reference

Fraleigh, Warren P., *Right Actions in Sport: Ethics for Contestants.* Champaign IL: Human Kinetics Publishers, Inc., 1984.

THE ETHICS OF EATING
AND EXERCISING DISORDERS

PASQUALE J. GALASSO

Physical activity professionals, undoubtedly, never dreamed a dozen years ago that there would be a need to raise questions about the procedures and practices used in promoting exercise and the avoidance of obesity, and to be aware of the potentially harmful outcomes. It was generally agreed that nothing short of an atomic blast would ever change the lifestyles of the vast majority of Canadians with respect to fitness. In fact early motivational efforts were quite unsuccessful. Nothing seemed to work nationally as a motivational mechanism. This was reinforced in a government document in which it was stated,

> Although we wholeheartedly endorse marketing campaigns to 'sell' physical activity to Canadians, we are concerned that the expectation of positive results may oversimplify an exceedingly complex situation.[1]

In this same government document, a strong interest in promoting success seems to have emerged through a paternalistic attitude and with the help of behaviour modification methods,

> Recreation Canada (the forerunner of Fitness Canada) should seek the cooperation of established 'professional behaviour modification agents' and agencies who could provide expertise in changing the value system of Canadians, related to physical fitness.[2]

To give some idea of the promotional impact, the federal government takes full credit in this statement:

> In an era when more people seem to question the cost, size and efficiency of government, we can point to one government program that has obviously worked, and is still working.
>
> Since Participaction was launched in 1971, and Fitness Canada convened the national conference on fitness and health in Ottawa in 1972, the results have been obvious. More than a decade later, we can see the signs of success

everywhere. In cities, towns, villages and hamlets across Canada, men, women and children are walking, jogging, running, cycling, swimming, and playing tennis, squash and racquetball as never before. You find them exercising in modern fitness centres, in their own homes, even in front of that one-time enemy of fitness — the TV set.

There is no doubt about it, we have gone from a sedentary society to one that is on the move. Studies and statistics indicate that more and more Canadians, an impressive one-third of the population, are getting — and staying — fit, and the general level of health in Canada is improving as a result.[3]

It is obvious that these and other motivational programs have been successful. A much higher percentage of the population is fitness conscious. Unfortunately, accompanying this behavioral pattern has been an epidemic of eating and exercise disorders such as anorexia, bulimia and over-exercise leading to many bone, joint and tissue breakdowns. Was the promotion of fitness oversold? Did the method and techniques used in promoting fitness create negative self-image problems?

The vast majority of those suffering from eating disorders are female. This is where the unfairness aspect arises in that the females in our society have been trained to be overly conscious of their appearance, and are more easily influenced to become fit and thin.

The individuals and organizations promoting fitness and thinness, no doubt, are thinking of the benefits that should accrue to the individuals who participate. It appears that thinness and fitness are looked upon as being good in themselves, and that any method used to motivate people to attain this status is justifiable. For example, making people feel guilty about their lifestyles is looked upon as a fair game approach to promoting thinness and fitness. The use of cartoons to lampoon various body types has also been looked upon as an acceptable practice. Health is also being promoted, but the fact that it is combined with these other motivational mechanisms and techniques is the focus of attention of this paper. Showing a rabbit with a paunch racing against a tortoise raises a question of propriety with respect to motivational techniques, in my view. This may influence people to hate their bodies, and could very well be a contributory factor associated with these self-image and eating disorders.

Use of material of a non-factual nature, that is, comparing the sixty-year-old Swede to the thirty-year-old Canadian, also raises questions. Using statistics as a fear prod would also raise questions of an ethical nature with respect to motivational techniques.

Eating and exercising disorders are difficult to causally analyze. How much of the blame can be attributed to parents, friends, idols, peers, and the individual affected is impossible to assess accurately. In examining the cause-effect relationships, as to which organizations may or may not be responsible for this sudden high level interest and motivation to be thin and fit, we could probably place all parties into two categories. On the one hand, we have the altruistic, professional, well-intentioned group made up of governments, human kinetics and physical education degree departments, parks and recreation departments, exercise physiologists, health educators, Participaction, Canadian Association of Health, Physical Education and Recreation Journal (CAHPER), Canadian Association of Sport Science and physical education teachers in elementary and high schools. The other group is made up of commercial enterprises motivated primarily by a desire to gain financially. In any case, the collective efforts to promote fitness and thinness have worked. Sadly, they have worked too well. No one would argue with the fact that a significant percentage of the population is either worried about and/or is doing something about becoming thinner and fitter.

We as professionals, cannot, we must not, ignore what is happening out there. We should not go on patting ourselves on the back for having motivated X thousands or millions of people to exercise and be thin when we have problems of an epidemic nature on our hands as a byproduct. We cannot go on leaving it to others to solve these problems and to pick up the pieces.

People have a right to knowledge, and government and professionals have a responsibility to provide information with respect to the dangers of overexercising and fat control. We need to create balance in our promotional campaigns and to warn people of potential outcomes and how to avoid them. It is not good enough to say that our job is motivation. We must assume responsibility for what is happening as a result of our promotional campaigns.

It would be interesting to determine whether or not organizations and individuals promoting fitness have, in fact, addressed these issues, or whether they are simply leaving the problem to other professionals and organizations. Conscious and deliberate actions or statements are in the moral sphere and therefore can be deemed either good or bad, or right or wrong. Thus, those who promote and motivate without assuming any responsibility for the outcomes, both good and bad, need to reconsider their position and strategies.

What Should Be Done

1. Ethics committees exist in universities to examine research proposals and the potential effect on humans and animals. One could very readily suggest that professional committees be struck to deal with ethical guidelines on advertising and promotion of all facets of health in order to avoid the excesses and damaging results which are occurring.

2. The Honourable Otto Jelinek, the former Minister of Fitness and Amateur Sport, took a major interest in fitness, judging by articles published in the *Globe and Mail* and other newspapers. We should recommend to his successor that he include, in addition to promotional material on fitness, guidelines dealing with moderation and the potential danger of overexercise and overthinness.

3. Practitioners in the area of fitness management should be provided with the latest information concerning these areas of potential harm.

4. Advertising by commercial enterprises should be monitored more closely under guidelines dealing with false claims.

5. Provincial ministers of fitness and recreation should also provide their employees with guidelines relating to the promotional material used. Ethical standards should be developed for the media to avoid unbalanced promotion.

6. University courses should include material and research dealing with these issues in order to apprise our students of the potential outcomes of thinness and fitness programs. All too often we think of the body as a test tube devoid of emotional and mental components.

Individuals themselves have responsibilities to monitor their own behaviour, and thus not 100 percent of the blame can be placed on the previously listed organizations and individuals. And it is for this reason that as we teach, coach and administer it must be done within the framework of developing autonomous individuals who are capable of self-determination within our social context. By producing dependent individuals there is a tendency to produce people who can easily be convinced and coerced, and it becomes easy to move them in a lifestyle direction that is harmful to them and to others associated with them.

What started out to be a basic belief in the goodness of thinness and fitness motivated on the part of the government to save the tax

III. Women, Sportsmanship and Relationships

dollar has now turned into a major health and financial problem which needs to be addressed. Inadvertently, we have produced people who are not only addicted to thinness and fitness, but who are also addicted to treatment by medical doctors, chiropractors, masseurs, as well as to drugs and other forms of treatment which are costing the taxpayer probably more money than if these individuals went back to their original lifestyles. It seems embarrassingly simple to state that moderation must prevail in all forms of health promotion. We have to seek another balance in bringing the pendulum back to a more midline position with respect to the issues of fitness and thinness. A task force should be set up by the Canadian Association for Health, Physical Education and Recreation (CAHPER) to examine the question of ethical guidelines for the motivational promotion of fitness and thinness.

Bibliography

1. "Motivating Canadians to Become Physically Fit." A Working Paper prepared by the Recreation Committee of the National Advisory Council on Fitness and Amateur Sport, Ottawa, Canada, June, 1975. p. 21.

2. "Motivating Canadians to Become Physically Fit." A Working Paper prepared by the Recreation Committee of the National Advisory Council on Fitness and Amateur Sport, Ottawa, Canada, June, 1975, p. 17.

3. "Fitness Works," Government of Canada, Fitness and Amateur Sport, in cooperation with Canadian Chamber of Commerce, Ottawa, Ontario, June 1985, p. 1.

INEQUALITY IN SPORT
AND THE LOGIC OF GENDER[1]

DEBRA SHOGAN

What is the best way to pay more attention to the ways in which our experiences in sport are organized by gender? Separate investigations devoted to understanding women's experiences in sport are important because women and men, girls and boys have different experiences in sport as a result of social structures which have created these gender specific experiences. When there is no inquiry into women's experiences, the experiences of men and boys are often taken as the only experiences or, at least, the only important experiences. Separate investigations dealing with the "woman question" in sport often serve to reinforce, however, the assumption that gender specific experiences in sport are somehow necessary or natural. Moreover, the organization of special investigations about women and sport in separate sections of books or manuals marginalizes women's sport. The impression is given that the other sections are about real sport — men's sport. When an attempt to understand gender is reduced to inquiries about women and sport, the point is missed that gender is an organizing principle which affects both women and men.

In this paper I outline how gender does affect both women and men, I briefly mention some ethical implications for women's experiences in sport and I point to some remedies for these. Even though I restrict my comments to ethical implications for women in sport, I am convinced that there will always be a "woman question" in sport until a real attempt is made to understand the "man question" in sport.[2] Since, as I discuss in the next section, gender describes a power *relationship*, any attempt to understand and remedy the effects of gender in sport which does not pay attention to both sides of this relation will necessarily be incomplete.

What is Gender?

There are a number of organizing principles which bring order to the lives of the members of a society. The scheduling of our lives, for example, in terms of the sequence, duration, and time of day events will occur is an organizing principle that most Western societies have adopted. Although there can be important social implications to this ordering which can't be pursued here, this type of ordering is often innocuous. Other organizing principles, however, such as those that situate members of a society in power relations with each other on the

271

basis of conventions and meanings which have been socially constructed are often harmful to some or all of those in the power relations. Gender is this kind of organizing principle. An individual who is considered to be either biologically female or biologically male is shaped to take on the conventional attributes of femininity or masculinity; to become a girl or a boy and then a woman or a man.[3] These contrived social conventions affect everything each of us does from the way we communicate, to the way we move, to the ways in which we work.[4]

That femininity and masculinity are social constructs and not immutable natural characteristics is clear when looking historically at what characteristics have been considered to be acceptable for women and men. Acceptable feminine and masculine attributes are historically variable. As Jean Grimshaw writes:

> Ideals of masculinity [and femininity] are variable and contested things, and although at certain times and among certain social groups specific and relatively homogeneous ideals can be identified, these are not historically constant.[5]

If the features of femininity and masculinity change over time so that those features considered to be feminine in one historical time period might be considered to be masculine in another, why is it that gender boundaries have not become indistinct as more individuals in a society take on those features with which they feel most comfortable? The reason for this is that gender does not simply organize our lives by defining which attributes are important at a particular social period.[6] Gender also organizes the *relation* between femininity and masculinity. Femininity and masculinity are relational concepts; neither has conceptual or organizing meaning without the other. As Robert Connell et al. write, gender is not "just a matter of existence of two categories of people, male and female, but primarily...a pattern of *relations* among people."[7] The force of gender is that it guarantees that those attributes considered to be masculine are more highly valued *whatever* those attributes might be for a particular society during a particular historical period. Genevieve Lloyd notes that, "gender is first an inequality, constructed as a socially relevant differentiation, in order to keep that inequality in place."[8] In other words, since gender describes a power relationship, it ensures that some people (those considered to have male genitalia) will be more highly valued than some other people (those considered to have female genitalia) regardless of what a particular society determines are to be the attributes each category should have. Hence, if at a particular time, convention has it that men are to hunt and women are to cook, hunting will be necessarily more valued as an activity. If at another time, cooking becomes a valuable skill for men, this skill is differentiated from the cooking women do by describing the activity and the men who do it differently even when the skills necessary for the activities are identical. Consequently, men are chefs and women are cooks and to be a chef is, according to the logic of gender, necessarily more valuable.

More sporting activities were designed by men for men and this has served to further differentiate what men do from what women do. As the logic of gender demands, sport has been a more important pastime than those activities which have been considered to be appropriate for women. With the involvement of women in sport, this distinction between feminine activities and masculine activities and the power relation reinforced by this distinction has been disrupted. Women's involvement in sport jeopardizes the relational force of gender achieved by having different women's and men's activities. Since women do participate in sport, it has become necessary to find ways within sport to differentiate between women and men. In order for the logic of gender to prevail, men's sport, even when not comparable in any way with some women's sport (how do you compare the skill of the lineman in football with the skill of the synchronized swimmer?) must be (and is) considered to be better by those whose lives are governed by the logic of gender. The assessment of men's sport as better, regardless of its characteristics, also leads to a very curious phenomenon. Regardless of how poorly skilled or unathletic an individual man is, he gains power from his identification with men's sport. There is an interchangeability of the individual, regardless of his particular attributes, with the perceived attributes of men.[9] Even when an individual man is less skilled and athletic than an athletic woman, he tends to identify with the characteristics of the most skilled and athletic men. If he is not "superior" to women athletes, it is likely that (depending on the sport) some men will be, and this is usually enough for the individual to claim his own superiority over women athletes. This identification with skilled men allows the unskilled man to argue with skilled women that, because some men are more skilled in some sports, there is justification for giving more resources to all men's sports, including his own. This example clearly shows that gender does not only have implications for women. When someone embraces the relational principle of gender that males are necessarily more valuable than and superior to females, this individual must see *himself* this way as well, despite the evidence from his own life.

Ethical Implications of Gender

By now we can see some of the ethical implications of gender for both women and men. Expectations that one must live up to a feminine or masculine ideal which is recognized as arbitrary and contrived has a devastating effect on the lives of many women and men. The ethical implications for women's lives, however, are more profound by virtue of being in the less powerful side of the gender relation. The implications of the devaluation of women's sport are that:

> Women's physical education has received less money for programs and personnel, and women have had unequal access to facilities. In general, women's sports have been underfunded, less well coached and equipped, and players have not had equal fringe benefits such as medical benefits, housing, food and travel allowances. Women have not had equivalent opportunities for athletic scholarships. In schools and in society, women's sports have been accorded much less status and attention than men's.[10]

These effects of gender are a necessary result of the logic of gender. The social organization of sport is far from being neutral on these matters. Insofar as sport, including women's sport, is almost always controlled by those men who have a vested interest in maintaining the relationality of gender, women's sport will continue to be undervalued and, consequently, underresourced.[11]

Gender Sensitivity

Because the effects of gender are so pervasive in all of our lives, it is not always easy to be aware of the ways in which gender organizes the way we look at the world. Remedies to inequality in sport cannot occur if gender is seen to be an irrelevant characteristic which we must ignore in order to be just. This is because inequality is a necessary condition of gender. If gender is ignored, so too will inequality be ignored. As Barbara Houston writes:

> The ideal of sex equality urged by those who advocate the gender-free strategy is one which gives gender the status eye color now has in our society. In short, gender is taken to be totally irrelevant to social organization. I have no special quarrel with the claim that this is precisely how a good, just society ought to treat gender. My worry is that this ideal is not especially helpful in the detection and elimination of present gender bias.[12]

To be gender blind in the classroom is to be unaware, says Houston, of who does the most talking, who interrupts whom, who determines what discussions will be and it is to reinforce patterns that discourage women from being actively involved in the educational process.[13] To be gender blind is to contribute to learning a "hidden curriculum" which indicates "who is entitled to talk in the educational arena."[14] So too in physical education and sport. To be blind to gender in sport is to send the message that women can be involved in sport as long as they are content to stay in the margins. Girls will not catch up in their motor skills if we don't notice the different expectations we have of girls because they are female. Co-educational classes and teams will be doomed to failure if we don't take notice that girls tend to be left out of game interactions regardless of their skill level. Women will not fill leadership and officiating roles in sport if we fail to notice the systemic obstacles to women because they are female. As Maureen Ford writes, gender sensitivity is not just a matter of ending discriminatory practices. To be gender-sensitive is to be skillful at recognizing the symbolic dimensions of gender at work in our lives.[15]

Who will be gender sensitive? All of us should have an interest in gender as an organizing principle if only to be clear that one has not blindly taken on certain conventions. It is likely, however, that those who will be sensitive to gender are those who have not entirely embraced the conventions of femininity and masculinity. To the extent that someone immerses oneself in the conventions of gender, the more difficult it will be to recognize the variability and hence artificiality of what the logic of gender demands. Yet the end of inequality in sport depends on gender sensitivity. If we are truly serious about ending inequality in sport (and elsewhere), we must become serious about investing in the gender sensitive education of our students and ourselves.[16]

Notes

1. I am indebted to Catherine Bray for her helpful comments as I wrote this paper.
2. For work in this area see, for example, *Jocks: Sport and Male Identity*, edited by Don Sabo, Jr. and Ross Runfola, Englewood Cliffs, N.J.: Prentice-Hall, Inc., and see Bruce Kidd, "Sports and Masculinity," in *Beyond Patriarchy: Essays By Men on Pleasure, Power and Change*, edited by Michael Kaufman. Toronto and New York: Oxford University Press, 1987.
3. For a discussion on variability in the manifestation of chromosomal sex, see articles in *Women: Sex and Sexuality*, edited by Catharine R. Stimpson and Ethel Spector Person, Chicago and London: University of Chicago Press, 1980.
4. Maureen Ford, "Gender-Bending is Political: Gender-Sensitive Education Reconsidered," unpublished manuscript, 1988, p. 7.

III. Women, Sportsmanship and Relationships

5. Jean Grimshaw, *Philosophy and Feminist Thinking*. Minneapolis: University of Minnesota Press, 1986, p. 62.
6. Maureen Ford, "Gender-Bending is Political: Gender-Sensitive Education Reconsidered," p. 12.
7. R.W. Connell, R.W. Askendin, D.J. Kessler, G.W. Dowselt, *Making the Difference*. Boston: George Allen and Unwin, 1982, pp. 34-35.
8. Genevieve Lloyd, "Woman as Other: Sex, Gender and Subjectivity," unpublished paper, 1988, p. 11.
9. See Marisa Zavalloni, "An Ego-Ecological Analysis of the Representation of Women: The Sartre-Beauvoir Interviews." *Trivia: A Journal of Ideas,* 9 (1986): 61-72.
10. Ann Diller and Barbara Houston, "Women's Physical Education: A Gender-Sensitive Perspective." In *Women, Philosophy, and Sport: A Collection of New Essays*. Edited by Betsy C. Postow. Metuchen, N.J. and London: The Scarecrow Press, Inc., 1983, p. 247.
11. Moreover, because sport was created by men for men, many of the structures of sport mirror the characteristics considered to be important characteristics for men. As well, many sports depend on physical traits such as strength and size which, until social structures change which encourage women to be strong and which also affect women's size, will guarantee most men's success relative to most women. "But even in societies where both boys and girls receive an adequate diet, the physical training of girls influences their adult height.... Other things being equal, athletic girls...tend to grow taller than girls who are less athletic...." (Alison M. Jaggar, "Sex Inequality and Bias in Sex Differences Research," in *Science, Morality, and Feminist Theory*, edited by Marsha Hanen and Kai Nielsen, *Canadian Journal of Philosophy,* Supp. Volume 13 (1987): 34.) Jaggar's comments are based on work by Marion Lowe in "The Dialectic of Biology and Culture," in Marion Lowe and Ruth Hubbard, eds. *Women's Nature: Rationalizations of Inequality*. New York: Pergamon Press, 1983.
12. Barbara Houston, "Gender Freedom and the Subtleties of Sexist Education," *Educational Theory* ,35 (1985): 366.
13. Barbara Houston, p. 363.
14. Barbara Houston, p. 363.
15. Maureen Ford, "Gender-Bending is Political: Gender-Sensitive Education Reconsidered."
16. Certainly sex inequality is not the only type of inequality. We must also be aware of the ways in which the conventions of class and race organize our lives and the effects these have on people's experiences in sport.

RESPONSIBILITY AND AUTHORITY IN COACHING PHILOSOPHY[1]

DENNIS NIGHSWONGER

The purpose of this paper is to begin to develop a justification of coaching activity in the form of a first principle for development of a consistent philosophical approach to coaching in sport. Is a coach responsible before or after acquisition of authority? In my view, authority could be more appropriately justified if it followed upon acquisition of certain specific responsibilities. Further, I suggest that every coach does, in fact, exercise whatever authority they might possess on the basis of a, conscious or unconscious, philosophical stand on responsibility. Also, given that there are often sanctions, applied to both the athlete and the coach, for faulty performances, the question of who is actually responsible for the athlete's performance is of additional importance.

Responsibility is largely an ethical concept. It involves the obligation to act or not to act; first, as a moral obligation to choose appropriate acts; second, as a legal obligation to act in certain ways considered appropriate by the whole of a society; third, as a political obligation, in management or participation in organizations, to act in accordance with directives of other individuals. Such obligations must, of course, necessarily presuppose the individual person's capacity for choice. That is, a person may be obligated to act or not act but he may actually do that which he is not obligated to do. Determining the locus of responsibility, that is "who is responsible," is to determine the origin or source of a particular act. Any normal individual has the ability to respond to many, if not most, aspects of at least the immediate environment by choosing one action over another. This is personal response ability. It may help to think of the meaning of the word responsibility in terms of the ability to respond.[2] That is, human action is not merely a reflex response. Rather, action is the result of what the person intends to do. Personal responsibility, then, is the origin of human action because of the individual capacity to choose among alternative acts.

Personal responsibility cannot be easily denied although theories of behaviourists have attempted to do so.[3] In fact, personal responsibility is used to determine the locus of other types of responsibility as mentioned above. Ethically, establishing an obligation is meaningless if we do not know "who" is obligated. Legal responsibility is determined on the basis of "who" is responsible. In systems of management, responsibility also depends on establishing who is or was obligated or authorized to act. This is the point at which responsibility and accountability are frequently confused.

Accountability is a consideration of actions which some person is expected to perform as well as punishment for that person if those actions are not performed. Responsibility, more correctly, involves a determination of who decided which actions to perform. A person is accountable if he is expected, by others, to perform certain actions. That person is responsible for those actions which he actually intends and initiates. This suggests that a person may be both responsible and accountable at the same time in one situation while he may be responsible and not accountable in another. A person may also be, in some situations, accountable while not being actually responsible.

The management concept of responsibility is concerned with an obligation to give directives and an obligation to obey directives. Major characteristics of management responsibility that should be noted include the following. There is a difficulty in separating authority from responsibility. There is also a need to distinguish between responsibility and accountability. Further, it is useful to consider the nature of directives from a "position" of authority regardless of any specific person occupying the position.

Further, the existence and appropriateness of personal responsibility has been challenged by these organizational systems. This challenge has been referred to by some as a crisis of responsibility.[4] In some organizational systems:

> [persons] are not conceived of as entities endowed with the ontological capacity for producing action....[5]

Any organization which uses a command system of management, as do military organizations, operates according to this view.

Determination of responsibility, as origin of action, is more appropriately derived from an agent who acts, a person who freely initiates that action. However, responsibility is commonly assigned, or ascribed, to a person who is perceived to be an agent of an action, regardless of whether that person actually performed a particular act. Now, responsibility is assigned to an agent of action by evaluation of that action. An action can be properly evaluated, by persons other than the agent of the act, only if that action is goal-oriented and that goal is commonly known. However, it is frequently difficult, if not impossible, to determine the goal of actions of individual persons. Therefore, actions of persons are commonly explained by ascriptive responsibility, and not by any causal description which refers to the intent or goal, of the individual person who initiated the action. In the use of ascriptive responsibility consideration of the individual, particular self is insignificant in an

278

analysis or explanation of acts, such that noting the occurrence of a rational act and accepting the origin of that act as that of an individual person makes no meaningful contribution to that explanation.[6] That is, in evaluation, we consider only who performed the action and do not consider his reasons for having done so. In this way, attention in evaluation of actions in social or organizational relationships, is shifted toward rule-following behaviour away from consideration of the intent of the person who performed, or initiated, the action. Evaluation of action, then, occurs largely according to the legal rules or laws. As such, persons are viewed more as being responsible, or rather, accountable, to the society as a whole. To be accountable, then, is to be subject to punishment for non-compliance of established rules. Through this attention shift, evaluation of social conduct becomes based on accountability as liability to punishment or sanctions for failure to comply with social/legal rules.

The athlete, then, as a person, would not be viewed as significant in explaining the origin of his own performance. That is, any intention the athlete might have regarding his manner of performance does not help explain why he performs in the manner he actually does. The athlete appears as only a minor character in the whole of his own performance.

If personal intentions in determination of responsibility are thought to be insignificant, how then do we ascribe responsibility? Joel Feinberg[7] describes two major aspects of ascriptive responsibility as authorship and liability.

Ascription of responsibility according to authorship involves reference to that person or persons with whom the action originated. However, as responsibility is commonly ascribed according to the expected behaviour and emphasis on the specific action itself, the concept of ascriptive responsibility also emphasizes performance. That is, the question of who performed the act is emphasized rather than who actually initiated the act. Authorship, then, refers to causal agency. Each athlete may be appropriately considered the causal agent of their individual performance. As such, each is responsible by authorship.

Ascription of responsibility according to liability refers to an ascription:

> either to the agent or to someone else, liability under a set of rules or customs to some further response for it.[9]

Feinberg notes further, that ascriptions of causal responsibility are frequently confused with ascriptions of causal agency. Feinberg states:

ascriptions of liability can be transferable, vicarious, or...independent of actual fault.[9]

Someone may, by some set of rules, be punished for an act he did not directly perform. For example, executives in organizations are reprimanded for faulty performances of their subordinates although the executives do not perform, or fail to perform, those particular acts. And yet, we should note, as Feinberg does, that:

> the most usual reason for holding a person liable for an action is that he performed it.[10]

In context, the coach is not a direct causal agent of the athlete's performance but is commonly ascribed causal responsibility for that performance. The coach is thought to be responsible for the outcome of the athlete's efforts in performance even though he does not participate directly in that performance.

The notion of ascriptive responsibility is such that someone is given or assigned the status of being responsible for an action and its consequences. It is important to note, then, that ascription is to a large degree discretionary.[11] The next obvious problem is that of who's discretion to apply.

The answer is relatively simple. Discretion in decision-making is exercised by persons in "positions" of authority. As the following quote from R.B. Perry illustrates quite effectively:

> It is a well known fact that we describe as the cause of an event that particular condition by which we hope to control it.[12]

This seems to be the case with ascriptive responsibility as it applies to the coach. Responsibility is ascribed to persons in "positions" that enable them to control the actions of others, at least to some degree. Now, although the athlete is the direct causal agent of his performance, causal responsibility for the athlete's performance is frequently, if not always, ascribed to the athlete's coach. This ascription follows upon establishment of the coach in a position of authority for the purpose of controlling the athlete's performance outcome. This is an important point as we can now see that ascription of responsibility commonly follows allocation of authority and not the reverse as some might suggest.

Coaching is an interventive activity engaged in for the purpose of enhancing an athlete's performance in competition. The term "performance" implies expectation of specific behaviour or action. That is, a specific behaviour or action is expected to be executed according to established, well-known rules that govern or guide that particular type of performance. It is further expected, or assumed, that the athlete's intent, if considered at all, is actually in accord with those rules. The coach, by virtue of the purpose of his activity, acquires a position of influence over the athlete in a manner which most effectively facilitates the coach's control over that performance outcome. The coach is subsequently subject to punishment if he fails, or rather if the athlete fails. Thus, a coach acquires or exercises some authority in order to fulfil the purpose of coaching activity.

The concept of legitimate authority answers the question of when one person may give directives to another such that the person being directed has an obligation to obey. Thus, the concept of legitimate authority is a moral justification of the exercise of authority. In order to attempt justification we need to know what kind of authority a coach either acquires or exercises. Four kinds of authority will be reviewed in turn.

The first type of authority to be noted follows directly from the above description of legitimate authority. It seems that the ultimate appeal to a justification of the exercise of authority is morality. There is, however, a question of what standards to use in evaluation. That is, whose principles do we use, or who is to say what is moral and what is not? This is a problem which needs to be addressed by each coach but is frequently interjected merely to defend a presumed right to some personal preference. However, I concur with Robert L. Simon who says:

> The obvious answer to 'Who is to say?' is that the individual
> with the best reasons has the best grounds for saying.[13]

I suggest that the answer lies not only with the individual views of the coach but also with society as a whole whom the coach is thought to represent. What, then, is the usual contemporary basis of a coach's moral authority?

I suggest that the usual basis of a coach's moral authority is derived from two sources. The first is that informal source of tradition which will be discussed shortly. The second is that formal source which is the defined purpose of the activity. Authority is commonly justified according to the purpose of the directive. As the supporting organization usually defines that purpose, parameters of moral authority for the coach may also be defined by that organization.

The second type of authority to be noted is epistemic authority. Justification of actions by epistemic authority involves an appeal to knowledge or to persons who are knowledgeable. An epistemic authority is one who has acquired knowledge that another or others have not. This does not mean, however, that the word of another is automatically accepted as a statement of fact.

The athlete is initially considered to be ignorant of both the demands of competition and his ability to meet those demands, as well as the value of sport and competition itself. The coach is thought to be knowledgeable regarding those items and therefore able to advise the athlete authoritatively to that end. The coach, then, would appear to be an epistemic authority. It seems as well that this is the most appropriate reason for establishing such a position. However, I suggest that epistemic authority is not the only source of a coach's authority nor is it, in many cases, the major source.

Arguments that attempt to justify epistemic authority include such considerations as unequal abilities and intellectual capacities, availability of data at any given time and place, the amount of data available exceeding one person's capacity to know, and the variable means by which each individual acquires knowledge, such as research, thought, experience and experimentation. These arguments provide practical reasons for accepting epistemic authority. It appears reasonable and appropriate to accept epistemic authority as invested in individual persons, but a position of authority itself does not ensure that implied epistemic authority is legitimate. Legitimacy here deals with the question of how we know that a person actually does know what he is claimed to know. What reason do we have for accepting what is said by "x" other than the fact that he occupies a position which declares him to be an epistemic authority, that is, a knowledgeable person. The position, or any accompanying certification, only supplies a *prima facie* reason for accepting the person as a legitimate epistemic authority. Is a coach's epistemic authority justified by appeal to his position or is it justified by his actual knowledge? If we do not rely on the position alone as an appropriate justification of epistemic authority then we must evaluate the actual knowledge of the coach. I suggest that the actual knowledge of a coach is evaluated by inappropriate means. That is, coaches are evaluated according to their effectiveness in developing their athletes' abilities to meet the demands of competition. The transfer of knowledge is not a primary concern and, therefore, is not used as criteria in evaluation of the coach's activity. This means that coaching activity is evaluated according to the success of coaches' athletes in competition and not by assessing knowledge, of any kind, which may have been gained by the athlete. Some might suggest that the athlete's performance itself is a kind of knowledge. Granted, learning to move in certain ways may be accepted as a form of knowing "how" to do some particular thing. However, the same performance result is possible and, I suggest, frequently pursued via techniques of modifying behavioural response without allowing athletes to intentionally modify their own behaviour.

Thus, behavioural learning is not consistent with the notion of personal responsibility which includes the individual's awareness and intent to act according to a choice made from alternatives. Performance alone, without intent on the part of the athlete in pursuit of that performance, is insufficient to justify any and all directives given by a coach to an athlete to that end.

The third type of authority to be noted is that of political authority. Political authority is concerned with what people do rather than with what they believe.[14] Michael D. Bayles attempts to clarify this concept of authority in terms of power.

The ordinary concept of power is the common view of controlling the conduct of others through the ability to enforce directives or commands given. This involves an intent to do harm to subjects who do not comply with directives and the intent to bestow benefits to those who do comply. This reward-harm model involving an ability to enforce directives is usually associated with coercion. Due to a dependence on coercion the "ability" to enforce directives, in itself, through this model, is not considered an exercise of legitimate authority.

The social scientific concept of power excludes the items of reward and harm but relies on persuasion to convince someone that it is best for him to comply with certain directives. By this model:

> x can get y to perform actions by telling, commanding, or ordering him to do them.[15]

The subject will comply with directives without being forced to do so because he recognizes and accepts that there are other good reasons for his compliance. On this view, the subject's autonomy is not violated.

The coach is established in a position of authority within the organizational structure of the sport group. By virtue of his position, the coach has the capacity to promise benefits or threaten harms to the athlete to further the purpose of enhancing the athlete's performance. Here we should note as Bayles does:

> authority over the supreme coercive power in a population or territory is necessary for the existence of political authority...[16]

It is, in addition, always implicit that that coercive power may be used to further the purpose for which the position is specified if *de facto* authority ceases or fails. It is frequently thought that a lack of coercive power weakens the capacity of the coach to further the purpose of his position. It seems that this alone is sufficient evidence that the authority of the coach is, to a large extent, political authority. But, does the coach really need coercive power to accomplish his purpose? Does the purpose of enhancing the athlete's performance justify a coach's use of coercive power to that end? I suggest that the answer to this question is usually offered with reference to the actual, defined, purpose of the organization which supports or has established the position.

Positions of authority are established by organizations for some specific purpose. However, obligations to obey directives are dependent upon the specific kind of authority and its application by persons occupying that position. Bayles notes:

> A position of authority is specified for a purpose. The person who occupies the position is responsible for promoting that purpose and is allowed some discretion in the method of doing so. Further, the sphere of his power is specified by the subject over which he may issue directives.[17]

Bayles concludes that justification of political authority lies in its function. He states:

> Thus, political authority is justified in terms of its function. The function of a thing is not merely what it does, but what it does as contributing toward a purpose. The function of authority is therefore specified by filling in the purpose and subject matter in a rule constituting a position of authority.[18]

In application, the political authority of a coach is usually justified in terms of the function of that authority. This appeal is understandable as rules that constitute the role of a coach are provided by the supporting organization. Rarely, if ever, are defined roles provided for the coach in constitutive rules of sport activity.

The fourth type of authority to be discussed is that of social tradition. Authority would seem to be initially a social phenomenon. If an individual could carry on his affairs entirely without any relation or interactions with other individuals, the concept of authority would be meaningless. It is this unavoidable interaction of social life that necessitates appeals to authority. There is a need for a reference point to guide the nature of and acceptable means of interaction between individuals. Also, there is need for provision for mediation between individuals when their interactions are not harmonious.

The social aspect of human beings is considered the "primary human condition."[19] Most of what we know about humans is derived from studies of interrelations or interactions between individuals or groups of individuals in various situations. W.D. Handcock in his discussion of authority in society notes the profound influence of tradition in our individual lives.

> Social tradition exercises an authority over us which none of us escapes, and which indeed provides the ground and scaffolding of our personal lives.[20]

The manner in which we conduct our affairs is guided by the way things have been done before and are normally done at the present time. Tradition gives us a starting point from which we develop our own individual place in society. Tradition provides us with various sets of role expectations for individuals in certain situations. We are expected to comply with those role expectations to ensure continuity in the established order of society without which social relationships would be chaotic. Therefore, tradition serves to maintain social order. Maintenance of social order and existing role expectations is facilitated to a large degree by unquestioned acceptance of tradition. It is generally accepted that most people do not subject their social experiences to philosophical analysis.[21] Another example of the strength of tradition lies in noting how people and organizations in general resist or react to change.[22]

Structure is the most visible aspect of authority. As such, structure is the aspect of authority with which we are most familiar. However, the source of authority, which we do not see as readily, and rarely question, is more expansive and complex. The source of authority is established over time and across the entire fabric of a society. Thus, the most influential source of authority lies in social tradition. I would argue that the influence of traditional role expectations outweighs that of any institutional set of expectations for a coach. Traditional role expectations, then, determine the structure of authority used by the coach.

The source of the coach's authority is twofold in this regard. First, authority is assigned to the coach by the sponsoring institution which is presumed to be an agent of society at large. Second, and a major factor, the coach's authority is defined and assigned through traditional role expectations associated with the term or designation of a person as a "coach." Ladenson[23] refers to this type of authority as command authority and suggests that it is not justified by appeal to any moral assessment. It would appear, then, that the authority of a coach is commonly justified by non-moral means with restricted perceptions as to the purpose of the activity. It seems that attempts to justify coaching activities as the exercise of authority, solely by appeal to social tradition, are deficient and require further examination and support by other means of acceptable justification.

To summarize, the actual source of a coach's authority is social tradition as supported and strengthened by the formal organizational structure of the sponsoring institution. Ascription of causal responsibility and accountability follows upon establishment of a person in a position of authority designated as a "coach."

Authority is commonly justified if it is successful in fulfilling the function for which it was established. The authority of a coach, then, is justified if the coach is successful in fulfilling the purpose of enhancing the athlete's performance. This conclusion involves the assumption that enhancing the athlete's performance is also the purpose of the sponsoring institution. However, justification of a coach's authority, by this view, does not involve a consideration of the means used by the coach to fulfil the purpose or function of his position. As such, there is little or no consideration for the treatment accorded the individual persons, the athletes, involved in the performance. Further, although the athlete is the direct causal agent of his performance, causal responsibility as well as responsibility in the form of accountability for the athlete's performance is frequently ascribed to the athlete's coach.

If a coach is responsible for an athlete's performance, that conclusion suggests two things. First, the athlete's performance is the result of some thing or things that were done to the athlete by the coach or other external agent. Second, the athlete's performance is explicitly not the result of any intent or choice of action on the part of the athlete himself. This conclusion further implies two things. First, the athlete's performance occurred in the only way possible. The athlete could not have done otherwise than what he did, at least from the point at which he came under the coach's influence. Second, the athlete cannot in any way claim any degree of responsibility, credit or blame, for his performance. In effect, regardless of the specific nature of the performance, the athlete is not seen as having any real, or significant, part in the performance. This conclusion, then, would be in opposition to the notion of personal responsibility.

If the athlete is responsible for his performance, that conclusion suggests that the athlete has the capacity, if not the ability, for free decision-making in the direction of his performance actions. The athlete may, however, be restricted in his capacity through lack of individual development or through other external influence. The coach is actually a minor figure in the athlete's performance. This conclusion, then, suggests that the authority by which the coach imposes his intervention may not be appropriately justifiable.

In my view, an appropriate role of the coach is that of mediating the influence of external factors and individual preferences as each affects or determines the nature of the athlete's participation and subsequent performance in sport. That is, coaches should be able to justify their activities properly according to the question of when one influence ought to override the other. Further, I suggest the specific nature of this role would vary according to the institutional context of any given coaching position. However, whatever the context, a view on the question of who is actually responsible for the athlete's performance and why that is the case is an essential part of a coach's philosophy. That is, a coach's view on responsibility should determine the extent, if not the type, of authority appealed to and exercised by the coach. As well, this view, once established would undoubtedly influence other factors of the coach's methodology.

In view of the nature of coaching activity and the authority used in carrying out that activity, the commonly accepted notion of responsibility is, to say the least, insufficient for a complete and appropriate consideration of the nature and role of responsibility in the development of a coaching philosophy. We need to clarify our views on the actual locus of responsibility, determine what specific obligations are involved for coaches in given institutional contexts and to whom, and then decide which type of authority is most appropriate to fulfil those obligations and to what extent. Personal responsibility is an accepted characteristic of human beings and is used as the basis of other types of responsibility in our society. It follows that talk of shifting responsibility to a locus where it already exists suggests that coaches incorrectly assume that they are responsible and must subsequently exercise some type of authority whether or not that authority is appropriate to the responsibility, as obligation, they actually do have. Due to this assumption of responsibility, I suggest that coaches need to consider further the appropriateness of those methods they use in attempts to enhance athletes' performances.

Following from the previous discussion, a major problem may be identified for coaches relevant to formulation of a coaching philosophy. How does a coach fulfil the demands of accountability in a "position of authority" while concurrently fulfilling natural demands of fair and just treatment of athletes? I do not intend to propose a specific answer to this question here. However, I suggest that a coach's response must be a blend of what I call theory of instruction and philosophy. I make this distinction to designate theory of instruction as a means of accomplishing a given end while philosophy involves a more rigorous justification of those means that are used as well as of the ends themselves. I suggest that through a theory a coach may apply what has been properly justified in a philosophy beginning with a principle of responsibility rather than a justification of authority. It is this starting point which I have attempted to provide in this paper.

III. Women, Sportsmanship and Relationships

Notes

1. The original version of this paper was prepared under the direction of Dr. J.D. Rabb, Chairman, Department of Philosophy, Lakehead University, Thunder Bay, Ontario, 1986/87 and received a Fourth Year Essay Prize in Philosophy for that year. This version, revised with the assistance of Dr. Debra Shogan, University of Alberta, was subsequently presented at the CAHPER conference, Edmonton, May 1988.
2. Herman, Daniel J. "Mechanism and the Athlete," *Journal of the Philosophy of Sport*, Vol. 2, September 1975, 102-110.
3. Buck, L.A. *Autonomy Psychotherapy: Authoritarian Control Versus Individual Choice*, North Quincy, Mass: The Christopher Publishing House, 1979, Ch. 2, pp. 25-40.
4. Horosz, W. *The Crisis of Responsibility*, Norman, Oklahoma: University of Oklahoma Press, 1975, pp. vii-xiii, Ch. 13, pp. 310-321, pp. 209-210.
5. Pols, E. *The Acts of Our Being*, Amherst: The University of Massachusetts Press, 1982, Ch. 1, pp. 6-23, Ch. 2, pp. 24-58, p. 8.
6. Pols, p. 53.
7. Feinberg, Joel. "Action and Responsibility," in White, Alan R., Ed., *The Philosophy of Action*, New York: Oxford University Press, 1968, pp. 95-119.
8. Feinberg, p. 107.
9. Feinberg, p. 108.
10. Feinberg, p. 111.
12. Feinberg, p. 113.
13. Simon, R.L. *Sports and Social Values*, Englewood Cliffs, N.J.: Prentice-Hall, 1985, p. 10.
14. Bayles, M.D. "The Functions and Limits of Political Authority," in Harris, R. B., Ed., *Authority: A Philosophical Analysis*, pp. 101-111, p. 101.
15. Bayles, p. 103.
16. Bayles, p. 106.
17. Bayles, p. 105.
18. Bayles, p. 108.
19. Handcock, W.D. "The Function and Nature of Authority in Society," *Philosophy*, Vol. XXXIII, No. 105, 1953, pp. 99-112, p. 102.
20. Handcock, p. 100.
21. Handcock, p. 100.
22. O'Donnell, D. and Bruce, G. "Change Agent Theory and Its Application to Recreation Administration," for 1974 Congress for Recreation and Parks, October, 1974.

23. Ladenson, R. F. "Legitimate Authority," *American Philosophical Quarterly*, Vol. 9(4), Oct. 1972, pp. 335-341.

Bibliography

Bayles, M.D. "In Defense of Authority," *Personalist*, Vol. LII, 1971, pp. 755-759.

Bayles, M.D. "The Functions and Limits of Political Authority," in Harris, R.B., ed., *Authority: A Philosophical Analysis*. Alabama: The University of Alabama Press, pp. 101-111.

Blau, P.M. "The Hierarchy of Authority in Organizations," *American Journal of Sociology*, Vol. LXIII, 1967, pp. 453-467.

Braybrooke, D. "Authority As a Subject of Social Science and Philosophy," *Review of Metaphysics*, Vol. XIII, 1960, pp. 469-485.

Davies, P. ed., *The American Heritage Dictionary of the English Language*, New York: Dell Publishing, 1972, p. 138.

De George, R. T. "The Nature and Function of Epistemic Authority," in Harris R.B., ed., *Authority: A Philosophical Analysis*. Alabama: The University of Alabama Press, pp. 77-93.

Feinberg, Joel. "Action and Responsibility," in White, Alan R., ed., *The Philosophy of Action*, New York: Oxford University Press, 1968, pp. 95-119.

Fuller, L.L. "The Forms and Limits of Adjudication," *Harvard Law Review*, Vol. 92, 1978, pp. 353-409.

Garver, N. "Rules," in *The Encyclopedia of Philosophy*, Vol. 7, pp. 231-233.

Gowan, G. "Coaching Philosophy and Its Effect Upon Coaching Performance," (2 parts) *Coaching Association of Canada Bulletin*, #11, Oct. 1975, p. 2, 14, and #12, Jan. 1976, pp. 2-3, 9.

Handcock, W.D. "The Function and Nature of Authority in Society," *Philosophy*, Vol. XXXIII, No. 105, 1953, pp. 99-112.

Harris, R. B. *Authority: A Philosophical Analysis*, Alabama: The University of Alabama Press, 1976, with extensive bibliography, pp. 142-170.

Hart, H.L.A. *The Concept of Law*, New York: Oxford University Press, 1961, Ch. 4 and 6.

Herman, Daniel J. "Mechanism and the Athlete" *Journal of the Philosophy of Sport*, Vol. 2, September 1975, 102-110.

Horosz, W. *The Crisis of Responsibility*, Norman, Oklahoma: University of Oklahoma Press, 1975, pp. vii-xiii; Ch. 13, pp. 310-321; pp. 209-210.

Kaufman, A.S. "Responsibility," in *Encyclopedia of Philosophy*, Vol. 7, pp. 183-188.

III. Women, Sportsmanship and Relationships

Ladenson, R. F. "Legitimate Authority," *American Philosophical Quarterly*, Vol. 9(4), Oct. 1972, pp. 335-341.

O'Donnell, D. and Bruce G. "Change Agent Theory and Its Application to Recreation Administration," for 1974 Congress for Recreation and Parks, October, 1974.

Pols, E. *The Acts of Our Being*, Amherst: The University of Massachusetts Press, 1982, Ch. 1, pp. 6-23; Ch. 2, pp. 24-58.

Popper, K. R. and Eccles, J. C. *The Self and Its Brain*, New York: Springer International, 1977.

Pound, R. "The Case for Law," *Valparaiso University Law Review*, 1967, pp. 201-214.

Pushkin, M. "Failure of the Young Distance Runner: The Coach's Responsibility," *Coach & Athlete*, Vol. 40(2), Oct. 1977, pp. 17-18.

Ravizza, K. and Daruty, K. "Paternalism and Sovereignty in Athletics: Limits and Justifications of the Coach's Exercise of Authority Over the Adult Athlete," *Journal of the Philosophy of Sport*, Vol. XI, 1984, 71-82.

Robison, W.L. "The Functions and Limits of Legal Authority," in Harris, R. B., ed., *Authority: A Philosophical Analysis*. Alabama: The University of Alabama Press, pp. 113-131.

Simon, R.L. *Sports and Social Values*, Englewood Cliffs, N.J.: Prentice-Hall, 1985.

Werkmeister, W. H. "The Function and Limits of Moral Authority," in Harris, R.B., ed., *Authority: A Philosophical Analysis*. Alabama: The University of Alabama Press, pp. 95-100.

White, Alan R., ed. *The Philosophy of Action*, New York: Oxford University Press, 1968, Introduction, pp. 1-18.

DISCRIMINATION IN SPORT: WHAT SO FEW SEE

MARGE HOLMAN

Introduction

For some time now studies have been conducted and articles have been written expressing concern for inequities which exist in sport. Objective measures have exposed a very clear picture. Statistics reveal that a gender imbalance does exist and becomes progressively more male dominant as the continuum moves from recreation to elitism and from participant and volunteer coach/administrator to paid or professional player/coach/administrator with a decision-making role. While we have recognized that equality in sport continues to elude us we have failed to adequately address the reasons for this happening which then limits our ability to facilitate positive change.

This paper explores the issues of discrimination within the system and how our failure to address these issues creates an environment which preserves the status quo. *Systemic discrimination*[1] excludes or has a negative impact on women (or other target groups) through policies, and procedures or practices which cannot be justified by job requirements. Such exclusion may exist whether or not it is intended and will have a similar effect in either case. Systemic discrimination creates barriers which are hidden and, although sometimes maintained for convenience or through neglect, is often unintentional. The end result of systemic discrimination and its effect is to discourage members of a particular group from becoming full participants within the system itself.

Women Within the System

Recent studies which have researched the existence of systemic discrimination have increased public awareness on the topic. This paper will focus on the ways in which women in sport are treated differently than men, specifically on those issues which create barriers. The attitudes and behaviours that each of us communicates within normal relationships convey a powerful message to women and to men that in the world of sport, which has been traditionally male, women are less capable and less valued as competitors, and less committed as coaches and less effective as administrators. Studies continue to show that positions which wield power and prestige still are disproportionately represented by males despite claims that strategies have been

291

III. Women, Sportsmanship and Relationships

established to ensure equal opportunity for women in sport. A review of the facts makes it readily apparent that the success of claimed strategies is extremely limited. In fact, what has happened is the creation of an environment which may be having the opposite effect. Figures reveal[2] that only 7% of our Canadian national coaches were women in 1985-86 and only 18% of "other coaches" were women. In sport governing bodies, only 24% of Chief Executive Officers and 17% of Technical Directors were women yet 62% of Co-ordinators were women within the same time frame. Canadian universities recorded[3] an equal number of male and female coaches for women's teams in 1985-86. The disturbing fact is that a five-year change showed the number of male coaches of women's teams to have increased by 15 percent and the number of female coaches of women's teams to have remained static. The role of athletic administrators within Canadian universities during this same time frame was represented by 73 percent men and 27 percent women. However, the overwhelming majority of these female administrators are co-ordinators, responsible to a male athletic director. The government and university environments provide the most opportunities for sport participation and sport-related careers. This does not speak well for Community Colleges or community recreation programs where the participation of women within the various ranks of their sport programs is negligible.[4]

Numbers — A Critical Issue

One of the problems women experience in sport as administrators, coaches, officials, competitors or other is *isolation*. For the professional, when women comprise only a few of the total group, the visibility of women becomes more apparent. Peers establish expectations and place women under constant review. Their performance in a professional capacity is evaluated and reviewed as representative of her gender. Under these circumstances, this evaluation may result in the generalization that one incompetent woman or poor decisions by a woman means that women are not capable of handling the job while one incompetent male or a poor decision by a male goes unnoticed within the system. When women enter a system as the only woman or one of a very few, they must prove their worth, yet the worth of men entering the system is assumed and must be blatantly disproved for them to lose status. Women are still considered an anomaly in sport leadership roles. This makes it very difficult to be comfortable in a position if every decision and action is to be scrutinized. If everyone was judged in this manner it would be quickly noted that each individual, regardless of gender, will expose strengths and weaknesses. One of the effects of this undue attention is the creation of a climate which discourages individuals from aspiring to leadership positions or continuing in them for any length of time.

When few women exist within the system, they may be called upon to represent women in general. This detracts from their ability to express themselves freely as an individual. It can also result in further alienation from the group if the opinion expressed is contrary to the traditional establishment even though that opinion may have been invited. Under such circumstances, it often becomes much easier to accept socialization to male values and compromise any advocacy position for women's sport.

At Work or Play — A Social Conflict

We have all been socialized to have certain expectations of ourselves according to gender and expectations of others according to gender. Generally, rules have been quite clear in a social setting. However, in a professional setting, it is often very difficult for males to view females as peers and place any value on their contribution as a professional. This is a natural process since the image of a traditional leader, e.g., athletic director, coach, athletic therapist, etc., is that of a male. Most positions in the past have been held by males, with the majority of women in support positions or assistant roles where they serve and are responsible to a higher status male. As a result, many men are not comfortable accepting women as equals and less comfortable accepting them as decision-makers.

When major issues arise, the opinion of women is often not sought or ignored when presented. The contributions of women are largely often undervalued. Women are usually denied credit for ideas generated by them. A female administrator, serving on a sport governing committee as one of two women with seven males, recalls an issue of debate for which she offered a proposed solution. This was quickly dismissed as impossible; however, following several more minutes of discussion, the same solution was presented by a male committee member. This time the proposal was unanimously accepted with no acknowledgement that it had been tabled earlier in the meeting.

By creating an environment which diminishes their personal and professional self worth, individuals within a group are discouraged from seeking access to that group or, in essence, are being denied access to that group.

Language

The manner in which we communicate often provides a message beyond the content of what is actually said or seen. Our choice of words or images and the way in which we convey them will often create

293

perceptions that reflect attitudes. In the case of references made to gender, language, be it written or verbal, can reinforce sex stereotyping which excludes one of the genders and therefore supports the existence of systemic discrimination. (From the University of Windsor Gender Inclusive Language manual, to be published Fall, 1988) Many yet still to be convinced that language is a limiting factor for females when defining their own opportunities and for males when defining the role which they perceive females should assume. However, as society grows, the components within it change. Language is in a state of transition. Sport is in need of incorporating broader gender-inclusive language to reflect its change in population. It is still very common to teach participants "man to man" strategies, easily accommodated for both genders with "one to one," or to cheer participants on with a phrase, "let's go guys" which easily can be changed to "let's go team." How often do we hear superior female athletes being praised with the phrase "she plays just like a guy"? Did those individuals ever consider the fact that females, too, can be good athletes and can play the game the way it should be played?

While words and phrases may create images for individuals or small groups, the titles assigned to identify an athletic program for women reflect an attitude descriptive of the status of women's sport within an organization. The use of "Lady" preceding the global team name used for male teams or the addition of "ette" at the end of this team name suggests secondary status. Since most women's programs have followed on the heels of men's programs, team names and the traditions associated with them have been established with good intent. The affiliate names have been developed to provide women's programs with their own identity. It would, however, be more appropriate to achieve this end through independent nomenclature.

Language and the method in which we address individuals can provide a description of the relationship between individuals. Professional titles should project a role and the status ascribed to the role regardless of gender. For example, in the educational environment, it is not uncommon to hear students or colleagues speak to or of female professionals on a first name basis. Yet males of equal status are normally addressed by "Coach," "Sir," "Professor," "Mr." or others rather than a first name.

Attitude — A Silent Barrier

Few will deny that discrimination against women in sport existed at one time; however, many believe that this discrimination has ended. An increase in the participation rate of females in athletic activities creates the image that equality has been achieved. However, while there are some women coaches, a few women officials and an occasional female administrator, equality is yet a long way off. The overt discrimination has been dealt with in most cases. However, the covert or indirect discrimination which exists within the system is more difficult to identify and more difficult to remedy. The subtle ways in which women are treated differently communicates to them and to those around that their status in the world of sport is less significant than that of their male counterparts. It is a subtle message and the method of conveying this message is one that silently protects the status quo.

Attitudes which have no single identifiable source prevail, placing limits and expectations on roles according to gender. In an educational environment, for example, the value of sport is still measured according to male standards. In a university environment where academic responsibilities are often combined with coaching responsibilities, one woman coach reported that male coaches were "allowed" to spend time coaching because they were expected to excel. On the other hand, while there was still the expectation for a woman to excel in coaching, there was a greater expectation for women to excel in areas other than coaching as well. Therefore, a male coach with a good record is excused for a poor performance in the classroom while a female coach with a good record was still expected to meet high classroom standards. There are a number of issues contained within this case. However, for our purposes, the variances in attitude based on gender is inappropriate. It creates a self-fulfilling prophecy which dooms women to failure.

The value given female athletes is secondary to that of male athletes. One male coach of a university women's basketball team resigned that position to "move up and coach a high school boys team." The media adopts this value system as well with the view that women's competitive results are inferior to the men's revealed in the exposure provided. One sports writer attended the end of a women's university game and the entire men's game. The next edition of the newspaper included a large article on the men's game as well as box scores and no results, even in the box scores, of the women's game "because it was not called in." Neither was the men's. Their claim is that the public is not interested. Women claim that the public will be interested in those events which the media feeds them. Administrators and sport information officers, most of whom are male, spend much time and energy promoting their identified high profile sports, i.e., hockey, basketball, football, and little effort promoting women's sport. They accept the media's reluctance to give adequate coverage to women's sport and reinforce the public image of the low status accorded women's sport. This is not a problem unique to women's programs. Sports within men's programs assigned the status of "minor" or "non-spectator" sports are confronted with the same value system. However, the gender issue lies in the fact that all women's programs normally fall within the "minor" category and are assigned coverage, and indeed all resources, accordingly.

When society perceives that the role of coaching is reserved for men, it is predictable that female athletes also expect males to be better coaches. With an automatic acceptance of a male as knowledgeable and competent in coaching skills, he is secure until he disproves these abilities. However, it is more difficult for a female coach who must spend time and energy establishing credibility and proving competence prior to acceptance. A more disturbing outcome of this attitude is the limitation it places on the aspirations of the female athlete. Young women who include sport within their career aspirations are quickly discouraged when they see few women within the system and when they see the low status ascribed to those women who are there.

Leadership is a prime quality for success in most roles within sport. Generally, leadership styles and behaviours have been defined according to a male model. It is difficult for us to perceive women in leadership roles particularly when both genders are represented. Women coaches with male assistant coaches are often mistaken as the assistant since we assume that the male will hold the higher status position. It is also difficult for us to accept women in leadership positions because the characteristics associated with strong leadership are viewed as male characteristics. An assertive, ambitious, high achieving woman often makes those around her uncomfortable and critical of her style. Those same characteristics within a male are praised rather than criticized.

When women have no administrative powers within the system, they have no voice, or a limited voice, in the decision-making process for programs that affect them. This becomes more significant with the recent trend to amalgamate men's and women's programs. Many profess that women have an equal opportunity to secure the administrative power but the reality of the situation reveals that it is an exception when a woman is appointed with responsibility for men's and women's athletics. There is a belief that women cannot be good administrators of men's high profile sports, i.e., football, hockey or even basketball, yet there is no question that men can administer women's sport, even synchronized swimming.

Hiring

Hiring is a major issue when creating change or maintaining the status quo. Again, attitudes and perceptions influence selections that are made and justify decisions that limit the opportunities for women. For example, it is commonly proposed that women have less of a commitment to sport than men; women may have higher levels of absenteeism or they may feel it is necessary to design their work schedules around family responsibilities; women are often stereotyped as more emotional and therefore incapable of dealing with the pressures of major decision making; women have leadership styles that reflect their personalities and run counter to the aggressive domineering male which limits their degree of success. These assumptions made on the basis of gender do not take into account any individuality and result in discriminatory behaviours that limit the opportunities for women in sport.

Further, while information systems become critical in ensuring equal opportunity, they can also be a limiting factor. At the time a position becomes available, the method of advertising becomes crucial. Within a predominantly male environment, the networking which represents the informal advertising of a position will yield a greater number of male applicants. In addition to being advantaged by special notification of an opportunity, these male applicants also have an advocate within the system when candidates are being considered. Without conscious efforts to alter this behaviour, the true opportunities for women will continue to be few.

Outcome

Despite some improvement, many things have not changed significantly. The effects of systemic discrimination have a major influence on how an employee feels about herself and her colleagues and how colleagues feel about her. The subtle behaviours that women experience on a day to day basis are often destructive to their personal and professional welfare. These behaviours may be inadvertent or may even be intentional but well meaning. However, the effect is usually viewed by the recipient as demeaning. Individually, an incident may not be significant — collectively, the impact can be devastating when such behaviours are part of the normal social and professional exchange of colleagues. Women become frustrated with the limitations established and begin to resent the message conveyed or begin to believe the message and accept the limitations. In either case, consciously or subconsciously, these behaviours erode the self-worth of women who are exposed to them as a normal part of the environment. They begin to question the value of their work and the contributions they make to the profession. This often results in a self-imposed increase in workload in an attempt to justify, to themselves and to others, their existence in and value to the sport environment. The lingering self doubt which results contributes to a lack of confidence and a reticence to seek advancement within the system.

Working with Adversity

It is important to realize that change is a slow process at best and that attitudes are difficult or impossible to change. It is therefore necessary to

III. Women, Sportsmanship and Relationships

direct personal energies in a manner which is most productive, confronting those issues where the greatest impact can be achieved, identifying those issues which cannot be immediately overcome and establishing coping mechanisms. Until there are more women in the system to work towards change and until a greater number of decision-makers have a complete understanding of the issues which result in the creation of limitations on women in sport, the situation will remain stagnant. The recognition that a lack of women in various sport roles as a *symptom* of systemic discrimination is critical in eliminating the systemic discrimination.

Immediate action can include a review of existing policies and procedures with the intent of eliminating discriminatory practices based upon policy gaps, precedents, past practice or reverse discrimination arguments. Other actions may include pro-active measures such as internal audits, goal setting, timetables, monitoring and evaluation to implement change. A number of studies[5,6] have offered recommendations which address the problem of the number of women in the system. Today, their effectiveness appears to be limited.

However, significant change generally provides long term solutions. In the short term, it is important to identify interim methods of coping which will also assist in facilitating change. Consideration of the following should be given by those who can relate to the content of this paper to ease the stress and prevent or diminish the loss of women in the system.

a) Work to increase the number of women involved in sport. This does not negate the fact that you will have many male colleagues whom you respect and interact with, or show any lack of appreciation for the contributions that many men have made to the development of women's sport.

b) Serve as a role model for other women who can relate to you.

c) Seek role models with whom you can interact and generate support. Their experience will reduce the isolation and stress, knowing that others have been subjected to the same frustration.

d) Direct energies and present positions where they will be heard rather than expending energy with individuals who are closed to the concept of equity for women in sport.

e) Set goals for yourself which are realistic and achievable.

f) Be an advocate for women in sport whenever the opportunity arises.

g) Establish priorities on those issues which need to be addressed, and focus energies first on those which are identified as most important.

h) When other women wish to pursue a vocation or avocation in sport in any capacity, it is important to encourage them to do so and even to take further measures to ensure that they feel welcome.

i) In establishing goals, intent must be followed by an action plan as a mechanism to ensure results.

j) Recognize that generally, women's lives are different than men's lives both socially and professionally and that both the system and individuals within the system must take this into account and be receptive to it.

k) As a woman in the system, especially as a woman who is in the system with some security and credibility, it is important to be sensitive to the issues other women experience even if in disagreement, or if they are not issues personally experienced. Do not assume your successes are automatically available to others.

l) In recruiting support for proposing change, recruit support from male colleagues who are sensitive to the reality of the environment and to the barriers with which women are confronted.

m) Maintain outside interests and contact with people who provide a distraction from the challenges within the system.

Bibliography

1. Ontario Women's Directorate. *Achieving Employment Equity: A Manual for Practitioners*, prepared by MacLeod Consulting Services Limited, Toronto, 1985, p. 1.6.
   and
   Employment and Immigration Canada. *Employment Equity: A Guide for Employers*. Glossary, p. 8.
2. Fitness and Amateur Sport Women's Program and the Canadian Association for Health, Physical Education and Recreation. *Women in Sport Leadership: Summary of National Survey*. Government of Canada, 1985-86.
3. Report of the CIAU Women's Representative Committee. *CIAU Comparative Study Update*. Fitness and Amateur Sport Women's Program, 1985-86.
4. Galasso, P.J. and Holman Prpich, M.J. *Equal Pay for Work of Equal Value and Related Issues in Sport, Physical Education and Recreation*. Ontario Women's Directorate and the University of Windsor, 1987.

III. Women, Sportsmanship and Relationships

5. Sopinka, John, Q.C., Chairman. *Can I Play?* The Report of the Task Force on Equal Opportunity in Athletics: Volume 1, 1983.
6. Sopinka, John, Q.C., Chairman. *Can I Play?* The Report of the Task Force on Equal Opportunity in Athletics: Volume 2: Schools, Community Colleges and Universities. 1984.

SECTION IV.

JUSTICE
AND
ETHICS

APPLICATION OF A SCIENTIFIC ETHICS APPROACH TO SPORT DECISIONS

EARLE F. ZEIGLER

Throughout existence the human animal has struggled for survival in a harsh physical environment. A recognizable semblance of victory has been won over difficult surroundings, but somehow we have not been able to remove the insecurity evident in our efforts to live together constructively and peacefully on our closed planet. In considering humankind's basic problems, Burtt (1965) believes that

> The greatest danger to his future lies in the disturbing emotions and destructive passions that he has not yet overcome; the greatest promise lies in his capacity for a sensitive understanding of himself and his human fellows, and his power to enter the inclusive universe in which the creative aspirations of all can move freely toward their fulfillment. (p. 311)

Thus, if our "distorting emotions and destructive passions" do indeed represent the "greatest danger" for the future, the application of a sound ethical approach to personal and professional living can be of inestimable assistance to people who are truly seeking a "sensitive understanding" of themselves and their fellows.

Evidence that others see the need for study in ethics comes from a variety of sources. Recently *The New York Times* reported that "nowadays students in many disciplines are enrolling in new ethics courses in a variety of undergraduate departments and professional schools....Part of the impetus for new programs stems from the social consciousness of the 1960s" ("The Growing Dishonesty," 1976). Whether this enrolment in ethics courses can be shown to have a relationship with the earlier social consciousness is an interesting question, but it is true that there has been a spate of indications that an interest in ethics is increasing. Some examples of this heightened interest are (a) Geoffrey Hazard's article on "Capitalist Ethics" (1978); (b) Henry Fairlie's book entitled *The Seven Deadly Sins Today* (1978); (c) James Chace's piece inquiring about "How 'Moral' Can We Get?" (1977); (d) Michael Blumenthal's statement that societal changes have occasioned "questionable and illegal corporate activities" (1977); (e) *The New York Times*' article inquiring whether the growing dishonesty in sports is just a reflection of our American society ("The Growing Dishonesty," 1976); (f) Derek Bok's request, as president of Harvard University, that courses in

IV. Justice and Ethics

applied ethics be taught (1976); (g) Amitai Etzioni's assertion that "the hottest new item in post-Watergate curricula is "moral education" (1976); (j) Rainer Maetens' belief that kid sports may currently be a "den of iniquity" (1976); (k) Ann Dennis' article explaining that the Canadian Sociology and Anthropology Association is considering the adoption of a code of professional ethics (1975); (1) *The Saturday Review* Special Report entitled "Watergating on Main Street" that assessed the ethics of congressmen, lawyers, businessmen, accountants, journalists, doctors and educators ("Watergating," 1975); and (m) Fred Hechinger's (1974) query as to "Whatever Became of Sin?" — to name just a few of the articles and statements that were readily apparent in a period of 18 months.

The term "ethics" is employed in three different ways, each of which has a relation to the other — and all of which will be used here. First, ethics classifies a general pattern or "way of life" (e.g., Muslim ethics). Second, it refers to a listing of rules of conduct, or what is often called a moral code (e.g., the "fair play" ethics of an athlete). Last, it describes an area of inquiry *about* ways of life or rules of conduct (e.g., that subdivision of philosophy now known as meta-ethics).

Ethics Yesterday and Today

History substantiates that ethics is a description of "irregular progress toward complete clarification of each type of ethical judgment" (Abelson & Friquegnon, 1975, p. 82). By this is meant the "search for the meaning and standards of good in general, and of well-being, right conduct, moral character, and justice in particular." How does one judge exactly, or even generally, how much "irregular progress" has been made since the development of Greek ethics began in the fifth century B.C. One may argue that the changing political, economic, and other social forces of that time required the introduction of a new way of conduct — just as today there appears to be an urgent need for altered standards of conduct during this evidently transitional period.

Today it would be an obvious exaggeration to say that there are as many approaches to ethics and/or moral philosophy as there are philosophers. Conversely, however, there is no single, noncontroversial foundation stone on which to build the entire structure of ethics. This is not to say that there are not some aspects of this branch of philosophy on which there have been fairly wide agreement. As Noel-Smith (1954) has explained, in the past moral philosophers offered general guidance as to what to do, what to seek, and how to treat others — injunctions that we could well keep in mind in the consideration of sport ethics.

As a rule philosophers have not tried to preach to their adherents in the same way as theologians have felt constrained to do.

304

Nevertheless, many philosophers have offered practical advice that included pronouncements on what was good and bad or right and wrong. Still, many have persistently searched for a true moral code, a normative ethical system, on which all people could and should base their conduct. The advent of philosophical analysis as a distinct approach during this century in the Western world has thrust the contemporary analytic philosopher right into the middle of the struggle between the ethical objectivist and the ethical subjectivist. The former asserts that the truth of that which is declared by an ethical statement is independent of that person, that particular time, and that place where it is used. The subjectivist, on the other hand, argues that moral judgments about people or their actions are judgments about the way we think or feel about these people or their actions. However, at the very time when the world is in such a turmoil with "hot" wars, cold wars, terrorists — at the very time when people of all ages want to know about "what to do, what to seek, and how to treat others" — the large majority of scholars in the field of philosophy are almost completely silent, avoiding the rational justification of any type of moral system and analyzing the meaning and function of moral concepts and statements only occasionally.

What we find, therefore, is that the dispensing of "ethical wisdom" in life is generally left to people who have given the topic much less scholarly thought than those related professionally to the discipline of philosophy. What we have as a result is a situation where theologians, dramatists, novelists, poets, medical doctors, politicians, sport figures, educational administrators — in no special order of importance — offer a variety of opinions from suggestions to dogma about all aspects of life including sports and games. Most notable among these amateur philosophers are scientists and comedians — people who may have earned justifiable fame, or even notoriety. I believe strongly that at least part of the professional output of sport and physical education philosophers ought to be directed pointedly at what might be called the lay public and also to their colleagues in educational circles.

All of us should be working toward the elimination of irrational ethical beliefs while attempting to discover the soundest possible ethical system for *our* evolving society. We recognize that the task of normative inquiry can be most difficult, especially when complex issues and conclusions tend to stray into the realm of meta-ethics. The person in the mother discipline of philosophy, the educational philosopher, and the sport and physical activity philosopher must assist the profession if we ever hope to be able to justify ethical theory in competitive sport. Such justification demands that the theorist state correctly, elucidate sufficiently, and defend adequately his/her moral or ethical claims and arguments about participation in competitive sport.

IV. Justice and Ethics

The Person's Implicit "Sense of Life"

How does a child's personality develop prior to the time when a young person gets a chance in our society to learn through education how to make ethical decisions in life? Rand (1960) offers an interesting analysis of what occurs in the life of a young person before any semblance of a rational philosophy develops. The human possesses a "psychological recorder" which is the integrating mechanism of a person's subconscious. This so-called sense of life "is a preconceptual equivalent of metaphysics, an emotional, subconsciously integrated appraisal of man and existence. It sets the nature of a man's emotional responses and the essence of his character" (p. 31). This human being is making choices, is forming value judgments, is experiencing emotions, and in a great many ways is acquiring an *implicit* view of life. All of this young person's conclusions or evasions about or from life represent an implicit metaphysics.

As people interested in the entire educational process, our hope is that all young people will have the chance to develop their rational powers. If this occurs, reason can then act as the programmer of the individual's "emotional computer" with a possible outcome that the earlier sense of life will develop into a reasonable logical philosophy. If the maturing child does not have the opportunity to develop rationality, or evades the opportunity, then unfortunately chance takes over. Thus we have a person who has matured chronologically, but who is "integrating blindly, incongruously, and at random" (Rand, 1960, p. 33). How important is it, for example, that in the development of a fully integrated personality the young person's sense of life matches conscious, rationalized convictions? What can the role of philosophy be — what *should* it be — in the formation of a fully integrated personality? Is not the goal of education an individual whose mind and emotions are in harmony, thereby enabling the person to develop to full potential and achieve maximum effectiveness in life?

Further, because a person is a social animal and because physical activity — often including sports and games — is typically part of everyone's life, we should give careful consideration to the problem of helping the young person to bridge the gap from an early sense of life with its embryonic, amorphous value integrations to the making of ethical decisions in sport and similar types of physical activity. We should be helping that person — the intramural or varsity athlete often involved in highly competitive situations charged with strong emotions — to develop conscious convictions in which the mind leads and the emotions follow to the greatest possible extent. It is at this point also where wise educational leadership can by example and precept serve as the best possible guide for the young person often confronted with difficult ethical decisions involving both speech and conduct.

Major Ethical "Routes" Available in the Western World

Having arrived at this point — position where we have stated that a young person in our society should be so educated that there is an opportunity to develop rationality as a "life competency" — we now need to ask ourselves what major, alternative ethical routes are available for our use in the Western world. We can all agree that we want to assist the young person to bridge this gap. Further, we would expect that the opportunity to achieve such comprehension within reasonable limits would be readily available to all aspiring young people in North American life today. Unfortunately, I am forced to state that nothing is farther from the truth based on my experience with young people over a period of years. I am forced to agree with Rand's earlier assertion that on all sides we find young people "integrating blindly, incongruously, and at random" about all aspects of life. No matter whether the question is one of taking drugs for presumably heightened experiences, or cheating on examinations or terms papers, or breaking the rules in competitive sport in one or more of a dozen overt or covert ways, the evidence points to an upbringing in which the young person has not received educational experiences in which an "ethical competency" could be developed.

Keeping all of the above factors in mind, I set out to determine what major ethical routes of a philosophical nature are available to the physical educator/coach today. A careful analysis of these approaches indicates great variation in terminology and emphasis. Terms that appear include ethical naturalism, ethical non-naturalism (or intuitionism), and emotivism (Hospers, 1953, p. 485); authoritarianism, relativism and scientific ethics (Fromm, 1967, p. 37); the legalistic, the antinomian and the situational (Fletcher, 1966, pp. 17-18); and religious absolutism, conventionalism, rational absolutism and utilitarian relativism (Abelson & Friquegnon, 1967). Further, Titus and Keeton (1973, pp. 59-60) use a threefold classification, but they do their best to avoid an "ism" nomenclature by stating that there are (a) those who live under the aegis of codes (e.g., God's word); (b) those who thrust aside codes and prescribed laws; and (c) those who seek to establish ethical norms through the application of reflective moral judgment. Finally, Patterson (1957) states that we can delineate correctly two divisional categories of ethical theories — where the knowledge comes from and the motive that prompts action. To add to this review of what might be called secondary listings, pertinent work of a primary nature was examined as follows: John Dewey (1929, 1946, 1948); Dewey & Tufts, (1932); G.E. Moore (1948); Simone de Beauvoir (1964); A. J. Ayer (1946);

IV. Justice and Ethics

C. L. Stevenson (1947-48); Joseph Fletcher (1966); Kurt Baier (1958); and John Rawls (1971).

As a result of this analysis, five presumably different approaches have been subsumed in Table 1. Each approach or "ethical route" has been described according to (a) underlying presupposition, (b) criterion for evaluation, (c) method for determination of ethical decision, (d) scientific ethics and (e) emotivism. No strong argument is being made here for five approaches as opposed to two, three, or four. This analysis represents only what might be called a consensual tabulation.

Underlying Rationale for Scientific Ethics Approach

My plan at this time — keeping space limitations in mind — must simply be one in which a brief discussion is presented as to why the application of scientific method to ethical analysis seems necessary at present. Men and women today are finding themselves in an unusually difficult position. All of us are discovering that there is indeed a "crisis of human values" in existence, and the confidence that we had previously in religion and philosophy has been seriously undermined. Daily we hear on the one hand that onrushing science and technology are our great benefactors. Then in the next moment we learn that science and technology may actually destroy life on this planet permanently — at least in the sense that we have known it to this point ("God and Science," 1977).

Further, we have learned that the twentieth century is a transitional one — that the old order has most definitely been replaced by the new! But what is not generally appreciated is that the rate of change in society is gradually accelerating and that this acceleration will continue to increase. All of this has led me to conclude that in the Western world we must eliminate the persisting dualism that has separated investigation about the physical world from the study of human behaviour in relation to moral values and virtues. In an evolving democratic society, I cannot personally find a strong rationale for any authoritarian or legalistic doctrine governing ethical behaviour — one in which ironclad conformity is required because of the presence of absolute good and rightness in the world. Such an assumption is a personal one on my part, of course. It is fortunate for me that our society guarantees individual freedom in such matters as long as the laws of the land are not abrogated.

I have considered the antinomial, relativistic position as well. As pleasant as it may be on occasion to rebel against society in a radical manner, antinomianism appears to be so far to the left on an authoritarian-anarchistic freedom spectrum as to be fundamentally "out of key" in a democracy. Despite the appeal of the emotivist approach and the logic of the language analyst, it is my position that society's present plight requires more than the application of this technique alone to life's many ethical problems. I believe that our failure to employ scientific method in the realm of so-called *moral* goods, as well as in the realm of so-called *natural* goods, keeps our world in a position where changes in values have come about accidentally or arbitrarily. Social theory has warned us continually about the powerful, controlling influence of societal values and norms. If in the near future we are only able to obliterate the idea that there is a difference in kind between what we have called "human nature" and what we have identified as the "physical world," we will then be able to bring the forces of science to bear more effectively on all human behaviour. What we need, therefore,

> is intelligent examination of the consequences that are actually effected by inherited institutions and customs, in order that there may be intelligent consideration of the ways in which they are to be intentionally modified in behalf of generation of different consequences. (Dewey, 1929, pp. 272-273)

> We need a faith that (a) science can indeed bring about complete agreement on *factual belief* about human behavior; (b) such agreement in factual belief will soon result in agreement in *attitudes* held by people; and (c) resultantly a continuous adaptation of values to the culture's changing needs will eventually effect the directed reconstruction of all social institutions (Dewey, 1948, p. xxiii).

I wish to explain further that placing our faith in scientific method in no way negates the work of the analytic philosopher who subscribes to the language analysis phase of the emotivist approach. Such analytic endeavor is actually scientific and can assist science in a vital way by dispensing with fallacious premises and nonsense terms so that hypotheses will be stated correctly and understood as completely as possible. However, it is at this point that a wholly scientific approach to ethics parts company with emotivism, because the problematic factual statements are not automatically referred to the social scientist. Indeed, the distinction between the so-called *factual* statements and the so-called value statements is not made in the scientific ethics approach — *it is explicitly rejected!*

With this approach the scientific method itself is brought to bear in problem solving. Reflective thinking begets the ideas that function as tentative solutions for concrete problems of *all* kinds. In the process a rapidly changing culture confronts the person who, as a problem-solving organism, must be prepared to make adjustments. Habitual and/or impulsive responses will often not be effective — and assuredly not as effective as reflective thinking that employs both the experience of the past and the introduction of creative ideas. Thus, as explained by Albert, Denise and Peterfreund (1975), the "criterion of truth is directly related to the outcome of the reflective process. Those ideas which are successful in resolving problematic situations are true, whereas those which do not lead to satisfactory adjustments are false" (p. 282). Viewed in this manner, we can appreciate what James called the "cash value" of an idea — the import that certain knowledge, having served as an instrument for verification for people, has for the fulfillment of human purpose.

An Application of Scientific Method to Ethical Analysis

At present when we encounter ethical problems in our lives, be they personal problems, work problems, or in situations relating to competitive sport — and assuming that we recognize that a problem is an ethical problem — we seem to be resolving any such issue on the basis of either authoritarianism, relativism, or perhaps on the basis of what might be called "common sense, cultural utilitarianism." One would feel somewhat more secure if only Fletcher's (1966) situationism embodying the principle of "God's love" were employed. How much better would it be, however, if we would avail ourselves of the opportunity to expand the mind's potential toward its true capability by using the experimental method for the solving of problems? Based on such a theory of knowledge — where the mind serves to form knowledge or truth by undergoing experience — we would have an approach that could be regularly employed with a much better chance of success.

Table 1
Major Philosophical Approaches to Ethical Decisions

Ethical approach	Underlying presupposition	Criterion for evaluation	Method for determination of ethical decision	Probable result
I. Authoritarianism (or legalism)	Absolute good and rightness are either present in the world or have been determined by custom, law or code.	Conformity to rules, laws, moral codes, established systems and customs.	Application of normative standard (or law) to resolve the ethical dilemma or issue.	*The* solution to any ethical dilemma can be readily determined and then implemented (acted upon).
II. Relativism (or antinomianism)	Good and bad, and rightness and wrong-ness, are *relative* and vary according to the situation or culture involved.	Needs of situation *there* and *then* in culture or society concerned.	Guidance in the making of an ethical decision may come either from "outside"; intuition; one's own conscience; empirical investigation; reason, etc.	Each ethical decision is highly individual since every situation has its particularity; there are *no* absolutely valid principles or universal laws.
III. Situationism (with certain similarity to I above)	God's love (or some other *summum bonum*) is an absolute norm; reason, revelation, and precedent have no objective normative status.	"What is fitting" in the situation is based on application of *agapeic love*; subordinate moral principles serve to illuminate the situation.	Resolution of ethical dilemma results from use of calculating method plus contextual appropriateness; act from *loving concern*; what is benevolent is right.	The best solution, everything considered, will result when the principle of God's love is applied situationally.

311

Table 1 continued
Major Philosophical Approaches to Ethical Decisions

IV. Scientific ethics (scientific method applied to ethics)	No distinction between *moral* goods and *natural* goods; science can bring about complete agreement on factual belief about human behaviour.	Ideas helpful in solving problematic situations are therefore true; empirical verification of hypothesis brings theory and practice union.	Use of scientific method in problem-solving; *reflective thinking* begets ideas that function as tentative solutions for concrete problems; test hypothesis experimentally.	Agreement in factual belief will soon result in agreement in attitude; *continuous adaption* of values to the culture's changing needs will effect the directed reconstruction of all social institutions.
V. Emotivism (analytic philosophy's response to problems of ethics)	Ethics is normative (i.e., moral *standards*) and therefore cannot be a science; the term "good" appears to be indefinable.	An ethical dispute must be on a factual level; *value* statements must be distinguished from factual ones.	Involves logical analysis of ethical (normative standard) terms; factual statements referred to social scientists; analyze conflicting attitudes to determine progress.	Ethical dilemmas can be resolved through the combined efforts of the moralist *and* the scientist; common beliefs may in time change attitudes.

Let us now follow this postulation with a series of theoretical steps that would be involved in the application of this approach to one persistent, truly vexing problem in competitive sport — the amateur-professional controversy. The steps followed in this experimental approach would be as follows:

1. *Theory — Step 1.* The smoothness of life's movement or flow is interrupted by an obstacle. This obstacle creates a problem, and the resultant tension must be resolved to allow further movement (progress?) to take place. Here we are faced with the problem (obstacle) that the concepts of "work" and "play" are typically strongly dichotomized in North America, and their usage is imprecise and muddled. Nowhere is the confusion (tension) more evident than when we are determining to what extent the nomenclature of "work" and "play" may be applied when dealing with the various levels of sport participation. This describes what may be called the "amateur-professional controversy" — a problem or obstacle that has been with humankind since ancient times.

2. *Theory — Step 2.* Humankind marshals all available and presumably pertinent facts to help with the solution of this problem. Data gathered tends to fall into one or more patterns. Subsequent analysis offers the possibility of various alternatives for action, *one of which should be chosen as working hypothesis.* First, the basic terms or concepts were defined carefully and then placed in a traditional play-work definitional diagram as applied to sport and physical activity. Differentiation was made among synthetic, analytic and pseudo-statements. Second, the status and a brief background of sport/athletics in North America were reviewed (with emphasis on the university level). Third, the possible relationship among the prevailing, pivotal social forces and the status of sport was considered. The differences in the interpretation of the various concepts in the three leading types of political state — democracy, communism and aristocracy — were explained. It was explained further why and how the terms "work" and "play" have become so sharply dichotomized. Still further, it became apparent that a need exists for reevaluation of some of our basic assumptions about the amateur code in sport. It was pointed out that the so-called professional in sport today is being professional in only a very limited sense of the word. There is typically no commitment as a true professional whose primary aim in life is to serve others through lifelong service. The argument was made that the amateur should be regarded as the beginner — not as the Olympic performer who somehow refrained

from taking cash (but who has somehow received all kinds of comparable support along the way). Fourth, as a result of the investigation described above, one alternative *(hypothesis)* was selected from the various courses of action open on the basis of the type of political state being considered (a democracy). Proceeding from this hypothesis, a *model* was recommended — one in which the concepts of "work" and "play" are altered, and one in which insurmountable problems do not arise in an evolving democracy. The model was entitled "Aspects of a Person's Active Occupation," with work, play and art included as the three appropriate aspects. These terms were related from the standpoint of a concept of the "unified organism." (see figure 1)

3. *Theory — Step 3.* The *hypothesis* must be tested through the application of the *model* developed to test its suitability. If one hypothesis does not solve the problem for our society, then another should be tried. A hypothesis that works — in the sense that it gradually achieves recognition as being fair and equitable — thereby turns out to be true. It offers a framework for organizing facts, and this will result subsequently in a central meaning that may then be called knowledge.

4. *Theory — Step 4.* The final step in this scientific approach to the resolution of sport decisions that are ethical in nature relates to acceptance of the working hypothesis as evidenced by changing attitudes on the part of the general public. The assumption is that determination of knowledge based on agreement in factual belief that is communicated to citizens in an evolving democracy should soon result in agreement in attitude. Admittedly, sociological progress is never a "straight-line affair," but continuous adaptation of values to the culture's changing needs should effect the directed reconstruction of all social institutions.

It is at this point that experimentalistic theory of knowledge acquisition merges with the value theory of scientific ethics. Knowledge acquired frees all people to initiate subsequent action furthering the process of movement and change indefinitely into the future (as adapted from Zeigler, 1964, pp. 72-74).

Figure 1
Aspects of a Person's "Active Occupation." (Play, Art, Work)

Level IV:	Freedom-Constraint Continuum	Freedom	Limited Freedom	Constraint (No Freedom)
Level III:	Amateur-Professional Continuum	Amateur	Semipro	Professional
Level II:	Goals Continuum	Short Range	Middle Range	Long Range
Level I:	Categories of Interest			

The

1. Physical education —recreation interests

Unified

2. Social education — recreation interests

3. "Learning" education — recreation interests

Organism

4. Aesthetic education — recreation interests

5. Communicative education — recreation interests

I believe that there is logic in a bonafide progression — if the person wishes to progress and is sufficiently capable — through the ranks of the amateur athlete to that of the semi-pro, and finally to that of the highly trained, proficient athletic performer. Such a person becomes a professional in at least one sense of the term. Based on the model employed, if a boy plays baseball after school (for example), his goals are short range and therefore conceived as "play." If he continues with his interest in high school and college and were to receive an athletic scholarship to attend college, play might soon take on many of the aspects of what we now call "work." Thus when the young man (and now it might be a young woman, too) goes away to college on an athletic scholarship, he may then be considered a semi-pro. This is logical because of the time being spent, because of the middle range goals attached to his athletic activity, and because of the level of performance he has achieved — as well as the fact that he was being paid an amount of money for performing the baseball skills he has mastered. If the young man is then chosen in a draft by the major leagues, he will then be forced to make a decision on Level II, the Goals Continuum, about moving on to the far right of the continuums at Levels II, III, and IV. Further, as shown at Level I (Categories of Interest), the same approach would hold for all aspects of a person's "active occupation."

Concluding Statement

We can all grant that these seem to be truly unusual times, that a world transformation is taking place, and that it is occurring rapidly because the tempo of civilization appears to be increasing exponentially. We are told that the "dialogue of freedom" may go on indefinitely, but the "solutions to our problems are not primarily ideological but structural.... They constitute a new political direction in the world — not left or right as in the past — but human and forward" (Platt, 1972, pp. 21-22). It is this type of reasoning that has rekindled my interest in the abolition of the longstanding, but probably unwise, distinction between what we in the past have called *moral* and *natural* goods.

We are exhorted further to prepare for a continuing technological thrust, and also told that "the only indispensable human component is the mind component for design, redesign, complex evaluation, and control" (Platt, 1972, p. 26). If these predictions have any validity, then as Platt states, "Yet millions of the older generation, alternately disgusted and terrified by these developments, will have to learn new values and a new language" (p. 26).

In this same vein, Callahan (1972) writes about searching for an ethic in a new culture that is on its way here, but that still does not yet exist. My general conclusion is that the scientific ethics approach, embodying careful application of language analysis at all appropriate points, offers the best and ultimately the most humane approach to the problematic situation our culture is now facing — that of new and continually changing values that will bring about a new and continually changing culture. Whether we are facing ethical decisions in our home life, our professional endeavor, or even in our competitive sport pursuits whether they be amateur, semi-professional, or professional, this approach offers everyone not a philosophy of life, but an explicit approach of philosophical understanding — a philosophy *for* the living of life today and tomorrow.

References

Abelson, R., & Friquegnon, M. *Ethics for modern life.* New York: St. Martin's Press, 1975.

Albert, E.M., Denise, T.C., & Peterfreund, S.P. *Great traditions in ethics* (3rd ed.). New York: D. Van Nostrand, 1975.

Ayer, A.J. *Language, truth and logic* (Rev. ed.). New York: Dover Publications, 1946.

Baier, K. *The moral point of view.* Ithaca, N.Y.: Cornell University Press, 1958.

Baker, R. "Good bad sports." *The New York Times Magazine.* Feb. 1, 1976.

de Beauvoir, S. *The ethics of ambiguity.* New York: Citadel Press, 1964.

Blumenthal, S.M. "Business morality has not deteriorated — society has changed." *The New York Times.* (Business and Finance), Jan. 9, 1977.

Bok, D.C. "Can ethics be taught?" *Change,* 1976, 8 (9), 26-30.

Burtt, E.A. *In Search of philosophic understanding.* New York: New American Library, 1965.

Callahan, D. "Search for an ethic: Living with the new biology." *The Center Magazine.* July/August 1972, pp. 4-12.

Chace, J. "How 'moral' can we get?" *The New York Times Magazine,* May 22, 1977, pp. 38-40.

Dennis, A.B. "A code of ethics for sociologists and anthropologists?" *Social Sciences in Canada,* 1975, 3 (1-2), 14-16.

Dewey, J. *The quest for certainty.* New York: Minton Balch, 1929.

Dewey, J. *Problems of men.* New York: Holt, 1946.

Dewey, J. *Reconstruction in philosophy.* Boston: Beacon Press, 1948.

Dewey, J., & Tufts, J.H. *Ethics* (Rev. ed.). New York: Holt, Rinehart, & Winston, 1932.

Etzioni, A. "Do as I say, not as I do." *The New York Times Magazine.* September 26, 1976, pp. 44-45.

Fairlie, H. *The seven deadly sins today.* Washington, D.C.: New Republic Books, 1978.

Fletcher, J. *Situation ethics: The new morality.* Philadelphia: Westminster Press, 1966.

Fromm, E. *Man for himself.* New York: Fawcett World Library, 1967.

"God and science — New allies in the search for values." *Saturday Review Special Report.* December 10, 1977.

"The growing dishonesty in sports: Is it just a reflection of our American society?" *The New York Times.* November 7, 1976, p. 9.

Hazard, G.C., Jr. "Capitalist ethics." *Yale Alumni Magazine & Journal,* 1978, 41 (8), 50-51.

Hechinger, F.M. "Whatever became of sin?" *Saturday Review World.* September 21, 1974, pp. 48-49.

Hospers, J. *An introduction to philosophical analysis.* Englewood Cliffs, N.J.: Prentice-Hall, 1953.

Maeroff, G.I. "West Point cheaters have a lot of company." *The New York Times,* June 20, 1976.

IV. Justice and Ethics

Martens, R. "Kid sports: A den of iniquity or land of promise?" *Proceedings, 79th Annual Meeting, National College Physical Education Association for Men,* 1976, 102-112.

Moore, G.E. *Principia ethica.* New York: Cambridge University Press, 1948.

Noel-Smith, P.H. *Ethics.* Baltimore: Penguin Books, 1954.

Patterson, C.H. *Moral standards: An introduction to ethics.* New York: Ronald Press, 1957.

Platt, J. "What's ahead for 1990?" *The Center Magazine,* July/August 1972, pp. 21-28.

Rand, A. *The romantic manifest.* New York: World Publishing, 1960.

Rawls, J. *A theory of justice.* Cambridge, Ma.: Harvard University Press, 1971.

Stevenson, C.L. *The nature of ethical disagreement.* Sigma, 1947-48, 1-2, 8-9.

Titus, H.H., & Keeton, M. *Ethics for today* (5th ed.). New York: D. Van Nostrand, 1973.

"Watergating on main street." *Saturday Review Special Report.* November 1, 1975, pp. 10-28.

Zeigler, E.F. *Philosophical foundations for physical, health, and recreation education.* Englewood Cliffs, N.J.: Prentice-Hall, 1964.

MORAL DEVELOPMENT OF YOUNG PEOPLE THROUGH SPORT: IS IT AN ATTAINABALE GOAL?

DEBRA SHOGAN

It is common for organizers of young people's sport to claim that sport provides an environment for moral development to occur.[1] Yet, we do not need to look far to see that abuses of rules, opponents and officials abound at all levels of sport, including young people's sport. Despite the claims for sport as a special moral environment, evidence from actual sport occurrences clearly shows that mere participation in sport does not bring about a moral conversion.

Unless sport leaders acknowledge that there is no guarantee that moral development will occur merely by being in a sporting environment, adequate attention will not be paid to the ways in which moral development might be facilitated by participating in sport. If direct attention is not paid to this, participation in sport will only accidentally contribute to moral development of young people. Moreover, it is quite likely that immoral behaviour will develop when the sporting environment is morally problematic.

To realize that moral development does not necessarily occur from participation in sport is not, of course, to say that participation in sport cannot contribute to moral development. In this paper I introduce some factors that must be attended to if we are to take seriously the moral development of young people through sport.

Moral behaviour will not be learned unless there are moral situations from which an individual can learn. What *is* special about competitive sport as an environment for moral development is that participants do encounter a number of moral situations that they would not normally encounter in the same time period elsewhere. Sport is a special environment in which moral development *can* occur by virtue of the number of morally problematic situations which arise in the practice of sport. To say something can happen is different, however, from saying it will happen. The fact that there are a number of moral situations confronting participants in sport is no guarantee that participants will learn moral behaviour. This is because people do not always, or perhaps often, respond morally whenever they are confronted with a moral situation.

In what follows I say something about what a moral situation is and consider whether these situations are found in sport situations. If moral situations encountered in sport are unique to sport, not only must

319

leaders be uniquely prepared for them but they also must refrain from claiming that these situations equip young people for moral situations outside sport.

Moral situations tend to be of two general types. One type of situation involves those instances in which others need help. They include, for example, those situations in which others are injured, starved, homeless, distraught, lost, confused, tormented and the like or when others do not suffer but there is an opportunity to help them flourish. The other type of situation is one in which fairness is at stake; for example when two groups or individuals conflict and adjudication is required or, for example, when an individual or group is measured against a standard of some kind such as measuring behaviour against the standards set out by game rules.

As I have said, a requisite condition for moral learning is that there are moral situations to encounter from which one can learn. Both moral situations occur in sport, although situations requiring fairness predominate because of the rule-governed nature of sport. Each sport is made up of rules which must apply in the same way to each person in the contest if the contest is to be fair. Even though the rules of games are based on the principle of fairness, fair treatment of participants is not guaranteed by the rules only. This is because participants can accept or reject the extent to which game rules will govern their behaviour. Consequently, a number of situations arise in sport in which a participant is in a position to decide whether to manipulate standards established by game rules for personal benefit and at others' expense. It is very likely that participation in sport introduces young people to more situations in which fair treatment of others is at issue than they would encounter in many other activities.

Even though sport clearly is an environment in which it is at least possible for people to be exposed to instances in which fairness is important, young people may not have the opportunity to learn from these situations if most decisions are made for them by coaches and officials. Since all but the most recreational games of sport are officiated, many opportunities for young people to respond fairly to others may be taken away. Participants are not often, if ever, responsible for reporting their own rule breakages. If not discovered by the official, they are expected to play on. The message from this both legally and morally is that something is wrong only if it is found out. Moreover, if expectations by leaders are that participants are merely to conform to rules reinforced by officials and coaches, young people will tend to learn that moral behaviour is what authorities say it is. Even though there are numerous moral situations requiring a fair response in sport, these are limited as learning opportunities for young people if these opportunities are pre-empted by coaches and officials.

There are not as many opportunities to develop *helping* behaviours in sport even though the physical nature of most sport makes it possible that participants will occasionally be injured. Instances in which players have opportunities to help others are to be distinguished from instances in which players refrain from striking opponents in retaliation or refrain from initiating excessive force in order to intimidate. These latter instances are usually covered by rules which establish fair behaviour in relation to physical contact.

There are occasions for participants to help each other during stoppages of play when, for example, someone falls or has been hit or even if someone is ejected. There are not, however, as far as I can see, occasions for helping behaviours during an actual play sequence. This is because it is not possible to continue as a participant in a particular play phase if one is helping someone. If, for example, a defensive player falls while defending against someone attempting to drive to the basket, the offensive player cannot both stop to help the fallen player and continue the drive to the basket. To stop to help someone in this type of situation is to cease to be involved in carrying out the prescribed movements of the game. If someone stops to help an opponent in this type of situation, he or she, in effect, decides that helping is more important than playing the game at this time.[2] Since certain significant helping behaviours can only be performed when one ceases to play the game, sport participation does not expose young people to the full range of moral situations which they will encounter in other life situations.

Central to any educational endeavour is the question how someone can be taught to see the point of an enterprise; how to teach someone else to be motivated to act because he or she sees the value of the activity and not in order to conform or because of fear of punishment. This is also the central question for the development of moral behaviour. Since it is possible that someone could recognize a moral situation as one in which helping or fair treatment of others is important and still not care about this, it is clear that 'teaching' moral behaviour is not a straight forward matter of explaining moral reasons for responding in a certain way. How *can* leaders 'teach' young people to care about the welfare and fair treatment of others? If leaders of young people's sport do not have some ideas about how this question might be answered, sport will be a vehicle for moral change only by accident.

If the concern is moral behaviour and not merely legal behaviour, it is not sufficient to instruct young people to follow rules. This is because keeping game rules for the sake of rules is a concern for legality only. Moral reasons for keeping rules, on the other hand, focus on the effect breaking rules will have on the *people* in the contest who are counting on others in the contest to keep the rules (counting on fairness to prevail).

IV. Justice and Ethics

Becoming motivated to help or to be fair is learned behaviour. This behaviour is not learned suddenly. As Iris Murdoch writes:

> Moral change and moral achievement are slow; we are not...able suddenly to alter ourselves since we cannot suddenly alter what we see and *ergo* what we desire and are compelled by.[3]

What someone is motivated by is affected by what he or she gives regular attention to over a long period of time. Someone who spends most of his or her life attending to depravity and violence, for example, is likely to develop values and desires commensurate with what he or she has 'looked at' and 'seen.' What is regularly attended to affects what one comes to find important. If the sporting environment to which a young person regularly attends is fraught with occasions of disrespect, deception, and violent behaviour, he or she may come to value this or at least accept it as the norm.

If leaders of young people's sport want sport to be a vehicle for moral development, they must be concerned with what young people attend to in sport environments. Even with the number of opportunities for participants to respond morally, sport will not be an environment for the development of moral behaviour unless participants are able to recognize moral situations when they do arise. One cannot respond to a moral situation if one does not see it as a moral situation. It is not always obvious, particularly to young people, when they might help others or treat others fairly or what is morally problematic about what they may do. A leader concerned with moral development in sport would need to point out these situations to participants. This would not include pointing out those situations in which it would be possible to break rules and gain an advantage, however. It would be inappropriate to point out to young people those situations in which it would be possible to benefit by cheating, for example. There are enough morally problematic situations which arise regularly in sport that one should not need to contrive examples in order to draw a young person's attention to stances of morally problematic behaviour.

Since values are shaped by what one regularly attends to, it is essential that young people's attention is regularly drawn to those situations in which participants act out of respect for each other and officials. If attention is to be drawn to instances of moral behaviour, an environment must be created in which instances of moral behaviour *do* occur. This means that leaders of young people's sport must not only rid sport environments of deception, violence and disrespect, they must work at creating an environment of honesty, joy in playing, and respect for

322

people. Moral behaviour will develop only by chance, if at all, if the leader is not actively involved in this process.

'Having one's eyes opened' so that one 'looks at' and 'sees' may happen through one's own efforts but this is more likely to happen through the influence of others. People often learn about moral behaviour by attending to the lives and actions of moral people. Someone who is admired, as a leader in sport often is, can change the significance of what might otherwise go unnoticed. Attempting to see what someone who is admired 'sees' about an enterprise is an important step in the process of moral development.

Since participation in sport makes up only a small part of a lifetime of attending to events and enterprises, sport is only one of many vehicles for the development of moral behaviour. And, it should be remembered, sport is limited as a vehicle for development of a full range of moral behaviours, particularly certain helping behaviours. Like any other enterprise to which people attend, sport will not contribute to moral development unless there are moral situations to which participants can attend and respond. Whether this is accomplished in sport will depend largely on the type of environment leaders create. It will also depend on whether leaders are involved in a deliberate effort to draw attention to the moral importance of moral situations as they arise in sport while providing an opportunity for young people to be moral agents. Sporadic attempts at any of this will be inconsequential.

Notes

1. As an example of this, the following is from an advertisement for a one week youth sport camp: we will "instill in each boy a sense of fair play and good sportsmanship. We also strive to further develop the qualities of good character and citizenship with every boy in our camp."
2. Bernard Suits describes an auto racer who, in order not to disqualify himself from a contest, runs over a child who has crawled onto the track. ("What is a Game?" In *Sport and the Body: A Philosophical Symposium*, 2nd. ed., edited by Ellen Gerber and William Morgan. Philadelphia: Lea and Febiger, 1979). Although it is reprehensible that anyone would value keeping the rules of a particular game more than the life of a child, the point is that attending to predicaments of others is often at odds with the continuation of a game of sport.
3. Iris Murdoch, *The Sovereignty of Good*. London: Routledge and Kegan Paul, 1970, p. 39.

CHILDREN IN ORGANIZED SPORT: RIGHTS AND ACCESS TO JUSTICE

PASQUALE J. GALASSO

SECTION ONE

RIGHTS OF ATHLETES

On the assumption that human rights exist as a concept within our society and are accepted by the vast majority, and secondly on the assumption that these rights should be enjoyed by athletes in general, the question arises, what are the extensions of these human rights in the field of sport. This question has been addressed by more individuals in the past five years than in preceding decades. Much of the work has probably been motivated by the autocratic mishandling of situations involving team selection and discipline by coaches and executive members of sport organizations. While some of these investigations are on the legal side, they have been initiated by deep concerns on the human rights side. They represent a recognition of the importance of rights to a system of justice as axioms are to deductive geometry.

The most extensive piece of legal work in this area has been produced by Kidd and Eberts. Another investigation by Sport Canada took place in the summer of 1982, where constitutions and rulebooks of national sport organizations were examined for equality of treatment of male and female athletes. In addition, Mr. John Sopinka, Q.C., a Toronto-based solicitor, and former professional football player, investigated the question of equal opportunity to both sexes in athletics in Ontario. The study covered community athletics and recreation; elementary and secondary schools; community colleges and universities; and professional athletics.

At this point it would be useful to enumerate and comment upon some of the changes and indications of change which have taken place over the past short while in the area of treatment of athletes, and the behaviour of competitors and non-competitors alike. To begin with, there seems to be an increased consciousness in the area of behaviour and ethics judging by the codes which have been developed for players, coaches and parents. The Canadian Council for Children and Youth produced a highly-popular pamphlet called "Fair Play Codes for Children in Sport." The pamphlet covers a variety of topics in the area of ethics, and covers fair play codes for players, coaches, parents, teachers, officials, administrators, spectators and the news media.

Honourable Mr. Justice John J. Urie, on the subject of civil liberties, included the following:

> CAHA bylaws provide for suspension of any player who goes to court with a complaint before a normal CAHA appeal procedure has been exhausted, although the CAHA decision on appeals has been said to be 'absolutely final and binding.' Also: players on junior teams who break team rules may be fined even though such rules may not be precisely defined in their contract.
>
> Players may be put on a club's protected list, in some area, without the player's knowledge, forcing the player to deal with that club or not at all. The player's freedom of movement or choice is limited by the wording of the contrast or player registration cards....
>
> The position taken by the CAHA and its affiliates that (human rights) legislation is not applicable to their organization seems somewhat incompatible with their acceptance of public funds and utilization of public facilities....
>
> The above clearly indicates the status of civil liberties and the respect for individual rights as shown by the CAHA.
>
> (Urie, p. 8-9)

On the other hand, the Canadian Olympic Association has made a significant advance in recognizing the essential part that athletes can play in providing information and in being associated with decision-making on a wide number of issues. For example, at the April, 1981 meeting of the Canadian Olympic Association, the Athletes' Advisory Council was formed. The purpose of the Athletes' Advisory Council is as follows:

> To broaden communication between currently active athletes and the C.O.A., and to serve as a source of opinion and advice to the executive committee and board of directors in regard to current or contemplated policies and programs of the C.O.A.
>
> (C.O.A. p. 1)

325

IV. Justice and Ethics

It is also interesting to note with respect to the Olympic Games that:

> No age limit for competitors in the Olympic Games is stipulated by the International Olympic Committee, unless there is an agreement between the I.O.C. and the relevant international federation to the contrary.
> (I.O.C. p. 16)

Another reference to the Olympic Games in the area of discipline reveals the following note:

> Team managers are responsible for the conduct of their athletes. Disciplinary action, if required, must not be initiated without the involvement of the Canadian Olympic Association through the Chef de Mission.
> (Mission Guidelines of Lake Placid, 1980).

On the matter of discipline and the relationships between the Olympic governing bodies and the athletes, when the formation of the Athletes' Council was announced, the following appeared:

> This is a new approach to athletes. It is in sharp contrast to the attitude of the late Avery Brundage and other I.O.C. leaders of the past, who treated the athletes like children who should be seen and not heard.
> (Athletes Given, 1981).

Clearly the winds of change are blowing strongly, and it augurs well for the rights of athletes, particularly at the international level among the elite.

In their legally-focused monograph, "Athletes' Rights in Canada," Kidd and Eberts cover a wide range of abuses of athletes as a basis for their recommendations to protect them. Specifically, they pinpoint one major problem area as evidenced by the Federal Government efforts to produce international gold medals and the pressure which then is transferred to the national sport organization:

> There is a widespread belief among national and provincial sports governing body decision makers that athletes enjoy few, if any, rights.
> (Kidd and Eberts, p. 11)

Galasso: Children In Organized Sport

In an effort to measure the interest in the concept of athletes' rights by national sport organization officials, interviews were held in Ottawa. In addition, discussions on this same matter took place with certain ranking officials associated with the production side of sport. No doubt, in the current acceleration of the incorporation of the rights of athletes in official and semi-official documents, certain remarks may be slightly outdated, nevertheless, it is worth noting there was a high level of acceptance of the concept at this time.

During the interviews it became evident that there is a widespread sensitivity to the rights of athletes in a general sense. This represented a change in the thinking of some of the national sport organizations and the contemplation of change in others. Public objections to the harsh treatment of certain athletes in recent incidents, and internal reconsiderations have led to policy guidelines being established in some sports to ensure fair treatment of athletes. However, as we all recognize, the publication of guidelines or even laws can be one thing and the application can be another. This is particularly true as it applies to the grass roots level of competition. The elite athletes who represent Canada in international competition, in most instances, are in a superior position to defend themselves as contrasted to children involved in minor sport programs. How influential these guidelines and programs will be at these earlier developmental levels remains to be seen.

Misinterpretations, and in fact different interpretations by those affected by these regulations will lead to conflict and confrontation. Uniform application will also present problems as conditions change. While not wishing to single out certain sports or individuals, nevertheless, the following case highlights the fact that further work has to be done before an acceptable total system is operational. In interpreting this case, one must recognize that objective, accurate portrayals of interviews cannot be counted upon at all times, and that disappointment and anger at being disciplined or ignored can affect dialogue. In any case, even if the case is partially verifiable and objective, it points out the need for a more rigorous effort on the part of those involved in making decisions not only to *be* fair, but also to *appear to be* fair. Walls of silence lead to suspicion.

In the spring of 1983, Mr. Don McRae, head basketball coach for men at the University of Waterloo, and head coach of Canada's women's basketball team, was fired by the Canadian Amateur Basketball Association. He was reinstated after Judge Keith Flanigan found that he had been dismissed without just cause. Judge Flanigan was appointed to assess the situation by the then Minister of Fitness and Amateur Sport, Mr. Ray Perrault. (McRae Returns, p. 1) This judgement and reinstatement occurred just prior to the world championships, at which time Mr. McRae selected the team and included the athletes who had left the team in protest just prior to the World University Games which were held in Edmonton in July, 1983. He excluded the athletes who had filled in at the University Games for those who had left the team in protest.

Questions have been put forward about the fairness of team selection for the world championships held in South America, and later about the selection process which included a tryout in May of 1984, just prior to the Olympics. Were these athletes dropped without just cause, and were the athletes who demonstrated loyalty toward the coach rewarded with a reciprocal gesture? Under the circumstances, one needs to take into account the fact these athletes were on the top national team through a selection process, but how long does this carry over into later championships and international competitions? It would be valuable to have Judge Flanigan's opinion as to the fairness of the process which led to the selection of the team for the World Championships in South America, and the apparent late scheduling of Olympic team tryouts in 1984. One can only speculate, based on newspaper reports, however, that if there is even a minute degree of truth to the complaint, it should provide those who create laws to give serious consideration to the comments. It would appear on the surface, at least, that coaches may receive the protection of the Fitness and Amateur Sport Minister, but that the process falls short when one considers the procedures such as team selection and the effect on athletes.

The above case, and there are others, clearly calls for rapid efforts to ameliorate the situation. It is obvious that goodwill on the part of paid executives and voluntary officials in itself is insufficient to guarantee that the rights of athletes are acknowledged and respected. The rather speedy reinstatement of Mr. Don McRae after an official judgement indicates that legal or quasi-legal protective mechanisms, that are at arms length from the sport governing bodies, must be set in place to protect the rights of athletes, coaches and officials alike.

It would be appropriate, at this time, to return to the Kidd-Eberts monograph to delve further into the legal aspects of athletes' rights. It is important in one particular sense in that they indicate that there is no single source to which anyone can turn to review a complete exposition of this concept, and the practical applications. What they do is identify and summarize these sources and comment upon them. In the text they cover athletes' rights in team selection and in discipline. These are the main focus. In addition, they deal with the "right to compete" when they refer to a case where people over thirty-five years of age are prohibited from competing by the Canadian Amateur Boxing Association. No mention is made in this section of suitable restrictions which should be in place to protect children who are too young to box. Where, in fact, it would be justifiable in light of potential damage during critical growth periods to place lower age limits to protect children against over-zealous officials and parents. In summary, the book is an excellent treatise on the legal aspects of athletes' rights.

In another phase of the study, sixty federal, provincial and local sport organization constitutions were examined. The focus of each constitution was determined by identifying the key words which prevailed in the sections dealing with philosophy and objectives. Where other sections seemed pertinent, these were also taken into account. The constitutions fell neatly into two groups. On the one hand, one set of constitutions concentrated on the development of the individual through skills, sportsmanship, citizenship, team play and so on, while the other set sharply emphasized the development of the sport, control of the sport, jurisdiction of the organization and officers, and authority of these same organizations and officers. In fact, in some of these latter constitutions, it was difficult to determine who or what was to be governed since they were not identified. There was also a stress on the legal approach, particularly where the organization was incorporated, and the standard form of incorporation was followed. The objective in this latter case was simply to protect the executive members, coaches and officials through incorporation. They might just as well have been talking about inanimate objects rather than people.

A constitution of a sport organization can be likened to a personality. A close examination of its intentions and beliefs can indicate clearly what behaviour can be anticipated in given circumstances particularly when it involves the rights of the individual and an accompanying objective appeal system, as opposed to the image, reputation or existence of the organization or sport. This is the critical decision fork in the branch of decision-making. Who or what comes first, i.e., what is the number one objective of the organization. Surely, it must be the individual — the athlete.

Clearly, a constitution must spell out the obligations of the executive members, coaches and officials, as well as the rights of the athletes and the appeal system based on objectivity. It should also contain reference to the obligations of the athletes given the objectives as they relate to their development. The participants should have access to full knowledge of the *modus operandi* of the team and sport. Relationships must be spelled out. The athletes must be looked upon as ends unto themselves. The constitution should spell out the minimum standard, at least, of the reasonableness and respect which must be shown toward the participant. And finally, the constitution must spell out what the organization is not about. For example, the constitution might indicate that the organization is not;

1)   a pro farm team
2)   a base for producing international gold medals

3)   interested in receiving grants from professional organizations
4)   willing to sacrifice the majority for the development of a few

This would be of inestimable help to the prospective participant and parents and is associated clearly with the right to knowledge.

SECTION TWO

ORGANIZED SPORT

In addressing the rights of children in organized sport and the concept of access to justice, the nature of both children and sport as well as the interrelationships must be examined. However, in order to initiate this process, key questions will have to be raised, and areas of concern identified.

By way of raising questions: Which principles are paramount in establishing the needs of children and their rights? Which is the most fundamentally important right which can be identified in this specific area of organized sport? What are the peculiarities and problems, if any, of the sport situations which warrant special consideration in this issue? Why does a special case need to be made for children? Is there a special case which needs to be made for female children? What influence does an absolute monopoly have by way of the authority of a sport governing body? Do governments have any responsibilities in addressing this question? Are there any practical solutions in protecting the rights of children in organized sport?

In response to the question, which principles are paramount in this issue, one would be compelled to recognize the freedom for the individual which emanates from living in a democratic society. This would focus on the development of each individual as being the quintessence of the meaning of life in such a society. This would entail the establishment and promotion of the essential rights and freedoms necessary to permit this development, and the recognition of the responsibilities which must be assumed by adults and governments.

In light of the above, it appears justifiable to designate the right to self-determination as the most fundamentally important right which impinges on the question of children's rights in organized sport. All other rights serve to undergird this right. All other rights appear to be secondary in importance in dealing with this question. The right to knowledge can readily be seen to be supportive to the right to self-determination. This has many overtones for those participating in sport.

The right to participate and the right to equitable treatment are also basic and fundamental.

There are peculiarities to the sport scene which require attention in order to understand the importance of studying the interrelationships which exist amongst children, rights, justice and sport. In the first place, the sport world for children is controlled exclusively by adults. Children have no direct or indirect control over rules, regulations, appointments of coaches, executives, referees and others. They are completely subject to the dictates of adults beginning with their parents and ending with their coaches who control them directly. If self-determination is to be accepted as the key right under consideration, then the role of adults in sport and their correlated responsibilities must be considered of paramount importance in discussing the rights of children in organized sport.

The monopoly held by sport governing bodies and their subsidiaries also represents a major contribution to the problems which arise when rights and justice clash with control. In many cases, choices and alternatives simply do not exist. If an individual is not prepared to "toe the line," then participation in that sport may be denied to him or her. Many athletes have had to back off in the past when their interest in certain competitions or participation on specific teams was thwarted by executive edict. International cooperation amongst sport governing bodies goes a long way in controlling the individual freedom of the athletes.

Another factor worth considering under this question, is that of enticement. The attraction of participation in sport, for the vast majority of children, is quite high. The peer group pressure which operates here, along with the pressures from professional sport, government programs, school programs, parents, and from adults in general, is difficult to resist by most children. Thus very early involvement in organized sport is a recognized and accepted phenomenon in our modern society. This has occurred chiefly in the past quarter century, and seems to be increasing with more government programs and those sponsored by the community. For example, municipal recreation departments are now more heavily involved in creating sport programs for children than in the past.

There is also a high financial cost to participating in organized sport. Pick-up games, on the other hand, because they take place in the area near the residences of the participants, do not require transportation. The cost of driving the children to practices and competitions amounts to a financial commitment on the part of adults, and thus they naturally expect more out of the activity than they normally would if the child were simply "playing." The initial cost of equipment, as well, also adds to the prior commitment by parents, even before the first competition takes place. This adds to the pressure caused by expectations and potential outcomes — pressure which is ultimately directed by adults toward children.

Once involved in organized sport, the parents begin to derive social satisfaction from this. The idea of meeting other parents at the place of competition or practice is looked forward to by the adults, and begins to increase the pressure on the child to continue to take part. It can become the main social function engaged in by adults and provides them with a great deal of satisfaction, in addition to the stimulation of watching their own children participate.

The above factors, and the general attraction of competition to human beings in general, serve to create a milieu which entices people to become involved, and adds to the peculiarities of the sport situation which serves as a focal point for many people. These factors, as well, need to be understood to allow us to recognize the situations children find themselves in and the difficulties which arise which prevent them from exercising their own choices as an expression of individual freedom.

The special case for children cannot be over-emphasized. When one considers the potential for both harm and good through participation in organized sport, and the fact that it is adult-dominated, highlighting the rights of children is imperative. Mechanisms must be put into place to protect their rights at all levels. The leadership must come from government along with the necessary funding. Overzealous parents living through their children also serve as a justification for identifying the importance of the right to self-determination for their sons and daughters. An ongoing educational process for the thousands of newly-involved parents must also be fostered and financed by sport governing bodies and governments at all levels. And finally, when one considers the danger elements for children involved in impact, collision and high ballistic action-type sports, there is further justification for ensuring their protection through emphasis on the right to self-determination.

There is a special case to be made for the female members of our society. Dworkin, whose monograph "Taking Rights Seriously," is based on the presupposition that not to take one's rights seriously is a moral affront, provides a suitable base for discussing this facet. It is the opinion of the writer that women as athletes are not taken as seriously as men. In fact, this begins in the home, where there is less concern with providing opportunities for female participation than for the male children. And this is not to say that organized sport is being espoused as the only venue for physical activity. But rather, if we were to survey attitudes toward providing recreational time and facilities for children, there would be greater concern expressed if these were unavailable for males as opposed to females as children in a family. Women must begin to take themselves more seriously as athletes and participants in recreational activity. If they do not, then the female children will be

332

deprived of the opportunity. This then is the focal point of contention with respect to making the case for female children. The right of equality of opportunity is paramount as a support right to self-determination. It is this right which has more meaning to the female than to the male.

The final question to be addressed in this section concerns the monopoly which exists as a control in the hands of sport governing bodies and their regional affiliates. Many studies and briefs have summarized the negative aspects of this control and have suggested remedies. However, the emphasis which must be placed on the concept of accountability has not received sufficient attention

In our society, where freedom should serve as a cornerstone, the accountability of sport governing bodies has been neglected. The magnitude of the control mechanisms over individuals as exercised by these bodies is overwhelming, when one considers the difficulties encountered by athletes, as adults, who challenge this authority, let alone the plight of children when placed in circumstances which warrant issuing such challenges. The emphasis must be on the development of the individual, not the sport, whatever that means, and the emphasis must be on freedom, not control. The wheels of progress are inhibited by inertia and the rust of neglect. The rights of children and access to justice in these sports as ruled by sport governing bodies must receive immediate attention to maximize the opportunity for self-development through the exercise of the right to self-determination. Monopolies can serve as the extremes of care or neglect. The tide is turning for adult athletes in this respect, but little effective legislation or emphasis on human rights has been witnessed with respect to children. The following section will summarize the importance of rights, along with a discussion of responsibilities and recommendations.

SECTION III

RIGHTS — RESPONSIBILITIES — RECOMMENDATIONS

This section contains a summary on rights, an identification of the locus(i) of responsiblity, and recommendations to potentially influential groups and institutions. Basically, there are three prospects open to those who advocate rights for children. In the first place, one could take the stance that the same rights accorded to adults should be extended holus bolus to children, and leave it at that. The second approach could be to tailor adult rights to the capacities of children. And finally, the third approach could be to create special rights for children over and above those enjoyed by adults. It is the author's contention that the second approach with suitable tailoring and modification would be most useful taking into account the impact of sport involvement.

The important point to keep in mind, while endeavouring to meet the needs of children, is that one does not trivialize rights, nor detract from their usefulness and importance as a social mechanism. It is also useful to prioritize these rights which are identified as being essential to children's welfare. And since personal development is so fundamental to the growth of children as human beings, then the most fundamental right would appear to be the right to self-determination.

It is not being suggested here that full autonomy be accorded to the child for all decisions which are to be made on his or her behalf, but rather in recognition of the developmental process that the child is going through, that a gradual introduction of the child to decisions affecting him or her is essential. This means that every opportunity must be created to enable the child to become autonomous through self-determination as quickly as possible. This cannot take place when adults unthinkingly superimpose their will on the children during the many ventures with which sport is replete. Rather, it requires a high degree of sensitivity to the process on the part of adults.

Very simply, if we believe in self-determination as the fundamental right, then those who do not should not be allowed to direct organized sport experiences for children, since the outcomes would be so different. Acceptance of the position of this right places a great responsibility on the adults to educate the children in the ways of understanding decision-making and how it affects them and others. Policies and procedures must be put into place to protect this fundamental right.

Basically, **The Right To Self-determination** has as its foundation the education of the child to make decisions which affect him or her as quickly as possible. This calls for educational sessions with the coaches covering all aspects of the activity and the various outcomes of different decisions which affect the individual and others as well. For this right to emerge as the fundamental focus of organized sport. Full recognition must be given to acknowledging that the development of the child is more important than winning. It logically follows that if the prime goal is winning, then the child tends to become a pawn or chattel. The coach must ultimately phase himself or herself out of the role of director and into that of consultant or advisor for the right to self-determination to emerge effectively as the fundamental right of children in organized sport.

Other rights which deserve support and which can be justified when keeping the child's freedom and development in the forefront are as follows:

The Right To Knowledge: children, and adults who are responsible for their development, need to know the basic philosophy of the sport organization. This is extremely important in that when a choice is made as to which activity is entered into or which team is selected, the child has a right to know what he or she is getting into and what they can expect to get out of it. Parents should insist on meetings with executive members and the coaches on both group and individual bases. Practice procedures and team selection criteria should be spelled out at these sessions. Other information concerning finances, discipline, transfers, and policy formation in general should also be made readily available. A copy of the organizational constitution and related documentation should also be distributed and explained to the children and parents.

The Right To Be Protected From Abuse: the child must be protected against overzealous parents, coaches and executive members. There must be an appeal system which is readily available, and without opportunity for reprisal, which children and their parents can avail themselves of in cases where a child's rights have been violated. The child also has a right, along with the parents, **to be present and to hear evidence with respect to discipline matters.** Kangaroo courts should be a thing of the past.

The Right To Try Out For A Team Or Position: Information should be made public so that all those interested can try out. Sufficient time and opportunity should also be made available to provide a fair chance to the child to be seen in the best light possible. Holding one practice, and then making cuts, is inadequate to support the above principle of fairness. Full criteria for team selection should be presented to the children and parents to avoid misunderstandings and to assist the child in routing his or her energies in the right direction. The team system or strategy should also be elaborated upon.

The Right To Have Properly Qualified Instruction And Leadership: adults with psychological hangups or those who place winning above the importance of the individual must not be allowed to take part in instructional and leadership roles in sport programs for children. It would be more beneficial to return to pick-up games for the sake of the children, than it is to subject them to the whim and fancy of adults whose philosophy of sport is off-base. The potential for harm simply is not worth it under these circumstances. A psychologically and physiologically healthy environment for sport programs for children is essential. Such an environment would include opportunities to strive for success. Sitting on the bench during entire games on end, and being shunted down to the other end of the playing surface in practices while the coaches concentrates on the "first string" for virtually the entire practice, does not meet this environmental qualification for development and learning.

IV. Justice and Ethics

And finally, **The Right To Be Involved In An Environment Where Opportunity For The Development of Self-respect, And To Be Treated With Respect** is imperative. This environment should be enhanced by the engendering of fun and enjoyment associated with effort and achievement through the establishment of realistic goals.

Responsibilities represent the obverse of rights when considering children. In light of this, the obvious focal point rests with the adults associated both directly and indirectly with organized sport. This includes parents, coaches, executive members of sport governing bodies and local organizations (both professional and volunteer), game officials, and governments at the federal, provincial and local levels. Attention should also be paid to the responsibilities of children.

Parents have a responsibility to investigate the sport organization, its operational behaviour, and its philosophy before enrolling their child in the sport. Attention should also be given to the instructors and the instruction to ensure that the qualitative levels are sufficient to sustain a proper program. This places an onus on the parents to educate themselves on what to look for and how to go about investigating the sport environment. This may appear to be a drastic measure to take. However, once the child is taking part it is very difficult to deal with decisions at that point.

Parents should also recognize that when they hand over a child to a coach they also hand over an obligation which the coach must assume to assist the child to develop as a human being. This handing over of responsibilities carries with it the right and obligation on the part of the parent to criticize the coach if the child's rights are violated. Any actions taken on behalf of the child must be free of reprisals. The ultimate responsibility for the health and welfare of the child must rest with the parent. However, this does not preclude government through its representatives from intervening on the child's behalf under certain circumstances

The coach has the responsibility to treat the child in a manner which enhances his or her development as a human being within an environment of fun and satisfaction. The coach must be mindful that the rights of children must be respected and that they must not be sacrificed at the altar of gold. The coach must also recognize a responsibility to the child to protect him or her against the overzealous parent through tactful and diplomatic interactions with both the child and the parental unit.

The coach must also be responsible for educating the children in the technical refinements of the sport. This entails a personal responsibility by the coach to become educated in this aspect of the sport as well as the nature and scientific aspects of the activity. The volunteer who agrees to coach must be made to realize from the outset that there are responsibilities that go with the task that go well beyond initial interest and enthusiasm. It must be recognized here that the volunteer does not have the time to develop competence as contrasted to the professional coach, but, nevertheless, the volunteer must acquire minimal fundamental technical and personal skills to enable him or her to achieve the goals of the organization and team.

No doubt, many volunteers will balk at the thought of assuming such responsibilities. However, if we accept the rights of children as carrying a fair weight in decision-making, and that they must be respected as individuals as the number one focal point of the activity, there is no way out for the volunteer coach under the circumstances. It is the view of the investigator, that it would be better to have the children return to self-directed competitions, rather than to have the current situation in organized sport continue.

Sport governing bodies and executive committee members of local sport organizations also have responsibilities associated with the rights of children. Both professional and volunteer members of these organizations have these responsibilities, and the volunteers must not be allowed to feel that they are off the hook because they are not being paid. Simply through the selection process for appointing coaches, the volunteer executive can do a great deal to protect the rights of children. The above, and other techniques and services, can assure a proper milieu for the child in organized sport.

The executive committees of these organizations are the control centres for the kind of environment that the child finds himself or herself in. Most people focus on the coaches when criticism is being levelled, but fail to realize that these executive committees appointed the coaches who seem to be creating the problems. There is a heavy onus on these committees to extend their influence beyond the mere selection of properly qualified coaches. There is also the responsibility of supervising them as well as suspending or releasing them as required. All too often executives simply do not reappoint the coaches in a subsequent year which means that the children have to endure the situation for the remainder of the season with their rights being violated in most instances.

Another area requiring consideration is that of game officials. These individuals, through a misinterpretation or reinterpretation of the rules, can do a great deal to create an environment which is not conducive to the maintenance or respect of rights. This is a two-way street, of course, with respect being required of the children as well. However, here again, the heavy onus is on the adults to educate themselves so that they are competent to handle the situation. This is an area where good officiating can serve to educate the child to respect the rights of others and to assume the responsibility for his or her actions.

IV. Justice and Ethics

This last point must be kept in the forefront when examining the area of responsibilities of children.

With the above in mind, and recognizing that there are major societal swings taking place as revealed through studying the Young Offenders Act, adults are beginning to recognize the importance of making children aware of their responsibilities much earlier in life. This should also be taken into account by all adults in organized sport. It has been recognized as well by social scientists that children are prepared to assume responsibilities much sooner in life than had previously been acknowledged. This should manifest itself through a rewriting of the rules, arranging for representation on committees, and above all, as much involvement in decision-making as possible in team strategy, procedures and rules. Sport exists as an outstanding opportunity to develop a respectful and caring individual.

The final identifiable group of adults which can be pinpointed as carrying the highest moral responsibility for protecting the rights of children in organized sport is government. Government at all levels, but particularly at the federal and provincial levels where the entire systems of sport governing bodies are harboured. No group is in a better position to do something about matters as they stand than government. This carries a heavy responsibility.

Government has the responsibility to intervene on behalf of minority groups which are being discriminated against. In this case, the enlightened members of society have recognized the potentially harmful outcomes of sport participation and the measures which must be taken to offset these, and in turn maximize the positive outcomes. Thus it is now in the hands of the government to recognize and exercise its duties to protect the rights of individuals involved in organized sport. The obligation is of the highest moral magnitude in this case because it concerns the highly malleable personalities of children. Government, therefore, has an obligation to develop and provide a system of justice for children to exercise their rights directly, or indirectly, with the assistance and interest of adults.

No doubt, there will be adults who will question the thrust presented in the above stated position and in the recommendations to follow. For it is recognized that it is easier in some ways to work with subservient, grateful children in sport. However, if it can be made clear to the adults involved in sport what their role should be, it may help them to sense the burden that autocratic directions place on the shoulders of children when they are included in the activity, let alone those who are excluded by capricious cutting methods or by being relegated to a role on the bench. What greater joy than seeing these children develop into autonomous adults rather than athletes wearing grey flannel uniforms. As for the argument about seeking gold and its

338

relative importance, the autonomous person will outstrip his or her opponents in the majority of cases.

RECOMMENDATIONS

In the areas of human rights and access to justice, change is taking place. Change is also evident, in general, with respect to the recognition of the importance of the individual. Unilateral decision-making is being replaced by dialogue, in many instances, before decisions are rendered. The reports which have been commissioned in dealing with these problem areas are being taken into account in producing these changes. These are indications of the recognition that the problems are widespread, and certainly do not exist as isolated cases of human rights being violated. Whether these initial attempts at communication translate into behavioural change at the practical adult-child level is another matter which will emerge over time. An example of change at the adult-adult level is the invitation sent to Nadia Comaneci by IOC President Juan Antonio Samaranch to join the International Olympic Committee athletes commission, which looks after the interests of competitors, some of whom are children. (Comaneci Agrees, Globe and Mail.) It is also a known fact that some of the national sport organizations and the COA (Canadian Olympic Association) have also organized advisory committees of athletes.

Special teaching units on rights and appeal systems should be added to elementary and secondary school curricula where appropriate. Specifically, physical educators should add these topics to their lectures or seminars as it pertains to sport. These topics and case studies would add interesting and educational material to a course.

Pioneering work in formalizing change in sport organizations which has been done by Drs. Moriarty and Duthie at the University of Windsor should be publicized.

Governments can and should provide assistance and direction in the following ways.

1. All grants being directed toward organized sport must be conditional. Only those committees and organizations which recognize and protect the rights of children through an objective system of justice should receive assistance. These and other means of exerting legitimate pressure must be used after initial efforts of moral suasion have been fairly tried and found to be unsuccessful. In recent discussions (August 13 and 14, 1985) with Sport Canada officials, it was stated that a prototype of an appeal

system was being investigated for distribution sometime in 1986. Additionally, guidelines on drug abuse and its consequences have been formulated.

2. Sport consultants, in a department separated from the 'quest for gold' department, should be hired with expertise in ethics and decision-making. This approach is being developed by organizations such as hospitals, where science is out-stripping accepted practices. These sport consultants should be involved in providing educational materials for sport organizations with respect to human rights and appeal systems. They should also be well-versed in change agent work and advising organizations on how they can help themselves. This department should be involved in providing training for executive members of sport organizations similar to the certification programs developed for coaches and referees. Government grants must be approved by this department to ensure that sport organizations and communities are recognizing and protecting human rights in sport and especially for children. It is essential that communities take pride in being "Equal Opportunity Communities."

3. The coaching certification programs should include a separate and distinct unit on athletes' rights and appeal systems. The impact on coaches attending these workshops will be much greater if this is highlighted in this manner rather than by diluting the area by spreading it amongst the other instructional units.

4. Finally, governments at the provincial and federal levels should set up offices for an ombudsman or arbitrator to facilitate access to justice. The role played by this person would be to settle disputes and conflict. The ombudsman must be given legislative support specific to sport to enable him or her to operate effectively. This ombudsman would not only be put in place to protect the rights of athletes, but also to protect the rights of others. The capacity to levy penalties against individuals must be written into such legislation for violation of rights. The widest possible jurisdiction should be incorporated within the scope of this office. Additionally, each minor sport organization should establish such an office to facilitate access to justice and to enhance the element of objectivity. There should be training programs for these people.

The rights of children in organized sport as a vehicle to an improved educational base for society is clear. The adults involved in these organizations, in general, and governments specifically, must recognize the heavy responsibilities which rest on their shoulders to effect the necessary changes to enhance these opportunities within the rights previously specified. The development of the autonomous individual through sport, and the provision of equal opportunities for all children with access to these programs are goals which are attainable for our society. It is the thrust of this project that government must spearhead the necessary changes which must take place.

Bibliography

Section One

"Athletes given a voice in running of Olympics." *Evening Telegram*. St. John's, November 7, 1981.

Canadian Olympic Association. Athletes Advisory Council. Terms of Reference.

Constitutional Examination. Sport Canada, May-September, 1982. Ottawa.

Fair play codes for children in sports. National Task Force on Children's Play, 1974-77. Dean (Emeritus) Neville Scarfe — Chairman. Canadian Council on Children and Youth, 1979.

Fletcher, D., Director General, Canadian Track and Field Association. (December, 1981. Interview.)

Gowan, G., President, Coaching Association of Canada. (December, 1981, Interview.)

International Olympic Committee. *The Olympic Charter*.... Item 28, p. 16.

Kidd, B., & Eberts, M., Ministry of Tourism and Recreation. *Athletes' Rights in Canada*. (Available from Ontario Government Bookstore, 880 Bay St., Toronto.)

Lewis, H., Executive Director. Canadian Amateur Hockey Association. (December, 1981, Interview.)

Mathieu, G., Manager, Games Mission, Canadian Olympic Association. (December, 1981, Interview.)

McRae returns as head coach of the women's national basketball team. July 18, 1983. Communique, Government of Canada, Fitness and Amateur Sport.

Mission Guidelines. Lake Placid, 1980. Canadian Olympic Association, p. 10, Item 3.

Sopinka, J., Q.C., *Can I Play? Report of the Task Force on Equal Opportunity in Athletics*. September 1983, 1.

Sorensen, O., Senior Sport Consultant, Sport Canada. Ottawa, Canada. (December, 1981, Interview.)

Smith, D., Technical Director, Canadian Amateur Hockey Association, (December, 1981, Interview.).

Urie, J., (Hon. Mr. Justice). Government of Canada. *A status report on the Canadian hockey review*. May, 1979.

IV. Justice and Ethics

Section Two

Dworkin, R., *Taking rights seriously*. 1977, London: Duckworth.

Section Three

"Comaneci agrees to join I.P.C. athletes commission." *Globe and Mail*, Tuesday, July 31, 1984.

RULES, PENALTIES AND OFFICIALS: SPORT AND THE LEGALITY-MORALITY DISTINCTION[1]

DEBRA SHOGAN

Coming to see that there may be a difference between the way a practice is legislated and the way a practice ought to be legislated is an important conceptual distinction that sport examples help to make clear. Legality and morality are not always synonymous. Legislative practices in corrupt societies, for example, do not assume moral worth by virtue of becoming laws. (A case in point is Nazi Germany.) Moreover, there are numerous human interactions, relationships and behaviours which have moral import but which are not, and likely could not be, codified into a legal system.

In this paper I show how examples from sport can be helpful in clarifying conceptual distinctions between legality and morality.[2] To accomplish this I say something about the function of rules, the role of officials, and the logical status of penalties including the so-called "good" penalty. As well I examine whether there is ever any justification for breaking rules.[3]

1. Rules

There are a number of different rule types associated with games. Regulatory rules, which indicate such things as size and placement of numbers on uniforms and stipulations regarding submission of team line-ups, make it possible to administer games more efficiently. Regulatory rules are very important in highly competitive game occurrences and much less important in more casual game occurrences. All games, whether highly regulated or very casual, are distinguished by their *constitutive* rules. Constitutive rules have descriptive, prescriptive and proscriptive functions all of which serve to outline what a particular game is. *Descriptive rules* describe the dimensions of the playing area and specifications about equipment size and shape. Descriptive rules in basketball, for example, describe the dimensions of the court, the height of the basket, the size of the ball, and so on. The game of basketball would be much differently constituted if these features were described in a significantly different way. *Prescriptive rules* prescribe those actions which a participant may perform when engaged in a particular game. Prescriptive rules in basketball indicate, for example, what entails a shot at the basket, what dribbling the ball is, what a sideline throw-in is, and so on. *Proscriptive rules,* on the other hand, proscribe actions which a participant must *not* perform when engaged in a particular game. Proscriptive rules in basketball include, for example, that one must not go outside of certain boundaries, that one must not stand in the key area longer than three seconds, and that one must not bump one's opponent when he or she is shooting.[4]

Actions which harm other individuals are proscribed in almost all sport. In hockey, for example, hitting others with one's stick is a proscribed action. In boxing actions which harm others are, on the other hand, prescribed by the rules. By definition someone is not boxing unless he directs blows toward another's body, or at least, he cannot win at boxing unless he does so. Those who box and, in doing so, conform to the prescriptive rules of boxing and those who play hockey, while not breaking the proscriptive rules of hockey, are both exhibiting legal behaviour but the boxer is arguably engaged in morally problematic behaviour. By conforming to the prescriptive rules of boxing, the boxer is doing nothing illegal but he is arguably doing something morally problematic because the rules of boxing prescribe actions which are harmful to others.

The rule-governed practice of boxing demonstrates that rules as such do not confer moral status on a practice. Some rules are moral and others, those which disregard the welfare or fair treatment of people, are immoral rules and are worth changing. The actual descriptive, prescriptive and proscriptive rules of most sport are morally neutral. In most sport prescriptive and proscriptive rules describe activities which are nonmoral — jumping over bars, throwing implements, aiming for targets.[5] To have these rules govern one's behaviour is to participate legally. What makes breaking a morally neutral rule a moral concern is if someone who is counting on you to keep a rule is harmed when you break the rule.

2. Penalties, Punishment and the Role of the Official

a. Penalties and Punishment

Breaking a prescriptive rule is usually an indication that a player is unskilled or unknowledgeable about when to use a skill in a game. Breaking a prescriptive rule does not have a concomitant penalty. The basketball rule book, for example, indicates what entails a shot at the basket. This is a prescriptive rule which describes what a shot is. There is no penalty for not taking a shot during a game nor for missing a shot when one is attempted. Although there are occasions when not shooting the ball is tactically inappropriate, there are no penalties administered by game officials for not recognizing when a prescriptive rule of this kind *is* appropriate.

To break a proscriptive rule is to do something the rules indicate must not be done. If a proscribed rule is broken with no loss to the rule breaker, the rule and hence the game loses its meaning. If, for example, a proscriptive rule indicates that a player must not touch the game ball with the feet but the game is allowed to proceed whenever the ball is touched by the feet, it would quickly become clear to players that this is not a proscriptive rule at all or, at least, not one to be taken seriously. If, however, the rule is not taken seriously and players use their feet, the game is no longer the same game. In order that proscriptive rules will be taken seriously, a penalty must be invoked when a proscriptive rule is broken.

Penalties ensure that the game, as circumscribed by its proscriptive rules, can continue within those boundaries at that time and in the future. Logically, a penalty is a good penalty if it corrects the inequity created when the rule is broken. In other words, game penalties must be *retributive* in order to restore order to the game.[6] Order is restored to a game when rule breakers are punished. Although they are conceptually related, a penalty and punishment are not the same. A penalty is concomitant to a proscriptive rule, both of which are written into the rule book. In any given game there may be no instances of players being punished if no proscriptive rule is broken. There must, however, be a formal indication of what the punishment will be in the event that a rule is broken in order that participants understand that proscriptive rules are to be taken seriously as proscriptive rules. This formal indication is the penalty which is written into the rule book. The penalty is invoked by punishing an offender when a proscriptive rule is broken.

It is important to note that penalties are invoked both for infractions (such as stepping out of bounds) and for fouls (such as bumping someone who is attempting a shot in basketball) and that they are invoked for both accidental and deliberate rule breakages. Someone cannot avoid the punishment stipulated by a penalty by claiming that a rule breakage is accidental.

The outcome of games can be affected by altering equipment and boundaries established by descriptive rules, and consequently proscriptive rules have been enacted which prohibit alterations to playing dimensions and equipment size. In addition to the descriptive rule in ice hockey which stipulates the thickness of goalie pads, for example, there is a proscriptive rule which indicates that this thickness must not be altered. And, since there is a proscriptive rule prohibiting alteration of pad size, there is also a penalty which specifies what will be the punishment if the proscriptive rule is transgressed.

IV. Justice and Ethics

b. The "Good" Penalty

Among the tactics of many coaches and players in the strategy of highly competitive games of sport is calculating how and when to deliberately break certain rules with the intention of being detected by an official for doing so. When reference is made to the actual rule breakage, this tactic is called a "good" foul or "good" infraction and, when reference is made to the penalty which is invoked, the tactic is called a "good" penalty. When, for example, a basketball player deliberately fouls an opponent near the end of a game and, by doing so, sends this person to the foul line, this is often referred to as a "good" foul because, if the opponent misses the foul shots, there is an opportunity for the fouling team to regain possession of the ball for another attempt to score a basket. The penalty for breaking the rule is thought to be a "good" penalty to invoke under the circumstances because there is a chance that the team will benefit from doing so and because the team will be at a disadvantage if the rule is not broken and the penalty is not invoked. The violator wants to be discovered breaking the proscriptive rule because it is to his or her advantage to have the penalty invoked rather than to have play go on. These situations arise because the punishment incurred by invoking the penalty may not be as severe as the consequences if the rule is not broken (bringing down a player on a breakaway in hockey), or because the administration of the penalty makes possible a benefit (obtaining ball possession from missed foul shots late in a basketball game). "Good" fouls occur in games and "good" penalties are accepted because the penalties are not commensurate with the rule breakage. They are not retributive. There would be no "good" penalty if, for example, the penalty for deliberately fouling in order to stop the clock in basketball was to award the opponent two free shots as well as ball possession. Nor would there be a "good" penalty if, after taking a player down on a breakaway, punishment was as severe as awarding an automatic goal to the fouled team. If players were punished rather than benefited, as the logic of penalties demands, there would not be "good" penalties.

A penalty for breaking a proscriptive rule can only be a *logically* good penalty, then, if it restores the order of the particular game thereby ensuring the future possibility that the game can be played as constituted by its rules. There is a logic to the so-called "good" penalty but the logic consists not in relation to game rules but in relation to an attempt to maximize outcome irrespective of the rules of the sport. The "good" penalty is logical when the goal is to be declared the winner of the game without actually playing the game as constituted by its rules. Understood in this way, the "good" penalty is prudentially good — it is a

346

tactic which is in the best interests of someone who is only interested in being *declared* the winner of a particular game.

c. The Role of the Official

The legal conduct of game players can be achieved through retributive penalties but the moral conduct of game players cannot. Moral retribution cannot be achieved in games because there is no independent system of moral punishment apart from the legal system of punishment. Officials are responsible for legal transgressions but not for moral transgressions. There is no equivalent authority who is entitled to punish a moral offence qua moral offence. Even if punishment for a moral offence operated independently from the punishment of a legal offence with independent authorities responsible for moral breaches, commensurate punishment for moral wrongdoing could not be easily determined. Commensurability of punishment occurs if punishment is severe enough to ensure that the rule breaker is at a disadvantage for having broken a game rule but without making the penalty so severe that participants would be discouraged from playing the game at all. It is not possible to construct a rational system of morally retributive penalties in a game because it is not clear just what type of punishment would be equal to the harm suffered by someone for, say, bringing that person down on a breakaway or by deceiving someone by moving your golf ball up the fairway. When a rule is deliberately broken, moral wrongdoing often coincides with legal wrongdoing, but punishment is a legal punishment and not a moral punishment. The individual is punished for breaking a game rule and not for treating an opponent unfairly. The wrongdoer can be morally blamed but penalties associated with game rules are there as legal punishment.

Retributive penalties do not assure the moral conduct of game players although they do assure legal and logical conduct because moral conduct, if it is to be moral, is based on motivation to respond in such a way that others are treated well or fairly. If individuals wish to avoid punishment, they can, of course, conform to certain kinds of behaviour but motivation to help or treat others fairly is likely not achieved by attempting to avoid punishment. Moral conduct of game players is a complex process which involves much more than the administration of game penalties. A coach concerned with moral development might further punish a player for a moral transgression by sitting the player on the bench, for example. Or, the coach may discuss the incident with the player, pointing out what may be the moral harm done. In either case, the purpose is not necessarily to punish the wrongdoer. The purpose of the legal authority (the official), on the other hand, is to punish the wrongdoer.[7]

IV. Justice and Ethics

3. The Legality and Morality of Deliberately Undermining Rules

Is there ever any legal justification for breaking rules? Is there ever any moral justification for breaking rules? There is no legal justification for someone to break a rule either deliberately, accidentally or from ignorance. This is because the logic of rules is that rules are to apply equally to everyone involved in an enterprise. It is not, therefore, the prerogative of someone to decide that a particular rule will not apply to him or her in a particular situation while it is to apply to others. There is, however, moral justification for breaking or undermining rules when rules proscribe activities which harm people in some way or when rules proscribe access by some to activities altogether.

The way in which rules may be justifiably undermined differs according to whether the morally objectionable rule is prescriptive or proscriptive. When one breaks a proscriptive rule on moral grounds, it is essential that one also recognizes that whenever one *deliberately* breaks rules, legal procedures *are* undermined. In order to continue to show respect for legal procedures, even when breaking a rule, the rule must be broken publicly and not surreptitiously. This is accomplished by accepting the punishment dictated by the penalty. Punishment is accepted in order not to undermine legal procedures and in order to force those who would punish illegal action "to engage in serious moral discussion."[8] When Kathrine Switzer broke the proscriptive rule against women participating in the Boston Marathon, for example, she did something illegal but in doing so she forced sport officials to engage in discussion about the morality of excluding women from this event. When Martin Luther King and others defied laws prohibiting Blacks from using public facilities, they performed illegal actions but, in accepting the ensuing punishment, they forced authorities to engage in discussion about the morality of segregation.

The Kathrine Switzer example shows that there may be justification for breaking proscriptive rules when they prevent certain people from being participants.[9] Are there other instances in sport in which it is moral to break a proscriptive game rule? There is never any moral justification for breaking morally neutral rules, as long as continuing to abide by the rules does not conflict with something of moral importance. There is obviously justification for a race car driver to break the morally neutral rule that drivers must stay on the race track, for example, in order to avoid running over someone on the track. There is, however, no moral justification for deciding that the rule against moving one's golf ball by hand up the fairway will not apply to oneself while it is to apply to everyone else.

I have found that the rule proscribing steroid use is helpful in seeing what is involved in breaking a proscriptive rule on moral grounds. There are those who argue that there should be no rule against taking steroids and they claim to make this argument on moral grounds. They argue that to have such a rule abrogates an individual's freedom and that freedom overrides health as the more important moral value in this situation.[10] If someone exhausts the normal procedures for changing rules which proscribe steroid use such as appeals to governing bodies, motions at rules meetings, the next step would be to break the rule but only if it is done in a public way so as not to undermine rules generally and in order to make those who enforce the subsequent penalty to discuss the moral justification of the particular proscriptive rule. If someone is not prepared to make public one's rule breakage, he or she undermines legal procedures and renders impossible any public discourse about the appropriateness of the rule.

If one disagrees on moral grounds with *prescriptive* rules of an activity, he or she must withdraw from the activity and undermine it from the outside since to participate is to do the activity one finds morally objectionable. It would be impossible for someone to take up boxing, for example, with the intent of breaking the prescriptive rules of boxing because to take up boxing is to utilize the prescriptive rules of boxing and to break the rules is to not box at all. Action designed to alter or abolish immoral prescriptive rules is action which occurs outside of the practice itself. If one believes that certain practices or enterprises are immoral, withdrawal or separation from the activity is what is morally required. To continue to be involved is to be complicit since this entails participating in the very prescriptive rules which one finds objectionable. To make this point another way, if one thinks, for example, that it is morally objectionable that women are not in a position to decide for themselves whether they will participate in certain activities, including boxing, but one also finds boxing immoral, the solution to the former problem is not to advocate boxing for women. The solution is to attempt to undermine the practice of boxing while also undermining patriarchal, paternalistic attitudes about women. So, too, the solution to women's exclusion from full participation in societal practices is not to advocate women's inclusion in practices which one finds morally objectionable, like armed combat. The solution is to work toward the end of armed combat and as well toward the dismantling of organizing principles, including rules and laws, which oppress women.

Conclusion

What is accomplished when sport ethics courses are offered, or any other ethics courses for that matter, is that students may come to understand

IV. Justice and Ethics

certain conceptual distinctions about ethics. There is little chance that such a course would affect any sort of moral conversion. A moral conversion in a sport ethics course is as unlikely as a moral conversion merely from participating in sport. Moral behaviour involves regular attention to matters which may include ethics courses and sport experiences but which go beyond these as well. Using sport examples may help people to understand ethics but understanding ethics is not sufficient or perhaps even necessary to being a moral person, in sport or elsewhere. This is because to understand the moral domain is an intellectual ability which both moral and immoral people may possess. Much depends on whether this understanding counts with a person and whether it counts enough to motivate behaviour.

Notes

1. Parts of this paper were presented by me at the Canadian Association of Health, Physical Education and Recreation Conference, Vancouver, B.C., June 11, 1987 and at the North American Society for the Sociology of Sport Conference, Edmonton, Alberta, November 5, 1987.
2. This paper is not an attempt to show how an understanding of ethics can improve moral behaviour of sport participants — a position which is, I think, problematic. Neither is this paper an attempt to show that involvement in moral situations in sport can improve moral behaviour — a position which I would want to defend but only after drawing out the complexities of moral education.
3. Although analogies can be made between rules of games and laws of a land, there is not an exact correspondence between the two.
4. An historical study would be helpful to show whether penalties have become more severe as deliberate rule breakage has become more common. It would be interesting to have an indication of the extent to which the number of proscriptive rules have increased as participants devise ways of making it difficult for opponents to fulfil prescriptive rules. I am reminded of Jim Unger's Herman comic in which Herman says, as he lies prone in front of the golf pin, "there's nothing in the rule book which says I can't stay here." By lying in front of the pin, Herman prevents his opponent from carrying out the prescriptive rule which indicates that players must play the ball into the hole by successive strokes. Moreover, if Herman and others do this action often enough, it forces rule makers to add a proscriptive rule prohibiting lying in front of the pin as well as an indication of how someone who breaks this rule will be penalized.
5. There is a sense, however, in which prescriptive rules limit who can be a participant since rules of most sport prescribe activities which,

at least at an elite level, can only be achieved by the big and strong. Prescriptive rules which do this are arguably not morally neutral.

6. There is no agreement that penalties for breaking societal laws should be retributive. Some would argue, for example, that the purpose of "punishment" is rehabilitation. See, "The Complexity of the Concepts of Punishment" by H.J. McClosky in *Philosophy* 37 (1962): 307-325.

7. The role of a legal authority in some other legal systems is similar to the role of a legal authority in games. If someone plagiarizes another's work in a university, for example, there must be a penalty if a rule against plagiarism is to be taken seriously. It is the role of an official to punish those who plagiarize. The role of a legal authority with respect to laws of a land are not as straight forward. Some would argue that the purpose of legal procedures, including the role of legal authorities, is to rehabilitate and not to seek retribution.

8. Ivan De Faveri. "The Virtue of Disobedience." *The Canadian School Executive* April (1983): 33.`

9. Clearly some activities are only interesting as contests because of rules which proscribe certain participants from taking part; for example, rules which create weight classes.

10. William Brown. "Ethics, Drugs, and Sport." *The Journal of the Philosophy of Sport* 7 (1980): 15-23.

SPORT ORGANIZATIONS
AND ETHICAL CONCERNS

PASQUALE J. GALASSO

Sport organizations are usually classified as professional or voluntary. In some instances, a distinction has been made in the sense of non-paid, but with a high level of expertise. In any case, in both scenarios the role labels are similar in that those who fall within the framework of the organization can be classified as players, trainers, coaches, spectators, relatives, medical doctors, or supervisors and executive members. A major deviation from this pattern has involved the hiring of people in amateur sport organizations who are paid, and usually in combination by the organization and by government. These employees, who carry titles such as executive director, are primarily centered in Ottawa at 333 River Road. Similar organizational patterns now exist at the provincial level. To what extent this has influenced the philosophic base undergirding the development and direction of these organizations at the amateur level would be an interesting study in itself. On the other hand, in professional sport organizations, the various roles of the members of the organization seem to be more clearly identified and delineated as to purposes and objectives.

In amateur organizations it is interesting and significant to note that behaviour and conduct, which could be classified in the ethical sphere, usually refers to player conduct on the field with minor allusions to spectator and parental conduct. Content of rule books associated with these organizations provides further reinforcement for this point of view. Very little is said about specific duties and responsibilities of adults involved as coaches and executive members, let alone the trainers and medical doctors as to their ethical behaviour. It could be, of course, that in reference to this latter class of individuals that the general medical ethics per se which apply are sufficient. However, some would argue that there is a specificity to the sport situation requiring specifically oriented statements as to behaviour and decisions in light of the influence of factors such as competition and winning. The playing of injured players under a variety of circumstances should be covered by the organization in its written material. Similar guidelines or ethical statements should be framed associated with the work of the trainer, coach and executive committee members as well. Why it is that these do not exist would be an interesting study in itself. It could simply be a genuine belief in the innate goodness of human beings, particularly if they are volunteers. Some would argue that because people are not being paid, demands cannot be placed upon them. That is, you get what you pay for — no pay — no commitments.

Ethical concerns themselves could be classified as including all consciously directed actions and outcomes generated by those participating in, or holding office in, these various sport organizations. This covers much more than most people realize that can be categorized as good or bad — right or wrong. It is interesting to note that when constitutions and by-laws are perused, one reads of various territorial rights, rather than the rights of the participants. There is greater interest in control of, rather than development of, the individual.

One major concern which should be addressed by every sport organization, particularly at the minor level, is the matter of moral development per se. If participation in the activity can affect the moral development of the child, either to enhance it, inhibit it, or misdirect it, then surely their moral development should be of primary concern on the part of the adults responsible for the running of the organization. And this applies to all adults involved. If an individual's value system serves as a base for all of his or her thoughts and actions, then as responsible citizens and adults they should be ensuring that mature, self-directed individuals emanate from these programs, or at least progress somewhat in the direction of moral development as described by Kohlberg and others.

For example, if it could be shown that the activity, based on the way in which it is conducted, inhibits the development of altruistic tendencies and in fact reinforces egoistic tendencies where winning is placed as the prime objective, and putting down the opponent becomes the means to an end in that the opponent is looked upon as an object rather than an equal, one could reasonably conclude that participants would develop egoistically oriented life styles into adulthood. What are the long term meanings of such outcomes, where after ten to fifteen years of minor sport, the individual is taught that it is all right, in fact it is encouraged, to take a "good" penalty or to get even? Is it any wonder that it is a schizophrenic development toward morality which ensues where the claim is made by those who come through this system, that what they do and how they perform on the ice towards the opponents, is not to be taken as a measure of their moral system, but simply as an isolated or pidgeon-holed part of their lives and something which does not carry over into their office or off-the-field activities. Do they really believe that if given somewhat similar circumstances in off-ice activity, they will behave differently than they do on the ice after having spent fifteen of their first twenty years being told that it is good, in fact it is required, that they do certain things to their opponents in order to come out on the upper end of the scoreboard? Surely, there is some measure of conditioning or transfer that takes place here in moral development.

IV. Justice and Ethics

And if it is true that there is a carry over, and if it is true that the whole aspect of morality is abused, and if it is true that this form of participation leads to a truncation of moral development, then why is it that citizens are supporting these activities? Governments, in fact, are pouring millions of dollars into facilities and programs associated with these organizations.

Who is going to speak up for the children? Who is going to bring forward the concept of responsiblity on the part of adults involved in these organizations, and what are the rights of these children? Who is going to bring forward a basis for establishing and identifying these rights which can then be entrenched in constitutions and playing regulations across the country at the Federal, Provincial and Local levels?

Is there an allegiance to something greater than the individual or the player associated with these organizations or activities? Is there a need, or some other need, of the adults involved that should and does take precedence? Do the adults think that the time they spend as volunteers is simply all that they can be called upon to put into the organization, or is something greater expected of them? When one looks at the thousands of children, both male and female, who are involved in these activities through organized sport, what of the society of tomorrow — will its character be changed by participation in these activities? When hundreds of hours per annum are spent in practice and in competition, so unlike two decades ago where very little coaching went on prior to the child's admission to high school, what happens to the participant?

One other area where ethical concerns such as rights should be addressed is that of individual and team discipline by coaches, executive members or other administrative members of the organization. Normally, if an individual is disciplined, such as being cut from the team, or being forced to sit out during the rest of that game or competition, or subsequent competitions, it is done through a unilateral decision by the coach and/or manager. International athletes, as well as minor sport athletes, have been disciplined in the past. The idea of being sent home without the opportunity to compete after having spent years in training and without any courts of appeal or due process can be a traumatic experience which stays with the person for life. And for every major incident that hits the headlines, there are many others which rarely see the light of day. A sense of fair treatment needs to be officially and formally inserted into the basis of human interaction between the participants and others involved in the activity or organization. All too often the coaches and managers are not that highly skilled in human relations and the athletes need protection.

354

The roles of psychologists and exercise physiologists associated with national and international athletes also need to be examined. Both short and long term possible effects on athletes must be taken into account prior to the application of any testing or research by these two subdisciplinary areas. When athletes as humans are looked upon as units of cost effectiveness in the development of programs associated with these subdisciplinary areas, it is time to take a second look and assess the worthwhileness of these investigations. The key question, here, of course, is, do the athletes really know what is happening to them?

In the same vein, and at the professional level, some of you might have noticed an article in the Toronto *Globe and Mail* on Tuesday, May 19, 1981, covering professional football and the use of think-tanks of a different variety. In these think-tanks used by the Dallas Cowboys, the players, on a voluntary basis, at least at this stage, are allowed to float in tanks containing saline solution on a type of raft arrangement with the water at body temperature for an hour at a time and with audio and/or visual input associated with their playing position. The objective is to rid the athlete of interfering thought waves to facilitate concentration and therefore learning. However, as one athlete indicated, "the difference inside the tank of the Cowboys' plan is that someone else is able to control what a player sees, hears and feels." The player also goes on to state, "Dallas feels that they have an infallible organization, except for one thing — the players. If they could play without the players, they could win every game. Landry (the coach) has to be in control." Of course, anyone who has observed the Dallas Cowboys knows just how much control really does exist even compared to other professional teams, in that all of the plays, both offensively and defensively, are called by the coaching staff. In fact, the very behaviour of the Cowboys on the field is quite mechanical and has a machine-like precision, as opposed to the spontaneity that usually emanates from the behaviour of the other teams.

The business of mind control is being tapped here as a resource and should be investigated as a form of intrusion in that when the participants become involved in these activities, it begins to generate great pressure on their peers on the team to become involved as well. Bob Ward, a Dallas assistant coach, who has a doctorate in physical education and is in charge of the team's conditioning as well as this part of the program, states, "*conditioning coach, the village shrink, anything that improves performance*," when describing his role, "whether it's physical or psychological." And as Tom Landry, the head coach said, "You just have to get an edge someplace." In summary, the length to which some individuals will go to achieve the Holy Grail of competition, be it an Olympic gold medal or a world championship, is of concern. And we know we will always have adults arriving and operating at the maximum level to achieve these ends.

One unfortunate aspect of this is the involvement of children in amateur sport under the direction of such adults. These children, as incomplete moral agents, can be made to appear as being highly motivated to achieve in certain directions. However, it is doubtful that they are exercising full free will here. At what point can we say that they are independent people with respect to decision-making? This is a difficult question and needs empirical work to clarify the issue. It would appear that in such situations the children need to be protected against themselves and that even at the international level in certain activities such as swimming and gymnastics for girls, that decision-making carries well beyond the ethical maturity of these youngsters. The balanced input of objective outsiders should be involved in helping to protect them, and to control the situation beyond the coaches and others directly involved.

How do we know such competition for these children is enjoyable? How do we know it is fun? How do we know that it is good for them? When does play become sport, and ultimately athletics? Who is taking the opus out of these experiences and introducing more of the labour component? Somewhere down the line, sport organizations and governments at various levels are going to have to face up to the responsibility of dealing with this issue of ethical concerns fairly and squarely. Too much is being left to the goodwill of the adults involved and not enough consideration is being given to the protection of athletes at all levels, including the professional and international.

In conclusion, if one is to project into the society of the future, we can expect to see hundreds of thousands of adults who were involved as participants in minor sport competitions now making decisions as citizens. This leads me to infer that long-term effects on moral development within the framework of egoism and altruism should be studied, with funds provided by the government, by scholars in our field to determine the effects of such competition. Unfortunately, at the moment the focus is on short-term goals, with the emphasis on technical knowledge and physical performance. This applies not only within the sport organizations per se, but also within the programs being designed and financed by governments at all levels. It seems reasonable to recommend that sport organizations place their prime emphasis on facilitating and enhancing the moral development of the children rather than on athletic achievement. In this respect, programs should be fostered and financed by government to assist in the education of executive members associated with sport organizations over and above those already in place for coaches, officials and participants. In addition, those clinics and programs for the latter group should be modified with the inclusion of a major thrust toward an understanding of the moral development of children. A society based on taking good penalties, clearing the man out from in front of the goal, and winning through intimidation, can only lead to more and more disfunctional conflict for us as a society in the future.

THE DIMENSIONALITY
OF AN ETHICAL CODE

EARLE F. ZEIGLER

Introduction

The discussion here is based on a presumably logical sequence of questions that would need to be answered by an individual or group of practitioners who accepted the task of developing an embryonic code for the consideration of the members of a professional society operative within a recognized political unit and geographical area. The following, then, are questions which the writer will strive to answer as precisely and succinctly as possible:

a) What is ethics?
b) What is a value?
c) What is an ethical code?
d) Is this the same as an ethical creed?
e) What is a profession in the 20th century?
f) What has been published about the professionalization of the profession and the possible need for a code of ethics?
g) Should the Canadian Health, Physical Education and Recreation Journal (CAHPER) develop a code of ethics as soon as possible?
h) How can ordinary norms be related to professional norms or obligations?
i) What might be a reasonable approach to the categorization of these professional norms or obligations?
j) Is a secondary categorization within the heading of professional obligations possible and/or desirable?
k) What are the major areas of concern in the development of an ethical code?
l) What are some examples of provisions that could well be included in each of the major areas of concern?
m) What conclusions may be drawn from this discussion?

Definition of Terms

The first 4 questions (a-d) will be answered under this heading:

a) *Ethics* is defined variously as a "pattern or way of life" (e.g., Christian or Muslim ethics); "a listing of rules of conduct or moral code" (e.g., medical ethics); or an "inquiry about rules of conduct in a society or culture" (i.e., meta-ethics).

It can be explained further that ethics has a direct relationship with values, to "right" and "wrong" as applied to individual or collective acts and to "good" and "bad" as applied to the *effects* of acts.

b) A *value* can be explained roughly as something that is regarded as "worthwhile" and "good" by a person or group. For example, the values of a democratic society might be as follows: (i) governance of law, (ii) autonomy or freedom, (iii) protection from injury, (iv) equality of opportunity, (v) right to privacy, (vi) concern for individual welfare, etc.

(c) An *ethical code* may be defined as a "systematic collection of rules and regulations (i.e., what's right and wrong, and good and bad) determined in relation to the values espoused in a *given society*." It should be noted that values expressed as norms often take the form of *laws*.

d) The answer as to whether a *code* is the same as a *creed* is both "yes" and "no." A creed can be defined as a *short* idealistic (in the non-philosophic sense) statement of belief, while a code is a longer set of more detailed regulations.

What Is a Profession in the 20th Century?

To this point the discussion has related to the subject of individual ethics. In this paper, however, the intent is to consider *professional* ethics as applied to the field of physical, health and recreation education. Thus, the following is a brief attempt to define a profession in the last quarter of the 20th century:

a) A profession can be defined as an occupation which requires specific knowledge of some aspect of learning before a person is accepted as a *professional* person.

b) It can be argued, however, that there is no generally acceptable definition today i.e., it is impossible to characterize professions by a set of necessary and sufficient features possessed by all professions and *only* by professions (Bayles, 1981, p. 77).

c) Also, there are *categories* of professions as follows: consulting, teaching, research, performing, etc. Physical, health, and recreation education would presumably be a combination of teaching, coaching, administering, supervising, and consulting.

d) The following may be considered as three *necessary* features of an occupation that can also be designated as a profession: (i) a need for extensive training; (ii) a significant intellectual component that must

359

be mastered; and (iii) a recognition by society that the trained person can provide a basic, important service.

e) Additionally, there are some other features that are common to most professions as follows: (i) licensing by state/province or professional body, (ii) establishment of professional societies, (iii) considerable autonomy in work performance, and (iv) establishment of a creed or code of ethics.

What Has Been Published About the Professionalization of the Field of Physical, Health, and Recreation Education and the Possible Need for a Code of Ethics?

If there is agreement that a young person in our society should be educated so that there is ample opportunity for him or her to develop rationality as a life competency, it is essential that such ability be available for use with the many ethical problems that arise in all phases of daily life. Thus a more basic concern, in the present discussion, is that the young adult be able to apply such competency to the ethical problems that arise in the course of his or her subsequent *professional service* to a chosen field.

I am not arguing that we (in physical, health and recreation education) as a profession are any better or any worse than most other professions with regard to the application of professional ethics to our endeavours. Perhaps it simply would be best to state that our western culture is confused in this matter, and it has just happened that way in our development. This tangle of ethics has developed because of a diverse inheritance of customs and mores from other lands, and we have simply added our own brand of confusion to this ill-suited mixture of moral systems.

Where does that leave the profession of physical, health and recreation education? The answer at this point must be, "In trouble!" Nevertheless, if our profession is to survive and continue to grow, it must serve society more effectively in the years immediately ahead. To do this our profession, along with all other professions, must be attuned to the all-important values and norms that have been established within the culture.

It is obvious that we need to take a hard look at ourselves, admittedly a difficult assignment. Responding to current heavy criticism of highly competitive sport — with which we are typically identified because of our involvement with educational sport — is indeed a humbling experience. Further, in some ways we are part of the teaching profession, and yet ideally physical, health and recreation education has a broad mission that extends from infancy to our oldest citizens be they "normal," "special" or "accelerated."

We do have many of the attributes of a profession (e.g., extensive training period; significant intellectual component to be mastered; and *some* recognition that the trained person can provide a basic important service to society). However, physical, health and recreation education has not done as well as some of the highly recognized professions in developing and enforcing carefully defined professional obligations that the practitioner must follow to remain in good standing with his or her fellows and with society.

In considering what we do have in the field that might be considered to be professional ethics, initially we must be careful to distinguish between a *creed*, or "statement of professional beliefs" and a *code*, or "set of detailed regulations of a more administrative nature" (Bayles, 1981, p. 24).

In competitive sport, for example, the National High School Athletic Coaches Association in the U.S.A. has developed what might be called an embryonic code. A similar brief code — with some overlap — has been adopted by the Minnesota High School Coaches Association. In Canada the Coaching Association, as part of the National Coaching Certification Program, has adopted what is called a coaching creed. It too is very brief and contains some elements that might more correctly appear in a code. However, that is the extent of this development, and there is probably no coach at any level who could repeat all or even the essence of these statements.

Unfortunately, physical education (i.e., sport and physical education in the U.S. and physical and health education in Canada) has usually been viewed only within the domain of the education profession. Several efforts have been made, in the United States, over the years to define what our ethical concerns should be. However, at present there appears to be no concerted effort underway to rectify a situation that is glaringly inadequate.

Several textbooks have been made available by Shea (1978), Fraleigh (1984) and Zeigler (1984), the latter book being divided equally between discussions of personal and professional ethics. However, there are very few courses in sport and physical education ethics offered in North America, and practically none that treat the subject of professional ethics for the teacher/coach in our field. (I do not know what the situation in Great Britain and the rest of the Commonwealth is in this regard. I am not aware of other texts along this line other than McIntosh's [1979] excellent volume called *Fair Play*.)

The field of recreation has made some (but not substantive) headway on a continuing basis in this area. A brief code of ethics was developed by the American Recreation Society a generation ago, and the Society of Municipal Recreation Directors of Ontario in Canada constructed a code in the 1950s as well. Typically, these codes receive lip service, and the societies most certainly do not enforce compliance with the codes' tenets.

In summary, therefore, we can report only meagre beginnings in an aspect of the allied professions that warrant significant attention at this time.

Should CAHPER Develop a Code of Ethics?

The review of the meagre amount of development and accompanying literature on the subject of coach/teacher ethics described above, as well as investigations carried out in the past several years (Zeigler, 1983a, 1983b, 1984a, 1984b, 1984c, 1985a, 1985b, 1985c, 1985d, 1986), has led me to the following conclusion. The physical, health and recreation educator as a professional person striving for public recognition, will increasingly have obligations to the public, to his or her profession, and to his or her clients. In addition to the *necessary* features for a profession as indicated above (e.g., extensive training), the establishment of a creed or code of ethics was included as another feature that was common to most established professions. History has made clear that such ethical codes appeared only after one or more professional societies within a developing profession had been established for a period of time.

Accordingly, it is logical to propose that the time has now come for the national professional association (i.e., CAHPER) to set about such a task carefully and extensively on a cooperative basis with closely related professions. This would simply be taking one more important step forward in the total professionalization process. Such a detailed code, as opposed to a short creed that could easily turn out to be "window dressing" (such as medicine's Hippocratic Oath), would not seem to be sufficient at this time. Such a code, as is being recommended, would be a *system of norms* describing what *should* be the case in an individual's profession.

How Can Ordinary Norms be Related to Professional Norms or Obligations?

It is important to understand that the term "norm" has several different meanings. Used in this sense it does not mean an "average," as one understands the term in the social sciences. It has more the meaning of one of a series of standards of virtue that are expected to prevail in the society or culture. Thus, persons in this society can be expected to be honest, fair, etc. — in other words they should possess these desirable traits. These would be considered to be *ordinary* norms as opposed to *professional* norms.

Further, it is also to be expected that the society's ordinary norms will have a definite relationship to the norms or obligations expected in a specific profession. Bayles (1981) explained that ordinary norms can have four possible relationships to professional norms. By adapting these for the present discussion, we might suggest something like the following:

a) *Identical to*: a professional should be *honest*;
b) *Specifications of*: a professional should be *honest* with his or her client;
c) *Functionally related to*: a professional should be *honest* when advising a client about his/her mental state prior to an involvement (e.g., an important contest);
d) *Independent of*: a professional may occasionally need to tell a "white lie" when making an unusually difficult decision about staff or personnel selection (i.e., employing a separate system of ethics).

What Might Be a Reasonable Approach to the Categorization of These Professional Norms or Obligations?

Professionals may presently be functioning as professional, semi-professional or amateur practitioners in physical, health and recreation education. (For the present, we should probably limit our discussion to those who earn their living entirely in the field.) Thus, in an effort to list or enumerate the variety and large number of professional norms with which an intelligent and dedicated professional may be confronted, it will be necessary to postulate an underlying approach to the categorization of such obligations. On the face of it, a good starting point is to seek to answer two questions: (a) what *should* one do? and (b) what should one *not* do? The responses to the former question would be considered as obligations; they are *prescribed*. Responses to the latter question would represent actions that a professional should *not* take. The former would be considered right and should result in a condition or state that is good. The latter would be considered wrong and would presumably bring about a bad result.

Of course, there are always choices to make in life where the situation and action to be taken are not clear-cut. Thus, if one category is that of *obligations*, a second category of norms could be designated as *permissions*. In this case, where action is debatable, and possibly right or wrong resulting in a good or bad state of affairs, the professional is offered the freedom to make a choice.

363

Is a Secondary Categorization Within the Heading of Professional Obligations Possible and/or Desirable?

A secondary categorization of professional obligations involves three specific subheadings that are designated as *standards, principles* and *rules* (Bayles, pp. 22-23). This approach should be very helpful to members of any profession (i.e., embryonic, developing or established) in the process of developing or upgrading its ethical code.

The stricture regarding the particular obligation is preceded by a designation of the *standard* virtue and/or vice involved. Then the approach moves from the general to the specific in that the ensuing *principle* allows for discretion and the accompanying *rule* is most specific.

More specifically, standards present desirable or undesirable character traits to be sought or avoided; principles state responsibilities that allow for discretion in the fulfillment of standards and may be balanced or weighed against one another; and rules explain duties that prescribe specific conduct and allow for very little discretion. As Bayles explains it, "principles can explicate standards, justify rules, and provide guidance in their absence" (p. 24).

The following might well be one example of how the above schemata could work:

a) *Standard of Virtue or Vice* (for the practitioner): a professional in physical, health and recreation education should be unselfish and beneficent in his/her dealings with a student or client.
b) *Principle of Responsibility* (this allows for individual discretion): a professional should use his/her power over a student/client carefully — not as a means to some other end.
c) *Rule of Duty* (this must be followed): a student/client should never be forced (i.e., made to feel) that he/she must do something because a third party's reputation is at stake (e.g., the teacher, the coach, the administrator).

What Are the Major Areas of Concern in the Development of an Ethical Code for Coaches?

One way to learn about some of the major areas of concern that ought to be in a profession's ethical code is to examine other such codes in existence. For example, there is "Ethical Standards of Psychologists" as developed originally and revised by the American Psychological Association (1977). There is no denying that this is an excellent statement with a fine preamble. It has been prepared carefully over a considerable period of time with numerous revisions along the way.

364

Interestingly, the initial *preamble* seems to be almost what has been defined in the present paper as a *creed* (see Definition of Terms above). This code contains nine principles to which the members of the Association have subscribed. These principles relate to the following aspects of the profession: (a) responsibility, (b) competence, (c) moral and legal standards, (d) public statements, (e) confidentiality, (f) welfare of the consumer, (g) professional relationships, (h) utilization of assessment techniques and (i) pursuit of research activities (Ibid.).

As good as the prevailing APA code is, it does not appear to clarify sufficiently among standards, principles and rules as Bayles has recommended. His plan (i.e., the format of standards, principles and rules) represents a significant improvement over the prevailing arrangement. The APA's code simply lists nine excellent principles, but makes no effort to categorize or arrange them as sequentially as could (should) be done. Also, the APA has not sufficiently delineated among standards, principles and rules. The result is a lack of clarity as to where one leaves off and the other begins. In other words, the ethical standards that have been developed make an effort to "throw a covering blanket" over the entire discipline and profession. This is fine, but the task should be designed more specifically to cover the duties, obligations and responsibilities of each of the sub-professional groups concerned (i.e., teaching, clinical, research).

What Major Areas of Concern Can be Recommended?

I agree that the listing of nine "principles" in a seemingly random order without categorization into major areas of concern is perhaps a satisfactory beginning. Nevertheless I believe that such a statement can be strengthened by further clarification. Consider, for example, the subsuming of the "principles" listed above under five major areas of concern as follows:

a) Bases upon which professional services are made available.
   Example: Is there a mal-distribution of services?
b) Ethical nature of professional/client relationship.
   Example: What constitutes trustworthiness?
c) Conflict-resolution when conflicts arise between professional's obligations to student/athletes/clients, and to third parties (e.g., his or her employer, the state or province).
   Example: Should a professional report his/her own student/client/athlete to his/her employer/supervisor if it is known that the individual has taken an illegal drug?
d) Professional obligations to society and to his or her own profession.

IV. Justice and Ethics

Example: Should a practitioner risk doing harm to his/her own profession's reputation by carrying out his or her duties in such a way that fellow professionals and the public view him or her as an unethical person?

e) Ensuring compliance to the profession's established ethical code.

Example: Should a member of the profession report a colleague who has undoubtedly been unethical in his/her actions so that possible action may be taken against him/her by the professional society?

What Are Some Examples of Provisions That Could Well Be Included Under Each of the Major Areas of Concern?

The following are some examples of provisions (i.e., standards, principles, rules) that could well be included under each of the major areas of concern (Table 1).

What Conclusions May Reasonably be Drawn From This Discussion?

In this paper there has been a sequential discussion and analysis of the developing professionalization of the field of physical, health and recreation education sport. In addition to a brief review of literature on the topic, a rationale and format for an ethical code has been presented. Having arrived at this point, the following conclusions may reasonably be stated:

a) That there is some recognition by society that a qualified professional in physical, health and recreation education can provide a basic, important service.

b) That there is a significant intellectual component to be mastered, and therefore an extensive training is required before a person becomes qualified as a professional in this field.

c) That this field is moving very slowly toward true professional status based on the following accomplishments:

i. Establishment of professional societies;
ii. Conferences and symposia held to improve the knowledge and competency of professionals;
iii. Publication of a variety of semi-scholarly ("professional") and scholarly journals;
iv. Discussions held and articles and books published on the subject of professionalization over a period of time;
v. Considerable autonomy in work performance.

TABLE 1. Examples of Provisions for an Ethical Code

Categories	Standards	Principles	Rules
a. Bases upon which professional services are made available.	A prof. should be *fair* and *just* in providing his/her services	A prof. should ensure that all students receive adequate instruction	A student needing help must receive it as soon as possible.
	Example: A professional shows bias toward a client and instructs/coaches him/her as little as possible.		
b. Ethical nature of prof.-client relationship	A prof. should be *honest* in his/her treatment of a client	A prof. should never treat a client as means to an end	A client must never be forced to take an illegal or unethical action because of fear of loss or status
	Example: In sport, a coach urges an athlete to continue playing by stating that a scholarship will be lost otherwise.		
c. Conflict resolution when conflict arises between prof.'s obligations to clients and third parties	A prof. has an obligation to be *truthful* in dealing with third parties	In checking eligibility of a team member, a coach should be most careful not to permit an inaccurate statement to be entered	A coach must never knowingly sign an eligibility form in which an athlete has committed perjury
	Example: A coach knows that an athlete's eligibility has been used up elsewhere, but signs the form nevertheless in which an athlete has perjured himself/herself.		
d. Professional obligations to society and to profession (i.e., duty to serve the public good)	A prof. should be *loyal* to societal values and those of the profession	A prof. has a duty and responsibility to preserve and enhance the role of the coaching profession	A prof. has a duty to upgrade and strengthen his/her knowledge by attending one or more clinics or symposia
	Example: A professional gives the profession a bad name by obviously falling behind in the knowledge area of his/her expertise.		
e. Ensuring compliance with the established obligations of the professional ethical code.	A prof. should practice his/her profession with *honesty* and *integrity*	A prof. should encourage his/her students to be honest within the letter and spirit of the established rules	A prof. who permits his/her client to cheat shall be reported and should be excluded from the profession if found guilty
	Example: A teacher/coach guilty of flagrant unethical practice shall be reported to the ethics committee of the professional society and to the administrators of the league in which his/her team is playing.		

367

IV. Justice and Ethics

d) That, to promote sound, long-range development, a specific *creed* for the profession should be developed, and that this should be followed by a subsequent expansion to a detailed ethical *code* as soon as possible.
e) That programs of *certification* at the provincial level and voluntary *registration* at the national level be developed as soon as possible. Future development of *required* licensing for all practitioners (both in the society at large and within education) would necessarily have to take place on a province-by-province basis.
f) That, in the development of such registration/licensing procedures, every effort should be made to avoid narrow discrimination on the basis of "professional/disciplinary labels" and training (i.e., unwillingness to accept obviously comparable course experiences from another profession/discipline as part of certification requirements).

What must be guaranteed, of course, is that an acceptable level of knowledge, competency and skill be determined, and that all who practise professionally possess such ability on a continuing basis.

In conclusion, may I repeat the message I have sought to convey throughout this paper. I feel that there is an urgent need for CAHPER to give the question of ethics serious consideration for the development of the profession.

References

American Psychological Association. (1977). "Ethical Standards of Psychologists." Washington, DC: American Psychological Association.

Bayles, M.D. (1980). *Professional Ethics*. Belmont, CA: Wadsworth.

Fraleigh, W.P. (1984). *Right Actions in Sport*. Champaign, IL: Human Kinetics Publishers, Inc.

McIntosh, P. (1979). *Fair Play*. London: Heinemann.

Random House Dictionary of the English Language, The. (1967). New York: Random House.

Shea, E.J. (1978). *Ethical Decisions in Physical Education and Sport*. Springfield, IL: C.C. Thomas.

Zeigler, E.F. (1983a). "Cross-cultural applicability of a model for applied ethics in sport and physical education." A paper presented at the Big Ten CIC Symposium, The Ohio State University, Columbus, Ohio, Oct. 14.

Zeigler, E.F. (1983b). "Strengthening our professional arsenal." In *Proceedings of the Nat. Assoc. for Phys. Educ. in Higher Educ.* Champaign IL: Human Kinetics Publishers, Inc.

Zeigler, E.F. (1984a). *Ethics and Morality in Sport and Physical Education*. Champaign, IL: Stipes, 1984.

Zeigler, E.F. (1984b). "A triple-play approach to ethical decision-making in competitive sport." A paper presented at Central Michigan University, Oct. 25.

Zeigler, E.F. (1984c). "Applied ethics in sport and physical education." *Philosophy in Context*, 13, 52-64.

Zeigler, E.F. (1985a). "The urgent need for sport and physical education ethics." A paper presented at the University of Saskatchewan, Canada, March 17.

Zeigler, E.F. (1985b). "Sport ethics in world perspective." A paper presented at the Ethics and Athletics Conference, Louisiana State University, April 7.

Zeigler, E.F. (1985c). "The development of an ethical code for sport psychologists." A paper presented to the Sport Psychological Academy of the Amer. Assn. for HPERD, Atlanta, Georgia, April 18.

Zeigler, E.F. (1985d). "Merging the triple-play approach and a jurisprudential argument in sport and physical education ethics." A paper presented at the University of Windsor, Ontario, Oct. 17.

Zeigler, E.F. (1986). "Dimensions of an ethical code for sport coaches." In *Coach education: Preparation for a profession* . London/NY: E. & F.N. Spon, pp. 79-90.

AUTONOMY THROUGH PHYSICAL EDUCATION AND SPORT

PASQUALE J. GALASSO

The quintessential human being in a democratic society epitomizes the concept of autonomy. Autonomy, within this framework, does not mean isolated and insensitive to the needs of others. Rather, the autonomous individual is prepared to make choices and live with them. In addition, the individual must be capable of divorcing himself or herself from the pressures that exist in society to the extent that the choice is, in fact, his or hers. This same person will also reflect at length in dealing with others to the extent that their concerns and rights are taken into account.

The autonomous person enjoys and defends freedom of choice in decision-making. This same person will contribute to the development of other autonomous individuals within society through the mechanisms such as Physical Education and sport to enhance opportunites for others. Opportunities in all facets of society to help engender the development of autonomous human beings will also be fostered and supported. Economic differences amongst families will also be taken into account in providing opportunities for those less well financially endowed to partake in the development of autonomy.

The essence of this person flows into the development of a society made up of caring autonomous individuals who are capable of providing the leadership and energy to create a better society and better world.

The Right to Knowledge and Right to Self-determination

The right to knowledge and the right to self-determination, when respected and fostered, lead to the development of the autonomous individual.

Within the educational process students must be given full knowledge as a base for decision-making within their own life sphere and the society in which they live. By the right to knowledge we are not simply referring to theories, facts and figures in the usual sense, but the in-depth knowledge and background that is required to understand oneself as well as other individuals and the universe itself as well as one can. Every method, every encouragement, every opportunity must be given to them, as well, to serve as a base for the opportunity to achieve self-determination.

Opportunities for Facilitating Education of Autonomy Through Physical Education and Sport at the Elementary and High School Levels

What opportunities are there in elementary and high schools for autonomous development? Do elementary and high school teachers really focus on the development of the individual or are they simply involved in the business of survival and making it from day to day, week to week, month to month, year to year, until retirement? This somewhat bleak portrayal of the situation is not far fetched.

Nevertheless, when one thinks of the wide variety of opportunities for educating for autonomy in the areas of sport and physical education in elementary and high schools, they must be taken. We are referring to required classes, intramurals and interscholastic activities as well.

The values education programs which have been initiated recently do provide an opportunity for children to deal with ethical situations involving choice. This is a move in the right direction in developing the high school curriculum to provide opportunities for autonomy to emerge. However, it is just that — a bare beginning and, unfortunately, many of the teachers themselves have not been prepared properly and look upon the opportunity as a way of avoiding preparing lessons.

Further opportunities exist and must be exploited. Students should be involved in choice of topics in health class. Seminars, debates, presentations, role playing, etc., should be added to the methods used in the classes. Students should organize the intramural program and officiate the games as well as dealing with discipline problems. Game plans and strategy in sport would be an excellent opportunity for development as decision-makers. Wherever there is choice, the students must be educated to make them.

Undergraduate Curricula — Factors to Consider in Designing for Autonomy

A perusal of the average undergraduate curriculum in kinesiology, physical education and related areas shows no basis or thrust towards developing an understanding of the meaning of autonomy and how it can be fostered, and its importance in sport and physical education. The usual curricular components can be found under the headings of motor learning, biomechanics, exercise physiology, history and so on. Unfortunately, the majority of programs do not have courses in ethics where decision-making and the impact on self and others can be delineated and with the students being assisted to understand the fundamentals of decision-making as an ethical issue. In growth and

371

IV. Justice and Ethics

development courses we find the outlines covering psychological and physiological growth and development but no thrust whatsoever in the area of the recognition and development of self leading to the understanding of the autonomous individual.

Cause-effect relationships in interpersonal dealings also tend to be neglected in the average curriculum across the country.

If ever there was an opportunity for our field to take a place of importance in education it is through this mechanism and opportunity to provide a base for the understanding of human beings and what they mean to themselves and others as they seek to become autonomous. We have the opportunity in our field to do an outstanding job of providing the citizens of tomorrow with the tools to deal with change. In this respect, lab situtations should be set up to a greater extent than they now exist in social science courses associated with our field in order to allow for the practical applications of theories and to provide opportunities for greater development and insights into this concept. We tend to think in terms of lab courses being associated with the hard sciences, and thus neglect this hands-on opportunity to provide for the human effort to seek the truth.

The effect of the recession and government cutbacks has had a dampening effect on innovative curriculum design. This has been particularly true with respect to fundamental skill and personal development which must serve as a base for our graduates who will be involved in all forms of education, including teaching, coaching, administration, counselling and so on. Without educating for autonomy through physical education and sport we have nothing more than a shell of information and no focus or direction. A few educators have, by virtue of individual effort, developed this concept within their own courses but there has not been an overall addressing of the issue at the departmental, school or faculty level. We also need more courses related to the area of ethics and lifestyle development to assist the student to develop along these lines.

The work of Dr. Wayne Dyer, "Pulling Your Own Strings," can serve as a basis for discussion and seminar groups along with presentations and defences that are tape recorded and re-examined by the students themselves. This will sensitize them to the degree and the ways in which others influence them. Being aware of this is the first step to being educated and becoming autonomous.

We must start with our own undergraduate curricula in allowing for the development of leaders to provide the impetus in this direction, and to make the significant contribution throughout our field as a whole.

Elite Sport and Autonomy

Another fascinating area of analysis is elite sport where you have, in most cases, individuals, adults, being coached at the international level by our national coaches who, unfortunately, in many instances, are afraid of losing control of the athletes. By virtue of their control of the knowledge which flows to the athlete they are able to control the athlete.

There are many developments occurring at the elite level whereby experts in biomechanics, sport psychology, administration, exercise physiology and strength development are providing information for the advancement of elite athletic performance. The sad part is that the national coaches, generally speaking, insist that all of the information must be filtered through them before it gets to the athlete. In this respect, they are interfering with the athlete's right to knowledge, and the athlete's right to seek that knowledge as he or she sees fit and to interpret it in his or her own way in consultation with the coach. Surely at this level, the coach should not serve as the funnel, filter or broker.

If the national coaches themselves were autonomous individuals with a sense of security in their own right, they would not be attempting to control the athletes through the control of information flow and with, in some instances no doubt, a sense of paranoia with respect to the potential influence of these other experts in their specific areas of knowledge. The autonomous elite athlete who breaks away from this somewhat oppressive milieu will no doubt become a better athlete and a better person. The elite athlete who is dependent simply never cuts it when the chips are down. This was exemplified at the Olympic Games where American sprinters were sitting in the lounge waiting for their coach to decide when they should leave the athletes' village to go to the stadium for their heats in the 100 metres. These athletes were shocked to see their event being called on television as they were watching. They never did get to the stadium to compete. This pathetic reliance on others for actions to be taken and behaviour to be exhibited does not, in the view of the author, lead to the development of the kind of human being who will serve as a leader in a society of autonomous individuals who also care.

This same kind of control exists at the minor sport level. Unfortunately, in sports where physical contact exists, this kind of control turns into violence and intimidation, which is a psychological form of violence, for the sake of winning. When winning takes over, autonomy goes out the window. It is only through the declared and stated objectives which are associated with the development of the autonomous individual that this, in fact, can take place when behaviour matches the words as written in some constitutions associated with minor sport organizations. Here, too, and this is on the basis of the author's four and one-half years of work on the rights of children in organized sport, it was discovered that the majority of minor sport organizations do not have constitutions. The constitutions that do exist are inadequately focused and are not understood to be effective.

Fear of Difficulties in Developing a Program Leading to Autonomy

As stated earlier, the coaches of elite athletes apparently have a need to control the situation and they do so by controlling information flow. This creates athletes who are dependent and, in the view of the author, not the kind of people who can come through in the crunch when they are on their own on the playing field competing against their peers around the world. Somewhere along the line, the Coaching Association of Canada should assist with this in working matters out with Sport Canada to ensure a greater degree of the use of this perspective in their educational materials, and particularly with respect to working things out with the national coaches. Unfortunately, national coaches are largely selected on the basis of their athletes' performances, without recognizing that such a wide variety of coaching styles can be associated with the production of outstanding athletes who in many instances could have gotten to where they did with little coaching. The education of national coaches has been rather neglected and it is the development of the autonomous athlete as an elite athlete that should be the key focus of such a coaching education program.

    Another area of concern in the educational field at the elementary and high school levels has to do with allowing for greater decision-making on the part of children. Questions have been raised with respect to legal liability in allowing children to make decisions on their own. In many instances this has developed as a form of cop-out on the part of the educators in fearing lawsuits. Needless to say, the promotion of the concept of autonomy is not taken as a kind of laissez-faire, disinterested approach, but rather, on the contrary, a very caring approach, but in full recognition that the only way in which autonomy can be developed is through providing for a maximum opportunity for decision-making and input in direction and focus of activities with which the children are associated.

    A caring educator will make the effort to investigate this focus and concept in order to provide the environment in which the children can develop fully.

    I am providing no cookbook formula for developing this concept. It is an elusive focus, but one which can lead in this direction through the collective endeavours of the creative people in our field who can formulate approaches and opportunities for the children. This concept applies all the way to elite athletes and it will allow them to adapt to competition much more readily. What a brutal sight it is when an international team falls apart and is unable to adapt on its own due to over dependence or control by the coach. The autonomous individual tends not to panic and lose sight of game plans and opportunities for the team to advance while taking advantage of a variety of opportunities as presented on the field of play.

Through the Coaching Association of Canada and the associated programs, through individual faculties, departments and schools in the development of their curriculum, and through faculties of education across the country, surely we should be able to develop a focus which will educate through physical education and sport in the development of the autonomous individual.

Bibliography

Dyer, Wayne. *Pulling Your Own Strings*. New York: Avon Books, 1977.

Galasso, P.J. *The Rights of Children in Organized Sport, Study for the Ministry of Tourism and Recreation*, Ontario, 1984.

Nault, Louis-Philippe. "In Search of Coaching Excellence." *Coaching Review*, January/February, 1986. Ottawa, pp. 29-32.

Sport Canada — National Coaches' Workshop, *Science and Medicine in Sport Workshop Report*, ed., Jacques Dallaire, Mont Ste.-Marie, Quebec, 1985.

A CASE ANALYSIS OF AN ETHICAL PROBLEM: THE REQUIRED TEXT

EARLE F. ZEIGLER

As we all appreciate, ethical case analysis in no way resembles an exact science. This may represent a situation which some might deplore, but in all probability the vast majority would find it desirable and wholesome. Nevertheless, we do deplore the current dilemma faced by the large majority of intelligent citizens in our society — a situation where typically one hardly knows where to turn for some sound basis upon which to formulate an answer to just about any ethical problem that arises. What we find, therefore, is that the developing child and young adult is making choices, is forming value judgments, is experiencing emotions, and in a great many ways is acquiring an *implicit* view of life based on a "sense of life" (what Rand called "a pre-conceptual equivalent of metaphysics, an emotional, subconsciously integrated appraisal of man and existence" (1960, p. 31).

In an effort to improve this situation for my professional students, I proceeded to provide them with an opportunity to develop rationality as a "life competency." Accordingly, I set out to place before them the major ethical routes of a philosophical nature that were available to undergraduate students today. Obviously any analysis of current sources resulted in great variations in emphases and terminology. I decided that a consensual tabulation was possible and took pains to present this material to my students in considerable detail. In the process I emphasized the underlying presupposition, the criterion for evaluation, the method for determination of an ethical decision, and the probable result of each of six approaches (i.e., authoritarianism, relativism, situationism, scientific ethics, "good reasons" approach and emotivism).

It had become apparent that I could not use all of these approaches to ethical decision-making in a first course of this type with undergraduates. Nevertheless I was determined to help students approach ethical decision-making in as explicit a manner as possible as a point of departure. I wanted this to be an approach that could be useful to them throughout their adult lives, and yet one that they could possibly build upon as well. Thus, over a period of time with the advice of Professor Richard Fox of Cleveland State University, Ohio, U.S.A., I devised a three-part plan of attack for ethical decision-making as explained in Zeigler, E. *Ethics and Morality in Sport and Physical Education.* Champaign, IL: Stipes Publishing Co., 1984. (I should point

376

out that I make it very clear that this is only one approach with which they are being asked to experiment as they move toward greater sophistication in this subject.) This plan of attack in its entirety includes the following three parts:

Part A. Determine through the employment of a "triple-play" approach — from Kant to Mill to Aristotle — what the ethical or moral issue is in the specific case at hand. That is, proceed from a test of *universalizability* to one of (net) *consequences*, and finally to a test of *intentions*.

Part B. Once Part A has been carried out, proceed with Part B, or the layout of the argument (recommended as a jurisprudential argument in S. Toulmin. *The uses of argument*. NY: Cambridge University Press, 1964). In doing this, insert the universalizability maxim for Toulmin's *warrant*, the net consequences result of the presumably unethical action for the *backing*, and the intentions test items as possible *conditions of exception* or *rebuttal*.

Part C. Thirdly, upon the completion of Parts A and B — *if there is time and if human relations appear to have played a significant part in the case problem* — I have asked students to work their way through an even more detailed, overall approach (Part C) to ethical decision-making (as adapted from Manicas, P.T. and Kruger, A.N. *Essentials of Logic*. NY: American Book Company, 1968 and Zeigler, E.F., *Decision-Making in physical education and athletics administration: A case method approach*. Champaign, IL: Stipes Publishing Co., 1982). There are seven steps to this overall approach of Part C as follows:

a) Determination of the *main problem* after consideration of the various *sub-problems*.
b) Analysis of the main problem keeping in mind that the *application* of the "triple-play approach" above (Fox) as *integrated* with the layout of the argument (Toulmin).
c) Analyze the various personalities and their relationships.
d) Formulation of only those *alternative solutions* to the ethical problem that appear to be relevant, possible, and meaningful.
e) *Elaboration* of the proposed alternative solutions involving the framing of *warranted predictive statements* (i.e., both pros and cons).
f) *Selection of* the *preferred alternative solution* (including initial tentative testing of the proposed solution prior to actual implementation — i.e., especially important if the case is actually a true one to be resolved).

377

IV. Justice and Ethics

g) *Assessment* and *determination* of currently useful *generalizations* for possible future use in similar situations.

A Further Note: In this analysis of "The Required Text," *only Parts A and B* will be employed because space is limited and also because the case presented has not (yet) been explained as a strongly human relations-oriented one.

Case Analysis

This is a case about a new instructor who learns that all instructors of a basic required course in physical education must use the same textbook, a text written by the senior instructor, a tenured full professor, who was also the coordinator of all physical education courses within the professional preparation program.

Application of Part A, Step #1. The first step in the recommended triple-play approach is to employ Kant's *universalizability* criterion — his most fundamental moral principle — in what might be called a test of *consistency*. In other words, is the course coordinator "acting only on that maxim which he might will to be a universal law"? The question is whether all required course coordinators everywhere should have the right to require the use of their own texts in all sections of courses that are being taught. Obviously the course coordinator, the professor who wrote the text and who also collects the royalties based on the number of copies sold, feels that there is nothing wrong with his decision to use his own text in *all* sections of the required course. (We might grant that this practice would be permissible in his own section of the course, but only if contrasting and/or conflicting approaches and positions were presented and openly and freely discussed.)

The Kantian ethic further requires that the "professor treat his student always as an end and never as a means merely" (Brubacher, 1978, p. 110). It could be argued, therefore, that the course coordinator/professor is treading on thin ice in this situation insofar as his personal ethical responsibility to all students taking the course is concerned. Over and above making a decision that he will use his own text in *his* section of the course, he has also decided that it shall be used in *all* sections! (Of course, we are not told whether the new instructor has even mentioned the idea of using another text to the course coordinator.) Shils sides with Brubacher in this argument by stressing that "the teacher has to be careful not to fall into dogmatism in the exposition of his subject or to attempt improperly to exercise influence on his students by demanding that they become adherents of his own particular substantive and methodological point of view" (1983, p. 45).

378

However, the new instructor who is forced to use this text disagrees with this position he finds himself in. He has used the book for two semesters and has found it to be inadequate and too simplified. The instructor can justifiably argue that continued, enforced use of this text does not take into consideration the academic freedom that he/she has a right to expect in western society. As Commager stated,

> ...We require you to avoid the temptation to serve those who may suppose themselves your masters, and devote your affluent talents to your true masters — the whole of society, the whole of humanity, the great community of learning, the sacred cause of truth. In order that you may do this, we give you the precious boon of independence which is academic freedom.... (1966, p. 37)

Shils updates the specifics of this freedom by pointing out that "the relations between senior and junior members of the teaching staff now run across the entire range of academic activities — the design of a course of study...the fixing of the syllabuses for the teaching of particular courses...." (1983, p. 52). However, he continues by pointing out that, despite the frequent "dispersion of authority within departments and within the university as a whole," some still seek to rule authoritatively in regard to various academic activities thereby distorting and often destroying desirable intradepartmental consensus on such highly important matters (Ibid.).

Thus, our conclusion in regard to Kant's test of consistency (Step #1) is that it is now not appropriate to encourage a practice such as this in western educational circles where the principle of academic freedom (*Lehrfreiheit* und *Lernfreiheit*) is presumed to prevail for both faculty and students.

Application of Part A, Step #2. Step #2 of this recommended approach has been taken from our heritage of philosophic utilitarianism. For the maxim "Act so as to bring about the greatest good possible," we are in the debt of John Stuart Mill, as well as another significant philosopher, Jeremy Bentham. Here we have what may be called a test of *consequences* to invoke — that is, what the total effects of the course coordinator's action might be. Further, we should be concerned with the promotion of the maximum amount of *net*, not *gross*, happiness (appropriately interpreted). Such thoughts come to mind as whether the professor's action to require the use of his own text in all sections of the basic, required course is fair, just, beneficient, and permits a desirable amount of autonomy on the part of the other instructors concerned (not to mention what would be most desirable for all of the students involved).

IV. Justice and Ethics

The logic of this basic utilitarian approach — only *act*-utilitarianism as opposed to *rule*-utilitarianism will be offered here — could be simply basic logic where "if all the premises are true, *then* the conclusion will be true." Thus, the following premises and conclusion would apply in this instance:

1. The act that — on the basis of the best evidence available at the time of acting — produces the greatest total good is right.
2. *This* act will produce the greatest total good.
3. Therefore, this act is right. (*modus ponens*)

Here, of course, we are asking the question whether the imposition of one instructor's text as the required text for all sections of a required course will produce the greatest total good insofar as the students' introduction to physical education is concerned — not to mention how this will affect the attitude of the other instructors who may be disturbed by such an imposition.

On this basis, therefore, I believe that the application of the test of consequences (Step #2) shows us that the continuance of such a practice will evidently not produce the "greatest total good." Further, we are arguing that the continuance of such a practice could easily result in students receiving inadequate, biased information, while at the same time the other instructors might feel frustrated and embarrassed in the presentation of what they perceive to be inadequate course information (based on their own knowledge of the subject-matter and their preferred individual instructional methodologies).

Application of Part A, Step #3. Step #3 of this approach we may call the test of *intentions*. For this advice we turn to Aristotle, who asked in the *Nicomachean Ethics*, "What were the conditions under which the act was performed?" Virtue, as defined by Aristotle, "is concerned with emotion and action, and emotion and actions that are *voluntary* are objects for praise or blame, while those that are *involuntary* are objects for pardon and sometimes for pity" (in Loomis, 1943, p. 113). Thus, the question to be asked typically is whether the presumably bad action was voluntary or involuntary.

Thus, despite what has been argued in Steps #1 and #2 above, it may well be that the course supervisor who saw to it that his own text was used as the required text in all sections of the required course was absolutely convinced on the basis of his experience that in this situation such a standardized course structure was the best approach. He might well argue that other approaches had indeed been tried, and in his opinion they had all been found wanting.

The course supervisor might also explain that he had been most careful to present all sides of the various questions and issues that were to be discussed throughout the course experience. It might be further indicated that he could argue that he was himself not profiting materially from the sale of the text that he wrote, that the profits were being used to purchase books for the department's reading room.

Conceivably the professor in question might also argue that he gave the various instructors using his text in the course opportunity for a full measure of input into the course planning, and that this had all been worked out democratically so that the end result was a reasonably standardized approach as to what content was to be included in the course and how the course was to be taught. He might argue that this was considered to be the most desirable approach in the hope that all students in the course would receive a similar, high-quality experience.

Application of Part B. Now that Part A, including the tests of consistency, consequences and intentions have been discussed, I will superimpose these steps (1, 2, and 3) on what Stephen Toulmin has called his "layout for a jurisprudential argument" (1964, p. 95). This is a formally valid argument in proper form that is similar to arguments employed in jurisprudence and mathematics and is "laid out in a tidy and simple *geometrical* form" (Ibid.). Here only the "bare bones" of the argument will be employed for illustrative purposes:

IV. Justice and Ethics

FIGURE 1. JURISPRUDENTIAL ARGUMENT LAYOUT (TOULMIN)

Data	Modal Qualifier	Conclusion
D	Q	C

So, presumably

A decision to enforce use of one's own text by the person in charge of all basic, required courses in physical education is an unacceptable practice in a democratic society

Efforts should be made to eliminate this undesirable practice as soon as possible

Unless

R

Since

W

The principle of academic freedom is presumed to prevail for both faculty and students in a democratic society

(universalizability)

(step #1)

the course supervisor whose text was required was convinced through his experience that such a standardized course structure was the best approach

and/or

On Account of

B

the continuance of such a practice could easily result in students receiving inadequate, biased information while at the same time instructors may feel frustrated and embarrassed in the presentation of course information based on their own knowledge of the subject-matter and individual instructional methodology

(consequences)

(step #2)

the course supervisor gave the various instructors an opportunity for a full measure of input as they all worked out through democratic practice a reasonably standardized approach as to what content was to be included in the course *and* how it was to be taught

and/or

the course supervisor, who wrote the text, was most careful to present all sides of the various questions and issues being presented in the course

and or

the course supervisor was not profiting materially from the sale of the text that he/she wrote, since the royalties were being used to purchase books for the departmental reading room

(intentions)

(Step #3)

Zeigler: A Case Analysis of an Ethical Problem

Key: Argument Layout (Toulmin, 1964)

D = **data** (a statement of a situation that prevails, including evidence, elements, sources, samples of facts)

C = **conclusions** (claim or conclusion that we are seeking to establish)

W = **warrant** (practical standards or canons of argument designed to provide an answer to the question. "How do you get there?")

Q = **model qualifier** (adverbs employed to qualify conclusions based on strengths of warrants — e.g., necessarily, probably)

R = **conditions of exception** (conditions of rebuttal or exception that tend to refute the conclusion)

B = **backing** (categorical statements of fact that lend further support to the 'bridge-like' warrants)

References

Aristotle. *Nicomachean Ethics* (Book III, Chapter 1). In Aristotle (L.R. Loomis, Ed.) New York: W.J. Black, 1943. (Translated by J.E.C. Welldon).

Brubacher, J.S. *On the philosophy of higher education.* San Francisco: Jossey-Bass Publishers, 1978.

Commager, H.S. "The nature of academic freedom," in *Saturday Review*, August 27, 1976, 13-15, 37.

Manicas, P.T., and Kruger, A.N. *Essential of Logic.* NY: American Book Co., 1968.

Rand, A. *The romantic manifesto.* New York and Cleveland: The World Publishing Co., 1960.

Shils, E. *The academic ethic.* Chicago: The University of Chicago Press, 1983.

Toulmin, S. *The uses of argument.* New York: Cambridge University Press, 1964.

Zeigler, E.F. *Decision-making in physical education and athletics administration: A case method approach.* Champaign, IL: Stipes Publishing Co., 1982.

Zeigler, E.F. *Ethics and morality in sport and physical education.* Champaign, ILL: Stipes Publishing Co., 1984.

NATURAL JUSTICE IN SPORT

PASQUALE J. GALASSO

I trust that this knowledge when applied will lead to fair treatment of the athletes and fewer legal hassles. In this respect, I wish to point out that I am not a lawyer, and that what I have to say has an ethical framework. However, if we keep in mind that the law itself fits into the ethical sphere, then it might make my position clearer. In any case, if my recommendations are followed, there is no guarantee that lawsuits will be eliminated; however, it could mean that there will be fewer legal confrontations in light of the fact that the athletes will feel that they have been treated fairly.

As to procedure, I requested information from Ontario sport governing bodies concerning their constitutions, by-laws, and any other material which would reflect on policies and practices dealing with appeal systems. The areas which interested me primarily focused on team selection, carding and decarding, disciplinary matters, and actual cases which had already been dealt with by each sport governing body. I sent out 46 requests and received 25 responses. In addition, I also interviewed around 12 individuals to get some further insights into the material I had received.

I also discussed the concept of natural justice with several lawyers and judges as well as doing library research on this topic. As part of the assessment of the material received, I discussed some of these reports and constitutions with these same lawyers and judges.

Based on the material received, one third of the Ontario sport governing bodies does not have an appeal system for decisions made in a variety of areas. Some indicate that the laws of natural justice will be utilized if disputes arise, and a few have quite well-defined procedures for dealing with these issues. Fewer still have codes of ethics. What this could mean is that some sport governing bodies will be scrambling for legal help at great cost at the last minute, and have a good chance of losing the case due to improper procedures having been followed.

An underlying assumption of this study is a belief that knowledge of ethical thinking could be an important basis for dealing with athletes. Simply following a list of steps in a procedure does not in itself guarantee a fair hearing, although it is probably safe to state that having procedural guidelines set down at least is better than not having them. Inherent within each decision in this process are value judgments which require our best, clear, logical and unbiased thinking to arrive at the best decisions.

My interest in the area is tied in with a sense of justice as I view the treatment of human beings engaged in sport. I have also been involved in a number of legal and quasi-legal cases. And when I think back to the exceedingly costly expenditure of time, money and emotion, much of it could have been avoided if certain steps had been followed. Increasing our knowledge of the law and ethics should be of assistance in a goal of amelioration.

Major trends seem to be evolving with a more litigious base serving to increase incidents of confrontation. Young and old alike are much more prone to question and challenge formerly accepted authority figures. Citizens are more aware of their rights. There is a rejection of paternalism. Athletes have sunk more costs in daily time and effort over a much longer span of time since they are staying longer in the sport. Parents and guardians are sacrificing much more in time, energy and money over a lengthy period of time. Just imagine the amount of travel time and cost associated with a 100 game schedule in minor hockey as an example. People recognize that there are bigger pay-offs from athletic success and thus they are more prone to challenge unfair treatment. In any case, the challenge is there, and what is done about it can pay off if handled correctly.

The coalescing of a number of different laws under the rubric of Administrative Law is a recent phenomenon which affects the decision-making of individuals and groups. The establishment of the Canadian Charter and changes in the Ontario Human Rights Code must also be taken into account. This isn't easy according to the legal experts whose words fill many books. We have to recognize that individual rights are becoming more important in judicial decision-making much to the chagrin of some of our sport governing body executives.

Frankly, I have great difficulty understanding why some sport governing bodies have nothing in place with respect to proper procedures: The Statutory Powers Procedures Act, which is used to judge the levels of fairness which have been exercised by groups, is available to check against currect practice and by-laws. Additionally, the Judicial Review Procedure Act, which deals with follow-up review procedures, is also available when setting up policy and procedural guidelines and when discussing appeals from the original decision. An excellent book, *Athlete's Rights in Canada*, written by Kidd and Eberts has been available since 1982 which covers the rights of athletes in Canada. Another Canadian book, *Sports and the Law in Canada* by John Barnes, was published in 1983. Legal cases are springing up all over the place dealing with athletes. Therefore, I am non-plussed as to why sport governing bodies haven't done a better job in protecting themselves by treating the athletes fairly and keeping their legal world in order.

IV. Justice and Ethics

Another good reason for the sport governing body executives paying greater attention to this phase of their task is contained in a letter I received from Canon Borden Purcell, Chairman of the Ontario Human Rights Commission. In it he outlined a resolution which had been passed in September of this year by the Canadian Association of Statutory Human Rights Agencies, which puts provincial and territorial amateur sports federations on notice that there are problems with some of their by-laws. CASHRA is conscious of provisions in federal and provincial human rights enactments that forbid discrimination on the basis of sex; and they are conscious of complaints received by several human rights commissions concerning the division by sex of amateur sport in Canada; and that the application of provisions allowing any form of discrimination in amateur sport must be interpreted restrictively and be based on an objective assessment arising from a real and proven need. In other words he seems to be saying that CASHRA will be keeping a closer watch on these problem areas, and that you should be aware that you are within the jurisdiction of the Ontario Human Rights Commission.

From an American procedural perspective, in cases involving significant potential penalites, it may be necessary that the affected person be accorded: the right to counsel, given a list of the charges that are to be presented, provided with a list of the names of and facts to be elicited from adverse witnesses, and be allowed to undertake reasonable discovery activities. Once the hearing has been held, the findings and conclusions which are rendered may have to be presented in a written report that is available for inspection. In short, the person subjected to enforcement activities should have the opportunity to appear, be heard, and make an intelligent and informed defence to the preferred charges. With respect to these various procedural rights, it is important to emphasize again that not all of the rights will be required every time a sanction is imposed. For example, if an athlete failed to observe a coach's rule requiring "hustle," and was suspended for one game, the only procedural steps that would appear to be required would be that the coach advise the athlete of his finding, and give the athlete an opportunity to respond, according to Weistart ("The Law of Sports," p. 97). Other good sources on this topic may be found in Waicukauski's monograph "Law and Amateur Sports," as well as a brief, concise article by Harry Mallios, "What is Due Process" in the summer, 1979 edition of *Athletic Administration*.

To give you an American example of a case dealing with due process and the terrible waste of human vitality, Tarkanian versus the National Collegiate Athletic Association, is an unusually poignant example. The timetable starts back in November 28, 1972, with the National Collegiate Athletic Association sending a preliminary letter of investigation to the University of Nevada at Las Vegas, and it ends with Judge Paul S. Goldman ruling in favour of Mr. Tarkanian. The NCAA announced it would appeal to the Nevada Supreme Court — all of this on June 25, 1984. The interesting aspect of this case was the involvement of the full-time bureaucrats in the NCAA, who seemed to be on a vendetta against Tarkanian, for which they were chided by the judge. A clear message emerges: "don't get the judge mad." This material is covered in the *Chronicle of Higher Education*, July 5, 1984.

On the Canadian Scene, Barnes in his book *Sports and the Law in Canada*, covers discipline matters and the procedures which should be followed by organizations in the area of sport in the following manner:

> These principles of judicial review will afford some protection to the athlete who has been seriously affected by a disciplinary action. In the sports context, it has been held on a number of occasions that disciplinary proceedings should observe the rules of natural justice, i.e., that both sides of the case should be presented in a fair hearing and that the decision should be arrived at by an impartial arbiter who has no interest in the outcome. The precise form of the procedures may, however, be flexible in structure so long as these basic principles are observed. It is not necessary that courtroom procedures be followed or that parties be legally represented, but the player or athlete must be fully acquainted with the case against him or her and be given an opportunity to deal with it in a fair hearing.
>
> It is also open to the courts to review disciplinary action that is overly harsh, i.e., punishment that is excessive considering the offending behaviour, or that does not allow for the possibility of rehabilitation. Such action would offend the principles of natural justice although the courts may consider the league's need to effectively deter activities that threaten the integrity of the particular sport.

Kidd and Eberts made recommendations to Sport Canada to ensure that the sport governing bodies establish the following procedures:

> A. In Cases where the proposed penalty is other than the loss of competitive privileges,
>
> 1. The national coach or a specifically designed official should be responsible for enforcing the agreement. Where it is alleged that the agreement has been violated, the coach

should meet with the athlete, state the charges against the athlete, and the penalty he or she plans to impose. The athlete should then be allowed to defend herself or himself. The coach then makes the decision.

2.   If the coach decides that a violation has been committed and feels the need to impose a penalty, the coach should immediately inform the athlete and the elected team captain.

3.   If the athlete wants to appeal the decision, the athlete should go to the team captain, and the team captain should talk to the coach about reconsideration.

4.   The penalty should not go into effect until the team captain has talked to the coach about reconsideration.

B.   In Cases where the proposed penalty is the loss of competitive privileges,

1.   The national coach or a specifically designated official should be responsible for enforcing the agreement.

2.   Where it is alleged that the agreement has been violated, the coach should meet with the athlete, state the charges against the athlete, the penalty to be imposed, and the time and place of a hearing. The athlete should be given at least 12 hours to prepare a defense unless the urgency of the situation dictates otherwise.

3.   A disciplinary panel should be established to conduct the hearing. It should be composed of the coach, the elected athletes' representative, and one other team official who is agreeable to both the coach and the athlete.

4.   At the hearing the athlete should be allowed to:

    a) call evidence
    b) testify personally
    c) make submissions and arguments
    d) cross examine witness(es) from the "other side"
    e) be represented by someone else

5. The panel must decide whether the charges have been proven. If the athlete is convicted, the panel may decide to withdraw the athlete's privileges or whether to impose some other penalty. If the violation arose out of circumstances that could have been avoided in any way, the panel should make recommendations to the sport governing body for improvement. The panel must keep a written record of the grounds for its decision. Where possible, it should keep an audio-visual tape of the hearing.

6. Neither the coach, nor the athlete, nor any other member of the association should release any information about the case until after the hearing.

7. If convicted, the athlete should be entitled to appeal the case, in writing, to the association's board of directors.

Other monograph sources on the subject of due process or natural justice would be *Administrative Law* by David J. Mullan, and *Canadian Charter of Rights and Freedoms — Commentary* by Tarnopolsky and Beaudoin. In addition, the Canadian Amateur Swimming Association has done a considerable amount of work on this topic and has produced a document which would be worth looking at.

The best source of the practical application of ethics in decision making may be found in the monograph *The Hard Problems of Management* by Mark Pastin. He uses concepts such as ground rules, end point ethics, rule ethics, and social contract ethics very effectively.

Summary

In summary, the concept of natural justice can simply boil down to being fair, and going that extra step to show that you are working at being fair. Technically, or legally, it involves a series of steps or procedures which have been enshrined in the statutes, which must be utilized to ensure fairness. If one were to follow all of the steps ensuring fairness in the Statutory Powers Procedure Act, the world would grind to a halt. We have to recognize that with volunteer organizations this would be unrealistic. In spite of this, the comments I received from a few lawyers and judges when viewing the procedures established by certain sport governing bodies, was that they should be reviewed in light of new cases and interpretations. How do we know when we have applied a sufficient number of steps or have applied the process with sufficient fairness? It might be helpful to have a round table with some top lawyers, athletes, executive directors and executive members. It might also be worth

IV. Justice and Ethics

having cases analyzed which have been lost to determine if there is a pattern to the steps which have not been followed in applying natural justice.

Other questions which arise have to do with the role of the executive director, and who is to be the judge, jury and police officer in such a system. In examining the steps, one needs to decide which ones are absolutely essential to include regardless of the level of the misdemeanour or issue in question.

Recommendations and Comments

Stating that natural justice will prevail in official documents and not spelling it out, in my opinion, is not enough. Those who may be affected have a right to be informed of the detailed procedures the sport governing body intends to use in handling cases. And they must know in advance.

The steps in natural justice to be used must be made available to all segments in the sport in order to help educate them as to what is expected in behaviour, and what to look forward to if they become involved.

Tribunals should be formed with as much distance as possible from the two parties involved. By setting them up in concert between the two parties, it will be seen as the fairest basis for decision-making. If one individual is to be appointed, then he or she must be mutually acceptable to both parties. Having a previously agreed-to list from which selections may be made can also be helpful.

An appeal system must expedite matters, particularly when it pertains to scheduled competition. I get the impression that greater co-operation amongst the sport governing bodies would be most helpful. The fact that some of the bodies have spelled out the appeal systems in detail while others have nothing on paper, indicates that there is room for co-operation and sharing. Why not have an expert in this field brought in to discuss the entire matter and evaluate those plans which already exist. I realize that each body wishes to maintain its autonomy, and I favour this approach in general; nevertheless, there comes a time when co-operation makes sense, and I believe that this is appropriate for such a move.

Justice delayed is justice denied. Undue delay is unfair and can be detrimental to the athlete concerned.

Criteria for team selection should be laid down as far in advance as possible to give the athlete time to prepare in every way for the selection period.

Consideration should be given to publishing manuals for all of the positions on the executive committee for each SGB as well as for coaches and everyone in the provincial office, and to spell out the duties and responsibilities as well as rights. Executive directors represent continuity in a sport governing body and hiring and firing should not be subject to personality problems or whim. In fact, the principles of natural justice should apply to the positions in the provincial office as much as they apply to the athletes.

I was surprised to find that only a few of the sport governing bodies have a code of ethics. These codes are helpful in delineating the prescribed behaviour for all segments of the sport and not just for the athlete. In some sports, codes are spelled out for parents as well as those more actively involved. The Royal Bank, for example, has a code of ethics for its entire staff, from top to bottom. Is there a code which has been developed for the Executive Directors?

And finally, I would like to address the question of the role of the executive director in appeals and disputes. In my view, due to the delicate position of the executive director, to expect him or her to be involved as an adjudicator as well as policeman just doesn't wash. The ED must remain as an advisor to the Executive Committee and the President. If this is not the case, then the delivery system which the ED heads up in working with the athletes directly or indirectly could break down due to lack of trust. I believe that there is more room for co-operation amongst the EDs with respect to learning from each other. In fact, in taking this whole package one step further, consideration should be given to forming an advisory body or small group to assist each other.

THE OMBUDSMAN FOR SPORT: AN IDEA WHOSE TIME HAS COME

PASQUALE J. GALASSO

In minor sport the resolution of conflicts and disputes can be simple and brief, or they can extend over years. The latter has been the situation in the Justine Blainey case, which was resolved on the side of the complainant, Justine Blainey, in her dispute with the Ontario Hockey Association. This case was initially taken to the courts through the Charter of Rights and Freedoms and ultimately was turned back at this level, and then fed through to the Ontario Human Rights Commission.

Disputes at the minor sports level are handled by the coaches, convenors of various leagues and/or executive members. While problems may fester, they usually take very little time to deal with, in light of the fact that the people involved in the adjudication are also those involved in the instruction and administration of the programs. Thus, it has both advantages in quickness of decision-making, and disadvantages in that individuals are dealing with questions that they themselves were involved in originally.

It is probably fair to state that very little is done to educate the players and parents as to what their rights are during these disputes.

Currently, at the provincial and federal levels, Sport "Province" and Sport Canada have pressured the sport governing bodies to deal with disputes and grievances through the proper application of the principles of natural justice. While this phrase is usually included in the bylaws or constitutions of the sport governing bodies, in very few instances, based on research I did on my sabbatical last year, do you find the actual procedures spelled out in detail. Usually you find an allusion to the application of the principles of natural justice written into the guidelines or bylaws, but never spelled out. In fact, at the provincial level in Ontario, one third of the sport governing bodies do not have written appeal systems.

Where these are not spelled out, the complainants, if they find frustration within the organization, have to take the legal route which can lead to an enormous expenditure of time, energy and funds.

The drug testing procedure has been set down in great detail through the Sports Medicine Council of Canada, in conjunction with Sport Canada. In spite of this, a recent ruling on athletes in track and field found the athletes not guilty. An arbitrator had to be brought in after a judge had sent the case back to the internal system.

According to the executive directors interviewed, more and more athletes are going the legal route with respect to disputes concerning discipline, carding, decarding and team selection. We will, no doubt, begin to see legal problems arising with respect to the concept of amateurism and professionalism associated with sponsorships and prize money.

It appears that the full-time paid executive managers, as well as the elected representatives to the various sport organizations at all levels, simply do not have the training and time to deal with many of the volatile issues that have erupted over the past few years. Some of them seem to feel that they should be exempt from legal responsibilities, let alone moral, by virtue of the fact that they are volunteers. They believe they should not be held accountable as if they were full-time professional owners. Unfortunately, for their interests, the law has seen fit to hold them responsible. Therefore, when confronted by issues, they have a tendency to run immediately for legal advice. This sets a very expensive chain of responses into action and the athletes, administrators, coaches and salaried professionals become spectators to the process while the lawyers and judges and tribunals become the real players.

It appears that the prime focus of the problem lies in the violation of fundamental rights through neglecting or avoiding consciously the application of the principles of natural justice. There are four sources of information which can be helpful here with respect to the principles of natural justice, and they are:

1) the monograph written by Bruce Kidd and Mary Eberts in which they refer to the rights of athletes in Canada;[1]

2) the proceedings published by the University of Florida through their publication, the *University of Florida Law Review*, Spring, 1987, Vol. 39, No. 2, p. 237:[2]

The Review contained an inventory of rights which should comprise a proper natural justice process as follows:

a) the right to adequate notice of a hearing;
b) the right to pre-hearing discovery;
c) the right to an adjournment;
d) the right to counsel;
e) the right to call witnesses and submit documents;
f) the right to cross-examine adverse witnesses and to refute prejudicial material;
g) the right to a transcript and, if requested;
h) the right to reasons for decision.

IV. Justice and Ethics

One way to state the presumption relating to bias or interest is that the decision maker

> a) would be free from any pecuniary, moral or professional interest in the outcome of the decision;
> b) would not demonstrate any prejudicial conduct in the hearing;
> c) would not be sitting in appeal of its own prior decisions;
> d) would not be exercising a hybrid role of prosecutor and judge;
> e) would not have made any prior delegation or engaged in any prior activity suggestive of attitudinal bias.

In the same document they refer to the idea of natural justice as containing two rules:

> *Audi alteram partem* (let the other party be heard) and *nemo iudex in causa sua debet esse* (let no man be a judge in his own cause).

> More colloquially, these rules were understood to ensure parties the right to adequate notice precedent to an opportunity to be heard, and the right to an impartial and disinterested decision maker.

> 3) A third source sould be *Sports and the Law in Canada* written by John Barnes (1983)[3] and

> 4) The fourth and the most definitive source would be the Statutory Powers Procedures Act for Ontario[4], where the procedures for fairness in dealing with the topic of natural justice are spelled out in very great detail, covering a wide variety of circumstances. Following all of the procedures in all cases is not necessary. However, it could certainly serve as a kind of ultimate resource for the administration of justice in sport.

During interviews with a number of executive directors at both the provincial and federal levels, the question was raised of the potential ameliorative role of an ombudsman for sport as a measure to avoid going the costly legal route. They were unanimous in support of such a position in the sense that if problems can be resolved equitably prior to taking the ultimate step, that this was preferable.

In order to provide some background on the concept of the ombudsman, two sources were selected: 1) "The Ombudsman as an

Administrative Remedy," by Mr. Kent D. Anderson, graduate student in the Master's Program, University of Dayton, Ohio, USA[5] — a paper received from the International Ombudsman Institute at the University of Alberta, and 2) "Variation on a Classical Theme: The Academic Ombudsman in the United States," by Carolyn Steiber, University Ombudsman and Associate Professor of Political Science at Michigan State University.[6] The following information is excerpted from the first source:

> Direct organizational ancestors of the modern ombudsman were created during the early eighteenth century. This period saw Peter the Great appoint a Procurator General for the Russian Empire in 1722. This 'Eye of the Czar' was charged not only with ensuring the enforcement of laws and edicts, but also with protecting the population from excessive official action.
>
> In 1713 Charles IXth appointed an 'ombudsman' for his Swedish Kingdom for the same basic reason, to be a legal safeguard against overzealous state administration. This office evolved through the 1809 Swedish Constitution into the model for today's ombudsman officers worldwide.
>
> The first ombudsman's office in North America was established in the Canadian Province of Alberta and was largely patterned after the New Zealand ombudsman's office. The first United States effort to implement this concept was undertaken in Nassau County, New York, where the county executive, a political officer, appointed a 'public protector' with ombudsman-like functions.
>
> However, because this office lacked the independence essential to effective oversight of administrative functions, he was not considered a true ombudsman. The credit for first creating such an office goes to the State of Hawaii in 1968. I think it clear to everyone that as far as North American standards are concerned, this is quite a recent phenomenon. 5 (p. 1)
>
> The legal concept of the ombudsman also enjoys widespread acceptance and agreement worldwide. The International Bar Association defines the ombudsman as 'an office established by constitution or statute, headed by an independent, high level, public official, who is responsible to

the Legislature or Parliament, who receives complaints from aggrieved persons against government agencies, officials and employers, or who acts on his own motion, and has the power to investigate and recommend corrective action and issue reports.'

An organization based in statutory law enjoys considerable official status and perceived public authority. In many instances this perceived authority is indeed fact, and the jurisdiction's legislative body has granted the ombudsman full powers to investigate all executive departments, make unfettered recommendations for corrective actions, and generally conduct their affairs with a great deal of independence. In some instances this authority extends to the subpoena power. 5 (p. 2)

Independence is the most critical determinant of an ombudsman's effectivenss. It is for this reason that an executively based ombudsman is the least desirable of all organizational forms. Statutes creating or authorizing ombudsman offices generally clearly remove the ombudsman from the administrative, financial, or policy review of its parent the government. 5 (p. 6)

After independence, the most next effective tool available to the ombudsman is the power to investigate, either in response to a client complaint or upon his own motion. This authority is seldom subject to any limitation in the ombudsman's charter. 5 (p. 7)

The third major means available to the ombudsman for effecting client remedies is the power of persuasion. Few ombudsmen at local or state government levels have the direct power to act or order an action in response to a complaint. Based on their investigative findings, ombudsmen present an objective view of the dispute to the appropriate agency and may recommend a specific resolution. Administrative agencies tend to be responsive to this approach, ideally for reasons of client service or professionalism, but also ultimately to avoid two other tactics available to ombudsmen to effect new change: the power to recommend systemic, policy or personnel changes to sponsoring governments, and the power to bring negative public attention to the agency through press reports. The potential negative impacts from the exercise of either of these tactics is so massive that ombudsmen seldom need recourse to them. Their mere existence is sufficient to assure cooperative relations in all but the most extreme cases.

The final tool available to the ombudsman is the office's credibility and it undergirds and reinforces all the office's other actions. So broad is the public acceptance of the ombudsman concept that an ombudsman of moderate disposition, positive orientation and unquestioned integrity needs few other grants of power. Failing any one of these character traits, the ombudsman will fail. That their possession, combined with independence and investigative authority, will almost always lead to success is the lesson found in the American ombudsman experience. 5 (pp. 7 & 8)

The second document, the one written by the ombudsman from Michigan State University, also contains a number of interesting variations on the concept of the ombudsman. She introduces a typology established by a University of Oklahoma professor, Larry Hill, who divides ombudsman models into two major categories: a) non-directive and b) directive. The non-directive model is further broken down into detached investigator, enabler/facilitator, broker/negotiator. Directive models encompass arbitrator, advocate, political activist. 6 (p. 1)

Prof. Hill's non-directive and directive models were formulated to describe classical ombudsmen, those individuals whose independence is assured by virtue of linkage to legislative bodies who appoint them and to whom they direct their reports. A classical ombudsman, once appointed for what is typically a long term, cannot be removed except by vote of an extraordinary majority.

The classical ombudsman was established in three Scandinavian countries long before a Carnegie Commission Report on Higher Education recommended that this concept be borrowed as one way to cope with some of the problems bedeviling American higher education in the turbulent decade of the 1960's. 6 (pp. 2 & 3)

IV. Justice and Ethics

Hill's non-directive model takes three forms:

1) detached investigator — investigation is the bedrock of an ombudsman's work, in academia as elsewhere. Investigation at Michigan State is facilitated by the fact that a fundamental piece of campus legislation assures the ombudsman access to everyone on campus and to all records except a few that are private by law, such as medical or police records. Unlike the classical ombudsman, a campus ombudsman does not possess subpoena power, but no requested record or other necessary information has ever been denied me. My counterparts at other universities report the same experience.

2) enabler/facilitator — all ombudsmen perform this role. Hill includes under this model careful explanation, which is an important part of every ombudsman's job. Often that may be all that is sought. He also includes referral, which, again, is a function both classical and academic ombudsmen regularly perform. Such referral gains much more usefulness in a bureaucratic hierarchy when the ombudsman 'paves the way' with some notice that he or she is doing the referring.

3) broker/negotiator — all ombudsmen from the most specialized to the most broadly based, constantly are called upon to perform this role. Depending on the circumstances, ombudsmen bargain, negotiate, mediate. As indicated above, Hill's non-directive models fit university ombudsmen very well. On the other hand, his directive models, in my view, seldom fit either classical or campus ombudsmen. 6 (pp. 3 & 4)

Annual reports are often a vehicle for raising critical questions of process and targeting procedures or policies which disadvantage one's clients. Such reports are a distinguishing feature of any ombudsman's office. Their distribution to those in a position of authority and the seriousness with which they are read can make the reports a powerful influence for change. To that extent, an ombudsman may be an advocate. 6 (pp. 5 & 6)

The power to persuade, orally and in cogent correspondence, is a prerequisite for holding the office. 6 (pp. 6 & 7)

Very few academic ombudsmen are lawyers, yet they, too, inevitably interpret legal matters and must have easy access to legal advice. 6 (p. 7)

Maintaining a high degree of confidentiality characterizes every ombudsman's office; this includes personal confidences. The opportunity to ventilate before a practiced listener is highly prized, by citizen and student alike; many clients want nothing further from the ombudsman. 6 (pp. 7 & 8)

Yet Canada, with a totally different political organization, has established classical ombudsmen in every province except Prince Edward Island, with a number of specialized offices at the provincial and federal level — ombudsmen for corrections, privacy, language, among others. A dense network of college and university ombudsmen also exists; in this group, even Prince Edward Island is represented. 6 (pp. 10 & 11)

In a flyer distributed by the Ombudsman's Office for the Province of Ontario, excepts have been taken from Bill 86, an act to provide for an ombudsman established in 1975. The following items are taken from this flyer:

1. In Ontario complaints about the Provincial Government may be investigated by the Ombudsman.

2. The Ombudsman's work covers a wide range of provincial concerns such as human rights issues, health, and social services. This includes workers' compensation, OHIP, expropriation of land for provincial projects, family benefits, retail sales tax, and many others. The Ombudsman cannot deal with federal matters such as postal service or unemployment insurance cheques or municipal matters such as garbage collection or bylaw enforcement and cases against private individuals or companies. Some provincial matters, too, are beyond the Ombudsman's power — courts, judges, cabinet decisions and actions taken by the government's legal advisors.

IV. Justice and Ethics

If the Ombudsman's recommendation is denied, the Ombudsman may refer the matter to the Premier and finally to the Legislature through the Standing Committee on the Ombudsman.

If the Ombudsman concludes that the complaint was not justified, a written explanation of the reasons why is provided.

In either case, there is no fee for the Ombudsman's service, and all information received by the Ombudsman is kept strictly private and confidential.

It is best to think of the Ombudsman as a last resort — the person who tries to help you after all other approaches have failed.

No one is turned away from the Ombudsman's Office. Every inquiry is responded to and a professional referral system is used and constantly updated and enlarged.7

The University of Waterloo published a report based on a review of the Office of the Ombudsman that was made in 1986. The Office of the Ombudsman was established at the University of Waterloo by the Federation of Students in May of 1982. Some of the advantages outlined in the report of the office at the University of Waterloo are:

1) The Ombudsman contributes to the image and efficiency of the University by:

i) recommending appropriate changes in University of Waterloo policies and procedures
ii) redirecting a situation which might go outside the University jurisdiction and into the courts
iii) resolving potential conflict informally

2) The Ombudsman helps to establish a more harmonious environment suitable to university study and research by:

i) explaining to people why a decision was made and what policies are associated with a decision
ii) acting as a mediator to bring conflicting parties together so that they might appreciate each other's positions

iii) gaining the trust and respect of the University community and acting as a symbol of partnership between students and administrators

3) The Ombudsman will assist in the long-range planning of student life at the University through/by:
i) listening to student problems and identifying patterns which lead to the deterioration of the quality of student life
ii) recommending necessary services which are not available to students (i.e., campus mediation, legal resources offices, etc.)

4) Making people feel comfortable with their surroundings by

i) listening
ii) understanding
iii) caring
iv) assisting when necessary from within the system

5) The Ombudsman saves time for University administrators and students by:

i) reaching informal resolutions to conflicts
ii) redirecting inquiries to the proper channels
iii) explaining to the student why they should accept a decision
iv) recommending appropriate changes in policy which avoid conflict.

The Ombudsman Review Committee recommends that the funding for the office at the University of Waterloo be split 50-50 between the administration and the student body. 8 (pp. 5 & 6)

There are three models for Canadian university ombudsman's offices.

1) The ombudsman is appointed by a search committee representative of all constituencies and the office is completely funded by the university (Toronto, Concordia, Laval, Manitoba, Quebec and Montreal)

a) The Ombudsman is officially available to any member of the university (Concordia, Toronto, Laval) or the

IV. Justice and Ethics

Ombudsman is officially available to students only (Manitoba, Quebec and Montreal) although others often use it.

2) The Ombudsman is appointed as above and the office is funded on a cost-sharing basis by the university and student associations (Carleton, Western)

a) The Ombudsman is officially available to any member of the university (Carleton)
b) The Ombudsman is officially available to students only (Western), although others often use it.

3) The Ombudsman is appointed and the office funded by the student associations (Waterloo, McMaster, Victoria, British Columbia and Simon Fraser). These offices are officially available to students only, although others use them.8 (p. 13)

The classical ombudsman is independent, neutral and separate from institutional administration. He or she has
• authority to investigate grievances
• power to do so (including access to necessary documents)
• the right to report publicly
• the right to act on a confidential basis. 8 (pp. 13 & 14)

We recommend therefore that the ORC and the University consider extending the mandate of the ombudsman's office to include all members of the University, student, staff and the faculty. 8 (p. 15)

How does all of this fit into sport? Who could handle such a task? Would training programs be set up for such people? What form of ombudsman would be most suitable in the area of sport? Would we be simply adding to the bureaucratic layers of decision making? Would volunteers feel too threatened by an ombudsman? These and many other questions need to be asked and ultimately dealt with by any sport organization seriously thinking of setting up an ombudsman's office.

The ombudsman that I would suggest should be part of a sport organization or serve as an independent extension of a provincial or federal government, would be the classical type of ombudsman. The reason I suggest this is that it appears to be the strongest possible position based on the experience of current ombudsmen and would work best with volunteers. A local sport organization or the government could appoint someone whose responsibility it would be to protect individuals against administrative decisions. Anyone who felt that they had been hard done by could, after going through the usual appeal channels, rest his or her case with the ombudsman. The ombudsman would then investigate the matter and attempt to arrive at the best solution through the means with which he or she has to work.

Also, as indicated previously, most appeals are handled by the same people who are administering, teaching or coaching in the programs. This violates one of the two central principles of natural justice. Consequently, the ombudsman would have a significant role to play, since the office seems to be highly successful in solving problems without taking the ultimate legal steps of confrontation and conflict.

The executive directors interviewed as part of this research felt very strongly that this type of person would be extremely helpful. The strength of the position would be in continuity and objectivity. At upper levels this should be a paid position because of the time involved, and the individual should be highly protected which could only see removal by a significant majority of the directors of the organization.

One key responsiblity of the office, over and above those previously mentioned, is the business of educating people as to process and their rights. I can recall being on a platform of a toronto subway station after having visited the ombudsman's office on Queen's Park Crescent. I noticed the flashing run-through signs that they have down in the subway. There was a message from the Office of the Ombudsman pointing out the role that he plays and the purpose of his office. It invited citizens of Ontario who had suffered from decisions of the Ontario government and its agencies to approach his office for potential solutions to their problems. This is the sort of thing that is sorely needed in sport, because very few athletes or parents at the minor sport level are made fully aware of or understand what their rights really are.

He or she would obviously be required to stand up to pressure and irrational behaviour, as well as being well organized in order to ensure that good records are kept to provide the organization with a sound report at the end of the year which, by virtue of its persuasive language, would carry some clout along with the specific individual efforts.

Obviously, the individual should be knowledgeable in the sport, as well as being highly respected and able to operate at an arms-length basis in decision making.

Just as we have the Coaching Association of Canada, clearly there should be room for setting up an educational process in order to produce ombudsmen.

Overall, I feel quite strongly, based on the investigations that I have taken part in, that an office like this would be helpful to the organization, as well as to the athletes. It would allow the organization to continue without the kinds of legal and quasi-legal blowups that tend

IV. Justice and Ethics

to occur from time to time across the country. If anything, it is worth an experiment for a limited period of time, and then a reappraisal.

Bibliography

1. Kidd, Bruce and Eberts, Mary. *The Rights of Athletes in Canada*, Ministry of Tourism and Recreation of Ontario, 1982.
2. *University of Florida Law Review*, University of Florida, Vol. 39, No. 2, Spring, 1987.
3. Barnes, John. *Sports and the Law in Canada*. Toronto: Butterworth & Co., 1983.
4. Statutory Powers Procedures Act for Ontario.
5. Anderson, Kent D. *The Ombudsman as an Administrative Remedy*, Master's Thesis of Public Administration, University of Dayton, Ohio, U.S.A., 1987.
6. Stieber, Carolyn. *Variation on the Classical Theme: The Academic Ombudsman in the United States*, Michigan State University, 1987.
7. Flyer distributed by Office of the Ombudsman, Province of Ontario, Queen's Park Crescent, Toronto, 1987.
8. *Report on Office of the Ombudsman*, University of Waterloo, Waterloo, Ontario, 1986.

THE PRISONER'S DILEMMA IN COMPETITIVE SPORT: MORAL DECISION-MAKING VS. PRUDENCE[1]

DEBRA SHOGAN

Regardless of the level of intensity of competitive sport, players are usually interested in achieving the purpose of the activity. In a basketball contest, for example, the goal is to shoot the ball into one basket while attempting to stop one's opponent from shooting it into the other. Most of the decisions a player will make in a basketball contest are decisions about how to enhance the likelihood of achieving this goal. That is to say that most decisions are self-interested or prudential decisions. As the basketball example shows, acting from self-interest is not necessarily morally problematic since decisions to achieve the purpose of a game do not usually affect the welfare or fair treatment of others.[2] If I decide to drive to the basket rather than shoot the basketball at the basket from a distance, for example, there is an effect on my opponent but the effect is of no moral import. To refrain from making a decision to enhance oneself in a situation of this type is to trivialize morality. Prudential decisions *are* morally problematic when others are harmed or treated unfairly as a result of one's decisions. This occurs in competitive sport when a player's goal is not simply to achieve the purpose of the game but to be declared the winner irrespective of rules or irrespective of the effects on others in the contest.

Both prudential decisions and moral decisions are *rational* decisions if they coincide with a person's goal. If a football player says, for example, that his goal is to compete with others while respecting their rights but he regularly harms others in order to gain an advantage, we can conclude that the means that this person uses are not rational given his goal. However, if his goal is to always be at an advantage regardless of harm to others, then decisions to achieve this goal, including decisions to harm others, are rational decisions. To deliberately harm another is to do something which is immoral but it is not to do something which is irrational as long as the player's goal is to be declared the winner of the contest irrespective of harm to others. The decision *is* irrational when one's goal is to compete while taking into account the welfare and fair treatment of others.

What I want to show in this paper is that, when one's goal is to enhance oneself irrespective of rules or harm to others, there are times when decisions to fulfil this goal paradoxically do turn out to be

405

irrational. I will illustrate how this manifests itself in competitive sport by first giving an account of how it works in mathematical game theory. There is an instance of a game in which an attempt by two individuals or two groups to maximize outcomes leads to a genuine paradox or dilemma. Both individuals or groups make rational decisions in order to maximize outcomes, and both find themselves in a situation which is not the best outcome for either. This paradox called the prisoner's dilemma after the antecdote used to describe the game has the following features. Two prisoners are charged with the same crime of which they will be convicted only if one of them confesses. The prisoners are told that, if they both confess to the crime, they will both receive five years in jail. If neither confesses, some trumped up evidence will put them both in jail for three years. If one confesses while the other does not, the one who confesses will receive one year in jail and the one who does not confess will receive ten years in jail.

By confessing, the worst outcome for each prisoner is to spend five years in jail. This is the outcome if both confess. The best outcome is to spend one year in jail, but this will only occur if the other prisoner can be trapped into not confessing when the other is confessing. By not confessing, the worst outcome is to spend ten years in jail. This happens when one prisoner believes that the other prisoner will not confess and is betrayed into not confessing while the other prisoner does confess. The best outcome for both is to spend three years in jail. This can only happen if neither confesses.

	Best Outcome	**Worst Outcome**
Confess	1 year in jail	5 years in jail
Don't Confess	10 years in jail	3 years in jail

Since each prisoner attempts to create the best self-interested outcome, each confesses to the crime and each receives five years in jail. The dilemma is that by attempting to create the best possible self-interested outcome, each prisoner is left with an outcome which is not the best for either prisoner. The best outcome for both would be not to confess and receive three years in jail. Because each prisoner knows that the other is attempting to create the best possible self-interested outcome, each chooses to confess for fear that the other will confess. Each knows that if one of them confesses and the other does not, the one who does not confess will be sentenced to ten years in jail while the other will be released after only one year. Neither wants to be trapped into this outcome.

Shogan: The Prisoner's Dilemma in Competitive Sport

Although the mathematical example of the prisoner's dilemma is contrived to make the point, one does not need to look far to see the paradox of the prisoner's dilemma in actual situations in our lives. Problems with pollution, over-population, conservation, and the arms race are all exacerbated by the fact that individual decision-makers do not trust others. For example, for a large company to spend the millions of dollars it would cost to control pollution emissions, those in charge would have to trust that competing companies will also control their emissions. If a competing company does not control its emissions, this company will be able to produce a product for less money. Company managers do not trust decision-makers in other companies to spend the money necessary for pollution control and so they make decisions which result in the pollution of our air, rivers and streams. Everyone, including those who make the decisions, are in a worse position since everyone is affected by the killing of the Earth's resources.

It is my contention that, when the goal of participants in competitive sport is to be declared the winner of a contest regardless of the effects of their decisions on others, they become game theorists in the mathematical sense of that term. When the meaning of competitive sport is found in the outcome alone as represented by win-loss records, medals and trophies accumulated, and championships and scoring races won, participants are likely to become trapped in the prisoner's dilemma. One becomes trapped when one's choices are either to respect the rules and others and almost certainly lose the contest, or to accept the effects of such practices as steroid taking, blood doping, puberty inhibition and psychological manipulation. Prudential decision-making requires one to take advantage of others before being taken advantage of. An environment is created in which no one trusts the other. An athlete does not trust opponents to refrain from taking steroids, for example, and consequently he or she feels compelled to take steroids for fear of being less competitive. To refrain from taking steroids is to risk having one's strategy weakened and one's outcome minimized. When the goal is to maximize outcome irrespective of rules or harm to others, a participant makes a prudential decision to take steroids in order to enhance personal outcome. Paradoxically, however, the person is left in a worse situation than if all participants would not take steroids. By taking steroids, a participant risks damage to his or health and mistrust is created among participants. Unfortunately, those whose goal is to attempt to win the contest within the rules become less and less competitive. It may very well be that there are few individuals presently competing in international weight lifting and throwing events who do not take steroids. An individual with outstanding natural ability who refuses to use such performance enhancers may have difficulty staying competitive. Those who break the rules trap those who don't. But those who break

407

IV. Justice and Ethics

the rules are also trapped for they harm their own bodies and undermine the very nature of the activity they claim to find important.

Achieving the purpose of a competitive sport necessarily depends upon acting according to rational self-interest. To do otherwise, would be to fail to take the activity seriously and would very often imply disrespect for one's opponent. If two players agree to determine who is the better squash player, for example, and one player merely lobs the ball back to the other player, the opponent would conclude that this player is not serious about the activity and/or that the player does not respect the opponent's interest in the activity. Earlier I said that to refrain for supposed moral reasons from making decisions about which manoeuvre would better allow one to take advantage of an opponent is to trivialize morality. It trivializes morality because there is no effect on another's welfare or fair treatment when someone acts on this type of decision. In saying this, however, I am aware of the important message of those who advocate co-operative games as a substitute for competitive games. Co-operative games have no place for self-interested goals, not even morally neutral self-interested goals. This is because the self-interest which is required when one is serious about achieving the purpose of a competitive activity is often confused by some players with unbridled self-interest. If we are to avoid developing unbridled self-interest in players, coaches and other sport leaders must be careful about what sort of message is given when players are encouraged to persevere in gaining an advantage over opponents. It is one thing to attempt to develop perseverance in participants and another to give the impression that perseverance can only be measured by a win. It is not a large step from concluding that perseverance must result in a win to concluding that a win must be accomplished, regardless of effects on others. When this attitude pervades a competitive activity, mistrust of opponents abounds and this mistrust leads to the prisoner's dilemma in competitive sport.

Is there a solution to the mistrust which escalates into the prisoner's dilemma? Part of the solution depends on participants changing their goals so that they do not feel compelled to make the types of decisions created by unbridled self-interest. Changing one's goal from being declared the winner of a contest irrespective of rules or harm to others will depend partially on understanding that deliberately breaking a game rule undermines the very structure of the game occurrence itself. This is because games of sport are constituted by certain rules which make the game activity possible. In high jumping, for example, although the contestants want to be on the other side of the bar, they do not use ladders and catapults to accomplish this. The goal is not to be on the other side of the bar *per se* but to do so only using the means permitted by the rules[3] which is to say that the goal is to get to the other side of the bar by high jumping the bar. Rules allow the activity of high jumping to

408

take place and consequently limit the ways one can utilize to get to the other side of the bar. When someone says that there are other ways to accomplish the end of a game which are not permitted by rules, they are under the mistaken impression that winning *per se* is the goal of the game.

Understanding that game activities do not exist without rules is important if someone is to change one's goals, but understanding this is not enough. Many people do have this understanding just as many people understand that certain of their decisions may result in harm to others. Yet, some people continue to act from self-interest because they do not care about rules or the effects of their actions on others. Influencing someone to change personal goals is to influence this person to change what is thought to be important. This cannot be done merely by explaining rules and expecting players to conform to them nor by pointing out that someone is affected significantly by one's action. Understanding that someone may be harmed as a result of one's decisions is not the same as having this matter to a person.[4] But care for rules and others must come to matter to participants if competitive sport is not to be the domain of only those who are highly skilled at trapping others in the prisoner's dilemma.

Notes

1. This paper is a revised version of a paper called "The Prisoner's Dilemma: Can It Be Avoided in Competitive Physical Activity?" which appeared in *Quality Programming in Health, Physical Education and Recreation*, vol. 2. Edited by John J. Jackson and H. David Turkington. Victoria: Morris Printing Co. Ltd., 1981.
2. In boxing, however, one achieves the purpose of the activity by striking one's opponent on the head or body.
3. Bernard Suits, *The Grasshopper: Games, Life and Utopia.* Toronto: University of Toronto Press, 1978, p. 31.
4. See my paper in this volume, "Ethical Development of Young People Through Sport: Is It An Attainable Goal?"

Among the authors:

Bruce Kidd is a member of the School of Physical Education, University of Toronto.

Patricia A. Lawson is Professor of Physical Education in the College of Physical Education, University of Saskatchewan.

Saul Ross is a member of the Department of Physical Education, University of Ottawa, Ontario.

Earle F. Zeigler is a member of the Faculty of Physical Education at the University of Western Ontario, London, Ontario.

Margaret Steel is a member of the Department of Philosophy, Kent State University.

Terence J. Roberts is Professor at Footscray Institute of Technology, Australia.

John C. Weistart is Professor of Law at the Duke University School of Law.

Debra Shogan is a member of the Department of Physical Education and Sport Studies, University of Alberta.

Pasquale J. Galasso is a member of the Department of Kinesiology, Faculty of Human Kinetics, the University of Windsor, Ontario.

Marge Holman is Associate Professor in the Department of Athletics and Recreational Services, University of Windsor, Ontario.

Dennis Nighswonger is a graduate student in the Department of Physical Education, University of Alberta.